HANCOCK HOUSE Encyclopedia of
Estrildid Finches

Matthew M. Vriends, Ph.D.
Tanya M. Heming-Vriends

ISBN 0-88839-493-4
Copyright © 2002 Matthew M. Vriends, Ph.D.

Cataloging in Publication Data
Vriends, Matthew M., 1937–
    Hancock House encyclopedia of estrildid finches

    Includes bibliographical references and index.
    ISBN 0-88839-493-4

    1. Finches. I. Heming-Vriends, Tanya M. II. Title. III. Title:
Encyclopedia of estrildid finches.
SF473.F5V74 2002   636.6'862   C2002-910144-1

Editing: David Bender
Production: Theodora Kobald, Ingrid Luters
Cover photographs: J. G. Blasman and Pieter van den Hooven
Illustrations: E. P. J. Meijer and Tanya M. Heming-Vriends

Published simultaneously in Canada and the United States by

HANCOCK HOUSE PUBLISHERS LTD.
19313 Zero Avenue, Surrey, B.C. V3S 9R9

HANCOCK HOUSE PUBLISHERS
1431 Harrison Avenue, Blaine, WA 98230-5005

(604) 538-1114   Fax (604) 538-2262
(800) 938-1114   Fax (800) 983-2262
Web Site: www.hancockhouse.com   *email:* sales@hancockhouse.com

HANCOCK HOUSE Encyclopedia of
Estrildid Finches

Soyons fidèles à nos faiblesses

Of course animals do not really associate bars with prisons and they are quite happy as long as there is something nice to walk or climb on, for they do not really notice that the environment is artificial. There is, of course, the well known line "A robin redbreast in a cage sets all heavens in rage;" but robins live longer in cages than they do anywhere else and they are probably perfectly happy.

—SIR PETER SCOTT
(in Martin, R. [ed.]. 1975.
Breeding Endangered Species in Captivity.
Academic Press, London)

Gouldian Finch (male, black mask) / *Chloebia gouldiae*

Contents

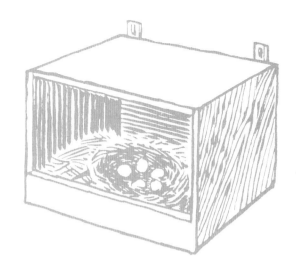

PART I

PART II

Preface

Every day more people discover the pleasure of keeping finches. Whether your plans simply call for a few birds in an attractive cage brightening your home, a fully furnished aviary, or something in between, this is a hobby that offers great satisfaction for everyone who enjoys being in close touch with nature.

In this book, you will find a detailed description of some of the most colorful and popular cage and aviary birds from the tropics and subtropics: waxbills, mannikins, munias, grassfinches, and parrotfinches, together forming the family of estrildid finches, or estrildines, Estrildidae. Many of these fascinating birds can be procured in the pet trade.

Market channels for these birds, and many other creatures, are changing, however. Increasingly, their countries of origin are realizing the ecological importance of their wildlife!

It is nevertheless frightening to know that "the world's rainforests will disappear altogether in 85 years if the present rate of 43,000 square miles per year continues," according to the Animal Welfare Institute in a warning issued some ten years ago. Nothing much has changed since then, although, as indicated, many countries are improving their wildlife resource management, strengthening provisions of existing wildlife laws, and enforcing laws to protect endangered or even all their species. We fully applaud this development!

Consequently, the importation of most animals, including the vast majority of the estrildid finches, will be cut off. Therefore, every right-minded fancier should try to expand the pet bird stock of our country so that domestic breeding will completely eliminate our dependence on importations of wild-caught birds. Many pet bird species, including various estrildid finches, have been domesticated, and imports of these species are no longer necessary. It is indeed time to roll up our sleeves and develop effective programs to propagate other species in cages and aviaries before it is too late! The time will come when the breeding stock needed for such propagation will no longer be available if nothing is done to maintain them.

This book will give you all the essential guidance you'll need to achieve success in finch culture. Here are answers to questions both scientific and practical to enable you to pursue the hobby as deeply as you wish, as well as a bounty of insights on the natural history of the species themselves. Let us work together to prevent the depredation of nature, so that it will remain dynamic in our time and that of our descendants!

We sincerely hope that this book will contribute to this effort. Readers' comments or suggestions to improve the text or expand it will be gratefully received, and we will consider using them for any later printings of this book.

—MATTHEW M. VRIENDS, PH.D. & TANYA M. HEMING-VRIENDS

Acknowledgments

We are very grateful to the many aviculturists, curators of zoological societies, avian veterinarians and finch enthusiasts who have so generously helped us with this book. Particularly, thanks are due to those who have so kindly allowed us to use many of their notes on feeding, breeding and general care: David Bender (USA), Horst Bielfeld (Germany), N. Brickell (UK), J. Buchan (UK), P. Hachemeister (USA), David Hancock (USA), Edward Heming III (USA), G.W. Iles (UK), C. Koepff (Germany), P. Kwast (Netherlands), P. Leijsen (Belgium), E.P.J. Meijer (Netherlands), E. Milnar (USA), H. Rubner (Germany), and the avian veterinarians B. Ritchie DVM, Ph.D. and B. Dahlhausen, DVM, M.Sc., both from the US, among many others. This book could not have been produced without the help of these and other wonderful people! Thanks a lot, folks!

All of the opinions and conclusions expressed in the following pages are our own, however, and any errors must be our own responsibility.

—M.M.V. & T.M.H.-V.

Important Note

The subject of this book is how to take care of Estrildid Finches in captivity. In dealing with these birds, always remember that newly purchased birds—even when they appear perfectly healthy—may be carriers of salmonellae. This is why it is highly advisable to have sample droppings analyzed and to observe strict hygienic rules. Also, many insects used as food by birds are pests that can infest stored food and create a serious nuisance. If you decide to grow any of these insects, be extremely careful to keep them from escaping from their containers.

Part I
FINCH AVICULTURE

**Understanding the Origin
of Your Pet Finch**

Housing, Management and Care

**Common Illnesses and Their
Treatment**

Food and Water

Breeding

Long-tailed Finch (male) / *Poephila acuticauda*

CHAPTER 1

Understanding the Origin of Your Pet Finch

Country of Origin

The members of the family Estrildidae, the waxbills, grassfinches, parrotfinches, mannikins, and munias, come from the Old World. The majority of the species originated in Africa some 30 million years ago, at the end of the Miocene period. Most representatives can still be found in Africa, south of the Sahara, and Malagasy (formerly Madagascar). Other representatives can also be found in southern Asia, northward to Taiwan, and in Australia, but not in New Zealand. In Australia, for example, there are 18 native grassfinches and one imported one, the spice finch *Lonchura punctulata*, which is one of the most well known pet finches. Australian grassfinches closely resemble the true finches of the family Fringillidae, the weavers and sparrows, but can be distinguished by the presence of 10 primary wing feathers rather than the nine found in the true finches.

We can also find estrildid finches in New Guinea, Indonesia, the Philippines, and many islands of the western Pacific. Naturally, people have moved various finch species from one area to another over the centuries. Some species, such as the previously mentioned spice finch, have adapted marvelously and become established in their new surroundings. In some instances, introduced species even displaced the original species, but more often they died out in time.

Estrildid finches inhabit various habitats, but the majority of species favors open country. They are also found along the margins of forests, in forested flat lands and fairly open forests. Generally, they are found near water, often in the immediate neighborhood of a brook, river or lake.

Many species prefer the tall growth of the water's edge, where they like to build their nests.

Some finch species follow man into his habitation, and you can find nests in fields, parks and gardens, and often under roofs, in rain pipes and other unnatural locations. Working in Australia, we also encountered grassfinch nests constructed in rather unusual (to say the least!) places. As examples, we found Bicheno finch *Stizoptera bichenovii* nests close to a wasp nest; black-throated finch *Poephila cincta* nests in the bottom of the nests of birds of prey; Sydney waxbill *Aegintha temporalis* nests in the rose bushes of a public park in Adelaide; and spice finch nests in a fissure of an old garden shed.

In Africa, we encountered many firefinches *Lagonosticta* spp. which were living close to human settlements, and we often found their nests under roofs, in the holes of telephone poles, and such. In Asia, we even found rice finches *Padda oryzivora* in stables and barns.

Estrildines are true children of the sun, since they originally come from tropical and subtropical climates. Even after several generations of domestic breeding, they are still extremely sensitive to temperature changes. Recently imported birds therefore must be gradually acclimatized (see page 23).

Often, the temperatures of the country of origin are totally different from those in the United States, Canada, and Europe. We will go into more detail later, but let us say here that in many areas, particularly those with cold and humid autumns and winters, you can't expect to keep estrildines all year in an outdoor or garden aviary. In early fall, they must be moved indoors and kept in a warm place at room temperature. Research has indicated that tropical finches really feel comfortable at temperatures between 65°F (18°C) and 82°F (28°C). The upper limit of this range is not essential for all species; you can look up the details under the individual descriptions of the various species (pages 73-252). Still, in our experiences, birds we have raised felt most at ease and comfortable within that range, even when they were aviary bred.

There are some species, the Gouldian finch *Chloebia gouldiae*, for example, that won't breed successfully in their country of origin unless the temperature reaches 104°F (40°C). Gouldians live primarily in the Kimberley District of Australia, where the temperature ranges from 107–122°F (42–50°C). If temperatures fall below 86°F (30°C) the birds continue to flourish, but not as actively as with a higher temperature. They become sluggish and droopy at temperatures under 60°F (15°C), which can be noticed clearly in wild birds during the rainy season. In the wild, they won't even attempt to breed when temperatures fall below 73°F (23°C).

Most bird fanciers in North America, Canada, and Europe therefore keep their birds in cages and aviaries located in attics, dens, enclosed porches, and even garages, where temperatures can be controlled. When birds are recently imported or shipped from Europe or Japan, for example, the new arrivals are always kept indoors in a temperature controlled bird room of at least 85°F (30°C). With temperatures that high, you should not forget to furnish several dishes of water or various humidifiers (see page 22) to keep up the humidity, which is essential for a proper finch environment. It is important to maintain a constant temperature and humidity in places where birds are bred or quarantined. The humidity in a bird room with 75°F (25°C) should remain between 65–70%.

There are finch species which are less sensitive in this respect than others, but none can tolerate large temperature changes. If you live in an area where the nights are cold and especially humid, you must provide proper shelter in the outdoor aviary by means of a night shelter (see page 31), a generous supply of nest boxes which can be used

for sleeping purposes, and dense bushes. Birds originating from wooded regions can't withstand changes in temperatures and humidity as well as birds from open country, where nights can be intensely cold, sometimes down to freezing temperatures. So listen to the weather forecast for predictions that can cause problems for your stock, and then take the proper precautions.

Food Sources in the Wild

You can tell by their more or less keg-shaped beaks that estrildines are principally seed eaters. This fact shouldn't be taken too literally by those of us who maintain birds in captivity. You can't just expect to keep them in excellent condition with a cup of some kind of seed mixture. To keep finches in good condition, you must supplement the seeds (see page 57) with a good commercial rearing or egg food, ant pupae ("ant eggs"), small chopped mealworms, white worms, fruits such as apple, pear, berries, banana, orange, date, soaked raisins, and green food such as spinach, chickweed, endive, sprouted seeds, as well as fine grit and cuttlefish bone. We'll discuss this topic in more detail later (see page 58); at this point, we merely want to emphasize that feeding only a tropical seed mixture is no guarantee that our ornamental finches are properly nourished.

A closer look at the beaks of the various types of estrildines shows that some of them have a strong, keg-shaped bill; we call them waxbills. Others, however, have a beak that is much lighter in construction; we call those grassfinches. There are others as well.

Even in the wild, finches do not live on seed alone. Especially in the breeding season, the birds look industriously for spiders, flies, mosquitoes, small bugs, termites and such. Therefore, although it is illegal in the United States, European fanciers often release red avadavats *Amandava amandava*, during the breeding season, so that they can busily look for all types of insects in the yard. They love it! Obviously, these finches must be full-time inhabitants of a garden aviary and completely accustomed to living there. Fanciers don't release their birds until the female finch has laid her first egg. Furthermore, they obviously never reduce the quality and quantity of the live food provided inside the aviary. The fanciers don't want to cause the birds to worry about getting a full meal for themselves or their young. Finally, the risk of an experiment like this, however, is considerable; the birds may fly off into the wild blue yonder with their offspring!

Wild estrildines look principally for ripe and nearly ripe grass and weed seeds. They particularly like various grass and grain varieties. It is a special sight to watch these colorful birds maneuver around the seedhead of a long-stemmed grain to pick at the seeds. It isn't hard to observe this behavior in the flatland species. Wild birds also like reed seeds as well as flower and leaf buds, various berries, young greens, and naturally sprouting grass and weed seeds. During the breeding season they prefer spiders and insects, especially when feeding their young.

Birds that live in the woods and along rivers and streams have a rich variety and quantity of seeds available almost throughout the entire year. Those living on the flat lands annually experience recurring periods of drought and thus have to make do with dry types of seeds. Many large flocks move to the coast or elsewhere to look for food, especially many Australian grassfinches. You can find the birds in large numbers at the strangest places, as long as there is a bountiful supply of food and water. Species which are normally considered nonmigratory can become nomadic during certain years when necessity forces them into moving sometimes hundreds of miles in search of sustenance. There is nothing abnormal about this. In addition to lack of food, a shortage of water is also reason enough to move on.

In the rainy season, of course, the birds don't lack for food and water. Barren regions transform into beautiful green habitats, where the birds have everything to their liking. They can find a good supply of their favorite insects. Flying termites and mosquitoes especially are caught and eaten by the thousands every day! This emphasizes that birds known as true seed eaters depend on insects as an important source of nourishment, especially because insects are used as food for the young in the nest. The parent birds generally strip branches and stems to find the insects, in addition to catching insects in flight or on the ground.

There are exceptions, however. We know of several finch species that won't have anything to do with insects! This is most particularly true of the pin-tailed parrotfinch *Erythrura prasina* of Indonesia and nearby regions, a totally seed-eating species. Even the young are raised entirely as vegetarians. At the other end of the scale, however, is the orange-winged pytilia *Pytilia afra* from East Africa, which is an exceptional insect eater even outside of the breeding season.

We could go on with more examples, but the birds themselves will show you where their preferences lie. Those with a somewhat pointed beak are, in addition to being seed-eaters, lovers of insects and small spiders, which they also offer to their young. Those finches with a more keg-shaped beak can generally be regarded as primarily seed-eaters.

Some finches drink their water in a way that differs from the scooping motion commonly seen in chickens and other similar birds. These birds can take in water in a continuous sucking motion. Among them are many Australian finches, including the diamond finch *Zonaeginthus guttatus*, the Bicheno or double-barred finch, the Gouldian finch, the black-throated or parson finch, the long-tailed finch *Poephila acuticauda*, and the zebra finch *P. guttata*.

The Breeding Season

Breeding is a natural instinct to maintain the species. When this instinct manifests itself, the breeding season begins. Generally, this occurs in spring, but there are birds that start earlier or later. Internally, the birds start this process with what can best be described as a fever, in the good sense of the word. The internal temperature rises, not throughout the whole body, but just in the areas where it is necessary, in the so called brood spots, which are pressed against the eggs during incubation. Brood spots, areas where a large supply of blood is found, differ sharply in various bird species. The way eggs are set on is determined, among other factors, by the shape of the nest, the location of the brood spots and their size and intensity, and the size of the clutch of eggs. Just look at the difference between a zebra finch and a water bird and you will immediately understand.

As indicated earlier, availability of appropriate food is a determining factor whether wild birds will start breeding. Species living on the flat lands will need to have insects available to feed their young, in addition to seeds. This food is available only when there is adequate precipitation. Rain promotes plant growth so that birds have available fresh grass stems, moss, plant down and other necessary nesting materials. If conditions are favorable in nature and the rains guarantee adequate vegetation, you can notice that in a short period of time the birds will raise two or even three broods, one after the other. You can tell that the birds are in a hurry by noticing that a female is incubating eggs while the young of the previous brood are still in the nest, now under the exclusive care of the male. Gouldian finches even have the young of earlier clutches help feed their brothers and sisters of a succeeding brood.

During the breeding season, large flocks of estrildid finches often separate to have plenty of food and nesting material available to all, even though most species don't break off the colony or group bond. It's a fact that these finches love company and therefore stay in groups and share feast and famine together. You can still observe this in the breeding season. They make nests in close proximity, sometimes even in the same tree or bush. This is a characteristic trait of Estrildidae, which differentiates them from the true finches, Fringillidae, where each pair sets up its own territory that is defended against any undesirable intruder, including members of the same species. One of the estrildid finches, the crimson finch *Neochmia phaeton*, a rather rare species in captivity, is an exception, however. This species is extremely territorial and chases out small and large birds, including members of its own species.

The social behavior of the estrildid finches can be noted clearly among zebra finches. These well-known birds conduct special meetings during the day in the breeding season, social hours in which they appear to discuss the events of the day with other zebra finches, while preening each other's feathers.

During the breeding season, the male goes in search of a mate, although the female determines the final choice of a partner. The search for a mate is called the mating dance. This dance is accompanied by song and/or the exhibition of certain, often colorful, parts of the plumage. Almost all of the grassfinches hold a blade of grass, a piece of straw, or a feather in the beak while performing the mating dance in front of the female.

Once mates are selected, the newly formed couples go off and spend much time close together. Especially in the early afternoon, they preen each other's feathers, or just sit pressed together on a branch, smooching while they sun themselves. It is believed that the majority of the Estrildidae in the wild form pairs that remain together for life. By the way, there are some finches that don't engage in any particular physical contact such as preening. The Gouldian finch, for example, never, or hardly ever, engages in bodily contact.

When the female is ready to start a family, you can see this clearly by her behavior. She presses herself down against a branch and quiveringly beats her tail in an up-and-down motion. In some species, the female also utters a few notes of song with head held high, or holds a long blade of grass, a feather, or a thin twig in her beak. This occurs, for example, in cordon-bleus *Uraeginthus* spp. and their relatives. During mating, and also frequently before mating, the female utters short, trilling sounds. It is consistently the female that invites the male to copulate. Mating can occur several times in succession.

After mating, the serious work begins. The male will look for a suitable spot to build a nest, and the female will inspect the potential sites he finds. She is definitely choosy, and may reject ten or more locations! Once she accepts a choice, the male goes in search of building material. The female usually takes the role of architect. Most nests are bullet or bottle shaped, and are covered by a roof. Most nests also have a small tunnel as an entrance. Usually, nests are built in the open in thorny bushes, trees, or among grass stems. There are some species that use tree hollows or abandoned nests of weavers and other birds. These adopted nests are almost always restored and reconstructed before being used.

Favored construction materials include fresh and dried blades of grass, moss, wool, plant fibers and down, twigs, and small branches. To line the nest, small feathers, plant down, soft grass, hair, wool, and moss are put to use.

The size and shape of nests vary sharply according to species. Most nests, however, are rather small, ranging from 7 in. (18 cm) or less down to about 3 in. (7–8 cm) in diameter. We do know of nests, however, with a diameter of 8–10 in. (20–25 cm).

The late Prof. Klaus Immelmann estimated that it took between 1800–2000 separate blades of grass, the principal construction material, to build an estrildid nest. Some ornamental finches have very specific nest sites, as, for example, in the neighborhood of wasp nests or the eyries of birds of prey. The diamond finch is a good example. Still other species move into abandoned nest tunnels in the banks of waterways or in holes drilled into trees by woodpeckers and other birds. There are even species that build nests in termite hills.

The height at which estrildines build nests is also characteristic. The large majority builds low, or even at ground level. We may take it as a general rule that nests will rarely be more than 13 ft. (4 m) off the ground. Only those species that increasingly move into human settlements are likely to build considerably higher. Zebra finches, spice finches, and star finches *Bathilda ruficauda* are good examples of this. Species that build very close to the ground include the munias and mannikins, and the cordon-bleus. One that builds right on the ground is the common, or black-chinned quail-finch, *Ortygospiza atricollis*.

Usually, nest construction takes several days, although there are species that take somewhat longer. The job doesn't have to be lengthy because the usual nest is quite small. Actually, the process is rather slow. The birds add just a bit of building material to the nest in any one day, and they continue the process even after the nest is in use. While they take turns brooding and looking for food, the two parents often bring along additional building material. They use these items to wave to one another and then work them into the nest, seemingly as a pastime. There are even finches that build nests outside the breeding season, but

generally these nests aren't built as tightly and are used only for roosting at night. Some finches also build sleeping nests during the breeding period for use by the young that have left the regular nest.

The eggs are generally pure white and are laid in clutches of four to six. Usually, both parents take turns incubating during the day, but at night they generally sit on the nest together. It can happen that the female broods alone during the night, while the male keeps watch nearby. We discovered that the masked finch *Poephila personata* also takes turns incubating the eggs at night, even if both parent birds stay in the nest. Each parent spends a period of about two hours incubating before being relieved.

During the day, incubation shifts can vary considerably in length. For example, red-eared waxbills *Estrilda troglodytes* take turns of approximately three hours, while other species incubate only for one or two hours per shift. Not all males are devoted participants, however, and some leave most of the job to the female. The incubation period takes 11–16 days, depending on the weather, the number and duration of breaks for socializing that many birds take during the early afternoon, the temperature and humidity, the time of year that breeding began and corresponding availability of food, and the intensity of brooding. Actual incubation does not begin until the third or fourth egg has been laid, which leads to a situation in which the first eggs laid hatch with only a time differential of a few hours, while the later eggs often hatch two or three days after the others.

Newly hatched young are blind and naked, although they may have sparse patches of down here and there. Therefore, the parents take great care during the first week to keep the hatchlings warm. After a week, the chicks' eyes open, and down starts to grow on their tails and wings. The smaller species of ornamental finches leave the nest at 18–21 days of age; the larger ones, at 22–25 days.

As stated earlier, many species build special sleeping nests during the period that they are brooding, so that the young have a place to sleep once they are ready to leave the parental nest. Some birds, however, direct recent fledglings back to the parental nest for the first few nights.

When the young have been out of the nest for two or three weeks, they can be regarded as independent. At that point, they may start to make playful attempts at mating, even with young of the same sex, but they can't by any means actually copulate.

The young birds will exchange baby feathers for adult feathers at three months of age and then, generally, they can't be distinguished from the parent birds. By this time even the beak, which at hatching is usually ivory, later becoming a black horn color, is in full adult color.

The plumage of young birds is not as colorful as that of the parents. At first, they look greyish, greenish, or brownish, which is a good camouflage against the predacious eyes of birds of prey and other hunting animals.

In general, all estrildid nestlings strongly resemble each other. Only the markings on the mouth, palate, inside lower mandible, and tongue differ noticeably from species to species. The most noticeable markings consist of knobby papillae in the corners of the mouth, which can be blue, yellow or white. In addition, there are black round and oval patches on the palate, tongue and on the inside of the lower beak. These markings enable us to distinguish between the young of various species. The young of the blue-faced parrotfinch *Amblynura (Erythrura) trichroa* have bright blue tubercles, without distinguishable markings on the tongue and palate. The Gouldian finch, however, has many markings on the tongue and palate. In short, the mouth markings of nestling estrildines are, as mentioned, characteristic for the species in both color and pattern. Furthermore, not all species have these markings. The orange-cheeked waxbill *Estrilda melpoda*, for example, is a species which has no mouth markings.

In most species these markings disappear once the young are independent, but there are species that do retain them, although generally in a less intense form. By the way, there is a pattern discernible in these markings. In general, the beak pattern consists of five round, black patches which can be seen clearly because the palate is pale pink. On the tongue, two dark patches can be seen, and on the inside of the lower beak, there is a half round series of small patches. The beak papillae

are often somewhat phosphorescent. The general purpose of the markings is to show the parent birds precisely where they should deposit the food they're carrying in. That's important, because the inside of the enclosed nest is almost completely dark. Furthermore, the markings stimulate the parents to bring food, and they recognize their own young by the markings without error. We discovered this clearly when we once had to move some nestlings to a foster nest. The adoptive parents were of the same species and were good providers. The foster chicks had somewhat deviant but very small markings. (Nature is not static, but dynamic, and individual animals differ, just as human beings do.) Well, the adoptive parents refused to feed the transferred babies! Let us quickly add that this behavior is unusual. Most parent finches accept foster babies from the same or closely related species.

The feathers of young birds that haven't molted have characteristic colors that differ among species. Often there is a lined or patchy design in yellow, white, red, or blue. In this connection, it is interesting to note that there are certain whydahs, finches of the genus *Vidua*, that parasitize members of the genera *Estrilda, Pytilia, Uraeginthus* and *Lagonosticta*. The young of the parasitic species cannot be distinguished from those of the host species, a fact to which we will return later (see page 19).

Young birds being fed in the nest can assume several begging postures. Zebra finches seem to be able to turn their head 180 degrees or lay it on the shoulder. Bronze-winged, or bronze, mannikins *Spermestes cucullatus (Lonchura cucullata)* beat their wings back and forth excitedly. Young of most species just move their raised head up and down in a rocking motion and utter an urgent begging cry; they don't move their wings, in contrast with the young of the true finches.

To feed the young, the parent bird regurgitates food, with pumping motions, into the throats of the nestlings, which close their beak onto that of the feeding parent. If the young bird doesn't swallow the food quickly enough (the swallowing reflex), the parent retracts the bit of food and inserts it into another opened mouth. The young that swallows quickly has an empty crop and thus is hungry. This technique seems to work excellently and all young are fed on time (a parent bird would be hard put to remember which of the begging little ones should get the next turn).

In addition to providing food, the parents brood the young the first 9–12 days to keep them warm, and, of course, also protect them. After a couple of weeks, the young have grown so much that there isn't enough room inside the nest any more. Often the young birds are somewhat bigger than their parents at that point; after all, they are extremely well fed and barely use any energy. So then the parents no longer bring food inside the nest, but feed them from the edge of the nest or from the entrance.

As fledglings, the young remain in close proximity to each other and continue to be fed, principally by the male parent, on the ground or on a low branch or twig. You can often see them sitting neatly in a row, enjoying the tidbits they are fed. Meanwhile, in most cases, the female has already started a new clutch.

Brooding Parasitism

We have made previous reference to the fact that a number of African estrildid species are maneuvered into becoming foster parents by brood parasites, of which various whydah species are the most well-known. The precise classification of these whydahs is still disputed among ornithologists. For our purposes here, we follow their traditional placement as a subfamily of the weavers, and thus are not related at all to the finches. We note, however, that recent DNA studies have indicated a closer relationship to the estrildines than was previously believed. Regardless of the exact relationship, the true offspring in the nest can't be distinguished from the interlopers, which have identical mouth markings as hatchlings, and later develop the same feather colors. They also have the same begging cries and assume the same begging positions. You can't tell them apart until they complete their first molt. Only when, as young males, they manifest their first bird song, can you notice a difference between the two species, and even that is true only for a rather limited number of species. The greater majority adopts the song of

the foster parent, so that whydahs sing like some of the estrildines!

Most of the whydahs have species-specific foster parents. For example, the paradise whydah *Vidua paradisea* only goes for the nests of the melba finch *Pytilia melba*, and the broad-tailed paradise whydah *Vidua orientalis obtusa* only parasitizes the orange-winged pytilia *Pytilia afra*. Let us add that the eggs of the parasitizing species also look identical in size and color to those of the hosts. This opens up a whole new territory for the aviculturist, especially for the one who lives in a warm area such as southern California or Florida, namely, raising whydahs with the aid of the appropriate foster parents. This, however, would obviously require other things like humidifiers and a quite roomy indoor or outdoor aviary.

Song

The song of estrildines is generally quiet and unobtrusive, in contrast with the true finches, which are real song birds that include some exceptional performers. The ornamental finches, however, do have a sometimes rich variety of enticing and whistling calls, each of which have a definite meaning. You can distinguish warning signals, begging, invitations for social contact, and others, which can be used alone or in combination.

Not all ornamental finches should be considered unmusical. The varied song of an African species, Dybowski's twin-spot *Euschistospiza dybowskii*, a bird that somewhat resembles the Australian painted fire-tailed finch *Emblema picta*, is quite well known, and has drawn considerable interest during the last 30 years.

The song of many birds has a quite specific function, namely, to establish boundaries for their territories and to warn away trespassers of their own species. The sound made by male estrildids can be heard best during the mating dance, when an enticement call is used to invite mating, and to begin nest building. Calls also serve as a way for mates to maintain contact, and are used as a social contact, as a warning, or as an invitation to form a flock.

It is interesting to note that the soft, hoarse song of the spice finch, or the near singing of the

Gouldian, appears to be solidly appreciated by members of the same species in the wild, even though it seems hard to hear, much less to understand, by the human ear. When these birds bring forth their aria, other males, particularly young ones, group themselves around the lead singer, in order to learn to sing properly, as it were. Females also appear to take lessons, but they can't learn to sing, at least not as well as the males. Why they attend these classes is anybody's guess, although listening to the different calls, they probably understand their meaning. Let us mention, however, that there are certain species of finches in which the females do learn a pretty good song; the cordon-bleu is an excellent example.

Life Expectancy

Research over the years has shown without doubt that the small species of birds seldom live more than three years in the wild. Many ornithologists believe they only attain a maximum of two years. This is easy to understand when we realize that most birds are exposed to all types of dangers. In this connection, we should not forget the negative role played by mankind through the ages, which continues today. Industrialization robs birds of entire habitats. To that, add water and air pollution, insecticides, noise, and many other factors that have been amply discussed and written about. They all have a negative influence, not only on birds, but on all animals and plants, and reduce their life expectancy considerably. Natural phenomena can also cause a great deal of damage to animals and plants; we are thinking about heavy storms, tornadoes, floods, tropical rain showers, hail, frost, and the like. All this affects the orna-

mental finches, as well as other animals! In particular, the large- scale deforestation being carried out at the moment, which ruins the natural habitat of many species, is devastating. In addition, the tropics and subtropics are home to many natural bird enemies that prey upon birds and their eggs and young. The effect of predatory birds, mice, rats, snakes and even insects, such as certain termites and ants, should not be understated. And finally, parasites like coccidia, bacteria, worms, and such also see to it that the life span of wild birds remains quite limited, at least as far as the majority of the estrildid finches is concerned.

It is very different in an outdoor or indoor aviary, or even a roomy cage, where the birds get optimum care, feeding and housing, and are protected from their enemies. In cold weather, they get heat; in sickness, they have access to our entire bird apothecary as well as to our well-trained avian veterinarians. Insecticides pose no threat, because their green food is carefully grown, raised organically and washed. So, it is of no great surprise that finches in captivity live at least twice as long as those in the wild. In an aviary environment, small finches that attain five to eight years of age are no exception. It is even possible to obtain good results when breeding with these oldsters. The hardiest species, like munias and grassfinches, can become 10–15 years old. Our professional experiences as zoologists and aviculturists have convinced us that aviculture doesn't harm nature. Rather, the fancier with his heart in his hobby is much more likely to be an effective force to preserve what remains in nature, especially if he makes a solid effort to breed the birds he is keeping so that we are no longer dependent upon wild-caught and imported bird species!

CHAPTER 2

Housing, Management and Care

Adequate Housing

Adequate housing represents a crucial part of what is needed for success in the bird fancy. A major reason is that good housing promotes proper environmental temperature, an important factor for breeding exotics, particularly finches.

Altogether, there are about 9700 species of birds in the world, and during the millennia they have become adapted to the conditions under which they have to live and raise their young. One major environmental factor that has affected the development of birds is warmth, and adaptations were made to provide proper protection against bitter cold or extreme heat. Penguins, for example, have a thick layer of fat that protects against cold and stores energy on which the birds can draw if it is necessary to survive for a time without food. By contrast, the tender exotics that live in the tropics have little to protect themselves against cold, and they must take in food frequently to maintain their body temperature.

One of the reasons why some fanciers lose their small exotics in winter is that they don't sufficiently realize that at that time of year there are at least 14 hours of darkness during which the birds can't eat. As a result, they cannot maintain their body temperature. Their crops are empty in the morning, and the cause of their death is often starvation. The solution is to provide several hours of artificial light in the evening, remembering, however, that a bird needs 10 to 12 hours of darkness each day to ensure adequate rest (sleep). However, since many birds in the wild, where there is never complete darkness, sometimes look for food or just fly about a little at night, it is essential that birds in

captivity have this same possibility. Therefore a small night light should be kept burning.

It doesn't take any special gadgetry to supply exotics with the environmental temperature they need. If these birds are properly acclimatized, they can live and breed under almost any climatic condition. And we must add that although most birds can't stand being exposed to direct, bright sunlight, this doesn't mean that they can't withstand high temperatures. It is quite hot in most tropical areas, even in the shade of trees and shrubs. This heat is often accompanied by a very dry atmosphere that can't be compared with the hot, humid weather we experience here during a summer heat wave. In most instances, reports of successful breeding of difficult birds indicate that the weather during the breeding season was exceptionally hot.

The body temperature of birds is about 10°F (5.6°C) higher than that of humans. All in all, we must create a situation for exotic finches that closely parallels the weather in their land of origin. Since in many areas we ordinarily don't experience hot spells that last more than a few weeks, we must find ways to create and maintain a high daytime temperature. Night temperature is not as important, since even in the tropics, this can fall quite a bit.

What's the best way to go about this?

One way is to set up a bird room with a thermostatically controlled heating system and electric ventilators. But the average breeder can't afford this level of luxury. The most available source of heat is the sun, and the facility for raising birds should be arranged so that maximum use is made of sunlight. The facility should not be too large, because a large volume of air is difficult to heat; also, heat is lost quickly if the surface area of the floor, walls, and ceiling is relatively large when compared to the volume of air the room contains. A space of about 12 ft. x 9 ft. x 6 ft. (approx. 4 m x 3 m x 2 m) is convenient and simple to heat. In a room this size, you can install a reasonable number of walk-in flight cages with, if possible, access to outside aviaries.

The building should be oriented with the front facing south, so that sunshine can warm it as long as possible. Also, the birds themselves enjoy the sun. It is amazing how much the indoor temperature can rise if exposed to even the relatively weak rays of the winter sun. If you have a bird house that uses available sunlight effectively, you then need to find a method to retain heat when the sun doesn't shine. It is a matter of proper insulation. There are several types of insulation available on the market to put on or between the walls. Yet, a basic requirement is that there is enough space between the outside and inside wall to retain a proper amount of still air. Pay special attention to windows. They are good to have, but if not made from double glass, lose heat easily. Therefore, install double glassed windows. A properly fitted door is also important for retaining heat and avoiding drafts.

A second important factor is proper ventilation. With higher temperatures, the atmosphere turns stale more quickly without a constant supply of fresh air. Air therefore needs to be circulated more frequently in the summer than in the winter, especially with an eye to retaining warmth in winter. The simplest method of ventilation is to have slots for air intake at the bottom on all four sides, with an exhaust slot in the roof, properly protected against rain. The slot should be closable with a slide so that the air flow can be regulated. The slots open to the wind should be closed immediately and the others should be completely opened. The openings should be covered with a fine, strong mesh to keep vermin out.

It is also essential to maintain proper heat and ventilation in winter if you want to keep your birds in good condition and in good health.

Heating, however, should not be overdone. The major purpose of a high temperature is to stimulate birds to breed, and that, of course, is not advisable in winter, anyway.

The best way to avoid problems with heat is to retain an inside temperature between 65–82°F (18–28°C), plus access to an open walk-in flight, so that the birds can choose for themselves. Even if there is much to attract the birds to the outside flight, the higher temperature inside will draw them there when necessary.

High temperatures have some drawbacks, but these can be overcome. First, you need to guard against food spoilage, particularly egg foods such as rearing foods, nectar, and such ready-to-eat foods as dead insects. Green food wilts fast and dries out, so provide these items in small quantities and replace them often.

Another factor is that water evaporates more rapidly in higher temperatures. We have found that replacing water early in the morning and late in the afternoon is usually adequate. We also recommend automatic waterers, called water bottles in the pet trade, which actually lose very little water through evaporation. Another way to reduce evaporation is to buy chick waterers, as they hold more water; in these utensils, however, never put more than 2 in. (5 cm) of water as some birds, while sticking their head through the waterer's opening, manage to drown themselves!

Birds don't have sweat glands in the skin, like humans. They will show you when they are sweltering by sitting with open beaks and drooping wings. If you see these signs, you must take steps immediately to lower the temperature. Actually, installing a reliable thermometer is useful for avoiding such stressful situations. Hang the thermometer at the height of the main perches, because the temperature can vary considerably between the floor and the ceiling. Also, remember to disturb birds as little as possible when the temperature is high, because body movements cause body temperature to rise, which can have tragic results.

If you need to catch birds in warm weather, do this early in the morning, or in the evening when it is cooler. Remember that heat dries out the air. Even though the humidity should be kept low for most finch species (approximately 55%), it pays to sprinkle water on the floor once or twice daily. Or you can place safe varieties of potted plants nearby and keep them moist to prevent the air from drying out.

Proper attention to environmental factors is extremely important, especially if you want to breed estrildines. Observe and experiment with the birds you want to raise, and you will be able to breed a variety of finch species. We want to urge you to progress from a keeper to a breeder of finches. Unless you've experienced it, it's hard to imagine how fascinating it is to observe courtship behavior and nest building, and how exciting it is to watch the laying of the eggs, the feeding of young, and the busy activities of enthusiastic bird parents.

Keep good notes and records to supplement published information about your birds. You will find an extensive list of reference books in the back of this book to discover all you need to know.

Well prepared and equipped, you will be able to extend the fellowship of breeders that are developing a good supply of birds independent of importation, which came to an almost complete stand-still recently. Responsible breeding in captivity can help prevent certain bird species from disappearing completely from the face of the earth. For example, many waxbills and Australian grassfinches are becoming increasingly popular, showing that the aviculturist can accomplish a great deal, when considering that importations of wild-caught specimens have been cut off for many years–since 1997 and 1964, respectively.

Acclimatizing Imports
(in case bans will be lifted or changed)
The importation of wild-caught finches for the pet trade has come to an almost complete stop; however, the importation of captive-bred estrildid finches from Europe and Japan is increasing rapidly in order to comply with the demand.

The cost of imported, captive-bred birds today is determined to a large degree by the cost of quarantine after their arrival in America. Government officials deem it necessary that every bird entering the country must be placed into quarantine for at least 30 days, whether it is an exotic finch or a par-

rot. The major concern is exotic Newcastle disease (VVND - Velogenic Viscerotropic Newcastle), a dreaded virus infection which several years ago caused major losses among chickens. There is no doubt that the poultry industry suffered millions of dollars in losses, so that it makes sense that the government releases imports into the domestic trade only after they have been medically examined and found to be free of this infection. Birds that die during quarantine are carefully examined and the cause of death is precisely determined. It is a system that works satisfactorily even though it raises opposition from time to time. There can be no doubt that it's important to bring healthy, virus-free birds into the domestic trade channels. And yes, it is expensive too, when you add all the direct and indirect costs involved, but much cheaper than acquiring an infected bird, and losing an entire collection.

While on the subject of regulations, be aware that in many places you need a permit or license to keep birds. There are neighborhood covenants that flatly prohibit the keeping of any pet whatsoever. There are also localities that limit the number of birds that you may keep in a residential neighborhood. Still other locations require that you get an occupational license before you can sell birds, even if you raise them yourself. Further, local ordinances may require commercial zoning if you want to sell birds. Some places permit the sale of birds, but not any advertisement on your property offering "Birds For Sale." If you live in one of these places, you have to place ads in the local newspaper, which is usually more effective, anyway. There are states requiring a state license to sell birds, even those you've raised yourself. Be aware of ordinances of this type. It may seem burdensome, but unless you stay informed, you may get into trouble sooner or later, which can be quite costly. Make inquiries from the local government and join a local bird club. Your fellow members will certainly provide you with full details about what may and may not be done. If they can't provide accurate information (and this has occurred far too often!), insist that the leadership informs itself fully and immediately on any restrictions and licenses that apply. Then insist also that all members be informed in detail on the existing situation. This approach will benefit the entire hobby.

If you do acquire imported, wild-caught birds, via legal permits or otherwise, it is important to give attention to their proper acclimatization. Birds arriving from other countries have been exposed to all manner of discomfort and danger during the trip. They will also be slow in becoming accustomed to new food sources, utensils, housing, etc.

Never house newly arrived birds with earlier arrivals. If they're housed in the same quarters, they could spread disease. Place the imports in separate, roomy cages and, if possible, house males and females separately. The best type of cage for this purpose is the so-called box cage that is well protected on all sides. Place an infrared lamp near the front. It will benefit those birds that "don't look so great" after a long, tiring journey, and it will also help those that appear well and in good condition. Place the lamp about 24 in. (61 cm) from the front of the cage and set things up so that the bird can move away from the heat if it so desires.

Almost all finches love panicum millet. Provide a dish of the small millet varieties, canary grass seed (= white seed), weed and grass seed, and niger seed. For drinking, provide tap water which has been boiled and allowed to cool. A disinfectant should be dissolved in the water, following the advice of your local avian veterinarian. We have had consistent success with fresh, cooled chamomile tea, which has a healthy quality which helps to offset mild intestinal and stomach disorders. We make it up fresh twice a day, and in the evening we replace it with the boiled and then cooled tap water with disinfectant. Remember that chamomile tea turns sour quickly in warm weather; that's why we make it fresh twice a day and do not allow it to sit in the cage overnight.

Place drinking cups in a location where no droppings can fall into the water. Overlooking this precaution can obviously lead to a lot of trouble.

After two weeks, we start providing only tap water. This is still boiled and then cooled to room temperature, of course. In areas with hard water, we suggest using spring water, which can be purchased in the super market or drug store.

Recently imported birds should not be allowed to bathe during the first two weeks. Wait till they perch healthy and lively before letting them bathe. Once again, we provide tap water at room temperature for this purpose and add to it one-third part of chamomile tea cooled to the same temperature. We do this because birds like to drink before they bathe. After a week, you can omit the chamomile tea. Chamomile tea also has a healing function in the bath water. If there are any patches of inflamed skin, which may be hidden from our view by the feathers, they will disappear when exposed to chamomile tea.

Since most finches feed, at least in part, on the ground, recently arrived birds will instinctively look for food on the floor. So when you provide food, sprinkle some on the floor and hang the seed dishes low in the cage or aviary, close to the main perches. Furnish drinking water in flat, earthenware dishes; the rim should be somewhat rough so that the birds won't fall into the water. Preferably, cover the dishes with wire mesh to prevent the birds from bathing in the drinking water.

To avoid intestinal upsets, don't feed new birds any greens or fortified food for the first four days. Sprouted seed, however, will be greatly appreciated.

Approximately one week after the arrival of the birds, scatter some sand on the floor of the cage. The sand should not be too sharp, and should be replaced daily. Or else, use fine oyster-shell grit. It can happen that recently imported birds take in too much sand or grit. If so, cover the floor with paper (not newspaper) because too large an intake of sand or grit can cause all kinds of stomach and intestinal disorders, as well as crop impaction. This can be prevented by giving the birds grit in an open dish once a week and letting them pick whatever they like for one hour only.

Keep the cage scrupulously clean, and wash all utensils at least once a day with hot water and then disinfect them with Clorox, Purex (1:32 solution; half a cup per gallon of water), One-Stroke, Environ, or Lysol.

Watch carefully for any sign of watery droppings, and if noticed, take immediate action. This symptom can be life threatening for birds. Add a 5–10% glucose solution to the drinking water and

Suggestions for a group aviary

1. Recommended for beginners who want a reasonable chance to breed successfully:
- British birds (eg. European goldfinch, serin, linnet)
- canary
- cardinal species
- crimson finch
- golden sparrow
- painted quail
- Pekin robin
- spice finch
- zebra finch

Keep all these birds in pairs and don't plan two pairs of any sort in the same aviary (to avoid constant bickering); three or more couples are okay.

2. Recommended for beginners who are not looking for immediate breeding results:
- cardinal species
- cut-throat finch
- doves (eg. diamond dove)
- Java sparrow (eg. white, gray, pied)
- painted quail
- weavers (the larger species)
- whydahs (the larger species)

A collection of this type could produce some breeding results, despite the description we gave it. Several species will breed satisfactorily, if they get the opportunity.

3. Recommended for somewhat experienced hobbyists:
- Australian finches and parrot finches
- canaries (for song and color)
- Chinese painted quail
- gray finch
- Pekin robin
- red-tailed lavender
- waxbills

4. Also recommended for somewhat experienced hobbyists:
- Australian finches and parrot finches
- Bengalese (in several color mutations)
- black-headed munia
- Chinese painted quail

- diamond dove (or similar birds)
- gray-headed silverbill
- yellow-faced grassquit
- zebra finch (in several colors)

5. Recommended for anyone who likes a well-stocked group aviary:
- Bengalese
- cherry finch
- Chinese painted quail
- common waxbill
- crimson-rumped waxbill
- golden-breasted waxbill
- gray singing finch
- gray-headed silverbill
- green avadavant
- green singing finch
  (Note, however, that this bird cannot be kept in an aviary also housing a pair of gray singing finches; these two species are almost always on the brink of battle with one another.)
- Indian silverbill
- nun species (the three popular species, black-headed, tricolored and white-headed, can be placed together without problems)
- orange-checked waxbill
- red-billed firefinch
- red-checked cordon bleu
- red-eared waxbill
- red-tailed lavender
- spice finch
- star finch
- strawberry finch
- violet-eared waxbill
- zebra finches (in various color mutations)

6. Recommended for the experienced hobbyist:
- African glossy starling
- British birds
- bulbul species
- cardinal species
- crimson finch
- doves (the large species)
- pagoda starling
- Pekin robin
- quail (the larger species)
- shama thrush (and other thrush species)
- song thrush
- weaver species (only the larger species)
- whydah species (only the larger species)

7. Recommended for hobbyists who prize song and color (while maintaining reasonable chances for breeding):
- Bengalese (in several color mutations)
- black-headed canary
- British birds
- doves (only small species)
- golden sparrow
- Java sparrow
- saffron finch
- weaver and whydah species (only the larger ones)
- yellow-faced grassquit

8. Recommended for hobbyists wanting to combine song, color, and breeding:
- Bengalese (in several color mutations)
- black-headed canary
- black-throated finch
- cherry finch
- Cuban grassquit
  (Note, however, that this bird should not be placed in the same quarters with the yellow- faced grassquit, even if there is more than enough space; sooner or later they'll start a "war.")
- diamond sparrow
- indigo bunting
- Java bunting
- lazuli bunting
- long-tailed grass finch
  (Note, however, that among this species there can be couples that are pugnacious, so it pays to watch them.)
- nun species
- quail (various species)
- red-headed finch
- red-winged pytilia
- saffron finch
- weavers and whydah species
- zebra finch (various mutations)

The listed combinations reflect our personal preferences. They will however, serve as a guide for creating your own collection, taking into account the size of the aviary.

provide some poppy seed in the normal seed mix. And don't forget to consult an avian veterinarian immediately.

We recommend providing a night light (see above), say 4–7 watt, so that the birds can see enough to eat and drink at night if they want to. Sometimes the infrared lamp provides enough light, so if you use one, be sure to leave it on day and night.

For an antibiotic, we recommend oxytetracycline Hc1:20 percent, at a dosage of five grams per liter of drinking water for one or two weeks. Another popular antibiotic used by most veterinarians is fluoroquinolones; Baytril is an example. Always follow your veterinarian's instructions; not following the prescribed course can be life threatening to your birds.

Once you have had your recently imported birds in quarantine for at least two weeks, you can start offering them chickweed for green food, and also small amounts of egg food (CéDé, for example, available in most pet shops). By the way, you can commence feeding insects (ant "eggs," mealworms, white worms, fruit flies, etc.) approximately ten days after arrival, provided the birds look chipper and healthy. But remember that any time birds are offered any new type of food, they should be monitored carefully for diarrhea and intestinal upsets; if problems are observed, discontinue the new food for several weeks before offering it again.

After two weeks, you can limit the use of the infrared lamp to night time. However, if you have any weak birds, keep the infrared lamp on day and night for several more weeks.

Birds become accustomed quickly to a caretaker, so during the acclimatization process, always have the same person clean the cages or flights and provide the food and water. This helps keep things quiet, thus avoiding stress.

If you keep the birds out of doors, be sure not to expose them to temperatures below 72°F (22°C) at any time. Aviaries should have a protective sleeping coop, called a night shelter, with plenty of sleeping boxes. Cages should be moved indoors, if necessary, when evening falls. In early spring and in the fall, don't house recently acclimatized birds outside at all. And don't force the birds to breed the first year after arrival; this would weaken them too much.

Cages

You can get to know your birds, their behavior and life experiences, only if housing and care are well arranged. Good housing promotes careful observation and record keeping, and that's important for all types of birds. Don't think that because they are so common, zebra finches *Poephila guttata* or society finches *Lonchura striata* var. *domestica* don't need to be observed, that nothing new could be found out about them. That's by no means the case. We need to know as many details as possible about all our birds because there are already a great number of countries that forbid export of their birds. Additional regulations are coming our way, so that soon we can expect to be limited to birds that are bred in captivity.

Most estrildid finches are rather small, and people are tempted to think that they can be kept in small quarters. Not so! There should always be enough room for them to exercise adequately. Small quarters lead to fat and listless birds that won't breed. This is particularly true for the diamond sparrow *Zonaeginthus guttatus*. Even the smallest finches should be given a cage of at least 30 in. x 18 in. x 20 in. (75 cm x 45 cm x 50 cm) high. Finches should always housed in pairs, if possible.

We prefer cages that are as long as they are wide, which would change the dimensions we just mentioned to 30 in. x 30 in. x 20 in. (75 cm x 75 cm x 50 cm). Cages of this size are appropriate for two pairs of different species (see page 25), or, in a pinch, for three pairs, provided the species are really small, like various waxbills. At that level of crowding, however, don't set your sights too high for breeding results.

Box Cage: The best type of cage is the so-called box cage, which allows birds to feel the most protected and the safest, as experience has shown. A box cage has some kind of wire mesh only on the front. The sides, roof and rear walls can be made of wood or other material. Paint the inside of the cage with a safe, lead-free, light colored paint. You can use paint intended for children's furniture, for example. This paint is easy to wash, which is an important consideration. For the outside, you can use any type of paint you wish. Over the floor, build a second floor of metal (zinc), hardboard, or the like, that can slide in and out. Then take a sheet of glass or hard plastic about 4 in. (10 cm) high and put it along the entire front of the cage to prevent spillage of seed hulls, sand, and feathers. Make sure that this sheet is easy to remove for cleaning.

In the sidewalls (and the rear-wall too, if you like), install some doors, so that you can reach all areas of the cage. Ideally, the front of the cage also should be constructed so that it can be slid open; as this helps simplify feeding and watering. There are ready-to-use cage fronts in various sizes, even with sliding doors, available in the better pet shops. You can hang a water bottle or even one of the well-known plastic bath houses in one of these doors, although, for bathing, an earthenware dish set on the floor will also be very much appreciated.

The location of the cage is quite important. Be sure there is enough light and fresh air, but definitely no drafts! Never place a cage close to an open window, because it is almost impossible to avoid a draft there. Also, a window location could expose birds to strong, direct sunlight, which can rapidly raise the temperature in the cage.

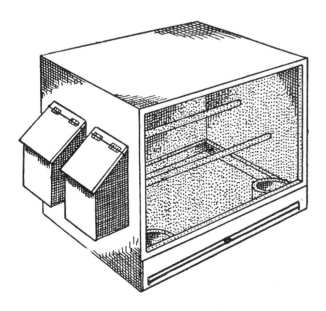

A bird feels most at ease if kept in a partly enclosed cage, the so-called box cage, a unit in which only the front is covered in mesh, the rest—the three walls, floor and roof—is totally enclosed. Such a cage must stand in a brightly lit, draft-free spot. Not in full sunlight, as such a cage can, in a short time, become like an oven. Box cages are ideal for breeding, and come in many different sizes and types.

Vitrines

Vitrines are currently quite popular. They are often advertised in the commercial bird magazines. And indeed, vitrines make fine quarters, provided they are constructed correctly and are large enough, especially for the more fragile exotics. The front is made of glass or plexiglass. The sides and roof are made partially of wire mesh. These parts should be equipped with shutters to regulate fresh air and ventilation. There should be several doors in the sides to permit all necessary tasks.

A vitrine is excellent for a living room, den, or study. Add some suitable, safe, live plants and you will have a really attractive exhibit.

You will need a thermometer to check the temperature in order to maintain it properly. We recommend that the glass front slopes, so that the vitrine is wider at the bottom than at the top. This way, droppings and dirt are less likely to spoil the view. The glass front really should be removable, so that it will slide out easily for cleaning. Make two parallel grooves on each side of the vitrine's front frame, so that before removing the glass plate you can install a solid piece of cardboard or a similarly sized piece of glass to contain the birds. The bottom of the vitrine also should have a floor that can slide out, as with a box cage, for easy cleaning.

Equip a vitrine properly. Furnish some live branches, such as willow or apple, placed in jelly jars filled with wet sand to keep them fresh. Make a wire-mesh cover, so that you can insert the branches easily. Have some containers solely for green food, and supply separate dishes for food, water and bathing. Also, install several perches separated by an appropriate distance.

Cover the floor with so-called bird gravel, not too coarse sand with just a little charcoal, which somewhat combats hyperacidity and sweetens the stomach, and oyster shell, which supplies calcium, about 1 in. (2½ cm) deep, and put some small stones (flagstones and such) on top.

You can backlight the vitrine if you'd like. Some people decorate the walls with nature scenes, but we don't recommend this. You can become bored looking at these after a while. We suggest you use a neutral light blue or soft gray color that will show off the birds well. Use washable paint, because the birds tend to splash while bathing and otherwise spread dirt. The glass front, of course, also gets dirty, and you need to count on washing it at least three times a week. Birds will be less alarmed if you insert the cardboard before sliding out the glass front.

Indoor Aviaries

An indoor aviary should have a surface at least 18 in. (0.5 m) square. Personally, we prefer aviaries twice that size, and even larger doesn't hurt. This size aviary can hold three to four pairs of estrildid finches. It is large enough even for the young that you expect later. Place the entire aviary on a platform at least 2 ft. (60 cm) high to avoid cold drafts.

As with any type of quarters, be sure that you have access to the inside of the aviary so that you can service it for food, water, nest boxes, clean up, etc., without disturbing the birds too much. Take this into account when you design and build the aviary.

Bird Room: A bird room is fun to set up, if you have the available space, especially if it has several windows facing south, southeast, or southwest. Make sure the birds you house together are compatible. You must plan your collection carefully to satisfy this precondition. You want to avoid fights that cause commotion, particularly during the breeding season.

Once you have independent fledglings in the bird room, move them to separate quarters, because many parents have the habit of chasing their young-adult offspring around. This again disturbs the peace that you want to maintain during the breeding season.

You can split the bird room into two, four, or six aviaries with a service aisle along the middle. This way you are able to maintain several collections and to have separate quarters available for quarrelsome birds, newly independent young, or for other reasons. It is also easier to observe your birds with such an arrangement. If you place all the birds together in one room, you usually get a situation where the aviculturist has to sit with his nose against the wire mesh on the door frame, often exposed to a drafty hallway or causeway.

Be sure to put screens on all the windows, so that you can open them safely to let in fresh air and direct sunlight. This is of prime importance for your feathered friends. Paint the walls with washable paint in natural, quiet colors, like light green or gray, pale blue, and such.

Decorate the corners with live plants in pots and barrels (see page 30), and install fabricated perches there too. This way you preserve maximum flight space. You may consider planting elder, willow, roses, all types of philodendron, reeds, bamboo, privet, or dwarf conifers. You will have to count on some damage inflicted by the birds, so that now and then you will have to

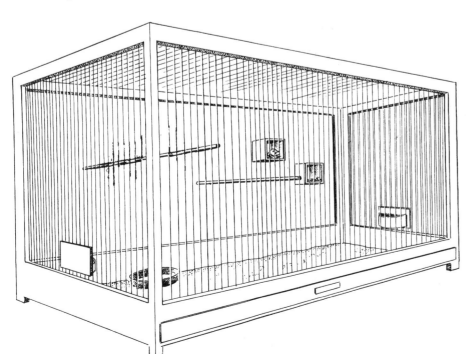

Indoor cages can never be too large. Ideal for three (never two!) to four pair of finches.

replace the plants. But actually, the damage isn't as great as you might think. You will need to spray the plants regularly with a water mister. We consider a bird room complete only if proper attention has been given to plants. You have a good chance that many types of birds will build nests there in the open, which is highly interesting in itself.

An ideal situation is to have a bird room on the ground floor with an outdoor aviary attached. This is the most appropriate set-up of all. Even if the exposure isn't ideal in such a case, we would still advise you to consider it. With the aid of glass on the outside, you can correct a less than ideal exposure considerably. On pleasant, sunny, windless days, you can open the windows and the birds can enjoy the fresh air and direct sunlight to their heart's content, a vital factor for exotic finches, as we discussed earlier. Ultraviolet rays on the feathers are beneficial, and birds that have been kept indoors for a long winter improve visibly when they can come back out into the open air and enjoy a daily sun bath. The outdoor run should have plenty of plantings also, so that birds can hide in the shade of the greenery if they need to. An excess of sunlight is not good, either!

Garden or Outdoor Aviary

The outdoor or garden aviary is currently the most popular type of housing for the serious aviculturist. As a result, you have a great variety of well-constructed aviaries to choose from (see also the ads in commercial pet bird magazines).

First, the minimum size for an outside aviary should be 6½ ft. high x 6½ ft. wide x 10 ft. long (2 m x 2 m x 3 m). A good outdoor aviary usually has a covered section and an open section. Let us discuss the open section first, which is often called the run. Situate the front of the run toward the south as much as possible; if you need to deviate, southeast is better than southwest. Even if the front is properly oriented, we would still suggest making part of it from glass, using only non-reflecting glass. Naturally, you want to place the aviary where you can view it easily, set attractively among some flowers, plants or bushes.

From the start, plan to make the outdoor aviary attack-proof against the entry of all vermin, wildlife, cats and owls. First, pour a concrete foun-

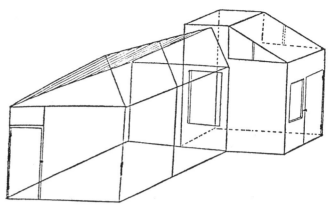

Diagram of a well-designed garden aviary with plenty of room for natural shrubs.

dation. The upright sides should be supported by metal T-beams. Wood is not so easy to make attack-proof, but if you need to use it, fortify the edges with metal strips. Build a wall of brick or cinder block on the foundation, about 12–18 in. (30–50 cm) high, on which you'll lay the floor. The best flooring is concrete, especially for the sleeping coop or night shelter. You can also use creosoted flooring and tiles. For solid walls or sections, we suggest using tongue-and-groove pine boards, but this can be rather expensive. The roof should be somewhat sloped. We recommend using roof tiles. If you build the aviary against an existing wall or fence, make sure that the roof extends over the wall, so that water doesn't gather in the cracks, although you could minimize this problem with a sheet of tarpaper.

Other materials you'll need are strong ½ x ½ in. (25 x 25 mm) wire mesh, wire, nails, and glass. For the semi-covered part of the outdoor aviary, use safety glass. We recommend a good metal or plastic gutter, also.

We suggest letting the environment dictate the size of the aviary. You're not keeping chickens or ducks, where it makes sense to let the size of the flock dictate the size of the coop. See what size aviary would suit the surroundings, then decide the number of birds you can keep. If you have enough space, you can try colony breeding, with several pairs of the same species, which is recommendable for many of the exotic finches, anyway, as certain species naturally breed in colonies.

In designing an aviary, maintain simple lines and construction that fits into the surroundings as

Some Poisonous Plants

acocanthera (fruit and flowers)
amaryllis (bulbs)
amsinckia (or tarweed; foliage, seeds)
anemone (all parts)
angel trumpet (flowers, leaves)
apple (seeds)
apricots (pits, inner seed)
atropa autumn crocus (bulbs)
avocado (foliage)
azalea (leaves)

balsam pear (seeds, outer rind of fruit)
baneberry (berries, roots)
beach pea (all parts)
belladonna (all parts, especially black berries)
betel nut palm (all parts)
bird of paradise (seeds)
bittersweet (berries)
black locust (bark, sprouts, foliage)
bleeding heart (foliage, roots)
bloodroot (all parts)
bluebonnet (all parts)
blue-green algae (some forms are toxic)
bottlebrush (flowers)
boxwood (leaves, stems)
buckeye horse chestnut (sprouts, nuts)
buckthorn (fruit, bark)
buttercup (sap, bulbs)

calla lily (leaves)
caladium (leaves)
cardinal flower (all parts)
Carolina jessamine (foliage, flowers, sap)
cassava (roots)
castor bean (or castor oil-beans; leaves and beans)
chalice vine (or trumpet vine; all parts)
cherry tree (bark, twigs, leaves, pits)
cherry laurel (foliage, flowers)
Chinaberry tree (berries)
Christmas berry (berries)
Christmas cactus (sap)
Christmas candle (sap)
Christmas rose (foliage, flowers)
coral plant (seeds)
crocus (bulbs)
croton (foliage, shoots)
cyclamen (foliage, stems, flowers)

daffodil (bulbs)
daphne (berries)
datura (berries)

deadly amanita (all parts)
deadly nightshade (all parts)
death camas (all parts)
death cap mushroom (all parts)
delphinium (all parts)
deiffenbachia (or dumbcane; leaves)
dogwood (fruit)
Dutchman's breeches (foliage, roots)

eggplant (all parts except fruit)
elderberry (foliage)
elephant's ear (or taro; leaves, stem)
English ivy (berries, leaves)
equisetum (all parts)
euphorbia (or spurges; foliage, flowers, sap)

false henbane (all parts)
fiddleneck (or senecio; all parts)
fly agaric (or amanita; all parts)
four o'clock (all parts)
foxglove (leaves, seeds)

gelsemium (all parts)
ghostweed (all parts)
golden chain (or laburnum; all parts, especially seeds)

hemlock (all parts, especially roots and seeds)
henvane (seeds)
holly (berries)
horse chestnut (nuts, twigs)
horsetail reed (or equisetum; all parts)
hyacinth (bulbs)
hydrangea (flower bud)

impatiens (or touch-me-not; all parts)
Indian turnip (or jack-in-pulpit; all parts)
iris (or blue flag; bulbs)
ivy (all forms; foliage, fruit)

jasmine (foliage, flowers, sap)
jasmine star (foliage, flowers)
jatropha (seeds, sap)
java bean (or lima bean; uncooked bean)
Jerusalem cherry (berries)
jessamine (berries)
jimsonweed (foliage, flowers, seed pods)
Johnson grass (all parts)
juniper (needles, stems, berries)

laburnum (all parts)
lambkill (or sheep laurel; all parts)
lantana (immature berries)
larkspur (all parts)
laurel (all parts)
lily of the valley (all parts including water in which they have been kept)
lobelia (all parts)
locoweed (all parts)
lords and ladies (or cuckoopint; all parts)
lupine (foliage, pods, seeds)

machineel (all parts)
marijuana (leaves)
mayapple (all parts except fruit)
mescal bean (seeds)
milkweed (foliage)
mistletoe (berries)
moccasin flower (foliage, flowers)
mock orange (fruit)
monkshood (leaves, roots)
morning glory (all parts)
mountain laurel (leaves, shoots)
mushrooms (most wild forms; caps, stems)

narcissus (bulbs)
natal cherries (berries, foliage)
nectarine (seeds, inner pit)
nicotine bush (foliage, flowers)
nightshades (all varieties; berries, leaves)

oak (acorns, foliage)
oleander (leaves, branches, nectar of blossoms)

peach (fruit pit)
pear (seeds)
pennyroyal (foliage, flowers)
peony (foliage, flowers)
periwinkle (all parts)
philodendron (leaves and stem)
pikeweed (leaves, roots, immature berries)
pine needles (berries)
plum (foliage, inner seed)
poinsettia (leaves, flowers)
poison hemlock (foliage, seeds)
poison ivy (sap)
poison oak and sumac (foliage, fruit, sap)
pokeweed (or poke cherry; roots, fruit)

poppy (all parts)
potato (eyes, new shoots)
privet (all parts, including berries)

redwood (resinoids, leached wet wood)
rhododendron (all parts)
rhubarb (leaves)
rosary peas (seeds)
rosemary (foliage in some species)
Russian thistle (foliage, flowers)

sage (foliage in some species)
salmonberry (foliage, fruit)
scarlet pimpernel (foliage, flowers, fruit)
Scotch broom (seeds)
senecio (or fiddleneck; all parts)
skunk cabbage (all parts)
snapdragon (foliage, flowers)
snowdrop (all parts especially buds)
snow on the mountain (or ghostweed; all parts)
Spanish bayonet (foliage, flowers)
Sudan grass (all parts)
star of Bethlehem (foliage, flowers)
sundew (foliage)
sweet pea (seeds, fruit)

tansy (foliage)
taro (or elephant's ear; foliage)
tiger lily (foliage, flowers, seed pods)
toad lax (foliage)
tobacco (leaves)
tomato (foliage, vines)
touch-me-not (all parts)
toyon berry (berries)
trillium (foliage)
trumpet vine (all parts)

Venus flytrap (all parts)
verbena (foliage, flowers)
Virginia creeper (sap)

wild parsnip (roots, foliage)
wisteria (all parts)

yam bean (roots, immature roots)
yellow star thistle (foliage, flowers)
yew (American, English and Japanese varieties; needles, seeds)

A garden aviary consisting of three sections:

1. Open section, the flight or run.

2. Covered section, the partially enclosed flight (the roof is covered with corrugated plastic sheeting or something similar

3. Enclosed shelter in the form of a sleeping coop or attached indoor aviary to serve as a night shelter.

much as possible. Actually, this advice also applies for other types of bird housing. The emphasis should be on the contents of the facility, and you should not install such "improvements" as projections, turrets, and the like. Try to let the aviary blend into the environment and adapt itself to its surroundings. Strategically, place plants, bushes, and flowers in the manner described earlier.

The standard aviary has, as far as we are concerned, three sections:
1. a completely open section, the flight or run;
2. a covered section, the partially enclosed flight;
3. a completely enclosed shelter in the form of a sleeping coop or attached indoor aviary to serve as a night shelter.

Sleeping quarters should always be furnished, if only to have a place to install heaters and lights. The covered section should have a watertight roof. The rest of the aviary is covered with wire mesh. The floor can be sand, but a floor of cement tiles covered thickly with sand also works excellently. If you use concrete or tile floors, place the plants in barrels. Bring in fresh willow branches, fruit tree branches, and such, plus various dense bushes that can be replaced when necessary. Be sure to supply sufficient perches.

The open area of the aviary should have perches even if you supply plenty of natural plantings

to perch in. All artificial perches should be sanitized regularly. Those in the open run will, of course, be washed by the rain. When you water the plantings, you can still rinse the perches with a soft spray from the hose. Check their condition regularly.

The windows in the night shelter should have reinforced glass, so that the birds will notice the glass and not fly into it. Plexiglass also works well. You can stick some colored tape or plastic decals to the glass so the birds will see it.

Separate a section of the coop as an entryway with a double door, to avoid escape. When entering, close the outside door before opening the inside door that enters into the run. No free-standing aviary should be without this safety feature.

The next section of the coop should have a floor, half of which should be raised. The upper part is the real sleeping area. The lower part can be split into two compartments, one to serve as a mating area, quarantine area, cooling off area for those who breach the peace, observation area, and so forth. The other section can be a storage place for nest boxes, perches, bowls, water bottles, and such. The floor of this lower section is best when made of cement or tile. The floor of the sleeping quarters should be cement, covered with a 2–3 in. (6–8 cm) thick layer of sand mixed with small sized grit and oyster shell.

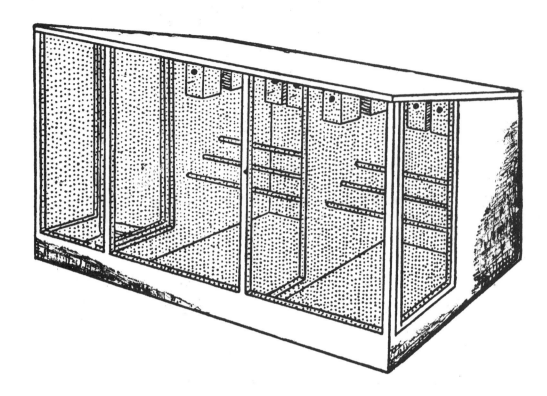

A covered aviary in two sections. Note the safety porch on the left which is an essential requirement to prevent the birds from escaping.

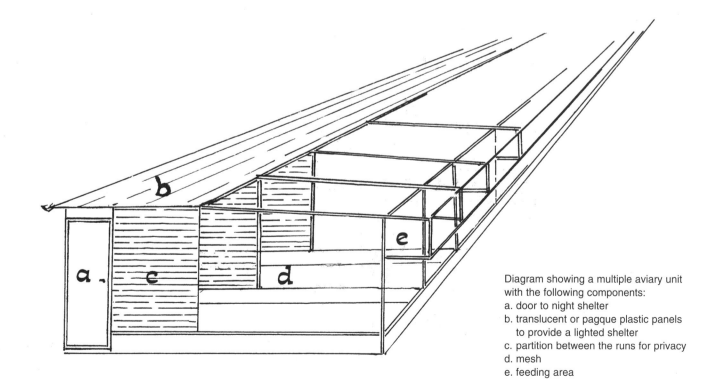

Diagram showing a multiple aviary unit with the following components:
a. door to night shelter
b. translucent or pagque plastic panels to provide a lighted shelter
c. partition between the runs for privacy
d. mesh
e. feeding area

Finches in an outdoor aviary. Although not an estrildid, the green singing finch *Serinus mozambicus*, right, can safely be kept with small estrildids such as these zebra finches and red-cheeked cordon bleus.
(J. G. Blasman aviary, Rozenburg, Netherlands [NL]) *Photo: J. G. Blasman*

RIGHT: Finch aviary with indoor and outdoor sections.
(J. G. Blasman aviary, Rozenburg, NL) *Photo: J. G. Blasman*

A nicely arranged garden with heavily-planted aviaries, ideal for breeding many species of estrildid finches. (F J. ter Horst aviary, Haaksbergen, NL)
Photo: J. G. Blasman

An attractive indoor garden aviary. (J. G. Blasman aviary, Rozenburg, NL)
Photo: J. G. Blasman

Another beautifully-planted indoor aviary. (H. van Os aviary, Birdtrader, Ridderkerk, NL) *Photo: J. G. Blasman*

Indoor aviary with small waterfall. (Birdparc Avifauna, Alphen a/d Rijn, NL)
Photo: J.G. Blasman

Small indoor aviary (rear) with breeding cages (left). (J. G. Blasman aviary, Rozenburg, NL) *Photo: J.G. Blasman*

Spacious and attractively planted indoor aviaries suitable for finches and other small compatible birds. (Birdparc Avifauna, Alphen a/d Rijn, NL)
Photo: J. G. Blasman

Birdroom with indoor flights, left, and breeding or holding cages. (H. van Os aviary, Birdtrader, Ridderkerk, NL)
Photo: J. G. Blasman

Interior view of garden aviary. (J. G. Blasman aviary, Rozenburg, NL)
Photo: J. G. Blasman

Well planted indoor aviary in a zoo setting. (Blijdorp Zoo, Rotterdam, NL)
Photo: J. G. Blasman

Small backyard gazebo aviary. (W. & E. Turner aviary, Surrey, Canada)
Photo: W. & E. Turner

Outdoor flights under construction. (W. & E. Turner aviary, Surrey, Canada)
Photo: W. & E. Turner

Grant Rishman's deck aviary made great use of available space.
(Victoria, Canada) *Photo: W. & E. Turner*

Elaine Turner's birdroom. Popholes lead to outside flights. (W. & E. Turner
aviary, Surrey, Canada) *Photo: W. & E. Turner*

A small garden aviary for finches. (C. Maarseveen aviary, Rozenburg, NL)
Photo: J. G. Blasman

Another attractive garden aviary. (J. G. Blasman aviary, Rozenburg, NL)
Photo: J. G. Blasman

A nicely-planted garden aviary. (B. Smetser, Gorile, NL)
Photo: J. G. Blasman

A large garden aviary will house a mixed species collection without problems.
(Birdparc Avifauna, Alphen a/d Rijn, NL) *Photo: J. G. Blasman*

A series of outdoor aviaries in a birdpark. (Birdparc Avifauna, Alphen
a/d Rijn, NL) *Photo: J. G. Blasman*

The simple wood-frame construction of these touraco aviaries is ideal
for finches. (Faske Aviaries, Texas) *Photo: David Hancock*

Seed cups offer a selection of seeds.
Photo: J. G. Blasman

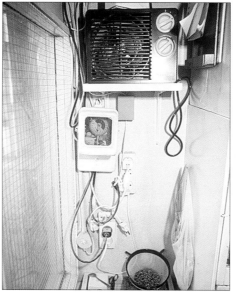

Heater, clock and sprouted seed.
Photo: J. G. Blasman

A commercially available hospital cage.
Photo: J. G. Blasman

The three-colored parrotfinch, *Amblynura (Erythrura) tricolor* likes a planted aviary.
Photo: J. G. Blasman

Indoor flight used as holding pen for finches and other compatible birds, such as small softbills and diamond doves *Geopelia cuneata*. *Photo: J. G. Blasman*

The gray-headed oliveback *Nesocharis capistrata*, an avicultural rarity, prefers a thickly planted aviary. *Photo: J. G. Blasman*

Rarely available and expensive species like this pair of crimson seedcrackers *Pyrenestes sanguineus* deserve a large planted aviary. *Photo: J. G. Blasman*

Breeding cages are useful for domesticated species such as zebra finches and society finches.
Photo: J. G. Blasman

Mealworms are indispensible for breeding finches. *Photo: J. G. Blasman*

An assortment of nesting materials. *Photo: J. G. Blasman*

Nesting diamond finches, *Zonaeginthus guttatus*. *Photo: J. G. Blasman*

Bird band (rings). *Photo: J. G. Blasman*

Banding a nestling finch. *Photo: J. G. Blasman*

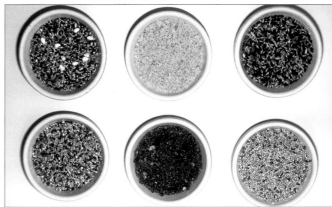

Soft or universal food, egg food, and various seeds. *Photo: J. G. Blasman*

All finches should have cuttlefish bone for calcium. *Photo: J. G. Blasman*

Spray millet is enjoyed by estrildid finches. *Photo: J. G. Blasman*

Water and seed cups. *Photo: J. G. Blasman*

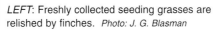

Ground oystershell and grit are essential for seed eating birds. *Photo: J. G. Blasman*

LEFT: Freshly collected seeding grasses are relished by finches. *Photo: J. G. Blasman*

Various types of nestboxes *Photo: J. G. Blasman*

A large desert garden aviary suitable for species which prefer a drier habitat. (Burger's Zoo, Arnhem, NL)
Photo: J. G. Blasman

Raymond Sawyer feeds touraco at Ezra-Sawyer Aviaries, England. *Photo: David Hancock*

Aviaries can be designed to fit the existing landscape such as this hillside aviary. (Harewood Bird Garden, England) *Photo: David Hancock*

A strong foundation will help keep aviaries rodent-free. *Photo: David Hancock*

Michal Klat Aviaries, England. *Photo: David Hancock*

Right: Opperman Museum, Windhoek, Namibia: A two hectare walk-through aviary with colonies of Society-weaver finches and other species. *Photo: David Hancock*

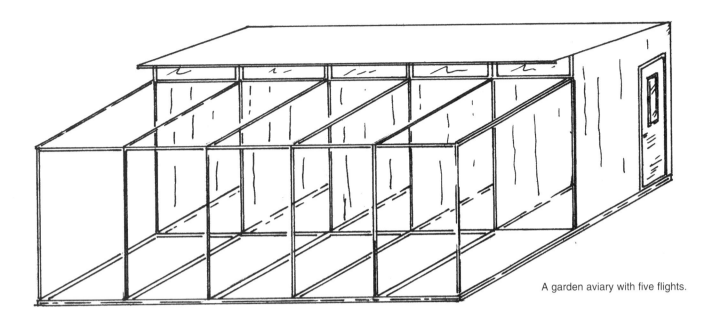

A garden aviary with five flights.

Bird House

The somewhat complex bird house is becoming common among more experienced bird fanciers and aviculturists. This consists of an indoor aviary in a separate building, with a quarantine room, an acclimatization room, and several attached outdoor aviaries. All these must be built and furnished in the same manner as a basic garden or outdoor aviary. We would recommend constructing the aviary relatively wider than longer. This allows young or weak birds to find a haven more easily if that becomes necessary, and you will be more able to make the necessary observations. A stretched-out aviary encourages the birds to make long flights, one after the other, and you will not be able to enjoy seeing much of their behavior and colorful appearance.

A bird house is best built of masonry and should have a good number of windows which can be opened. The windows should be covered with permanent screens to make sure the birds can't fly out when the windows are open, or hurt themselves by flying against the glass. The inside aviary can be arranged as described above for indoor aviaries (see page 28).

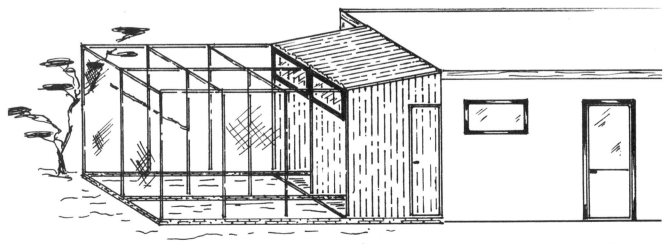

A practical design for a double finch aviary.

Catching Birds

Trying to catch an exotic finch in an enclosure is always a nerve-wracking task. If you tackle the task with a plan, it will certainly become easier after you have gained some experience.

Get a good net with a short grip. The rim should be heavily padded. Then get some lessons from an experienced aviculturist or watch how an experienced pet store manager does the job, and talk over his method with him.

Catching birds in a roomy aviary is easier than doing the job in a cage or small vitrine because you have more operating room. Remove all artificial perches and other utensils from the aviary before going to work because you don't want anything in your way. You'll have enough trouble with just the plants!

We catch our birds in stages when there are several to catch, as when they need to be brought indoors for the winter. As one person enters the aviary, a number of birds will naturally fly off into the sleeping coop. Close the door on them, and go to work on the birds that remain in the run. When you have caught them all, open the sleeping coop again, step inside, and let another group of birds fly into the run. Then, close the door once more, and catch those birds. You keep up this routine until you have caught all of your birds. We always catch them in flight, not while they are resting on a perch, or hanging against the wire netting.

Be sure that you don't have a net with too large a mesh because the birds can get terribly tangled. If that ever happens, it causes a real strain on your nerves, not to speak of the effect on the birds before they are properly disentangled.

Purchasing

When examining birds you're considering buying, never put your nose right up against the wire mesh of the cage holding a bird you're interested in. Even if the bird is at death's door, it will sit straight and hold its feathers in tight when it suddenly sees a human face several inches away.

Rather, do your inspection at a reasonable distance, say 6–8 ft. (2–2½ m) from the cage. Don't be taken in by sales talk. Birds that have puffed up feathers or are easily caught by hand are at best dubious cases. Don't believe suggestions that these birds are just "tame" or "friendly."

Do take in your hand a bird that interests you. Blow aside some breast feathers and check that the breast is meaty and full. Look at the legs; they should be smooth, not scaly. The beak should look normal and the eyes should be clear and bright.

Once you decide to buy, put the bird promptly in a shipping cage. Wrap the cage in newspaper or packing-paper and head for home as quickly as possible. The shipping cage doesn't have to be fancy for a short trip. You can safely carry several finches together in a shoebox in which you have poked some ventilation holes. Put some millet spray and moist wheat bread in the bottom.

Shipping

If you need to ship birds a considerable distance by commercial carrier, find out what type of container is required by the carrier. Generally, they prefer flat, wooden shipping cages with a small strip of wire mesh in the front. Shipping cages are usually equipped with a round perch and two compartments for seed and wet wheat bread. You don't want to put water inside because it would spill in transit. Wrap the cage in thick paper and poke some holes in it for ventilation. That will let in some light but keep it dark enough to help quiet the birds. In bright cages they tend to fly around.

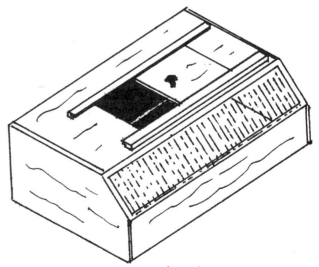

A travel cage should be constructed so that the birds are as safe from fright or injury as possible.

We suggest you pad the inside of the top of the cage with foam rubber to avoid injury if birds do fly up.

Mark the outside of the cage with labels indicating "Live Birds," "Handle with Care," "Don't Drop," "Don't Bump," and "This Side Up" (with an arrow). You probably can get them from the carrier for the asking; if not, make them yourself.

Be sure to check ahead of time on the shipping rules of the carrier you intend to use. Many airlines allow you to take a single pet into the cabin with you, provided you can fit the cage under your seat. You'll probably have to make reservations ahead of time and generally you'll have to pay an extra charge.

If you have several birds, or large birds, they'll have to travel in the cargo hold. Be sure to wrap the cage well in such cases because the temperature in the cargo hold can drop severely. We would line the entire inside of the shipping cage with indoor/outdoor carpeting.

Don't cage birds together if they are at all likely to harm each other. And don't overcrowd the shipping cage. Group birds of similar size together to avoid the danger of the larger birds pushing the little ones against the wall, which can have serious consequences.

If someone ships birds to you, be especially cautious when this is done in winter. Cold temperatures cause the temperature to drop inside the hollow bone structure of the bird. You have the natural tendency to put a chilled bird up close to a toasty heater, but actually, that is the most dangerous thing you could do. The air in the bones expands in response to the sudden increases in temperature, which causes the birds a lot of unnecessary pain. It could even kill them!

In making shipping arrangements, remember that exotic finches need to eat every single day, and they should always have access to seed and water.

New arrivals should not be put into the aviary right away. Keep them separate in a location where the temperature is pleasant and where they can recover from the journey in peace. Feed them generously, using food sent along by the seller. Then, gradually convert to your own menu if this happens to be different (and better!). Also, don't

forget to offer drinking water, at room temperature. Keep the birds warm with an infrared lamp and keep a close eye on them.

If you buy birds close to home, transport them early in the day, so that they can use the rest of the day to become adjusted to their new environment.

When the time comes to integrate new birds into the rest of your collection, place the newcomers, cage and all, into the aviary. Keep them inside the cage half a day, from about 7:00 AM to 1:00 PM. This way the birds can get used to one another before you release the newcomers. Then watch the situation closely. It can happen that the established group will not accept the newcomers, seeing them as challengers to their territories.

Watch what happens for a few days; if the rejection continues, remove the new birds and then reintroduce them gradually after another few days have passed. Generally, new birds won't cause problems in the aviary, provided it isn't overcrowded. Be aware, of course, that you shouldn't introduce new birds during the breeding season. You are really asking for trouble if you do that!

If you have new birds in the aviary, place water and spread some seed here and there on the aviary floor because finches instinctively look for food on or near the ground. Keep this up until you are sure that the newcomers have found the food bowls. The old birds show the new ones by their actions where to find food and water, and they learn by example.

Escape

A final word of advice on escapes. We have mentioned that the aviary should have a safety porch. Still it can happen that a bird escapes. If it is one of a pair, then it shouldn't ordinarily be difficult to catch the escapee. Use a cage with a trap door and put the remaining partner in the closed part of the cage. Then put some snacks and seeds in the part with the trap door. The bird in the cage will send out contact calls and it won't be long until the escaped bird is attracted to the cage. First of all, it ordinarily won't have flown far from the aviary. When it observes its partner in the cage and if it discovers familiar food in the cage as well, it will return to captivity quickly. Even if the escapee isn't paired, another bird of the same species can still serve as bait. If two paired birds both escape, the situation is a bit more difficult. Still, the process is the same. You put another bird of the same species in the trap cage to attract one of the escaped birds, which then in turn serves as bait for the other.

If you don't have any success with the trap cage, you have to wait until evening or night-time. Note precisely where the escaped finch goes to sleep. Then shine a flash light directly at the escaped bird. The sharp light seems to freeze the roosting bird in its resting place and you usually can lift it off the branch by hand. However, this technique does not work all the time!

Often when a finch escapes from a cage, it is enough to remove all other inhabitants temporarily from that cage and set it outside, with the door(s) open. Hunger and thirst will tend to drive the escapee back to the trusted cage after a few hours to take advantage of the feed and water it finds there.

Equipping Facilities for Exotic Finches

You should get two different types of perches, anchored ones and swinging ones. The swinging perches are for play, the anchored ones are for resting and roosting, and, during the breeding season, for mating.

Aviaries with good plantings naturally provide perches in the form of a variety of branches for sitting and sleeping. Many finch species will even build nests in the plants.

In the indoor aviary provide anchored, round perches; flattened on top for a better grip. Such perches should likewise be provided for the covered part of an outdoor or garden aviary. In other parts of the outdoor aviary, you can provide sleeping boxes in wind- and draft-free locations.

Perches should be made of hardwood dowels and, as already indicated, slightly flattened on top. Hardwood is recommended because it is less likely to harbor lice and mites. The perches should not be too thin. They must be thick enough to keep the toes of resting birds from closing around them completely, otherwise the birds can't relax well.

We suggest you supply perches of varying diameters. This will help to keep toe nails trim and leg muscles limber (see also page 00).

Don't skimp on places to perch and sleep. You don't want your birds to get into fights over them. Don't install one perch over the top of another. You don't want birds perching above to foul the ones below. For the same reason, never install perches over food and water bowls and baths.

For natural perches, we recommend branches from fruit trees such as apple or pear (no cherry!), willow, hazel, elderberry and sycamore. Remember to replace them regularly, because after awhile, cut branches lose their elasticity. If you have birds that have quick growing nails, like, for example, Java rice birds *Padda oryzivora* and other munias or mannikins, we recommend reeds and similar plants that help keep their nails trim. Flagstones or other rough stones serve the same purpose, and should be included in any aviary or bird cage.

The garden aviary should be further furnished with plants (see page 46). First of all, this will give it a natural appearance. Second, it provides nesting places. Third, the plants attract all types of small creatures such as aphids, spiders, bugs, and others. This comes in handy especially at breeding time, when most birds absolutely require insects for the proper feeding of the young. Observations in the wild and examinations of bird crops have shown that the young even of seed-eating finches are fed almost exclusively on insects and spiders the first period of their lives.

Many plants you can consider for the garden aviary also have the advantage of providing berries. Suitable examples include elder, cotoneaster, and firethorn. Birds love the berries. The only disadvantage of planting live bushes in the garden aviary is that they take up a relatively large amount of space that otherwise could be used as flight space for the birds. Besides, several types of birds tend to be hard on bushes, making them look pretty rough even after a short time. Years of experimenting led us to a satisfactory solution for minimizing the drawbacks of live bushes in finch aviaries by using the well-known firethorn *Pyracantha coccinea* exclusively. Firethorn has the advantage that it can be trellised, meaning that the branches can be led along walls and fences. It works particularly well along a closed rear wall. If the rear side is made of stone or solid wood it is easier to train the firethorn along its expanse. Plant the firethorn as close to the wall as possible, even against the wall of the night shelter. Then spread the branches against the wall and attach them. Resistant branches can be cut close to the stem. This way, you train a plant to grow tightly against the wall. If you keep attaching new growth consistently, it won't be long until the wall is completely covered. After awhile, this living wall can become a foot (30 cm) thick. You can place sleeping and breeding boxes between the branches. Training branches takes extra work and patience, but it is worth the trouble!

In May and June, the firethorn will reward you with countless white blossoms that resemble those of the perhaps better known hawthorn. These fragrant blossoms attract a lot of flies and other bugs that are hunted down by many birds. In the summer, the berries start to form, and by fall they will ripen and your back aviary wall will be festooned in glowing red, orange, or yellow, depending on the variety you planted. The ripe berries contain many small pits, which provide a welcome addition to the diet of the birds as soon as they become used to the taste.

Canaries and parakeets (budgerigars) need to be kept away from the firethorn because they gnaw too much. We don't recommend that you keep parakeets in the same aviary with estrildid finches, anyway! If you want to protect the firethorn, build a second rear wall about 2 in. (5 cm) in front of your "firethorn wall." Make this second wall of so-called parakeet mesh, which is one mesh size bigger than the half-inch mesh. The majority of the tropical finches are small enough to get through the mesh and enjoy the firethorn, while the somewhat larger canaries and such are limited to gnawing on whatever branches project from the living wall and grow through the wire-mesh. But again, it is inadvisable to house parakeets and canaries in an aviary with finches.

In case you're concerned about the thorns of the firethorn, they pose no problem for small finches. (Thorn birds exist only in legends). We have never come across an instance where finches

hurt themselves on the thorns, even though they often like to take a rapid dive into a firethorn branch. Humans, however, should take precautions. When you train the bushes, always wear gardening gloves because you could get scratched painfully by the thorns.

If you want to do something special, you could try decorating the open run of the garden aviary with tall-growing grasses or reeds. Reeds, for example, combine well with a small pond. Ponds are fine, provided you take precautions against drowning, particularly of fledglings. Make sure that the pond has extremely shallow spots that are at the most an inch (2 cm) deep. You can create these shallows with flagstones, other flat stones, or gravel. Also, build the sides with a long slope, so that a bird that falls in can get out again easily. Finally, be sure that you install a drain at the deepest point of the pond. You need it in order to remove and freshen the water and clean the pond. For this reason, construct the pond on the highest spot in the aviary, if possible, and attach a garden hose to the drain, so that you can lead the waste water away from the aviary.

Feeding and watering utensils come in many shapes, sizes, and colors. The best ones are made of white porcelain or hard plastic, are oval, and measure about 4 in. (10 cm) in diameter. You can consider automatic feeders, provided they really work well. Automatic waterers or drinking vessels are good too, and are really better than bowls because birds can't foul them. Large, glazed bowls or plastic containers are useful for sprouting seeds, universal food (rearing or egg food), and other supplements that are provided in small quantities to prevent spoilage. Separate vessels for grit and oyster shell must also be provided. Use flat bowls for bird baths. If you don't have them, you can adapt deeper bowls by putting flat stones or gravel in them. You want to prevent drowning, particularly of young birds!

In cages, insert all utensils in the sides and in door openings, or specially made openings. The well-known plastic food dispenser that hangs against the door is a good example.

In aviaries, put utensils close to a door, near, but not too near, the nest, to minimize the chance of escape and of attack by cats. Again, this is for

Some Aviary Plants Worthy of Serious Consideration

American arborvitae
Thuja occidentalis
Excellent hedge for community aviary with small birds. Plant only young ones.

Austrian pine *Pinus nigra*
Many finches like to build their nests in pines, especially if you help them get started with a base of woven rope, or the like, placed between the branches or in a fork. Regular trimming keeps the plant low.

Bamboo *Sinarundinaria* spp.
Quite decorative; mannikins and other small finches whose nails tend to grow fast like to frequent bamboo.

Beech *Fagus sylvatica*
When fully grown, the tree can provide needed shade in large aviaries. It is generally best not to grow a beech in an inclosed aviary because it grows too large. For an inclosed aviary, we would like to recommend a European hornbeam *Carpinus betulus*.

Boxwood *Buxus sempervirens*
Does especially well as a strip of hedge about 3 ft. (1 m) in length. Many finches, particularly the various Australian grassfinches, like to build nests in boxwood hedges.

Broom *Cytisus scoparius*
Cut the bushes, tie them together loosely, and attach them to the roof of the aviary. Hollow the sheaf out a little, and the birds will love to build nests in it. You can plant wild and cultivated broom in the aviary, and it will do quite well if it gets full sun. Broom requires a sandy, acid soil.

Buddleia *Buddleia davidii*
Use only young plants; birds like to nest in them or use them for an overnight shelter. To keep the shrub from growing too large, cut it back each year to a height of about 10 in. (25 cm). The shrub attracts countless insects, including many that the birds relish.

Climbing rose *Rosa multiflora*
An excellent aviary plant. It makes a good hedge. Actually, you can use all types of cultivated roses inside and around the aviary. They give extra color and life to your collection. In addition, many varieties are quite susceptible to aphids, which provide a special feast for all finch species.

Cotoneaster *Cotoneaster* spp.
We recommend the use of these richly branched shrubs. They demand little and don't take up much of the garden. There are a number of varieties, evergreens as well as deciduous. There are also dwarf and tall varieties. The plants produce pitted red fruits that are a treat to fruit-eating birds, particularly the thrushes; larger finch species, however, also like them..

Douglas fir *Pseudotsuga taxifolia*
Suitable for an open aviary. Select young plants.

English hawthorn
Crataegus monogyna
The bullet-shaped berries are popular with the birds. The shrub is easy to grow; a sunny location is preferable.

English holly *Ilex aquifolium*
This evergreen is a bush that can grow into a tree up to 25 ft. (7 m) tall. It is extremely well suited to all types of outside aviaries. You need both male and female bushes to produce the scarlet-red berries that are so loved by the birds. Some aviculturists, however, claim that the berries are poisonous.

European elderberry
Sambucus nigra
Berries are black and are readily eaten by all types of birds (and humans). Another important characteristic is that the plant attracts aphids. If birds have access to the shrubs, they will scour them for aphids and small spiders. Otherwise, you can provide your birds many hours of pure joy by cutting down several aphid-infested branches and putting them in the aviary or cage! This is particularly good to do at breeding time. Actually, we consider it is essential for tropical and subtropical finches!

European hornbeam
Carpinus betulus
This is truly an ideal plant for the aviary, especially because birds love to nest in it. In the fall, the leaves turn an attractive brownish-yellow. They tend to stay on the shrub for a relatively long time, giving birds some protection against wind and rain. When there is a heavy frost, the leaves drop off rapidly.

European larch *Larix decidua*
This tree is suited to aviaries, including those with poor soil, and so is widely used.

False spirea *Sorbaria sorbifolia*
Use only dwarf varieties for the aviaries, as they can grow up to 10 ft. (3 m). The related *Sorbaria aucuparia* is also frequently grown in aviaries; its' berries are a special attraction and avidly eaten by birds, particularly thrushes, larger finches and related species.

Firethorn *Pyracantha coccinea*
If you have a cement wall on your aviary, pyracantha is one of the plants that will grow against it quite well. The plant has magnificent flowers that are followed by red berries, the latter being a special taste treat for your birds. It can form a dense growth that makes an excellent nesting place for large finches, thrushes and related species, estrildid finches and many more. Various of our tropical doves like to nest in the plant! For more details, turn to page 00.

Golden laburnum *Laburnum* spp.
The main reason for mentioning the golden laburnum in this list is to warn you to avoid it at all cost, even though it is very popular in ordinary gardens and parks. Both the leaves and the pods are poisonous!

Hydrangea *Hydrangea* spp.

A hydrangea can add considerable color to your plantings with its canopy of pink, blue, or white flowers. The plant is quite prolific and can be grown in sandy soil, provided it is well-tilled with peat moss. It should not, however, be planted in direct sunlight.

Ivy *Hedera helix*

This climbing evergreen is attractive and quite useful. Ivy has round, blue-black berries, and many birds eat them avidly. Tropical finches will nest in ivy, especially if some rope is wound between the branches to provide a nesting base.

Japanese spirea *Spiraea japonica*

This shrub is considered an ideal plant for the aviary because it has a thickly branched type of growth. Many birds like to construct their nests in this shrub.

Jasmine *Philadelphus* spp.

This is a widely appreciated plant, not only for its white blossoms, which can be single or double, but also for its strong, yet very appealing fragrance. Birds like to flit in and out of the branches.

Juniper *Juniperus communis*

This evergreen shrub can grow up to 33 ft. (10 m) and more, displaying fanciful forms. Birds often build nests in it, or use it simply to spend the night.

Lilac *Syringa* spp.

The lilac can be made to grow as a bush or tree. It tends to grow tall quickly, so it may be better to place it outside the aviary rather than in it, for example, next to the night shelter. It attracts various insects which will be welcomed by many finches!

Oriental (or Chinese) cedar *Thuja orientalis*

Birds enjoy nesting in this bush, particularly if several (at least three) are planted close together, forming a large, interlocked hedge. Breeding birds feel safe and secluded there.

Oregon holly grape *Mahonia aquifolium*

Birds love the round, dark blue berries. The shrub can be grown in almost any location and soil type, but does require a large amount of water on a regular basis.

Privet *Ligustrum vulgare*

The common privet originated in southern Europe and Asia Minor, and is generally deciduous. Its leaves are sturdy, oblong, lancet-shaped, and about 3 in. (8 cm) long. Many large parakeet species, especially cockatiels, but also canaries and large finches, like to eat the leaves and/or buds, which are a good supplement to their regular diet. Tropical birds, and finches in particular, consider this plant an ideal location for breeding, and canaries and large finches like to spend time in privets on sunny days. The shrub blooms in April or May, showing small, whitish flowers that grow in rather tight clusters. The wood is hard.

The privet is one of the most popular aviary plants in Europe. In a well-limed soil, the plant does exceptionally well. The pied privet also performs admirably; it can be used as a hedge or as a solitary plant.

Snowberry *Symphoricarpus albus*

This native shrub has round, white berries that stay on the bush, even in winter. Blackbirds, pheasants and large quail like to eat the berries. Many tropical birds, finches included, like to nest in these shrubs.

Viburnum *Viburnum* spp.

Shrubs of this family, which are rather large, have been used in aviaries, although we don't recommend any of them for that purpose. We particularly counsel against using the well-known *V. opulus*, a deciduous shrub that can grow up to 10 ft. (3 m) tall. Besides being too tall, it is poisonous to birds. Many of them (even in the wild!) stay away from this bush instinctively, but we wouldn't chance it under any circumstances. The berries are a shiny, transparent red and hang down in bunches. The leaves and bark are poisonous as well.

You can consider Viburnum species for outside the aviary because they attract all kinds of insects which can be expected to pass into the aviary to be caught and eaten by its inhabitants. The shrub requires a somewhat moist soil and a shady location.

Weeping fig *Ficus benjamina*

A beautiful tree for a large aviary; birds like to make their nests in it or spend the night.

Willow *Salix* spp.

There are various species of willow, and any of them can serve as an aviary plant. They can be bushes or trees. If you keep lovebirds, cockatiels, conures, parrotlets, and other parrots and parakeets, you should not pass up the opportunity to place a willow in the aviary. Even a dead stump will do. Hookbills just love to hack and gnaw at the wood, and they like the bark. Many species, such as lovebirds *Agapornis* spp. use willow bark for constructing their nests. Willows thrive in moist, loose soil, and they need to be trimmed. Give the smaller twigs to your birds; they will love everything about them! Many finches like to nest in willow bushes. If you'd like to know more about this plant, please consult our book *The Parrotlet Handbook*, page 61 (Barron's, 1999.).

your convenience, to check on the food supply and to add to it without causing unnecessary disturbance. Do check on the utensils daily. Fill food bowls daily and put fresh, clean water in dishes and bird baths several times daily.

Some exotic finches don't like to stay on the ground if they don't have to, except to drink. Therefore, build a platform about 30 in. (75 cm) off the ground to put feeding dishes on. Bottle-shaped automatic waterers (the so-called water bottles) can be hung up; they will be well used. In larger aviaries, build several feeding platforms to minimize fighting at the food dishes. The platform should have a 4 in. (10 cm) rim to keep the dishes from sliding off. Drill some holes, about ½ in. (1 cm) in diameter, in the platform so that rainwater will present no problems, although it is obviously advisable to place at least one platform in the covered section of the garden aviary. The one in the open run should have some kind of roof as protection.

Place egg food or rearing food, grit, limestone, and other supplements in separate vessels. Cuttle bone is provided and hung against the outside wall of the sleeping shelter. During the breeding season, hang small baskets with nest-building material in the same place. Don't just put supplies on the ground; this gives the aviary an unattractive appearance. You can also buy special racks for providing green food. Branches (with aphids!) and bunches of weeds (for seeds) can be put in deep flower pots filled with wet sand.

Provide good lighting, particularly in the sleeping coop or night shelter. Finches are just plain lovers of light. In fall and winter, when it gets dark early, provide extra light so that birds can continue to eat and drink. Exotic finches should have at least 12–13 hours of light each day. Also, install a small, 4–7 watt night light in the night shelter, so that birds that fly up when they are startled can find their sleeping spot again. When you turn off the lights, dim them gradually.

A heater that can provide the required temperature safely is very important! In the detailed section on the various exotic finches (pages 73 to 252), we will indicate precise temperature requirements. Most species cannot tolerate temperatures below 50°F (10°C). Keep alert to the weather forecast, a suggestion we shared earlier.

Make It True To Nature

If you're planning to set up an aviary, make it as true to nature as possible by adding a few good bushes. Finches use plants to play in, as shelter from the rain, to shade themselves from strong sunlight, or just to perch in. In addition, natural perches play an important role at mating time, and bushes also provide good nesting places.

Obviously, you should select sturdy bushes that will tolerate a certain amount of gnawing by the birds. Actually, you can considerably reduce the tendency of birds to destroy vegetation by regularly (preferably every day!) furnishing fresh green food (see page 58).

We do not mean to imply that birds will leave bushes entirely untouched, even if you have extensive planting. That would be far from the truth. Many of the larger finch species, for example, have a lust for the buds of the common privet, and most birds like the berries, leaves, or buds of bird cherry and elder. Still, you can minimize the damage to growing plants by furnishing fresh greens daily.

Proper plantings take good planning. For example, don't plant rhododendrons in aviaries housing parrots and parakeets. These inveterate gnawers could be poisoned by the leaves of this plant. For other birds, hence all finches, rhododendrons are no problem. They are excellent plants for an aviary containing estrildid finches.

There should also be a patch of grass in every aviary. It's decorative, but it's also a necessity for species like quail, which weave a tunnel through long grass in which they nest. Among the finches, all Australian grassfinches love to search for insects in the grass, while many African finches just like to sit in it, taking a sun bath. Larger finches also value the grass patch. You will see them after a rain, rolling enthusiastically through the wet grass, all the while screeching exuberantly.

Consider planting rushes and corn plants in one of the corners of the aviary. Mannikins and other *Lonchura* species, among many others, really appreciate these plants, and they help control the nail growth of these birds. Also, plant some conifers and trees of the *Prunus* species, selecting varieties that are sturdy and don't grow too high. They are especially appropriate for a garden aviary of small exotics!

It's a good idea to get advice from a gardener or local nursery before placing plants in the aviary. Not every type of soil is suitable for the plants (see box) we are recommending.

It's equally important to maintain the plantings, or you run the risk that the place will become overgrown. Trim plants regularly and consult gardening centers and books for proper pruning and maintenance techniques.

Group Housing

Certain bird species can be kept together, others cannot. In the detailed descriptions that follow these introductory chapters, we will indicate whether the finches under discussion are prone to fight, and if so, when in particular. Often you can safely house pairs of different species together, but you may have war when you house finches of the same species or very closely related species together, especially if you put only two pairs together. However, if you put three or more pairs together, many species, such as the zebra finch and the Java sparrow will live together in harmony. Guard carefully, on the other hand, against placing an extra male into the collection. And don't bring new birds into the community in midseason, because this will upset the territories the various pairs have established, with resulting ill effects. (Yes, aviary birds do establish territories!)

In this connection, watch your birds carefully. If you notice any fights of consequence or wild chases, you will know that there are bad actors in the group and you should remove the culprits immediately.

As a general rule, you can assume that birds originating from the same country are likely to get along. The biggest bully among exotic finches is, without doubt, the crimson finch *Neochmia phaeton* from northern Australia. The male is aggressive not only during the breeding season, but at other times as well. He even attacks his own mate frequently outside the breeding period. To others of his species, he is everything but friendly or gentle. In Australia, where the crimson finch takes up a large habitat, he doesn't hesitate to attack birds five or more times his size, and he knows how to scare the devil out of them if they invade his territory. Also watch out for the following trouble makers: all species of mannikins of the genus *Lonchura*, diamond fire-tailed finch, cut-throat finch *Amadina fasciata*, red-headed finch *A. erythrocephalus*, melba finch *Pytilia melba*, orange-winged pytilia *P. afra*, masked finch *Poephila personata*, black-breasted fire finch *Lagonosticta rufopicta*, Java sparrow, and zebra finch, among others.

Chores for the Aviculturist

Daily
Provide fresh and generous supplies of fresh food and drinking water, bath water, and, during the breeding season, a variety of nesting material and good lighting and, if necessary, heating. All utensils for eating, drinking and bathing must be cleaned and disinfected. Also, check if there are any sick birds or provokers of unrest.

Weekly
Clean cages and aviaries, except during the breeding season. During this period wait and observe the right time to clean up, with consideration for birds that are incubating and youngsters about to leave the nest. The task involves replacing sand, cleaning and sanding perches, using rough sand paper, and replacing loose or broken perches. Live plants must be sprayed, trimmed, or replaced when necessary.

Monthly
Do a close and careful check on the birds and carefully check their quarters for vermin. Check toe nails and clip them when necessary. Rake the sand and replace it as necessary when the flooring is made of concrete or tile. Grass areas must be resodded as needed.

Semiannually
Disinfect the entire facility, timed before and after the breeding season. Clean and disinfect all sleeping- and nesting-boxes. When possible, replace components that are broken and burn them. Disinfect the aviary and check for breaches in the mesh and wooden partitions and posts. Consider replacing perches and plantings.

In general
It is best to set definite days on the calendar for all tasks to be done; that way, you won't forget something important. Feed birds at the same time each day so they can get used to a routine. The best feeding time is about 7:00 or 8:00 AM. Keep up the schedule even when you're not there by telling the substitute caretaker when to do what. Be particular about the feeding schedule, because birds shouldn't have to wait for their food just because you're not there. It can happen when birds are feeding their young that they stop doing so if the caretaker is several hours late with rearing or egg food, or other special feed you're furnishing for feeding the youngsters. Also, during the breeding season, things have to be managed as quietly as possible. Bring in food and water quickly but gently; the same goes for other chores on your list.

CHAPTER 3

Common Illnesses and Their Treatment

Introduction

Often the first sign that a bird is sick is listless behavior at the feeding station, where it drops more food than it eats. In most cases, you will also notice swollen or dull eyes. You'll also frequently notice puffed-up feathers. Sick birds often look like pitiful balls of feathers cowering in a corner or under a food trough, sleeping with the head buried deeply in the feathers. In short, they have lost all interest in their surroundings, have no appetite (anorexia), and persist in staying near the feeding utensils (polyphagia); their breathing is rapid.

Your first action should be to remove the bird, and keep it separate in a heated hospital cage. Then look for remedies or – the best action – contact an avian veterinarian. Keep an eye on the droppings and collect some for examination. Droppings may change color and may be loose, probably because the patient suddenly starts drinking more than normal. If, however, you notice that the amount of droppings is noticeably less than usual, also keep close watch on the bird. This can be a sign that it isn't eating. That's important to know, because a bird must continue to eat, no matter what. If necessary, furnish its favorite food.

The Hospital Cage

A hospital cage is completely closed, except for the front, which has wire mesh or glass with outlets. You can cover the front with a cloth, if that seems advisable. Put a dark, infrared lamp of 75, 150, or 250 watts at a distance of 12–18 in. (30–50 cm) from the hospital cage. Check with your hand to make sure that the inside of the cage isn't getting too hot.

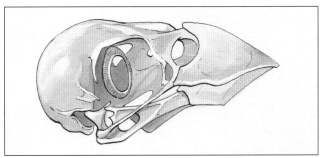

A rapidly flying finch must see extremely well, possess superior motor coordination, and make quick decisions. Therefore, finches, and all other flying birds for that matter, must have large eyes and a large brain.

The well-known aviculturist, the late Mr. C. af Enehjelm, designed a cage 14 in. x 7 in. x 12 in. (35 x 17 x 30 cm high). He separated the cage into a large living area and a small "basement" 4 in. (10 cm.) deep, which was at that time (in the early 1950s) still covered with asbestos on all sides. In the rear wall of this basement he placed three lamps, with switches on the outside. Along the sides, he attached three slats that permitted sliding several floors into the cage. The lowest floor consisted of a sheet of asbestos with various holes drilled into it; next came a frame holding a linen cloth to catch droppings and dirt; finally came a grate on which a bird could rest without the possibility of fouling itself in its own droppings. The living space had two perches, a removable glass front and a door in one of the sides. Both sides had openings for a feeding dish and a water vessel and, higher up, a row of ventilation holes that could be closed with a slide, partially or completely. He further installed a thermometer on one of the side walls. The lamps he used had a wattage of 15, 25, and 40, so that he could vary the temperature as necessary.

Since this early design, numerous models followed, many of which are now available in the better pet stores; however, all are based on af Enehjelm's first model. If you don't have two left hands you can make a hospital cage yourself, using a substitute for asbestos.

The best temperature for the living space in the hospital cage is 104°F (40°C), with as little variation as possible. As soon as the sick bird gets better, the temperature can be dropped gradually. Dissolve a water soluble antibiotic in the drinking water. Aureomycin and Terramycin are commonly used, or you can consult your avian veterinarian.

One or more hospital cages should be essential equipment for every dedicated aviculturist!

Some Diseases and Illnesses

Anemia

This problem occurs from time to time, especially if you inbreed too much, particularly with Bengalese (society finches) and zebra finches. The condition can also be brought on by insufficient nutrition, extreme cold, or vermin. The birds appear unattractive, have dull eyes that are some-times a little inflamed, and the color of the beak, legs and skin has faded. The breastbone often protrudes considerably. Affected birds often sleep with their heads buried in the feathers, which tend to be puffed up.

In this case, immediately clear vermin out of the facility. Change and improve the diet. Add vitamin C, low-salt grit, a good grade of finch egg food, Avilac (Eight In One, Hauppauge, New York), and a lot of greens. Keep the affected birds warm and expose them to direct sunlight as much as possible. Be sure to furnish fresh bathwater daily, but only during the warm hours of the middle of the day. Add a few drops of an antibiotic to the water; this will help return the glow to the feathers.

If you get medication from your veterinarian, be sure to follow instructions precisely. We have known people who have used medication in the exact opposite way as directed on the package. So, take time to read and understand how medication is to be used. Don't be afraid to ask as many details as possible. Your veterinarian is there to help your sick birds. But remember, there are obviously no wonder drugs that can save every bird.

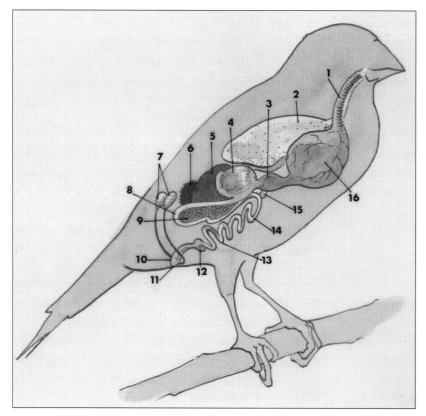

Internal Organs

1. esophagus
2. lungs
3. proventriculus
4. ventriculus or gizzard
5. liver
6. spleen
7. kidneys
8. duodenum
9. pancreas
10. cloaca
11. anus or vent
12. caecum
13. small intestines
14. jejunum*
15. gall
16. crop

Knowing a finch's anatomy and the various parts of its plumage is useful not only for conversations with veterinarians, but also for describing different bird species.

(*The middle portion of the small intestine extending between the duodenum and the ileum.)

Bald Spots

Feathers can drop out to create bald spots due to vitamin deficiencies, mite infestation, or calcium deficiency. To deal with the problem, make sure the rations are adequate. We suggest you add low-salt grit to the diet. Be sure that there is enough vitamin A, D and B in the offered food. If there are mites, get a good miticide (ask your pet dealer for advice). Put antibiotics into the drinking water (ask your avian veterinarian).

Bronchitis

This infectious disease is caused by colds, sudden, drastic changes in temperature, bath and drinking water that's too cold, or other infections. Affected birds resemble pitiful, shaking balls of misery; they gasp, cough now and then, and attempt to shake off the slime that exudes from the beak and/or nostrils.

Immediately separate the stricken birds into a warm spot or hospital cage to avoid infecting the rest of the flock. Thoroughly disinfect the cage or aviary. Consult an avian veterinarian immediately. Add a few drops of antibiotic to the drinking water, including the drinking water for birds that have remained healthy.

Broken Legs

The legs of small exotic finches are generally thin and quite vulnerable. A leg can break easily, especially during a mishap in the catching process. Birds such as mannikins, which are frequently troubled by overly long nails, often break one or both legs when they become snagged on something.

Your first response, naturally, is to capture the patient with the utmost care. Then, splice the leg with a moderately thick feather shaft (like a chicken feather), or a plastic drinking straw cut lengthwise. Attach the splint with woolen yarn or surgical tape and then make it rigid with collodion, surgical glue, or plaster of Paris. Put the patient in a small hospital cage. Cover the floor with a layer of paper and sand. Place food and water on the floor, so that the bird can reach it easily. Remove all perches. Provide extra supplement of limestone, cuttlefish bone, and vitamin D. You can take off the splint after approximately 20 days by dissolving it in acetone (ether is not as good, and danger-

ous). Be extremely careful, as the fumes may be harmful to the patient. If the leg hasn't turned black, you can assume that the operation was successful. Be sure to remember that when you wrap a broken leg, you shouldn't do this too tightly. It is advisable to consult an avian veterinarian.

Broken Wing

Broken wings are hard to correct. If the bird involved is valuable, go for help to a veterinarian. If you want to try a home treatment however, cut away the feathers around the break and disinfect the area of the break with antibiotics. Carefully hold the broken parts together and join them with a small piece of surgical tape. Put the finch in a small cage with its food and drinking cups on the floor. Remove all perches. Be sure the diet is optimally balanced (see Broken Legs). Remove the tape after approximately 20 days.

Chlorosis

This problem occurs through insufficient nutrition, or improper sanitation. The birds look anything but attractive as their feathers look bedraggled. The beak and legs lose their color. In many cases, small eruptions form on the skin and sometimes on the legs.

The only remedy is a drastic improvement in the diet. Provide chickweed, lettuce, endive, and sprouts daily; be sure they are fresh. Add several drops of an antibiotic to the drinking water. Get rid of lice in the bird facility. Eruptions on the skin and legs should be lanced with a disinfected needle. Empty out the pus with sterile cotton or gauze, then cover the affected area with pure glycerine.

Constipation

Constipation frequently results from feeding too much egg food, especially if it is too dry. An excess of poppy seed may also cause problems. Other causes can be spoiled or old seed.

Birds with constipation puff up their feathers and stay perched or nervously run up and down. Sometimes it is clear that they can't relieve themselves. The rear of the body may even be swollen. They stop eating and act sluggish. Remedy the problem with green food, a lot of fruit, and rape seed rubbed in fat (mix crushed eggshell with rape seed and suet, for example). Add antibiotics to the drinking water and vitamins to the food. Above all, be sure that the food you furnish is top quality and fresh.

Diphtheria

This infectious disease requires immediate remedy! Affected birds pant heavily and cough, produce slimy droppings, and have inflamed eyes. The nose exudes a slimy moisture that hardens quickly. The birds tend to sit constantly at the drinking fountain to slake their thirst, caused by fever. The most common cause is a cold. Capture the sick birds, and cage them separately in a warm spot. Add antibiotics to the drinking water, and follow the directions of the avian veterinarian.

Take steps to avoid a repeat infection. Examine the aviary carefully to detect openings that promote drafts. Be sure that the diet is correct. Disinfect the aviary and dig and turn the dirt floor good and deep. Incinerate dead birds.

Give sick birds antibiotics once or twice daily.

Egg binding

Egg binding is the condition where the female can't expel an egg that's ready to be laid. A major cause is breeding a female too young. We warn against this practice at several points in this book for a good reason. Never breed female finches younger than 10–12 months of age. Old hens should not be used for breeding, either; five years should be considered the maximum age for breeding finches.

Other possible causes of egg-binding include breeding females that have gotten too fat or too weak, or have a serious calcium deficiency. Cold, drafty sleeping quarters could also be a contributing factor. Finally, it is possible that the oviduct isn't developed properly or has become infected. If this last condition is at fault, there is little we can do about it; the only thing we can do is not breed with these females.

To help expel a "stuck" egg, gently dip the lower half of the female's body in alternately cold and lukewarm water. Dab some vegetable oil under the tail (in the vent). Put the patient in a hospital cage at 90°F (32°C). After the egg is laid, reduce the temperature slowly to normal.

Whatever you do, don't take a chance on breaking the egg inside the bird's body, as this could have fatal results. Add antibiotics to the drinking water. If you have to artificially promote laying, be sure not to use the eggs produced that way for breeding. In all cases, it is better to consult an avian veterinarian immediately.

Egg pecking

Birds will peck at their own eggs or those of other exotic finches when we don't furnish enough cuttlefish bone, limestone, grit, crushed eggshell, and vitamins during the year, but especially during the breeding season. Boredom also can be a cause. Be sure the supplements we just mentioned are in adequate supply, and provide extra vitamin A and D. Counteract boredom by using your imagination to vary the diet. Hang up jute rope or, once in a while, a piece of raw red meat to attract their interest.

Eye infection

If a bird has an eye problem, for example excessive tearing, place the bird in a darkened cage and treat the infected eye with five percent boric acid ophthalmic ointment (Neosporin or Neopolycin, for example) after first rinsing out the eye with lukewarm water or a 0.9% saline solution. Add vitamin A and D to the food. Eye infection is often caused by bacteria, so keep perches and housing clean.

Feather picking

Birds sometimes pick the feathers of another bird in more than an occasional way. This can be caused for example, by boredom, stress, overcrowding, or deficiencies in vitamins, protein, or calcium, or other mineral deficiencies. The result is bald spots on the victim's body.

First of all, immediately improve the diet drastically; with emphasis on an improved vitamin and mineral content. Add rearing food to the diet, preferably year-round. Add antibiotics to the drinking water, after consulting an avian veterinarian. Combat boredom by adopting the suggestions given under "Egg pecking." If you're overstocked, thin out the collection or construct more bird housing. Be sure to immediately remove all loose feathers that lie on the floor. If the problem persists despite your countermeasures, a light spray with Bitter Apple (available in pet shops) may help. Be sure not to get any spray in the birds' eyes. Whatever you do, don't wait before you take action against feather picking.

Intestinal infections and diarrhea

These disturbances can be caused by bacterial infections, coccidia, and worms, and therefore are quite contagious. The infection is actually in the intestinal lining. Diarrhea can be caused or worsened by insufficient rations, drinking and bath water that is too cold, egg food or green food furnished too wet, or large changes in temperature.

Affected birds are in poor condition, have listless eyes, act sluggish, and have thin, slimy droppings that are generally yellowish-green or white. In many cases, the cloaca (vent) is infected. The thin droppings cause the feathers of the lower body to become dirty and sticky.

Remove oil-rich seed from the diet for two weeks. Separate the sick birds and keep them warm. Furnish extra poppy seed. Add antibiotics to the drinking water, as well as to the bathing water. Remember, diarrhea is only an indication that something is wrong with your finches' digestive systems, or it may be caused simply by a case of mild indigestion if there are no other symptoms. To be on the safe side, it is always best to consult your avian veterinarian when a case of diarrhea occurs.

Jaundice

This illness is caused by a deficiency in vitamins or a shortage of food. The skin of the affected bird is yellow, particularly the lower part of the body. The skin can also be quite swollen. Jaundice often follows intestinal catarrh.

Isolate infected birds in a warm spot and provide antibiotics in the drinking water. It helps to provide wheat bread soaked water. Make sure the diet is first quality. Provide extra rape seed and a good-quality egg food. Also, offer a daily supply of chickweed, lettuce or endive. When the birds recover, keep them apart from the rest of the flock until the weather outside is warm and dry.

Mite infestation

Red mites *Dermanyssus avium* are the worst. This blood-sucking arachnid surfaces from all types of

dark hideaways during the evening and night. Favorite hiding places are cracks and seams, especially in nest boxes and under perches. In case of heavy infestations, mites may even stay on the birds during the day, so it isn't always good enough merely to transfer affected birds to another, uninfested facility, even if it is thoroughly disinfected. It also doesn't help just to let an infested facility stand empty for a few weeks in hopes of getting rid of red mites; they can live without eating for at least five or six months!

A red mite infestation is easy to notice. The birds are restless at night and peck and scratch continuously. If you shine a flashlight at the birds or their perches, you will be able to see the red parasites easily in most cases. Take good care that you do not personally pick up any mites, because they can cause an irritating, burning eczema in humans. A heavy case can even cause anemia.

Mite infestation can be brought in by wild birds or new purchases and can progress rapidly, since a single female mite can produce approximately 2600 eggs in its lifetime. So it pays to keep on the alert. During daylight, run a pocketknife through cracks and crevices. If you don't get any blood on it, then there's no trouble. Or else, lay a white cloth in the sleeping coop or on the cage floor and look for mites on this cloth the next morning.

The moment you confirm a mite infestation, remove all birds from the facility and spray it with a contact insecticide. Ask your pet store manager to recommend a safe product. Be sure to spray all holes, crevices, joints, perches, wire mesh, nest boxes, food and water dishes, especially the sides and bottoms, as well as all other utensils and equipment in the facility. Remove all nesting material and burn it. After letting the insecticide work its benefits for several days, wash everything thoroughly with soapy water. Rinse cages with boiling water. Make sure that your storage areas are also free of mites, otherwise a new infestation will be launched from there. Treat your birds with a powder insecticide or with a commercial, safe spray. Be sure to follow label directions. Under no circumstances should you use Lindane. You can get good results with a 0.15% solution of Neguvon.

Use the same remedies for feather lice, feather mites, and shaft mites. These species live on the carotine (protein) of the feather shaft, causing the feathers to drop and general growth and development to be stunted. We can't stress enough that absolutely proper sanitation in the bird facility is the only lasting remedy.

Another nasty mite is the Airsac mite *Sternostoma tracheacolum*, a blood-sucking arthropod that frequently affects Gouldian finches *Chloebia gouldiae*, diamond sparrows *Zonaeginthus guttatus*, parrotfinches and, to a lesser extent, canaries and other large and small finches. The mites infest the trachea, lungs, and air sacs of the bird. The affected patients have their necks stretched out and have visible problems with swallowing. They appear to sneeze and jerk their heads, puff out their feathers, cease to sing, and slowly lose body condition. In a later stage, as the mites infect the lungs and air sacs, the birds will develop obvious breathing difficulties (dyspnea). The birds will make swallowing noises, will wipe their beaks repeatedly on perches and twigs, and will attempt to remove the mites from their air passages by coughing and spluttering. As the infection develops, the birds' labored breathing will be accompanied by wheezing and peeping sounds, intermingled with little sneezes. In acute cases, the birds can suffocate from a literal plug of mites in the air passages. A microscopic examination will reveal numerous, dark-colored mites in the nostrils, the trachea, and all respiratory organs. Young mites are usually found in the nostrils.

The treatment is fairly problematical. Most avian veterinarians use Ivermectin. The entire flock must be treated at the same time and the premises cleaned. Some forms of Ivermectin dissipate rapidly and should be used within a specific time period after mixing. Inquire as to the usage if you treat the patients at home. According to Dr. Roger W. Harlin, an avian veterinarian, Ivermectin can be easily overdosed and losses can be alarming if it is used carelessly. Be sure a professional has advised you as to the right mixture or has mixed it for you.

Rheumatism

This malady is caused by drafts, wet floors, thin perches, and colds. Affected birds suffer consider-able pain, practically stop eating, and have visibly inflamed ankles.

Remove the affected birds from the collection immediately and place them in a warm hospital cage. Exposure to a lot of sun is one of the best remedies. If perches are too thin, they naturally have to be replaced (average thickness should be 1½ in. (4 cm). Swollen ankles should be treated with a topical application of spirits of camphor. If the swelling starts oozing pus, follow the suggestions given under "Swellings." Add antibiotics to the drinking water, and consult an avian veterinarian.

Swellings

Swellings typically are a hardening of the upper skin layer and are filled with pus. They can be caused by a variety of irritants, such as insect bites, scrapes, and blood poisoning. Treat swellings with an antiseptic remedy. When the swelling has ripened, lance it carefully and apply antibiotics. Separate the patient in a cage placed in a warm location. For awhile, don't feed seed, but provide wheat bread soaked in water, a variety of green feed (especially spinach), rearing food, and for seven days, Eight In One's Avilac for finches. Provide aftercare for the wounds with some Stay (Mardel). Consult an avian veterinarian.

Tuberculosis

This is one of the most feared and most infectious diseases. The major cause, often, is a cold. Immature birds also can get tuberculosis. The sick birds look unattractive, have a rasping respiration that obviously is quite painful, and have slimy droppings tinged with blood. They practically stop eating and become visibly thinner as a result.

Remedies help only if started early. Immediately segregate the sick birds. Administer drops of a strong antibiotic (consult your veterinarian) into the throat, generally twice per day, as directed. Be sure to disinfect the entire bird facility and dig up the soil in unpaved areas. Also put antibiotics in the drinking water, including the water for healthy birds. Burn dead birds immediately!

CHAPTER 4

Food and Water

Seed for Finches

Estrildid finches are principally seed eaters, that is, they feed on numerous varieties of grass and weed seeds available in their countries of origin. Finch species with small, weak beaks seem to prefer the soft types of millet, like Senegal millet and spray millet. Birds with somewhat stronger bills prefer silver, Morocco, and La Plata millets. All types of exotic finches, however, love to snack on spray millet, the seed heads of panicum millet. They also like white seed or, as it is usually called, canary grass seed, not to be confused with commercial canary seed, a term which refers to a mixture of seeds for canaries. Further, a good commercial seed mix must obviously contain ripe and unripe grass and weed seed. Many finches also like niger seed, but this should always be offered in small quantities because of its heavy fat content; excessive consumption can cause liver problems. But since it is rich in minerals, it should not be omitted. Oats, in the form of oat groats or hulled oats, can also be fed, especially in the diet of larger finches like the Java sparrow *Padda oryzivora*, but it is best to limit this food to birds housed in a large aviary. Birds in cramped quarters can grow fat too easily on oats.

Personally, we like the following seed mixtures:

For large finches
5 oz. canary grass seed (not canary mixture)
1 oz. La Plata and red or white millet
1½ oz. oat groats
The above seeds are high in starch and comprise 75% of the mixture.
½ oz. rape seed
½ oz. cole seed
0.8 oz. niger seed
0.3 oz. sesame seed
0.3 oz. linseed
0.1 oz. hemp seed*
These oil-bearing seeds comprise 25% of the mixture, by weight.

An alternative mixture for large finches is:
40% canary grass seed
30% white (German) millet
15% Japanese (or red) millet
10% panicum millet
5% hulled oats

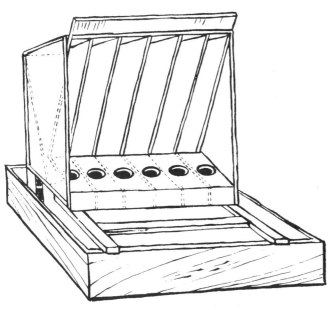
Seed feeder in which the seeds can be offered separately.

Seed mixtures for small finches
55% Senegal millet
15% panicum millet
15% white pearl millet
10% canary grass seed
3% hulled oats
0.5% sesame seed
0.5% poppy seed (blue)*
0.5% plantain seed
0.5% niger seed

Seed treat for all finch species
5% poppy seed (blue)*
5% canary grass seed
5% hemp seed*
5% lettuce seed
10% thistle seed
20% niger seed
10% black lettuce seed
10% linseed
10% weed seed
20% sesame seed
* usually commercially available in sterile form,
  for obvious reasons

Sprouted Seed

Sprouted seed is extremely useful, especially millet, niger seed, grass seed, and weed seeds. You may not be able to buy weed seeds commercially everywhere, although most garden centers will be able to help you. But you can always gather your own, of course!

To grow sprouts, take a rather thick, smooth towel and wet it with lukewarm water (white paper towels without designs will do excellently, too). Spread the towel out over a tray or flat plate. Sprinkle the seed on it and put it in a humid place. As the sprouting seeds burst open, after approximately 48 hours, take it off the towel and rinse it in lukewarm water. The easiest way to do this is in a colander. Then feed the sprouted seed to the birds in a separate dish.

Don't provide more sprouted seed than the birds can use up in a single day, and if there are leftovers in the evening, take them away. You don't want your birds to eat soured seed, which can cause intestinal upsets.

You can even plant some weed seeds on the floor of the garden aviary. As it sprouts and germinates, the birds will relish it. For this reason, don't remove all the spilled seed from around the feeding dish. The sprouted seed will create a green corner in which the birds will love to root around.

Green Food

There should never be a shortage of green food. This term includes chickweed, a favorite of most finches, collards, leaf and Bibb lettuce, endive, spinach (see box), cabbage, pieces of carrots and carrot tops, celery leaves, dock, shepherd's purse, groundsel, plantain, water cress, broccoli, and dandelion. The whole dandelion plant can be given, hence leaves, stems, flowers, seed and even the roots!

Always provide fresh greens and remove any leftovers around the time that the birds go to roost. Make sure you provide organic greens. If you don't have a sure source, grow them yourself.

> **Spinach** is an excellent green food but not all finches like to peck at whole leaves. Therefore, roll the leaves into a tight ball and slice them thinly with a sharp knife, just like you cut onions, and watch your fingers! Prepared this way, even the finicky Gouldian finch *Chloebia gouldiae* will accept this green with gusto.

Fruit

Many estrildid finches love to nibble on pieces of apple, pear, banana, tomato, orange, melon, cherry, grape, grapefruit, berries, raisins and currants. The latter two items may also be furnished soaked. If you provide big fruit pieces, cut them in parts, hammer a few nails through a board and stick the fruit pieces through the pointed ends. This keeps the fruit clean. Greens and fruit can also be provided in wire baskets, which are sold commercially for this purpose. However, be aware that some of the contents will usually fall out.

Food of Animal Origin

Practically all exotic finches like to eat food of animal origin. Insects, or man-made substitutes such as egg food or rearing food, are readily accepted. This type of food becomes a necessity during the breeding season, but many fanciers provide it all year-round.

In nature, birds also like termites, ant pupae ("ant eggs"), small spiders and similar live food. You can provide these to your captive birds as well, plus small cut-up mealworms. Better pet stores also sell dried or frozen ant eggs, small shrimp, etc. You have to prepare dried ant pupae for feeding by first pouring boiling water over them and letting them soak for a half hour. Frozen ant pupae and shrimp must be thawed for at least three hours.

A good menu should also include moths, fly larvae, and white worms *Enchytraeus albidus*. You can provide variety by sometimes substituting tubifex, red mosquito larvae, and water fleas, which you can buy in pet stores that sell aquarium supplies, and tackle stores. Rearing or egg food is also best bought commercially. If you wish, you can enrich it with finely diced boiled egg and small insects.

Vitamins, Minerals and Trace Elements

Birds living free in their country of origin select from a great variety of insects, spiders, seeds and fruits to complete their diet. Away from home in captivity, it is difficult to duplicate all these dietary elements, hard as we may try. One of the most likely deficiencies concerns vitamins. You can buy all types of multivitamins commercially, and these are essential for keeping your birds healthy. Green food and grass- and weed seed are also extremely important food sources. Furthermore, your birds need to have access to supplements with minerals and trace elements, which are essential for proper plumage, good bone structure and healthy internal organs. You can provide this supplement by furnishing finely ground boiled egg shells, cuttlefish bone, finely ground oyster shell, enriched limestone, and commercial low-salt grit (without charcoal, because some scientists believe that charcoal removes the vitamins A, B2 and K from the intestinal tract, thus contributing to vitamin deficiency).

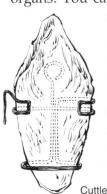
Cuttlefish bone.

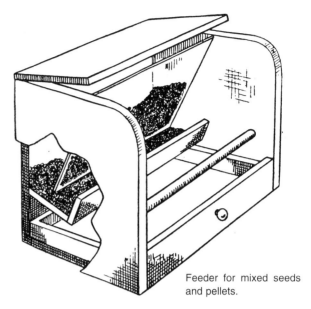
Feeder for mixed seeds and pellets.

Pellets

In recent years serious attempts have been made to improve the standard of pet bird feeding. There has been a tendency to adopt European methods favoring a far more representative diet, with more emphasis on energy producing ingredients and less concern for high protein content.

From 1985 to 1994 an ambitious research program was carried out in which the problem of pet bird feeding was examined in depth at various food production centers. The result is the pet pellet/crumble, which is balanced in vitamins, minerals, protein and carbohydrates, comes in various fruit flavored and attractive colors and shapes, and is fortified with *Lactobacillus acidophilus* and yeast cultures in order to prevent the depletion of beneficial gut microbes and maintain normal intestinal conditions.

Feeding Instructions for Pellets/Crumbles

Blend the new diet with the old (seed) mixture and gradually reduce the old diet over a period of 16 days as follows:

Days 1–4	25% pellets + 75% current seed mix
Days 5–10	50% pellets + 50% current seed mix
Days 11–15	75% pellets + 25% current seed mix
Day 16	100% pellets

Moistening with fruit juice may help the birds in adjusting to the new pelleted diet, but wet food should be removed after four hours and replaced with clean, dry food. After 16 days the birds should be completely converted to pellets/crumbles, although experience has proven that finches in general are very difficult in this respect and will seldom eat pellets/crumbles exclusively. If your birds are difficult to convert, return to the first step in the conversion process.

Most pellets/crumbles are nutritionally balanced and designed to be fed as the sole diet. However, offer fresh fruits and vegetables daily in small amounts as well as treats and a variety of bird seeds. Keep food fresh by filling the feeders daily. Food should be available at all times, meaning pellets/crumbles and seeds, greens, cuttlefish bone, etc. During the year, and especially during the breeding season, insects, spiders, etc., have to be on the menu at all times! Clean feeders at least every other day to prevent mold, and refill with fresh pellets and fresh seed, or a mixture of the two. Keep waterers clean, and have fresh water available for bathing.

Drinking water

The aviary waterer we like best has a little rock with running fresh water and a small gutter to drain excess water. This set-up is rather costly to install and needs to be shut off in the winter. Most bird fanciers, therefore, make do with earthenware dishes and such. This solution isn't very hygienic, however, because birds will bathe in their drinking water, and dirt and dust can mess up the water. Small water fonts and automatic bird bottles can also get dirty, but not as badly because they keep providing fresh water. And, of course, birds can't bathe in them.

If you choose to use open dishes, cover them with wire mesh. This is especially important in winter in colder climates, as you don't want to run the chance that birds bathe in their drinking water and end up freezing to death.

Check at least once every day to make sure that the water supply is in order, more often (several times per day) during hot summer weather.

To give your birds a special treat, dissolve some honey or grape sugar (glucose) in the drinking water several times per week. And now and then, give the finches a small dish of fruit juice.

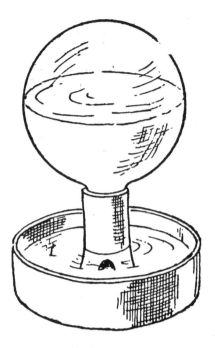

Drinking vessel.

Cover these dishes with a lid made of wire netting, otherwise the birds might bathe in them!

If your water is highly chlorinated, supply rain water instead of tap water. Boil it, cool it for at least three hours, and only then give it to the birds. Spring water, available commercially in various brands, is also excellent.

Bath Water

Many finches like to play and jump in wet grass or sit on the edge of a water container and take a shower by dipping their heads quickly in the water and throwing it all over their bodies. A handful of wet grass on the floor of the cage, or some wet lettuce leaves, will really be appreciated by most finches. For cages, there are the well-known plastic bath houses which can be mounted in the entrance of the cage. In aviaries, shallow dishes can be used, but always put some gravel or flagstones in these dishes to avoid accidents (see page 45). Bath water must be replenished several times each day. Bathing utensils can get dirty rather quickly and must absolutely be cleaned regularly (see also page 24).

Feeding Your Finches

■ Nothing is as important as getting your birds accustomed to a fixed daily routine. Furnish drinking water, bath water, and food at definite times each day, and maintain the same appearance. In other words, if you wear glasses, always wear them. If you wear a hat in winter, wear it in summer too. Wear a dust coat to protect your cloths and to standardize your appearance. If it wears out, try to buy a replacement in the same color. Then keep up this appearance whenever you do any work in the aviary, bird room, or anywhere near your birds.

■ Feed the birds at a regular time each morning, when they are hungry after a night's rest. Commercial rearing food and other soft food can also be furnished at that time of day. This way, it can be consumed as needed and is freely available if any nestlings have to be fed. Also, chances of spoilage are minimized, because you set it out before sunrise or while the sun is still weak. Remember spoilage, and check each evening at a regular time whether any perishable food is left over and throw it away. If you are feeding pellets, check for spoilage, especially when furnished in garden aviaries.

■ Provide seed (and pellets) in open dishes or in an automatic seed hopper. Before adding fresh seed, blow away empty hulls. You can get automatic feeders in pet shops; they should have a glass front so that you can check on the food supply that's left. Check these to see that the flow of seed isn't jammed when the unit is in use, and refill as needed.

■ When you provide fresh bathing and drinking water, wash out the dishes and vessels. As you do these chores, softly whistle a tune or talk softly to the birds to keep them calm. A regular routine, including regular whistling or humming, regular cloths, and a regular chore time, will accustom the birds to your presence, and they will not become upset even if you need to look into a nest during the breeding season or when you need to do any chores near them while they are incubating or feeding their young.

■ Take the opportunity to individually examine birds in your collection to see how they are doing. Pick a time other than the breeding season, or do it when you are moving birds indoors from the garden aviary. Lay the bird on its back in the palm of your hand, and then blow aside some breast and stomach feathers. This allows you to inspect the skin. The breast and stomach should have a healthy red color without any yellow discoloration. If you do see some yellow, this generally indicates that the bird has grown too fat because you have been feeding too many oil-rich seeds. Improve the situation by adjusting the diet gradually and by housing the fat birds in a facility where they have more room to exercise.

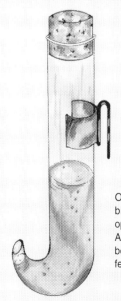

Only the larger-type hummingbird feeders, with a large opening may be used by small African finches with small beaks. Situate those types of feeders near perches.

CHAPTER 5

Breeding

Never commence with breeding too early. Many species of estrildid finches have the capacity to begin breeding as early as about five months of age. However, if you start them off that young, you will run into egg-binding, weak young, and other troubles. You will be far better off not to start breeding until your finches are at least a full year of age.

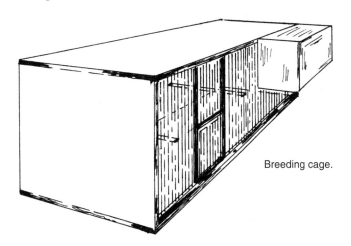

Breeding cage.

Preparations

A good-sized breeding cage, about 40 in. (100 cm.) in length, is required for effective breeding. Some species may even require more room. Keep only one breeding pair in a cage and provide a choice of nesting places. Your results will be considerably better, however, using one of the various types of aviaries, especially garden or outdoor aviaries. In the first place, the birds have more flying room there, and secondly, they can enjoy fresh air and sunlight.

Stick to the general rule that there needs to be at least one cubic yard (or meter) of space per breeding pair. Some pairs seem to prefer an aviary to themselves for breeding; others show better results if they cohabit with other pairs, colony style. You will receive specific advice on this topic in the description of the individual species.

Nest boxes and nesting material

Many exotic finches like to build a free-standing nest in the dense foliage of trees and shrubs. To satisfy this preference, consider providing a variety of plantings (see page 46). The seclusion offered by plants is a definite plus.

The birds will use all types of man-made nesting places, however. You can consider nest boxes, baskets, heather, and reeds. The majority of exotic finches prefer the so-called half-open nest box, still others like to breed in a closed nest box with a round entrance hole. Use boxes measuring

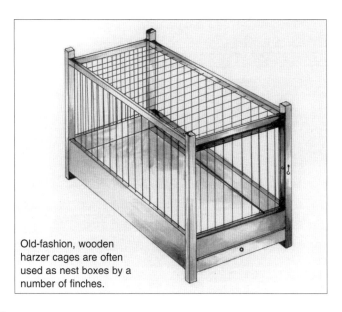

Old-fashion, wooden harzer cages are often used as nest boxes by a number of finches.

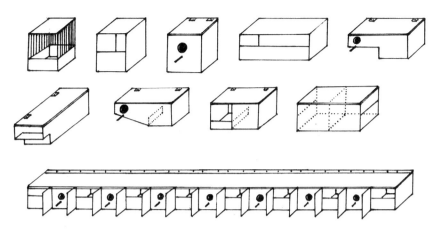

Depending on individual requirements (and personal experience!), there are indeed many types of breeding boxes for finches.

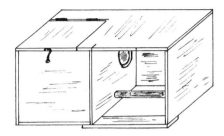

Breeding box for *Estrildidae* species. When made with a half-open side instead of an entrance hole the box becomes ideal for Australian grass finches.

approximately 6 in. (15 cm) cubed for the smaller species. The larger ones should have 7 (18 cm) cubed or 7 x 7 x 8 in. (18 x 18 x 20 cm) boxes.

If you use commercial baskets, consider only those with a diameter of about 6 in. (15 cm). Each pair of birds require at least two nest boxes or baskets, because there should always be a choice.

In the aviary, spread out the nesting receptacles as much as possible, in the night shelter as well as in the outside run. Don't hang them close together, but do hang them at various heights off the floor. Feel free to provide nest boxes of several types, because a breeding pair from a species generally known to prefer a nest box with a small entry hole may, as individuals, actually prefer to use a half-open nest box or basket. If you have dense bushes or trees, hang up some wire baskets or canary baskets, half a coconut shell, and other equipment that the birds can use as foundation for a free standing nest.

Provide an ample amount of nesting material. Include both dried and fresh-cut grass, coconut fibers, pieces of hemp rope up to 3 in. (6 cm) long, sisal *Agave sisalana* fibers, moss, tree bark, leaf veins and whole leaves, goat hair, and small feathers. Some finches also like to use small, thin twigs or needles from conifers. Others like small stones, charcoal, lumps of soil, and peat moss. For more details, see individual species descriptions.

Mating behavior

We heartily recommend you take time to observe the mating dance of your exotic finches, using binoculars when your birds are housed in an outdoor aviary. Most species are well worth watching! You will note that generally the male sings a full-throated song, often holding a blade of grass or a twig in his beak. He hops in a circle around the female, beating his tail. Often the mating dance is the only sure way to determine the sex of the birds that are not differentiated by color. Several of the parrot finches, among others, also like to chase heir beloved at amazing rates of speed, especially in a roomy aviary.

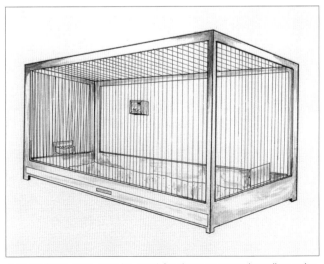

A large flight cage may be used for three or more breeding pairs. Never place two couples in the same cage or flight.

After mating, the birds start carrying all types of building materials. They inspect many nesting sites. The male repeatedly sounds off with his summoning cry, inviting the female to come and inspect sites that he has found. Quite often, the female is not satisfied with the location, so that the male has to go look for a new site for the future nest. You will be able to see that a certain nest box or other location is satisfactory if both birds sit at the site for about 45 minutes. Mating (copulation) often occurs in the nest, but is also possible on a branch, perch, or on the ground.

Nest and eggs

Nest construction can be carried out within several days, but may extend surprisingly long, as much as a week or longer. Most birds definitely don't stay with the task constantly; they take breaks regularly to eat, fly around a little, or to just rest and socialize. Many species keep rearranging the nest regularly even if eggs have already been laid. Generally, the male brings the building mate-rial while the female does the actual construction. Most nests are carefully put together, but we have also encountered large, rough nests with thick walls and long entry tunnels.

It's important that you furnish a variety of nest building materials. If you don't, the birds may give up on the job or steal nesting materials from other birds in the aviary. Often the female lays her first eggs before the nest is completely finished.

The first egg can be expected three to five days after mating has occurred. The female will continue laying one egg a day until the clutch is complete. Clutches can vary between two and nine eggs, but usually will range from four to six eggs. After the third or fourth egg is laid, incubation begins. The clutch is incubated for 11–16 days before the young hatch.

Incubating (Brooding)

While incubating takes place, give your birds complete quiet. Interruptions of any kind can cause the parents to abandon the eggs or the young. For this

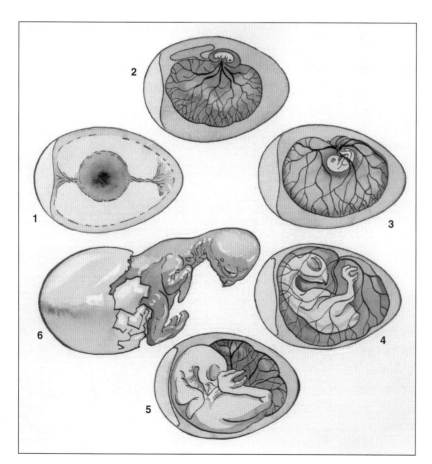

The development inside an egg

1. Internal view of the finch egg after approximately 20 hours of incubation.

2. Finch embryo after about 48 hours.

3. After about 50 hours.

4. After about 7 days.

5. After about 10 days.

6. After 12–14 days. The egg hatches and the chick pulls itself all the way out.

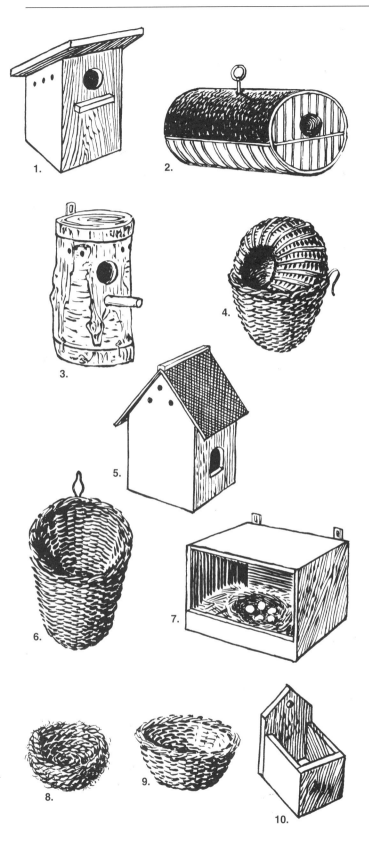

1. Zebra finches, society finches and *Lonchura* species.
2. Australian grassfinches, all small African finches and mannikins.
3. Zebra finches, Australian grassfinches and *Munia* species.
4–6. All species mentioned for 2. Regarding next box 6, note that the basket should be half filled with nesting material.
7–10. All larger finches (zebra finches, canaries and similar).

reason, we suggest you don't make close-up inspections of the nest. You should be able to tell by the actions of the parents whether everything is going right. Some birds are more tolerant of nest inspections, especially when done in the bird room, with the various breeding cages where a quick peek a few times per day is easily realized. However, this doesn't mean that it is wise to actually make these inspections in the aviary. Merely entering the aviary creates at least some unrest. The tolerant species include zebra finches *Poephila guttata*, long-tailed grassfinches *P. acuticauda* and society finches *Lonchura striata* var. *domestica*.

In the bird room you need to maintain a temperature between 65° and 80°F (18–28°C), and a humidity between 60–80%, depending on the species.

Young birds

For the first 7–10 days after hatching, the young birds are kept warm day and night. That's understandable, realizing that most hatchlings come out of the egg naked, or with just a little down. The young of many species very quickly start their begging cries; others are rather quiet, especially for the first three days. At a week to 10 days, the first feathers break through and the eyes open. From then on, the young develop rapidly, and they leave the nest box or basket after about 21 days.

The parents feed the young regularly, provided the right food is available. Unlike the practice of other birds, the parents of finches often won't remove droppings from the nest. Rather, the young themselves, once they are about four days old, make the proper movements to deposit droppings on the edge of the nest, where they dry up quickly. This way the droppings won't pose the danger of infections or contamination.

Once the young fly out, they will spend a lot of time on the ground the first few days. Toward evening , however, most of them will get back into the parental nest to sleep. There are species, to be sure, where the young do not spend the night in the nest but stay outside or in a dark, wind-free spot in the aviary. As mentioned earlier, it is therefore very important to maintain the right

Band Sizes

The band sizes should be considered approximate sizes for an average bird, as listed below. Diameter (in millimeters) is the internal band/ring measurement.

2.0 mm
Orange-cheeked waxbill *Estrilda melpoda*, red-eared waxbill *E. troglodytes*, crimson-rumped waxbill *E. rhodopyga*, St. Helena waxbill *E. astrild*, red-cheeked cordon bleu *Uraeginthus bengalus*, red avadavat *Amandava amandava*, and birds of similar size.

2.3 mm
Red-winged pytilia (aurora finch) *Pytilia phoenicoptera*, melba finch *P. melba*, all parrotfinches *Erythrura* and *Amblynura* species, violet-eared waxbill *Uraeginthus granatina*, common quail finch *Ortygospiza atricollis*, double-barred finch *Stizoptera bichenovii*, red- tailed lavender finch *Estrilda caerulescens*, Indian silverbill *Euodice malabarica*, African silverbill *E. cantans*, pearl-headed silverbill *Lonchura griseicapilla*, spice finch *L. punctulata*, long-tailed finch, masked finch *Poephila personata* Gouldian finch, all American siskin *Carduelis* species (which are not estrildids), and other bird species of a similar size.

2.5 mm
Cut-throat finch *Amadina fasciata*, red-headed finch *A. erythrocephalus*, chestnut-breasted finch *Lonchura castaneothorax*, society finch (Bengalese), diamond sparrow *Zonaeginthus guttatus*, and other species of a similar size.

2.9 mm
Saffron finch *Sicalis flaveola*, song-, color, and various posture (form-) canaries, common bullfinch *Pyrrhula pyrrhula*, greenfinch *Carduelis chloris*, black-headed canary (alario finch) *Serinus alario*, various tanager species, and bird species of a similar size.

3.5 mm
Java sparrow, pekin robin *Leiothrix lutea*, bulbul species, shama thrush *Copsychus malabaricus*, Norwich, Yorkshire, and Lancashire canaries, and bird species of a similar size.

temperature, not only in the bird room, but also in the night shelter of an outdoor aviary. Make sure that if there are young birds in a garden aviary, they spend the night in the warm sleeping quarters when the weather outside is not as it should be.

After one to three weeks, if all goes well, the young become independent and will be fed by the parents only rarely. In many species, young should be removed from the parents at that stage, because otherwise the male will start to chase them around. This prevents the parents from starting a new breeding cycle. However, in cases where the parents like to have their young around, don't hesitate to leave them together; that way, the young learn about life from their parents.

Leg banding
Even though you want to disturb breeding finches as little as possible, you will have to take the young in hand at least once, namely to band, or ring, them. Many bird societies require birds entering into shows to be banded with a closed ring or band. These leg bands can best be purchased directly from the various bird societies.

The band will be marked with information such as your personal identification code, the individual bird's number and the year of the bird's hatch. This gives you clear evidence that a certain bird comes from your breeding establishment, as well as a reliable indication of the bird's age. Many bird fanciers prefer an open, plastic, colored band to identify their finches. These are placed on birds after weaning, allowing the fancier to avoid the risk of undesirable side effects from taking the young out of the nest to band them. Problems that could occur include the parents' refusal to come back to the nest, refusal to feed the youngsters, or throwing the banded young out of the nest. Many bird parents take fright when they encounter their young in the nest with a shiny band. Because they endeavor to keep the nest clean the first few days, they regard the band as a foreign object and try to remove it. The fact that a young bird is attached to the band seems to be of no significance to the cleaning bird!

Estrildid finches are best banded at seven or

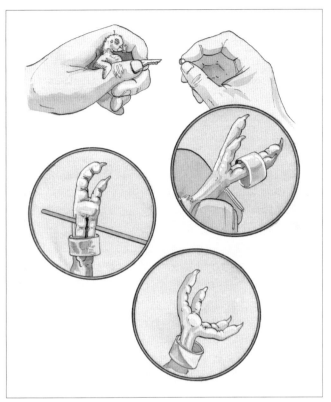

Banding a finch. Take the finch's foot between your fingers in such a manner that the back tow points toward the back and the other toes are stretched together towards the front. Rub a **little** petroleum jelly, salad oil, or saliva on the toes. Now place the band over the three front toes, slide it backwards, over the back toe, and continue a little further up the leg as well. If the back toe is still "trapped" under the band, release it with a somewhat pointed matchstick. The band is now correctly positioned around the chick's leg. After you clean the leg, put back the chick into the nest.

eight days of age. Blacken the band with a black marker before banding.

Not everyone has the knack for proper banding. Observe the process at the hands of an experienced bird fancier. Start the process at the onset of dusk when the female has become less intent on keeping the nest clean. That way you can almost surely avoid the young being thrown out of the nest. In any case, it pays to check every morning for a couple of days whether all chicks are still in the nest, and not laying on the aviary floor or on the bottom of the breeding cage.

The proper steps are as follows. Rub a little petroleum jelly on the leg, using it to "glue" the first three toes together. Then "glue" the small rear toe against the leg. This creates a straight line, so to speak. Now slide the band over the toes and the ball of the foot onto the leg. Then use a pointed match or toothpick to flip the small toe out care-

fully from under the band. Clean the leg and toes thoroughly with a cotton ball, position the band correctly around the chick's leg, and "operation banding" is complete.

Use a small band, with a diameter of 2.0, 2.3, 2.5, 2.9 or 3.5 millimeters, depending upon species (see box); if you use bands that are too large for the birds, you run the obvious chance of losing the bands sooner or later.

First molt

Once the young are four or five weeks old, they acquire their colored beaks. Earlier their beaks are usually black, or in the case of some parrotfinches, yellow. At six weeks of age, the first juvenile molt begins; it can last from one to two months, depending on the species. First the small stomach feathers and the feathers on the abdomen acquire their definite form and color, followed by breast, rump, and upper tail feathers, back, and flanks, in that order. Finally, the wing, head, and tail feathers complete the molt.

During molting, your birds require special care. Provide the proper temperature, sunlight, and a well-balanced diet with a sufficient amount of animal protein. A sudden change in temperature can cause the molt to be interrupted, which in turn can cause the birds to become sick, and even die. The diet absolutely must include oyster shell, vitamin-enriched limestone, ground shells, cuttle bone, sprouted seed, green food, yeast, minerals and vitamins. Another absolute must is exposure to direct sunlight/daylight; if that's impossible, use a fluorescent bulb. Do not use a sunlamp, however, as these are injurious to birds' eyes. Switch the heat lamp on for limited time periods only, perhaps 3–15 minutes a day, starting with 3 minutes and gradually working up to the given maximum. Place the lamp so the bird can also sit out of its glow, should it so desire.

Artificial light is also recommended, especially if new birds arrive during the fall or winter. The whole idea is to provide them with daylight as long as possible, allowing them more time to eat and get used to their environment, not to mention the new colleagues and the new keeper (see also page 26). Do not, however, place the cage directly in the sunlight; although finches like warmth and sun, they also need to have shade. On the other hand, it is not sensible to place the cage in a location where no sunlight comes in at all.

Crossbreeding

The Australian grassfinches and various waxbills are extremely well suited for crossbreeding. Many crosses occur spontaneously, in some cases, even in the wild. Crossbreeding in captivity, however, entails a sizable risk, namely to the racial purity of bird species, especially so when you cross species that resemble each other closely. Purposeful crossbreeding, in order to create hybrids, has no place in aviculture, especially when it concerns rare bird species. Bird importation has been severely restricted, hence every serious aviculturist should cooperate in the breeding of pure avian species, so that the hobby can continue into the future with a clear group of bird species which can be used for further breeding.

Hybrid
The result of crossing two different bird species, or of well-marked varieties within a species, is called a hybrid.

Mule
Any cross involving a canary and another species is called a mule. In Britain the mule is a hybrid resulting from crossing a canary with a certain British species, for example: canary x bullfinch.

Use of foster parents

It is generally known that society finches, or Bengalese, often serve as foster parents for other exotic finches. Nevertheless, you should do all you can to motivate the finches in your collection to do their own brooding. Nothing excels brooding with natural parents. We are strongly opposed to the practice of consistently employing foster parents for raising birds of high commercial value, like Gouldian finches, for example. We feel that going about the business in this way has no place in aviculture. The inevitable result is that the females of valuable finches are sooner or later converted into egg-laying machines; obviously this practice becomes a cropper and the "mechanized" female dies, usually from egg binding. It doesn't work either to first use females to produce as many eggs as possible and then later to let them brood and raise a set of youngsters on their own. Even if they do raise these young successfully, they are usually quite weak and in bad condition, which is understandable!

It has also been proven over the years that species that have been raised generation after generation by foster parents lose much of their own brooding instinct. In other words, they are barely able to raise a generation of young on their own. The first symptoms are incomplete nest building, egg pecking, and poor sexual drive.

If you provide proper housing and diet, you will be able to breed most of the estrildid finches in captivity. You will have to work, and work hard, for this goal. Some finch species are easier to breed than others, but they will give you good results with some extra attention on your part!

Still, occasions may arise that give you no choice but to make use of foster parents. At that point, you will have to weigh the advantages of foster parenting against the risks outlined above. Consider whether you are willing to lose a few eggs or young to promote nature's plan. Don't forget that young raised by foster parents often adopt the behavior of their foster parents, including song, mating dance, search for nesting sites, and choice of building material, among others.

The German-born ornithologist, the late Dr. Klaus Immelmann, as well as the senior author of this book, and others, have conducted experiments showing that breeding behavior is literally imprinted on zebra finch young in the first 50 days of their life. If zebra finch eggs are incubated by Bengalese which continue to care for the hatchlings, the young zebra finches receive the imprint of the Bengalese. Naturally this will lead to great difficulties later on, when the foster young start breeding their own. This problem is even greater if the foster young are paired, in order, for example, to prevent unnecessary inbreeding, with birds raised naturally. Both partners will have had a different education! Immelmann demonstrated that a mistaken imprinting could be corrected up to approximately the 50th day of life, provided that the young zebra finches are kept exclusively with members of their own species, without having any Bengalese within sight or hearing. As far as we know, imprinting works this way for most exotic finches. Once it is acquired, whether from natural parents or from foster parents, it is a determining factor for life. Nonetheless, we should do everything possible to try to change the imprinting of foster young to the proper type for their species.

To do this effectively, remove foster young from their foster parents as soon as they can eat on their own, and put them with birds of their own species. If you can manage this within 50 days of hatching, the chances are good that a proper imprinting will be achieved. Young that stay with the foster parents beyond the 50th day of life are not likely later to exhibit much interest in others of their own species. Rather, they will be attracted only to the species of their foster parents. If you plan to breed with birds raised by foster parents, you will definitely avoid many difficulties by matching individuals raised by the same species of foster parent (but again, avoid inbreeding). African silverbills (page 209) and, to a lesser extent, zebra finches, (page 224) can also be used as foster parents.

Even though Bengalese (see page 198) are favorite foster parents, you need to know certain points to succeed with them. You can't just shove eggs or young underneath them and expect to succeed.

Say you have eggs from a clutch that has been abandoned and you also have a pair of Bengalese that is brooding. The first step is to remove the eggs from the Bengalese and distribute them to other brooding Bengalese. Make sure that the clutches involved are not too far apart in the length of time they have been incubated (keep

score of all your breeding birds!). Then take the abandoned eggs to the Bengalese nest that has been emptied. If you have young that have been abandoned for some reason by the natural parents, you can transfer them to Bengalese only if these have youngsters of about the same age. Again, you will have to distribute the young of the adoptive parents among the nests of other Bengalese. In case you don't have enough breeding pairs, cooperate with a colleague.

If you have experience with Bengalese, you will know that two birds of the same sex, two males for example, can function as a pair. They build a nest together and will incubate imaginary eggs. This type of odd couple can also function very ably as foster parents, especially if you provide them with some infertile or, better still, artificial, stone eggs, while they act as a brooding pair. This stimulates their brooding behavior so that you can then bring young from other exotic finches to them for foster care. Once the young hatch, it can happen that the natural parents will feed them, provided they are housed in the same facility. They will be attracted by the begging cries of the young, and to have them share in their care can only promote proper imprinting.

Most young of the estrildid finches need insects, small spiders, and similar food while still in the nest. It is therefore essential that foster parents are familiar with this necessary animal protein. It is unfortunate that not all Bengalese are willing to feed live food; it is therefore absolutely essential that all your Bengalese are familiar, way before the breeding season, with egg food, which is available commercially in various brands. Fortunately, Bengalese have no problem eating this food and feeding it to their own young or foster babies.

Bicheno's Finch (male) / *Stizoptera (Poephila) bichenovii*

Part II
ESTRILDIDAE

ESTRILDINAE

Estrilda	Waxbills
Amandava	Avadavats
Uraeginthus	Blue Waxbills and Grenadiers
Lagonosticta	Firefinches
Cryptospiza	Crimson-wings
Nesocharis	Olive-backs or chickadee finches
Oreostruthus	Mountain Finches
Spermophaga	Bluebills
Nigrita	Negro Finches
Parmoptila	Antpeckers
Pyrenestes	Seedcrackers
Ortygospiza	Quailfinches and Locust Finch
Clytospiza	Brown Twinspots
Euschistospiza	Dusky Twinspots
Hypargos	Twinspots
Mandingoa	Green-backed Twinspots
Pytilia	Pytilias

AMADINAE

Amadina	Cut-throat Finches
Munia	Munias and Mannikins
Lonchura	Mannikins
Padda	Java Sparrows
Heteromunia	White-breasted Pictorellas
Lepidopygia	Dwarf Mannikins
Spermestes	Magpie Mannikins
Odontospiza	Gray-headed Silverbills
Euodice	Silverbills

ERYTHRURAE

Zonaeginthus	Diamond Sparrows
Neochmia	Crimson Finches
Poephila	Grassfinches
Stizoptera	Double-bar Finches
Chloebia	Gouldian Finch
Aegintha	Red-browed Finches
Aidemosyne	Cherry Finches
Bathilda	Star Finches
Reichenowia	Green-tailed Parrotfinches
Erythrura	Real Parrotfinches
Amblynura	South China Sea Parrotfinches
Emblema	Firetail Finches

Estrildidae

Introduction

The family Estrildidae, or Old World finches, contains the small seed-eating birds known variously as waxbills, grassfinches, parrotfinches, mannikins, munias and allied species belonging to the suborder Passeres, the songbirds, in the very extensive order Passeriformes, the perching birds. While the new system of classification established by Sibley, Alquist, and Monroe, based on DNA studies, has drastically altered the traditionally accepted relationships of many groups of birds, the actual relationship of the species within some groups, including the estrildid finches, has changed very little. There has always been a certain amount of controversy over the exact placement of certain species in the various genera, and, indeed, the number of genera that should be recognized. Basically, this book follows the more traditional approach of such ornithologists as Wolters and Immelmann, still upheld by most finch enthusiasts, with a few modifications of our own, based on years of experience and research into this family. We will chart our conclusions for comparative purposes with the S-A-M system of classification.

At one time, waxbills were placed with the weaver finches, because they had several traits in common with the true weavers of the family Ploceidae. Thorough research has shown, however, that the estrildines possess some characteristics that diverge from those of the weavers. They can be separated on the basis of anatomical details, such as the structure of the syrinx or vocal organ. Behavioral differences, especially in association to nest building, incubation, and chick rearing, are significant. Estrildines are monogamous, with both parents involved in incubating the eggs and feeding the chicks, while various weaver species are polygamous, with the females largely responsible for incubation and chick rearing. Additionally, relationships to other birds has had an influence in justifying the change in nomenclature, as have many important differences in feather structure, as well as ecological considerations involving the relationship between organisms and their environment.

The separation of estrildines from the weavers is logical, actually, especially if we compare methods of nest building. The males of true weavers begin by weaving a few blades or stems of grass around a twig. Only then do they form a ring-shaped construction to serve as a side wall. When the birds have completed that part, they start building the roof, and only when the outside is completely finished do they commence paying attention to readying the inside of the nest. Weaver males build several nests before they begin their courtship song displaying their skill to their hens, which in turn pick one nest in which to raise a family.

The waxbills go about nest building in a completely different manner, and only after forming pairs. First they build a dish-shaped construction in a tree fork, and then they follow with the sides and roof. Rather than building a succession of nests for females to choose from, most waxbill males gather nesting material for the female to arrange into a nest. Estrildid finches never truly weave their nests in the manner of true weavers. That's why associating them with the weaver finches is rather confusing, and it is better to classify them with such similar birds as the family Estrildidae. Minor differences between the typical waxbills and the Australian grassfinches, the parrotfinches, and the mannikins and munias has resulted in the further division of the family into several distinct subfamilies, including the Estrildinae, the Amadinae, and the Erythrurae.

Once this modified classification was arrived at, you could also reclassify the waxbills and their relatives, and so arrive at 49 genera that together have approximately 130 species.

Subfamily Estrildinae

The subfamily Estrildinae includes the typical waxbills, avadavats, firefinches, pytilias, cordon-bleus, twinspots, crimson-wings, seedcrackers, bluebills, olivebacks, and related species. With the exception of two of the three species in the genus *Amandava*, the avadavats, which occur in Asia, and the single member of the genus *Oreostruthus*, the crimson-sided mountain finch from New Guinea, the members of the subfamily Estrildinae are confined to Africa and the surrounding islands.

Genus *Estrilda* (waxbills or typical waxbills) Swainson, 1827

LAVENDER WAXBILL *Estrilda (Glaucestrilda) caerulescens* Vieillot, 1817

DK: Rødhalet Astrild, Grisbleu NL: Grijze astrild, Blauwgrijsroodstaartje FR: Benali Gris-bleu, Astrild Lavandre
DE: Schönbürzel, Blaugraues, Rotschwänzchen • IT: Coda d'aceto

▸ *photo page 97*

Description: Male. Gray-blue, darker on the back, lighter on the cheeks and throat. Underside black with white along the flanks. Rump, under tail coverts, and tail red. Little black periophthalmic ring; black lores. Eyes brown, beak red with a black tip; legs light brown. The female is generally less intense, which allows visual sexing without much difficulty. Length: 4½ in. (11.5 cm).

Distribution and habitat: from Senegal to the Cameroons in West Africa. It is found particularly in grassland and steppes, picking around in low bushes and clumps of grass in search of insects, grass and weed seeds. It is also encountered frequently in hedges and on lawns in parks and gardens, and even along busy highways.

Aviculture: This species is rather fragile. The birds never looked very robust when they arrived from overseas, and always required special attention. But in somewhat heated vitrines and indoor aviaries they always developed quite nicely.

Lavender waxbills are among the best acrobats in the bird world. They are uniformly cheerful and lively, and always ready to perform their simple song. The mating call of the male distinguishes the sexes, which otherwise are somewhat hard to tell apart, especially when young. Lavender waxbills perform a pleasant night-time routine. Once the sun has set, the male and female sit close together at their usual roosting place, then nod good night with definite head movements and utter a somewhat monotonous but pleasant-sounding "chew-chew-chew." The summoning calls differ between the sexes. The male calls with a "shee-tooey," while the female utters "shee-shee." If you sepa-

rate the two, these summoning calls can be heard constantly.

In the wild, as well as in the aviary, lavender waxbills build a round nest with a small, narrow entryway near the bottom. It is desirable to provide adequate space for this species. Placing them in cages that are too small often results in their losing head and neck feathers from plucking each other. The same problem also occurs when one ships the birds to shows.

This species does very well in a group setting. Be sure to furnish them separate sleeping nests and baskets. Put some nesting material inside, so that they have cover against the cold at night.

As an aside on the subject of breeding, there has been repeated successes in crossing the lavender waxbill with the red-billed firefinch *Lagonosticta senegala*, which we don't like to encourage! If these species are kept together, it is advisable to make sure they are correctly sexed and properly paired.

The female lays 3–5 eggs (see Red-eared waxbill, page 85) in a nest box or roomy basket, but they often construct a free, round nest in a thick bush. Provide grass, hemp and coconut fibers, and small feathers and such. In the wild, we often found nests where, in the outside layer, one or more dead young were used as "decoration" (or is this done for distraction purposes, so enemies won't go inside the nest?).

At about two weeks of age, the young leave the nest, but are still fed by the parents for a considerable period of time. For quite a while, the young have gray-blue papillae (mouth markings). Once the young are independent, at about a month of age, remove them from the parents. They unfortunately tend to do some feather picking, especially, as stated before, if the facility is too cramped. To minimize the problem, add extra cuttlebone, finely ground egg shell, and vitamins A and D to the food.

Food: These birds should be offered a top-brand commercial seed mixture for small finches, as well as sprouted seeds, a good variety of egg-food or universal food, ant pupae, real egg yolk that has been cooked and crumbled, finely cut mealworms, white worms *Enchytraeus albidus*, greens such as endive, chicory, chickweed, and dandelion, and millet spray. The ant pupae can be given fresh as well as in the dry form. This food is indispensable, particularly during the breeding season. Throughout the year, but especially during the breeding season, these birds like hummingbird nectar mixtures.

Other names: Red-tailed lavender, Lavender finch.

GRAY WAXBILL *Estrilda (Glaucestrilda) perreini* Vieillot, 1817

DK: Sorthalet Astrild NL: Blauwgrijs zwartstaartje FR: Astrild de Perrein DE: Schwarzschwanz-Schönbürzel
IT: Astrilde di Cinderella coda nera

▶ *photo page 97*

Description: Male. Very similar to the lavender waxbill (page 73) but lighter to white around the beak and bib, and under the eye. Tiny black spots just under the mandible. Tail and under tail coverts black. Rump and upper tail coverts red; there are often very small white dots on the flanks. Lores and eye stripes black. Eyes dark brown, beak dark steel blue with black tip; legs black brown. The female is similar to the male. Length: 4¼ in. (11 cm).

Geographic variations:

■ *E. p. perreini*, as above. Distribution: western Tanzania, northern Zambia, and from Angola to southern and western Zaire, and in northerly direction through western Congo to southern Gabon.

- *E. p. poliogastra* (Reichenow). Much lighter than the nominate form, especially in the face. Distribution: southern Tanzania, Mozambique to the eastern parts of Zimbabwe and into northeastern South Africa.
- *E. p. incana* Sundervall. Very light and somewhat smaller. The under tail coverts are gray. Hens have often darker under tail coverts. Distribution: eastern part of South Africa (Zululand and Natal).

Habitat: Found in pairs or in small flocks (up to 24 birds) near grassland, woodland and forest, high in trees and large bushes in which they build their beautiful retort-shaped nests. The nest is built from dried grasses and seed heads, and lined with fine grass and small feathers. The entrance tunnel protrudes from the top of the nest. The birds often roost in old nests of other bird species, especially weavers.

They like to catch flying insects on the wing, and are often seen with various other small bird species, like the greater double-collared sunbird *Nectarinia afra* and the pale white eye *Zosterops palidus*.

Besides various insects, gray waxbills like nectar, flowers, fruits and a variety of grass and weed seeds. They often use old weaver nests to raise a family; the hen lays 4–6 white eggs. Youngsters are much duller in color, and don't have the black chin spot, nor the black tail feathers. All red colors are much duller, and their beaks are brownish gray.

When the young hatch they are flesh-colored with some down feathers on the head and back. After 3–4 days their bodies are gray; after 8 days, black gray. This species lives a secret life, and not much is known about their behavior.

Aviculture: The gray waxbill is fairly well-known in aviculture. It must be acclimatized with great care, at a minimum temperature of 77°F (25°C) with a relative humidity of 60–70%. The species is friendly toward other small finches and members of its own kind. In order to achieve breeding results, house three or more pairs together in a well-planted indoor aviary. Birds keep constant contact with each other with a short "psee" (ee as in sea) or "psu" (u as in you). During the beginning of the breeding season the male tries to impress the hen, while flying around with a long blade of grass in the beak, with a warbly "pu u u u u-pee ee ee ee, pu u u u u, pee ee ee ee" or "p u u u u t" or "p u u wi wi wi wi." The species is very active and likes to search for food on the bottom of the aviary. The female lays 6–8 white eggs. Both parents incubate the eggs for 13–14 days. When the young are approximately 21 days old they will leave the nest. After 3–4 weeks they go into their final molt and are no longer distinguishable from their parents.

Food: See red-billed firefinch (page 149). Small insects are essential throughout the year, but especially in the breeding season.

Other name: Black-tailed lavender waxbill.

CINDERELLA WAXBILL *Estrilda (Glaucestrilda) thomensis* Sousa, 1888

DK: Cinderella Rødhalet Astrild NL: Cinderella astrild FR: Astrild de Cinderella
DE: Cinderella- Schönbürzel IT: Astrilde di Cinderella

Description: Male. Light grayish blue with a red reflection on the breast and back. The black lore continues past the eye into the neck, as is the case in the lavender waxbill. Rump and upper tail coverts red, as are the flanks. Halfway across the belly, the color changes to black, which continues across the abdomen. Eyes brown, beak red with a black tip and black edges, legs black. The female has less red, especially along the flanks. On the breast, she may lack the red coloration altogether. The abdomen and the lower covert feathers of the tail are more gray-black. The song is almost identical to that of the lavender waxbill. Length: 4 in. (10 cm).

Distribution and habitat: Western Angola to the Cunene River. Occurs in pairs and small family flocks, up to 25 individuals, in mountainous, wooded areas up to 3000 ft. (900 m), especially along the edge of forests and in clearings. The species lives on half-ripe grass and weed seeds and many types of small insects and spiders.

Aviculture: Until 1963, when several individuals were sighted, it was thought that this species was extinct. They were imported into Europe and bred successfully in 1970. They must be kept in a roomy inside aviary with the temperature around 85°F (30°C). Both parents-to-be will construct a large, rather flimsy, oval-shaped nest from dry grasses, with a small entrance, which often has perches in the form of protruding grass stems. The 3–5 white eggs are incubated by both birds for 12–14 days; the young leave the nest after 19–22 days but will still be fed by the parents for another 2–2½ weeks. Further care and feeding are identical to the recommendations for the lavender waxbill.

Other names: São Thomé waxbill, Neumann's waxbill, Red-flanked lavender finch.

DUFRESNE'S WAXBILL *Estrilda (Neisma) melanotis* Temminck, 1823

DK: Sortkinded Astrild NL: Zwartbekje FR: Astrild de Dufresne, Joue noire
DE: Schwarzbäckchen, Angola Schwarzbäckchen IT: Astrilde guance nere dellángola

▶ *photos page 98*

Description: Male. Head, breast and flanks blue-gray; wings and tail olive-brown gray. Rest of the underside beige to yellow. Chin, throat and cheeks black. Eyes dark brown, upper mandible black, lower mandible red, legs black. In the female, the black is lacking. Length: 3½–4 in. (10 cm).

Geographic variations:

■ *E. m. melanotis*, described above. Distribution: eastern and most southern part of South Africa, and in isolated small flocks in southern Zimbabwe.

■ *E. m. quartinia* (Bonaparte). The Abyssinian green waxbill, has been offered in the trade since 1960, or a little earlier in Europe. Unfortunately, this subspecies is no longer imported, but at one time it was raised successfully, particularly in indoor aviaries and large vitrines. Acclimatization, however, takes a lot of care. Use infrared lamps to keep the temperature at 85°F (30°C) for at least two months, after which you can gradually reduce it to 68°F (20°C). Abyssinians breed well and make good use of half-open nest boxes. Distribution: Ethiopia and the southeastern part of the Sudan. In the wild as well as in captivity, the birds like to use grass, sisal, and other fine nesting material; the nest bowl is furnished with small, soft feathers. Eggs are incubated for 12–13 days. The young are raised almost entirely on insects or substitute animal proteins such as commercial egg foods. After 19–22 days, the young fly out, but they return to the parental nest for several nights after fledging. After another 15–20 days they are independent and can be safely separated from the parents. The color of the Abyssinian green waxbill is, as the name already indicates, olive-green; the underparts are yellow; the rump is red, as are the upper tail coverts. The upper mandible is black; the lower mandible is red. The female is a little less intense in coloration than the male. Length: 3½ in. (9 cm).

■ *E. m. kilimensis* (Sharpe). Green waxbill. This is another well-known cage and aviary bird, especially in Europe among experienced finch fanciers. Don't confuse this subspecies, however, with the green avadavat *Amandava formosa*, which is sometimes also referred to as the green waxbill. This race is mainly gray with a greenish gray back and a red rump and upper tail coverts. Throat clear white; lower body yellowish white. Flanks yellow-green, wings brown, tail black. The beak resembles that of the Abyssinian. The female is a bit lighter in hue on the underside. Distribution: from Uganda and Kenya to eastern Zaire. Length: 3½ in. (9 cm).

■ *E. m. stuartirwini* (Clancey). The main difference with the previous subspecies is the lighter olive-green color on the head, back and wings. Distribution: from the southern parts of Tanzania through Malawi and eastern Zambia to eastern Zimbabwe and western Mozambique. Length: 3½ in. (9 cm).

■ *E. m. bocagei* (Shelley). Especially noticeable are the bright, olive-green back with a little dark wave design and the yellow belly. Distribution: western highlands of Angola southward to the Namibian border. Length: 3½ in. (9 cm). The hens of this well-known cage and aviary bird, as well as all the other females, have light gray heads and breasts; the rest of the underside is yellowish; chin, throat and border above the breast are white.

Habitat: All subspecies occur in mountain forests, preferably in low bushes and on the ground. They are also encountered in gardens and parks, particularly in hedges. They nest in bushes and hedges, constructing mainly with grass. They feed on all types of seeds and small insects and spiders.

Aviculture: The Dufresne's waxbill has become rather rare in captivity as well as in the wild. The bird is known for its fast movements, but it certainly is not aggressive, even though some ornithologists may not agree with this statement. We believe that it can properly be housed with other small finches. We experienced no difficulties in keeping a pair very active in an outdoor aviary for more than seven years, from 1971 through 1978.

Treat this bird right and it quickly becomes quite trusting. It is an excellent cage and aviary bird. In an outdoor aviary it does better than most finches, as it is quite hardy. Still, we definitely recommend moving it out of the garden aviary into a lightly heated facility during the winter.

The general care is similar to that recommended for the two previous species. Let us add, however, that Dufresne's waxbills are sensitive to disturbances during the breeding season, so leave them in peace. They are easy to start breeding if there are enough live plants and bushes in the aviary. They prefer to build a free nest, although some will use nest boxes and baskets. Incubation takes 12–14 days. The 3–6 young leave the nest after 21 days. At that time they still have black beaks; after three months they come into their adult plumage.

Food: Provide all types of small millet seeds. Further, furnish grass and weed seed, half- ripe, soaked and sprouted seeds. A rich variety of greens is highly important. In the breeding season especially, and also at other times, they should have a daily ration of all types of animal proteins, including small, cut-up mealworms, white worms, insects, spiders, commercial egg food or universal food, etc. Offer food on a little platform, say about 20 in. (50 cm) high, because the birds don't like to forage on the ground, in contrast to their behavior in the wild.

Other names: Yellow-bellied waxbill, Swee waxbill.

BLACK-CHEEKED WAXBILL *Estrilda (Brunhilda) erythronotos* (Vieillot, 1817)

(See also *E. charmosyna*, page 79)   ▶ *photos page 97*

DK: Alfeastrild NL: Elfastrild FR: Astrild a moustaches noires DE: Elfenastrild IT: Astrilde guancia nera

Description: Male. Breast, flanks and abdomen crimson pinkish gray, slowly grading into black. Forehead light gray, crown darker; cheeks and ear patch, and part of the throat, light reddish gray. Eyebrows and cheeks form one black part. It seems as if the bird has a moustache, and the French call it "l'astrilda à moustaches noires," which translates to "waxbill with the black moustaches." Primaries doe-brown to gray-brown. The rest of the wing gray to white with brown undulations. Back and rump bright red. Tail black. Eyes red to dark brown, beak steel-blue with brownish hue and a black tip, legs brownish black. The color of the female is a little less intense; the underside is more grayish black. There is no red on the back and breast, and the other red areas are less bright. The birds have a rather monotonous song that goes "doo-duh-doo-oo-oo." Length: 4½–5 in. (11.5–12.5 cm).

Geographic variations:

■ *E. e. erythronotos*, as above. Distribution: South Africa, from northern Cape Province through Orange Free State and Transvaal to southwestern Zimbabwe.

■ *E. e. soligena* Clancey. Red areas brighter and more extensive, but generally duller than the nominate subspecies. The undulations are brownish, not black. Belly spot, black-brown, but smaller. The back of the hen is deeper gray with dull brown feather-borders. Under tail coverts light gray with undulations. Length: 5 in. (12.5 cm). Distribution: from northwestern Botswana and southwestern Zambia to southern Angola and most of the northeastern parts of Namibia.

■ *E. e. delamerei* Sharpe. Brighter, with light red upper tail coverts and rump. Clearly visible white and black wing undulations; whitish forehead. The black cheeks have small white bottom and side borders. Underside dull gray; under tail coverts whitish. Hens lighter than those of nominate form. The young look like their parents, only duller without the undulations, except on the wings. There is no red, only some brownish red, on the upper tail coverts and rump. The beak is still black as in other waxbill chicks. Length: 5.4 in. (13 cm). Distribution: northern and central Tanzania, eastern Burundi and Ruanda; also in Uganda and southwestern Kenya.

Habitat: It is a typical steppe dweller that builds a pretty keg-shaped nest out of straw, grass, and wool. The nest, which has a long, downward facing entryway, is built in thorny bushes, between 13–20 ft. (4–6 m) from the ground.

Aviculture: This species is one of the foster parents of the pintailed whydah *Vidua macroura* and the Senegal combassou *Hypochera (Vidua) hypocherina*; in other words, these two bird species lay their eggs in the nest of the black-cheeked waxbill and various other species of waxbills. This is a classic example of brood parasitism, the laying of eggs by one bird species in the nest of a host species which rears the "changelings," sometimes at the expense of some or all of its own young, although this seldom occurs in waxbills. This behavior has also been called nest parasitism, but this term is easily mistaken to mean nest piracy, the appropriation of one species' nest by another.

It is rather difficult to obtain a good breeding pair of black-cheeked waxbills. First, they may not be available at all because there is no regular supply chain anymore, and European breeders are not too keen on shipping the species overseas. Secondly, they have always been expensive. And beyond that, it is hard to sex them, so that you must always be sure to have an arrangement with the breeder or seller to allow an exchange if you didn't acquire a true pair. You can tell the male by his mating dance and his piercing contact call: "tooooeyt-tooooeyt."

We have raised them successfully in a regular community aviary. The birds build a keg- shaped nest. The two clutches we raised had four white eggs that were incubated 13 days, in turn by the male and female. The young left the nest after 12 days, and two weeks later they were independent.

These birds love to sit in the sun, where they will stay for hours, holding their wings low. If you want to raise these birds indoors, you must definitely work with infrared lamps. They like searching about in dense bushes and also spend a lot of time on the ground. The black-cheeked waxbill is particularly sensitive to dampness. That is why it's important to raise the surface of the garden aviary above that of the surrounding yard, so that the surface doesn't stay wet after a rain shower. Further, the sleeping coop has to be absolutely watertight, and damp-free, too.

We consider this tender species suited only for experienced breeders and fanciers, as the birds are hard to keep in good condition, not to speak of breeding. Success in breeding is dependent on a good source of insects for food. Before the start of the breeding season, supply spiders, ant pupae, small cut-up mealworms, white worms, universal food, and the like.

In the winter months, house them in a lightly heated facility, preferably with an infrared lamp.

Even in summer, we think it best to keep the birds at a temperature of about 77°F (25°C), especially if they have arrived recently from Europe. You can gradually drop the temperature to 68°F (20°C). On nice, sunny days, they can make good use of an outside aviary, but they need to have a sleeping coop year round.

They are quite trusting, so that they can be kept indoors in roomy cages; there, however, you can't count on successful breeding, which is chancy anywhere. They build free nests and also make use of nest boxes and baskets. The problem with them is that after several days of steady brooding, they may abandon their eggs; or they may stop feeding their young after they are half raised! In any case, peaceful surroundings are of the utmost importance, as is proper diet. It is also wise to change the drinking water to spring water, and add several drops of commercially available avian vitamins to it. Refresh the water several times a day, and offer only water that is room temperature.

The mating dance is interesting to watch. The male dances around the female in full song, with a blade of grass in his beak. If the blade is long, he holds it off the ground (or off of the branch) with one of his legs.

Food: All types of small millet seeds, grass and weed seeds, and a rich variety of animal protein. They also accept flower leaves. The general feeding is similar to that for the red-eared waxbill (see page 85).

RED-RUMPED WAXBILL *Estrilda (Brunhilda) charmosyna* (Reichenow, 1881)

DK: Fee Astrild NL: Feeënastrild FR: Astrild des fées DE: Feenastrild
IT: Astrilde guancia nera (see previous name!)

▸ *photo page 97*

This species is better known as the black-cheeked waxbill, a name already given to *E. erythronotos*. Some authorities consider the two species conspecific, with *charmosyna* relegated to subspecific status, and the subspecies listed below also becoming subspecies of *erythronotos*. See Black-cheeked waxbill (page 77).

Description: Very similar to the black-cheeked waxbill. The throat is crimson pinkish with white, as are the breast, belly and under tail coverts. Tail blackish; cheeks black, bordered with white. Crimson rump and upper tail coverts. Eyes brown to reddish brown, beak blue-gray with a black tip, legs dark blue-gray. The female is duller with less red, especially in the under tail feathers. Length: 4½ in. (11.5 cm).

Geographic variations:
■ *E. c. charmosyna*, as above. Distribution: from Cameroon to Kenya and Tanzania; Somalia and east to Tanzania.
■ *E. c. nigrimentum* Salvadori. Somewhat darker and with more gray. Duller forehead. Many scientists don't consider this a subspecies but a darker form of the nominate race. Distribution: southwestern Ethiopia to southeastern Sudan; further in northeastern Uganda and northwestern Kenya.
■ *E. c. pallidior* Jackson. Lighter, especially on chin and throat, and with more red; nevertheless, difficult to distinguish from the nominate subspecies. Distribution: northern and central Kenya.
■ *E. c. kiwanukae* van Someren. Rather dark with little white horizontal stripes in the wings; by far the darkest representative of all the *charmosyna* subspecies. Distribution: southern Kenya, and northern and central Tanzania.

Habitat: Found in thorn scrub country below 3300 ft. (1000 m).

Aviculture: Care and management essentials are similar to those required by the black-cheeked waxbill.

Other names: Black-cheeked waxbill, Pink-bellied waxbill.

FAWN-BREASTED WAXBILL *Estrilda paludicola* Heuglin, 1863

DK: Sumpastrild DK: Moeras astrild FR: Astrild de marais
DE: Sumpfastrild, Rotsteissiger Astrild IT: Astrilde paludicola

Description:
Male. Forehead, crown and upperparts brown-gray, darker on back and wings, often with a somewhat red reflection. Rest of head and neck light gray, and almost white on chin and throat. Underparts yellowish white with a blood red patch. Flanks grayish yellow. Tail black with white edges; upper tail coverts red. Eyes brown, beak red, legs brown. The female has less intense red coloration. The young are generally grayer and still have a black beak. The song is a loud chirp; they also use a variety of communication calls that are performed by chirping and whistling. Length: 4 in. (10 cm).

Geographic variations:
■ *E. p. paludicola*, described above. Distribution: western Kenya, northern Uganda, northeastern Zaire, southern Sudan, and the eastern part of the Central African Republic.

■ *E. p. ruthae* Chapin. This subspecies has a lighter forehead and crown; back and wings brownish. No yellow trace on breast and belly; more grayish white. Length: 4 in. (10 cm). Distribution: eastern part of Congo and western Zaire, where the rivers Congo and Ubangi flow into each other. Smaller than the nominate form.

■ *E. p. roseicrissa* Reichenow. Male, forehead, crown, nape, back and rump light reddish brown. Barely visible little cheek. Chin, throat and breast whitish to silver gray; belly and flanks reddish orange; under tail coverts white. Hens lack the red colors. Length: 4 in. (10 cm). Distribution: southern Uganda into Zaire, through Ruanda and Burundi to northwestern Tanzania.

■ *E. p. marwitzi* Reichenow. Like the previous subspecies, but with much more chestnut brown; underside almost pure white. Length: 4 in. (10 cm). Distribution: interior of Tanzania.

■ *E. p. benguellensis* Neumann. Forehead, crown, nape, back and rump dark blue gray, as are the wings. Around the eyes and underside yellowish; vague yellow cheeks. The red belly color is stronger than in the nominate form. Length: 4 in. (10 cm). Distribution: most parts of Angola, in southeastern Zaire and in northern and western Zambia.

■ *E. p. ochrogaster* Salvadori. Known as the Abyssinian fawn-breasted waxbill. Male. Head, neck, and upperparts yellowish brown; yellow throat, much lighter on the breast. Flanks and rump red. Female duller in coloration. Red beak, eyes brown, legs and feet light brown. Length: 4 in. (10 cm). Distribution: high in the mountains of middle and western Ethiopia. Rather rare in aviculture.

Habitat:
The species lives along water, in swamps, near the edges of light woods, along roads, and the like, where they feel at home in the grass and reeds. We have found them also high in the mountains, up to 6700 ft. (2000 m). The nest is built on or close to the ground and resembles that of the red-eared waxbill. In the breeding season they occur in pairs or small groups; afterward, they form large flocks at times.

Aviculture:
This species looks deceptively like the orange-cheeked waxbill *Estrilda melpoda* (page 81), only a bit larger. After proper acclimatization, it proves to be a strong bird that will build a free nest in dense bushes without much difficulty. It will also breed in nest boxes and baskets, and even tolerates nest inspection, provided you don't do it too often.

You can achieve good results housing three or more pairs together in one roomy facility. They live mainly on the ground and like to crawl in grass and reeds. For further details on breeding, consult the sections covering the orange-cheeked waxbill and the red-eared waxbill (pages 81 and 85, respectively).

Food:
See Red-eared waxbill, page 85.

ANAMBRA WAXBILL *Estrilda poliopareia* Reichenow, 1902

DK: Anambra Astrild NL: Anambra astrild FR: Astrild de Anambra DE: Anambra Astrild IT: Astrilde di Anambra

Description: Similar to the fawn-breasted waxbill *Estrilda paludicola* (page 00). Wavy flank-design. Tail and beak shorter than in *paludicola*. Generally gray-brown with light orange-red upper tail coverts. Face, chin, breast clear yellow; belly and under tail coverts yellow gray-brown. Beak red, eyes brown, legs gray-brown. The hen is grayish with no red on the flanks. The young resemble their mother when they first leave the nest. Their beaks are still black. Not much is known about this species, except that they host the pin-tailed whydah, *Vidua macroura*. Length: 3 in. (10 cm).

Distribution and habitat: Lives in a rather small area along the Niger River in southern Nigeria.

Aviculture: Unknown.

ORANGE-CHEEKED WAXBILL *Estrilda melpoda* Vieillot, 1817

DK: Orangekindet Astrild NL: Oranjekaakje, Oranje wangetje FR: Astrild Bengali à joues orangées, Joue orange   ▶ *photo page 97*
DE: Orangebäckchen IT: Guance arancio

Description: Male. Mouse-brown, lighter on crown and nape. Chin, throat and breast grayish white; belly yellow to orange-yellow. Rump orange-red, tail blackish blue, cheeks light orange-yellow, lores orange-red. Eyes brown, beak red, legs pinkish. The cheek spots of the female are often somewhat smaller; she is, in general, also duller in coloration. Only the male sings. The young have black beaks and possess more brown and black in their plumage. Length: 4 in. (10 cm).

Geographic variations:

■ *E. m. melpoda*, described above. Distribution: western central Africa, from Senegal and Mali to western and southern Nigeria, western Cameroon and western Angola. Some years ago, escaped birds established themselves in the Caribbean.

■ *E. m. tschadensis* Grote. Paler upperside, lighter on breast and belly than nominate form. Red-orange cheeks. Length: 4 in. (10 cm). Distribution: southwestern Chad, northeastern Nigeria, and northern Cameroon.

■ *E. m. fucata*. Neumann. As nominate species but with clear red cheeks. Length: 4 in. (10 cm). Distribution: Zaire, except the western part. Also in Camaroon, southern and western Central African Republic, and northeastern Angola.

Habitat: This species lives in light forests, grassland, agricultural areas, large parks, and gardens. During the breeding season in pairs, outside this time in small groups.

Aviculture: A true pair fairly often comes to breed in a well-planted garden aviary with low bushes and high grass. The birds like to construct their oval-shaped nests with a rather long tunnel-like entrance, about 6 ft. (2 m) from the ground; some pairs prefer a half-open nest box in which they build a round nest of grass, wool, horse hair, plant fibers, etc. Two males or two females may act as a pair. The female usually lays 2–4, but sometimes up to seven, eggs; incubation time 11–12 days. After 2–3 weeks the young leave the nest. Don't disturb the breeding birds, as they are very sensitive to disturbances. The young assume their full plumage at the first molt, which is after approximately seven weeks. Acclimatization takes some time; house the birds in large cages or indoor aviaries at a minimum temperature 73°F (23°C). Cross-breedings with red-eared waxbills *Estrilda troglodytes* and common waxbills *E. astrild* are possible, but not recommended.

Food: As red-eared waxbill (see page 85). In order to achieve breeding success, a variety of small insects, weed seeds and sprouted seeds are absolutely essential.

COMMON WAXBILL *Estrilda astrild* Linnaeus, 1817

DK: Helena Astrild NL: Sint-Helenafazantje FR: Astrild ondulé, Astrild de St. Hélène
DE: Wellenastrild, Helenafasänchen IT: Astrilde ondulato, Becco de corallo di St. Elena

▸ *photos page 98*

Description: The nominate subspecies has a dark gray-brown crown and nape; the back is somewhat lighter. Cheeks, throat and part of the breast light brownish white; red stripe through the eyes. Crimson belly; flanks and underparts dark gray-brown, washed in pink. Practically the whole body is covered with fine dark brown undulations, except for the throat and ear patches. Eyes brown, beak red, legs brownish gray. The female is somewhat smaller, with lighter markings and with less pink on the abdomen and less intensive color on the belly. Length: 4½ in. (11.5 cm).

Geographic variations:

■ *E. a. astrild*, as above. Distribution: southern Botswana to South Africa, outside the areas where subspecies *tenebridorsa* occurs.

■ *E. a. damarensis* Reichenow. Upperparts paler than in the nominate subspecies, especially forehead, crown and upper tail coverts. Upper breast and throat also paler. Distribution: southern Namibia and northwestern Cape Province.

■ *E. a. ngamiensis* Roberts. An extremely pale-colored race with whitish ear coverts and throat, and with a small red belly stripe. Somewhat larger in size than the nominate form. Distribution: southern and southeastern Angola to northern Zambia, Zimbabwe and northern Botswana.

■ *E. a. jagoensis* Alexander. Lighter than the nominate subspecies; with more gray and smaller undulations. The red of the belly is vague and washed out. Distribution: along the coast of western Angola. Introduced and established on Cape Verde Islands.

■ *E. a. angolensis* Reichenow. With much red on tail, wings and belly, and with dark undulations. Distribution: in mountainous region of western Angola; imported on São Thomé and Principé islands.

■ *E. a. rubriventris* (Vieillot). Brownish on the underside with a clear red belly patch; all other red colored body parts are also much more intensive. The hen looks much like the nominate hen and is perhaps somewhat browner and has a trace of red on the belly. Distribution: northwestern Angola to western Gabon.

■ *E. a. occidentalis* Jardin & Fraser. Underside dark light brown, upperside much darker. Some reddish tone on the belly. Chin, throat and face whitish. Distribution: southern Sudan and northern Zaire west to Central Africa, and from South Cameroon to Equatorial Guinea, and from there spreading westward into southeastern Nigeria. This subspecies could very well be synonymous with the following subspecies.

■ *E. a. kempi* Bates. This form is somewhat lighter, especially in the upperparts. Distribution: from West Africa east to the Ivory Coast.

■ *E. a. macmillani* Ogilvie-Grant. Looks like the following subspecies, but has much darker brown upperparts, although practically no red on the underparts. Distribution: southwestern Ethiopia and southeastern Sudan.

■ *E. a. peasei* Shelley. Dark brown, without red on the upperparts; dark red on breast and belly. Chin, throat, and face whitish. Distribution: remaining parts of Ethiopia (see previous subspecies) and bordering Sudan. Also in northern Somalia.

■ *E. a. massaica* Neumann. Forehead, crown and neck gray; back and wings brown. All underparts barely show any undulations while the red belly patch is vague or not existing at all. Distribution: southeastern Uganda, and in the mountains of Kenya and northern Tanzania.

■ *E. a. minor* (Cabanis). A rather gray-colored bird with a small red belly patch. Chin, throat and face white. Length: Up to 4 in. (10 cm). Distribution: southern Somalia to the coast of Kenya, and eastern and central Tanzania. Also on Zanzibar and Mafia Islands.

- *E. a. muenzneri* Kothe. Upperparts like previous subspecies. Chin brownish. Dispersed red patches on underside. Distribution: Uganda, Ruanda and Burundi, western Tanzania and bordering eastern Zaire.
- *E. a. schoutedeni* Wolters. Pale brown underside with vague red patches. Upperside light brown. Distribution: central and southern Zaire.
- *E. a. nigriloris* Chapin. Known as the black-faced waxbill, this subspecies is accorded full specific status by some authorities. Black lores and eyebrows, bordered with a thin white and red line. Upperparts medium brown with fine undulations. Underside with dark red; no belly patch. Distribution: occurs in a rather small area around the upper course of the Lualaba River and Upemba Lake; all in all an area of approximately 2600 km².
- *E. a. cavendishi* Sharpe. Chin, throat and face white. Forehead and crown uniform gray. Very dark undulations. Rather dark crimson-red belly/breast patch. Distribution: central and southern Tanzania to Southeastern Zaire, Malawi, northern and eastern Zimbambe, and Mozambique north of Delagoa Bay to eastern Transvaal and northern Zululand (South Africa).
- *E. a. tenebridorsa* Clancey. Back and mantel darker than in the nominate subspecies; the undulations are barely visible and strongly washed with olivaceous brown. Distribution: South Africa in the Transkei, highlands of Lesotho, Natal, Zululand, eastern Orange Free State, Swaziland, southern and eastern Transvaal; also in southern Mozambique.

Habitat: This species is now feral in Portugal and parts of Spain (Europe!). In Africa they live primarily in savanna woodland, grassland and cultivated areas, in large flocks, except when breeding. They are completely fearless of man! Common waxbills were imported in the 19th century in St. Helena. Parasitized by the pin-tailed whydah *Vidua macroura*.

Aviculture: In the aviary the male builds a pear-shaped, loosely woven nest from moss, grass, hay, small fibers, hair, and feathers in a low, thick bush or in a half-open nest box. The birds frequently construct on top of the main nest an additional chamber known as the cock's nest, which is used as a dormitory for nearly fully-fledged youngsters to roost. Nest boxes should be hung high. The female lays 1–5, sometimes up to 10, white eggs, although the large clutches are probably by two hens; incubation time 10–13 days. After 17–22 days the young leave the nest, but will be nourished by the parents for yet another 10–14 days. It is advisable to house only one pair in a community aviary to avoid troubles, as they can be rather aggressive during that time, even toward larger birds. All *Estrilda* species must have access to a daily bath.

Food: See Red-eared waxbill (page 85). Animal protein and sprouted small seeds are essential throughout the year, but especially during the breeding season.

Other names: St. Helena waxbill, Red-bellied waxbill, Common African waxbill, Barred waxbill, and Brown waxbill.

CRIMSON-RUMPED WAXBILL *Estrilda rhodopyga* Sundevall, 1850

DK: Tøjleastrild NL: Teugelastrild, Teugelstreepastrild FR: Astrild à dos rouge
DE: Zügelastrild IT: Astrilde dal groppone rosso

▸ *photo page 99*

Description: Crown blue-gray; cheeks and throat somewhat lighter. Tail red; under tail coverts dark brown with a reddish sheen. Red eye stripe. Underparts white-yellow; wings and back dark brown-gray. Central tail feathers with crimson edges as well as the inner secondaries. Very similar to *E. troglodytes*. Eyes brown, beak and legs dark brown. The sexes are alike, but the red eye stripe in the female may be smaller and the light blue-gray throat patches are less extensive. Young birds are browner and don't have much red in their plumage. Length: 4½ in. (11.5 cm).

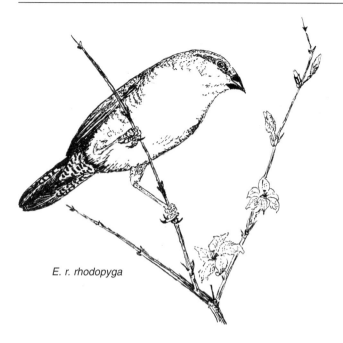

E. r. rhodopyga

Geographic variations:

■ *E. r. rhodopyga*, as above. Distribution: East Africa, northern Somalia, northern and central Ethiopia to the Sudan.

■ *E. r. centralis* Kothe. Somewhat darker brown but difficult to differentiate from the nominate subspecies. Distribution: southeastern Sudan and southern Ethiopia through Kenya, Uganda, northeastern Zaire, Ruanda and Burundi to central Tanzania.

■ *E. r. frommi* Kothe. Head and overall appearance grayer than the nominate subspecies. Distribution: southwestern Tanzania and northern Malawi. Likely in northwestern Mozambique.

Habitat: Grassland, farmland, open country, up to 4800 ft. (1450 m), and near villages; in small groups.

Aviculture: These birds must be acclimatized with care, at a minimum temperature of approximately 86°F (30°C), but after that period they are excellent for a garden aviary, although females are known to suffer easily from egg-binding. In an aviary as well as in the wild they often take the nests of the orange-cheek waxbill but will also build their own nests from wool, plant fibers, small feathers, grass, hay, and the like. They also construct, like *E. melpoda* and *E. troglodytes*, small nests in the immediate vicinity of the breeding nest; these can be regarded as decoys. For more breeding details see *E. troglodytes*. Parasitized by the pin-tailed whydah *Vidua macroura*.

Food: As for the red-eared waxbill. Egg food and universal food are essential although not always appreciated. Various small insects and spiders are a must throughout the year, but especially during the breeding season, as are grass and weed seeds, both fresh and sprouted.

Other names: Rosy-rumped waxbill, Ruddy waxbill, Sundervall's waxbill.

BLACK-HEADED WAXBILL *Estrilda (Krimhilda) atricapilla* Verreaux, 1851

DK: Sortkappet Astrild NL: Zwartkopje FR: Astrild à tête noire
DE: Kappenastrild, Schwarzkappenastrild, Schwarzköpfchen IT: Astrilde nonnette testo nero

▶ *photo page 99*

Description: Crown and face glossy black, as are the tail feathers. Back dark brown with black feather tips. Rump and flanks red, wings dark brown with black specks. Underparts blue-gray, darker toward the under tail coverts. Eyes dark brown, beak dark gray with a red spot on the lower mandible, legs dark brown. Females are usually paler on the upperparts, with paler red flanks. Young birds are fully colored after approximately six weeks. Length: 4 in. (10 cm).

Geographic variations:

■ *E. a. atricapilla*, as above. Distribution: southeastern Nigeria, southern Cameroon, Gabon to northwestern Zaire.

■ *E. a. avakubi* Traylor. Lighter, with broader undulations on wings and back. Chin, throat and cheeks white. Distribution: extreme northeastern Angola through most of Zaire with the exception of the eastern parts.

■ *E. a. graueri* Neumann (or *E. a. kandti*

Reichenow). Much darker than the nominate subspecies in all the red colors; white cheeks, and a little white chin. Very thin horizontal lines on the wings. This race is sometimes accorded full specific status as Kandt's waxbill *Estrilda kandti*. Distribution: extreme eastern Zaire, and in Uganda and Ruanda.

■ *E. a. keniensis* Mearns. Red-colored parts are replaced with light brown. Generally lighter than the nominate form or the above subspecies. Distribution: eastern Uganda and western and central Kenya; in small groups. Rarely seen in the wild!

■ *E. a. marungenis* Prigogine. White face, chin and throat. The red-colored parts are very dark. Distribution: southeastern Zaire.

Habitat: Along and in forests, gardens and parks, and close to roads and water; also in grassland in the mountains, up to 11,500 ft. (3500 m), in pairs or small flocks. Nests in thick bushes, creepers and such; some 6 ft. (2 m) off the ground. The nest looks like an American football with a long, narrow tunnel, often with a cock's nest on top of the original nest .

Aviculture: This species looks very similar to the black-crowned waxbill (page 86). It is, however, rarely seen in aviculture. It is an excellent and lively bird for large cages or well- planted aviaries, where it is friendly toward most other small African finches. In the breeding season it sometimes is somewhat quarrelsome. Clutch: 4–5 white eggs. During fall and winter this species is best housed in an indoor facility with an average room temperature.

Food: During the breeding season a rich animal protein diet is absolutely necessary; also small millets, spray millet, and grass and weed seeds throughout the year.

RED-EARED WAXBILL *Estrilda troglodytes* Lichtenstein, 1813

DK: Gråastrild NL: Napoleonnetje, Koraalbekje FR: Astrild centré, Astrild gris
DE: Grauastrild, Grauer Astrild, Astrild IT: Becco di corallo

▸ *photos page 98, 139*

Description: Neck and back dark gray-brown; cheeks beige-brown; crimson eye-line; wings dark gray-brown with black-edged primaries. Tail black. Throat whitish with a vague pink sheen. Underparts grayish white with a pink sheen, and reddish on the belly. The red color becomes more intense during the breeding season. Eyes light brown, legs brown-gray. The red in females is less intense. Length: 3½ in. (9 cm).

Distribution and habitat: from Senegal to Sudan and northern Ethiopia. A subspecies, which has more red in the underparts, lives in the southwestern parts of Saudi Arabia and parts of Yemen. Known as the Arabian waxbill *E. t. rufibarba*, it is accorded full specific status by many authorities. The red-eared waxbill is found in semi-arid areas, swamps; and in Ethiopia up to 6600 ft. (2000 m) in the mountains. This species may be seen in pairs or in small wandering flocks of up to 100 birds. Parasitized by the pin-tailed whydah.

Aviculture: An excellent, lively cage and aviary bird which is especially at home in large facilities. They are friendly toward other finches. The female lays 3–5 eggs in a nest box or in a freestanding, bullet-shaped nest in a bush. It is constructed from grass, wool, moss, fibers, and small feathers. The eggs hatch after 11–12 days; incubation is alternately performed by male and female, generally for periods of three hours duration. After two weeks the young leave the nest, but accept food from their parents for another ten days or so. Young birds still have black beaks, and all red coloration is missing. After six weeks, the youngsters are fully colored. During the breeding period the color of the male becomes more intense red, and his eyebrows become darker. He then goes through his display, holding a blade of grass or something similar in his beak, dancing in circles around the female. As soon as the breeding season starts, it is advisable to separate the various pairs and give them each their own large aviary, which must be well-planted. The partners communicate with a harsh "pee-chee, pee-chee." During fall and winter the birds must be housed indoors at a minimum temperature of 77°F (25°C). Cross-breedings are possible with various finches; most commonly with the orange-cheeked waxbill, red-cheeked cordon bleu *Uraeginthus bengalus*, African golden-breasted waxbill *Amandava subflava*, and crimson-rumped waxbill. We, however, don't like to encourage hybridization.

Food: Various small millet varieties, spray millet, fresh and sprouted grass and weed seeds, canary grass seed, niger seed, greens such as spinach, dandelion, chickweed, etc., ant pupae, white worms, small maggots, daphnia, cut-up mealworms, small moths, fruit flies, green flies, commercial egg and rearing food, cuttlebone, and vitamins and minerals.

Other names: Black-rumped waxbill, Gray waxbill, Pink-cheeked waxbill.

BLACK-CROWNED WAXBILL *Estrilda (Krimhilda) nonnula* Hartlaub, 1883

DK: Nonne-astrild NL: Non astrild FR: Astrild nonnette, Astrild à cape noire

DE: Nonnenastrild, Weissbrustiges Schwarzkopfchen IT: Astrilde nonnette testa netra

▶ *photo page 99*

Description: Almost similar to the black-headed waxbill (see page 84), but with less or no red on the flanks, especially after the birds have been living in captivity for some time. The black beak has red edges. Young birds are primarily brown. Length: 4 in. (10 cm).

Geographic variations:

■ *E. n. nonnula*, as above. Distribution: from southeastern Cameroon and southern central Africa and the Sudan to northern Congo and Zaire, to western Kenya, Uganda and Ruanda, Burundi and northwestern Tanzania.

■ *E. n. elizae* Alexander. Somewhat grayer than nominate subspecies. Distribution: exclusively on the island of Fernando Po.

■ *E. n. eisentrauti* Wolters. Looks identical to *elizae* but is grayer than *nonnula*, especially on breast and belly. Distribution: southeastern Nigeria and Mount Cameroon.

Habitat: Usually found along the edges of forests, in savannas and farmland; also fairly high in the mountains. They search for seeds and insects in bushes and on the ground; during the breeding season in pairs, but outside this period in small, probably family, groups.

Aviculture: A charming, lively bird that is exceptionally well-suited for cage and aviary life. During the day they like to take sun baths. The bird's song consists of a series of high chirping calls. For more details, see preceding species.

Food: As for the red-eared waxbill (see page 85). They have a special fancy for poppy seeds, which should be supplied, however, only in very small quantities! Also offer the seeds of dandelions as well as various small insects and spiders. A large selection of insects is especially necessary during the breeding season and molting time. Grit, calcium, and vitamins are musts for this species.

Other names: Black-capped waxbill, White-breasted waxbill.

Genus *Amandava* (avadavats) Blyth, 1836

GOLDEN-BREASTED WAXBILL *Amandava (Sporaeginthus) subflava* Vieillot, 1819

DK: Guldbryster Astrild NL: Goudbuikje FR: Astrild à flanes rayés DE: Goldbrüstchen
IT: Beagalino, petto d'oro, Ventre arancio

▶ *photos page 99*

Description: Male. Olive-brown above; bright yellow below. Red rump; orange breast; yellow throat. Red streak through the eyes. Bright red upper tail coverts and blackish tail. Eyes brown, beak coral red, legs brown. The female is much duller in coloration. Length: 3½ in. (9–10 cm).

Geographic variations:

■ *A. s. subflava*, as above. Distribution: Senegal and southwestern Mauretania, and around Moti in Mali (close to the Niger River).

■ *A. s. miniatus* (Heuglin). Deep orange to orange-red on breast and belly. Distribution: from Guinea-Bissau through various western states to Yemen and central Ethiopia, and to western Kenya, Uganda, and northern and northeastern Zaire.

■ *A. s. clarkei* (Shelley). Underside yellow (although we have seen birds with orange-yellow undersides as well), and lightly orange-yellow under tail coverts. Clear orange spot above the breast. Distribution: southern Somalia and Kenya, south to the eastern part of South Africa, and in westerly direction to Tanzania, Ruanda, and Burundi to southeastern, western and southern Zaire, southern Gabon, and northern Angola.

■ *A. s. niethammeri* Wolters. Like the nominate species; all orange colors however, are missing, except in the under tail coverts; even the breast patch in the male. Distribution: Zambia, southern Zaire and southern Africa.

Habitat: These birds keep to the ground a lot, and the nest is constructed close to the ground in a grass clump or in a small, dense bush. They will also take over nests of other finches, which they renovate somewhat and adapt to their own needs. After the breeding season, they can be encountered in large flocks, especially in grass and along waterways.

Aviculture: This easy-to-keep bird has the qualities of rich color, a loving disposition, and good breeding success. The subspecies differ only slightly and get mixed up in the bird trade. This is a real pity. We wish dealers would distinguish between the small differences in color and shape, because this would be a plus for specialized bird fanciers. Remember that *A. s. clarkei* is less sturdy than the nominate form. But it can be brought to breed successfully, provided that the bird is well acclimatized. That means that newly arrived birds should be placed in quarantine for at least 30 days, and then gradually acclimatized to the local outside temperature. The bird must spend the winter in warm conditions, around 65°F (18°C).

In most cases, all gold-breasted waxbill subspecies will move into a closed nest box, but at times a pair will build a nest in bushes. At first view, the nest looks quite ramshackle, but despite

A. s. miniatus

its rough, unattractive appearance and construction, the nest is absolutely safe. A free nest is round and enclosed, with a small, narrow entry way. Eggs are laid in clutches of 3–4, and are incubated by the female as well as the male. The young hatch after 11 days, or perhaps 12–13 days in colder weather. While parents are feeding young, be sure they have a good quality rearing food and/or egg food available as well as a variety of small insects and sprouted seeds. They should also get fresh greens, especially sprouted niger seed.

When the young have become independent, remove them from the parents to stimulate the female into starting a new clutch. The golden-breasted waxbills are usually pleasant toward other finch species, but during the breeding season they may be somewhat quarrelsome with other birds. If the aviary is not too densely populated, and there is enough plant life to provide hiding places for those birds that want it, there should be no difficulty.

The species sings, without interruption, its not unattractive song. They are continually cheerful and friendly, and they treat each other pleasantly. They do especially well in large cages and vitrines.

Food: Furnish all types of small millet, spray millet, and panicum millet in particular. Grass and weed seeds are also important, as is animal protein, which is particularly essential during the breeding season (see the notes on this matter under red-eared waxbill, page 85).

Other names: African orange-breasted waxbill, Zebra waxbill.

GREEN AVADAVAT *Amandava (Stictospiza) formosa* Latham, 1790

▶ *photos page 100*

DK: Olivengrøn Astrild NL: Groene tijgervink FR: Bengali vert
DE: Olivastrild, Grüner Tigerfink IT: Bengalino verde

Description: Male. Upperparts olive-green with a golden sheen on the rump and upper tail coverts. Tail black. Underparts greenish yellow, with dark green and white bars on the side. The female is duller, with a grayish hue on the underparts and face. Eyes brown, beak red, legs pinkish.

Young birds still have a black beak and lack the design on the flanks. Length: 4–4¼ in. (10–11 cm).

Distribution and habitat: central India. The bird occurs in grassland, cultivated land and cane fields, where it also builds its nest. During the breeding season, it lives in pairs; at other times in small groups.

Aviculture: This bird is now frequently offered in the trade, in part because of its friendly disposition and attractive colors. We have consistently found it a quiet aviary bird that doesn't have complicated demands and that breeds well, provided it is properly cared for. It doesn't cause any problems for other birds during the breeding season. In a group aviary, it doesn't associate much with other birds but tends to stay on the floor, under bushes and in grass clumps. In the winter, it requires a lightly heated facility. In the wild, they build a large, round nest in cane fields or long grass tussocks, but in captivity they seldom get to building a free nest. They like half-open nest boxes placed in a well-planted aviary.

Don't disturb the birds during the breeding process. The female especially is quite nervous and will leave the nest at the slightest disturbance. She will, however, return once everything has become peaceful and safe again; this nervousness is one reason why the green avadavat is not very well suited as a cage bird.

Recently imported birds from European breeders must nevertheless be first housed in a warm, roomy indoor aviary, at 70°F (22°C); after approximately six weeks they can be placed in a well-planted outdoor aviary. During the fall and winter, however, they must be housed indoors again. The female usually lays 4–5 eggs. The species will certainly come to breed if their aviary offers the necessary privacy.

Food: Provide ample animal protein, especially during the breeding season. For additional advice, see the next section on the red avadavat.

RED AVADAVAT *Amandava amandava* (Linnaeus, 1758)

DK: Tigerfinke NL: Tijgervink, Amandave FR: Bengali rouge, Bengali moucheté
DE: Tigerfink, Tigerastrild IT: Bengalino moscato (dell'India), Bengalino comune

▶ *photos page 100*

Description: Male. Fiery red; back and wings are a light reddish brown. Rump red, tail black. Lower belly and under tail coverts dark brown or black. Lores and border of the eyes are black. There are clear white spots on the neck, along the flanks, and on the rump. The tips of the primaries are also white. After the fall molt, the feathers are an even brown because the new feathers have brown edges that wear off only in late winter. This may give the impression that a new molt is taking place, but this is not the case. The female has a "dirty" yellow underside. The rump is yellowish orange; the upperside is greenish gray. The wings are dark greenish brown. The white dots are noticeably fewer, and occur only along the flank, on the end of the primaries and wing coverts. Eyes and beak are red, the legs grayish brown. The young closely resemble the female, but they still have a black beak. Length: 4 in. (10 cm).

Geographic variations:

■ *A. a. amandava*, see above. Distribution: India, Pakistan, southern Nepal, Southeast Asia except Malaya, and parts of Indonesia, including Java and the Lesser Sundas; introduced in Sumatra, Singapore, Mauritius, Reunion, Fiji, Spain (!), and many other places.
■ *A. a. punicea* (Horsfield). Brighter red with little white dots; lores red or dark red, more pronounced in females. No white spots on the upper tail coverts; belly and under tail coverts black.

Distribution: island of Hainan, southern Vietnam, Cambodia, and eastern Thailand. Also on Bali and Java (Indonesia).
■ *A. a. flavidiventris* (Wallace). Lacks the black on the lower belly; this area is yellowish. Upperparts browner than in the nominate subspecies; upper tail coverts have white spots which are smaller than in the nominate form. Distribution: Burma to southwestern China (Yunnan), and the Indonesian islands of Timor, Flores, Sumba, and Lombok. For more details, see below.

Habitat: This bird occurs in grass and reeds, in fields and meadows, and even in parks and gardens. It builds nests in clumps of grass, in dense, low bushes, and even on the ground, well hidden among vegetation.

Aviculture: The species is quite popular, in part because of its colorful appearance. Beginning fanciers can expect good results with these birds, including active breeding. General care, especially during breeding, requires one's full attention, of course. Beginners probably do well because the species has been bred in captivity for many years. Especially in a densely planted aviary, birds raise two, or even three, sets of young. We have had the best success, while living in the Netherlands, in a small aviary, where we housed only one pair of red avadavats. As soon as the nest was completed and there were young in the nest, we allowed the parents to fly free in our garden. This practice, by the way, is illegal in the United States as well as in the UK. In the garden they went hunting for small insects and the like among the leaves and in the ivy. Still, we made sure that they could find all types of protein food, such as ant pupae and white worms, within the aviary. We also provided mosquito larvae, spiders, water fleas (daphnia), all types of seeds, especially panicum millet, greens, sprouted seeds, grass and weed seeds, and fruit. Just prior to the time that the young were ready to leave the nest (hence, keep records!!), we closed the aviary again to avoid the risk that parents and young would escape. Both sexes have an attractive song. The female doesn't trill as loudly as the male. The mating dance is also interesting. The male goes about with a stretched out head and a drooping, spread tail.

The red avadavat is more likely to build a free nest than the green avadavat; it does so in a bush or in ivy. It also uses half-open nest boxes. The free nest is keg-shaped or bag-shaped, with one or two entry ways of about 4 in. (10 cm). Generally, the female lays 4–6 eggs. If you find clutches of more than 6 eggs, you may be dealing with two females. Several eggs from a large clutch belonging to a true pair may be fertile.

Provide a quiet environment for breeding birds. They are nervous breeders that can quickly decide to leave the nest to start again elsewhere. Don't house them in an overly large collection.

The male defends the nest aggressively, and when he considers the nest to be endangered, often by other birds in the near vicinity, the pair will get so upset that nothing much will come from their breeding.

When you buy red avadavats, be especially sure that you are getting a true pair. Outside of the breeding season, the male is not easy to distinguish from the female, but in breeding color, the male attains a beautiful red color with white little dots. Outside of the breeding season, you can find all kinds of gradations between the normal, "off-color" and the "fancy" in-season red color, hence few males resemble each other. Many have large amounts of yellow, and others have red or brown. A number of dealers have taken advantage of this situation and have artificially colored their birds red, green, purple, and other colors. They give these counterfeit birds all sorts of fancy sounding names and charge high prices. Federal laws ban these practices but nevertheless we see these colored birds quite often in real bird states like Florida and California. So be aware!

The subspecies with the yellow belly, *A. a. flavidiventris*, is occasionally available in the bird trade. Once, in 1986, we had the opportunity to work with a pair of these birds, and we found that the behavior and breeding habits were almost identical to those of the nominate race. The subspecies can justifiably be called the yellow-bellied tiger finch. Both subspecies prefer to breed in an aviary planted with clumps of grass, dense bushes, and ivy, where they have the opportunity to build a free nest. In good weather, there is no reason to avoid keeping either subspecies in an outside aviary, but in the winter months they should be kept in a lightly heated facility, at about 65°F (18°C). They are peaceable toward members of their genus and other small finches as well. With good care and management, they can get quite old; there are known cases of birds achieving 8 to even 17 years of age.

Food: We made reference to good feeding practices earlier in this section. Further, be sure to supply sufficient amounts of vitamins and minerals, especially cuttlefish bone, to avoid egg binding, to which the female is rather susceptible. For further suggestions, see Golden-breasted waxbill, page 87.

Other names: Avadavat, Red munia, Tiger finch, Strawberry finch.

Genus *Uraeginthus* (blue waxbills and grenadiers) Cabanis, 1851

ANGOLAN CORDON BLEU *Uraeginthus angolensis* Linnaeus 1758

DK: Angola-Sommerfuglefinke NL: Angola blauwfazantje FR: Cordon bleu dángola
DE: Angola-Schmetterlingsfink, Blauastrild IT: Astrilde blu dellángola

▸ *photo page 100*

Description: Almost identical to the red-cheeked cordon bleu *U. bengalus*; this species, however, lacks the crimson-red ear patches. Tail and rump blue; upper parts mouse brown; breast and flanks sky blue. Lower breast and abdomen whitish brown. Eyes brown; beak reddish gray, with a black tip; legs light brown. The females are somewhat paler in coloration and have creamy underparts, but are difficult to distinguish from the females of other cordon bleu species, although their beaks are usually a much brighter pink. Length: 4½ (11.5–12 cm).

Geographic variations:

■ *U. a. angolensis*, as above. Distribution: from Cabinda and Congo River through western and southern Angola into northern Namibia.

■ *U. a. cyanopleurus* Wolters. Upperparts more brown than in the nominate form, and duller and with more gray than *natalensis* and *niassensis*. Distribution: southern Angola and northeastern Namibia through southwestern Zambia, northern and eastern Botswana southward to Orange Free State (South Africa) and the northern part of Lesotho.

■ *U. a. natalensis* Zedlitz. Lighter brown, even the belly and under tail coverts. Distribution: Natal and eastern Transvaal (South Africa) and southeastern Zimbabwe.

■ *U. a. niassensis* Reichenow. Somewhat smaller but otherwise almost identical to the previous subspecies. Distribution: eastern and southeastern Tanzania, Malawi, as well as the northern and eastern parts of Zambia through northeastern Zimbabwe and Mozambique.

Habitat: This species occurs in scrub country and cultivated areas, including gardens and parks, sometimes in large flocks. Their oven-shaped nests are loosely built of strong grasses with the leaves still attached, and other dry vegetation; the inside nest layer consists of fine grasses and inflores-

cences, and often small feathers as well, usually from domestic poultry or guinea fowl, but also from crested francolins *Francolinus sephaena*, gray loeries *Corythaixoides concolor*, and cattle egrets *Ardeola ibis*. Both parents continue to bring feathers to the nest during incubation and even when the young are newly hatched. There is usually a porch-like side entrance made of grass. The nest is often situated close to a wasp nest. The species has been introduced into Zanzibar and São Thomé.

Aviculture: Excellent for large aviaries and cages, where they brood in half-open nest boxes. The female lays 3–4 white eggs. For further details see Red-cheeked cordon bleu. This species is usually very friendly toward other small African finches, although they are sometimes antagonistic toward the red-cheeked cordon bleu. Although sudden temperature changes can chill these birds, they resist lower temperatures far better than *U. bengalus*. During fall and winter, the species belongs indoors, however, with a minimum temperature of 65°F (18°C).

Food: Similar to that of the red-cheeked cordon bleu (page 92).

Other names: Blue-breasted waxbill, Blue-breasted cordon bleu.

BLUE-CAPPED CORDON BLEU *Uraeginthus cyanocephalus* Richmond, 1897

DK: Blåhovedet Sommerfuglefinke NL: Blauwkop blauwfazantje FR: Astrild à tête bleu
DE: Blaukopf-Schmetterlingsfink IT: Astrilde testa blu, Astrilde dal capo blu

▸ *photos page 101*

Description: Male. Very similar to the Angolan cordon bleu, but with a splendid blue-colored head, flanks and breast, and dark sand-brown upperparts. Tail blue. Eyes reddish brown, beak pink or crimson-red with a black tip, legs light brown. Females lack the blue head, although quite often some blue on the forehead may be seen. Young birds miss all the blue colors and still have a black beak. Length: 4½–5 in. (11.5–13 cm).

Geographic variations:

■ *U. c. cyanocephalus*, as above. Distribution: the northeastern half of Tanzania, through Kenya (except the northern and northwestern parts) and southeastern Uganda.

■ *U. c. muelleri* Zedlitz. Somewhat smaller than the nominate form. Duller blue, and lighter sand-brown-yellow on both the upper- and undersides. Distribution: northern Kenya, and bordering Somalia and Ethiopia.

Habitat: Found in arid grass and thornbush country. The birds search primarily for grass and weed seeds, small insects and spiders. Their nests are mostly constructed in thorny bushes, often close to wasp nests.

Aviculture: This species is somewhat shyer than the Angolan cordon bleu. If acclimatized properly, this species breeds regularly in a large, well-planted aviary. For more details, see Angolan cordon bleu.

Food: See Red-cheeked cordon bleu (page 92).

Other names: Blue-headed cordon bleu, Blue-headed waxbill.

RED-CHEEKED CORDON BLEU *Uraeginthus bengalus* Linnaeus, 1766

DK: Sommerfuglefinke NL: Blauwfazantje FR: Cordon bleu
DE: Schmetterlingsfink, Schmetterlingsastrild IT: Cordon blu

▸ *photos page 100, 101*

Description: Male. Underside brownish gray; cheeks, throat, flanks, breast, and upper tail coverts sky blue; tail duller blue. Crimson ear patches. Abdomen whitish brown. Eyes brown, beak pink-reddish with an ashy-black tip, legs light horn colored. The female is somewhat paler and lacks the red ear patches. The red ear patches in young males appear when the birds are approximately 10 weeks old. Length: 4½–5 in. (11.5–13 cm).

Geographic variations:

■ *U. b. bengalus*, as above. Distribution: from western Senegal to southern Sudan and northern Zaire.
■ *U. b. perpallidus* Neumann. Less red-sandbrown on belly; upperparts with yellow-brownish hue. Distribution: southeastern part of the Niger Republic, and from Nigeria to northern Cameroon, through Chad and the Sudan to northern Ethiopia.

■ *U. b. schoanus* Neumann. Lighter blue in both males and females. Distribution: Uganda, Sudan, and Zaire.

■ *U. b. brunneigularis* Mearns. Medium brown upperparts, lighter on the underside and under tail coverts. The hen has a brown face, chin and throat, sometimes with a few blue feathers. Distribution: highlands of southwestern Kenya.

■ *U. b. littoralis* van Someren. Somewhat smaller

than the nominate subspecies. Males are duller brown and blue; the ear patch is smaller. Females too are duller in coloration, and the ear patch often has little blue feathers. Distribution: southern Somalia through the coastal areas of Kenya and northern Tanzania.

■ *U. b. ugogoensis* Reichenow. The brown colors of the nominate form are in this subspecies yellowish brown. The females have some small yellow stripes in the throat area. Distribution: Ruanda and Burundi to the southwestern parts of Kenya, and in a southerly direction to central and southwestern Tanzania.

■ *U. b. katangae* Vincent. The males have very dark-red ear patches, but are otherwise identical to the previous subspecies. The females are blue only on face, chin and throat; breast and flanks are yellowish brown. Distribution: southwestern Zaire through northwestern and northeastern Zambia.

Habitat: These birds prefer open country, savanna, woodland, semi-arid thornscrub and cultivated areas. In the wild, nests are often found in the immediate vicinity of wasp nests, which serve as a natural protection against nest predators.

Aviculture: Acclimatization must be realized with the greastest of care, even when the birds are imported from European breeders. The first few weeks after arrival, the birds must be housed in a box cage or indoor aviary at a minimum temperature of 75°F (23°C). This species can't be kept in housing facilities where the temperature is below 65°F (18°C). Provide new arrivals with small millets, oranges, and bananas. We sprinkle universal or finch-rearing food over the fruits. This way the birds get accustomed to these new foods. Acclimatized birds are far from fragile and may be kept in outdoor aviaries during the late spring and summer months, together with other small finches. This species prefers to breed in garden aviaries with thick vegetation and a variety of box nests and half-open nest boxes. We have known birds that lived for more than 10 years in captivity! Although the birds occupy various types of nest boxes, provided they are placed high in the aviary, they sometimes build a free nest in a thick bush. Offer long stems of dry grass, moss, wool, coconut

Uraeginthus bengalus

fibers, small feathers, and the like. The female lays 4–6 eggs; larger clutches are usually from two females. After 16–19 days the young hatch; after 30–40 days, the young males can be distinguished from the females, as the red ear patches become visible.

The song of this species is pleasant and clear. During courtship the male dances in front of the hen with a long blade of grass in his beak. Throughout the day, both partners brood alternately, but toward the evening and night, usually only the female is on duty. On warm days, the parents often cover the eggs with nesting material and leave the clutch to its fate for many hours. Hybrids are possible with Bengalese, St. Helena waxbills, Angolan cordon bleus, and blue-headed waxbills, but we seriously want to discourage you from attempting this type of breeding. Toward the end of summer, cordon bleus are best housed in indoor aviaries or large cages.

Food: All kinds of small millets, spray millets, grass and weed seeds, germinated seeds, greens and, during the breeding season, various small insects, spiders, finch rearing and egg food, soaked brown (wheat) bread, cuttlebone, etc. Without animal protein, however, breeding successes will be rare to nil, and the young will be thrown out of the nest at an early stage.

PURPLE GRENADIER *Uraeginthus (Granatina) ianthinogaster* (Reichenow, 1879)

DK: Violbuget Granatastrild NL: Purpergranaatastrild FR: Grenadin à poitrine bleue

DE: Veilchenastrild, Purpurgranatastrild IT: Granatino violaceo

▸ *photos page 102*

Description:

Head, neck and upperparts chestnut. Breast blue with red and reddish brown spots. Eye-ring red with a sky-blue patch above and below the eye. Wings dark brown, tail black, rump blue. Chin and throat reddish brown; underside violet. Eyes dark brown, beak red, legs anthracite-colored. The female doesn't have any blue coloration, except for the rump; forehead and around the eyes little purple-white feathers. The breast often has some brown-yellowish and whitish specks. Young birds still have a black beak, and lack all the blue. Length: 5–5½ in. (13–14 cm).

Geographic variations:

■ *U. i. ianthinogaster*, as above. Distribution: central and eastern Tanzania through southeastern and eastern Kenya.

■ *U. i. roosevelti* (Mearns). Upperparts, chin, throat, breast and belly of male dark blue, interspersed with red-brownish spots. The female is darker red-brown than the nominate subspecies, with a blue hue on breast and flanks. More blue around the eyes. Distribution: southeastern Uganda, southwestern Kenya to northern Tanzania.

■ *U. i. somereni* (Delacour). Upperparts gray-blue. There is less blue on breast and belly. Females are lighter, especially on the underparts, sometimes with white. Distribution: northwestern Kenya and northeastern Uganda to southeastern Sudan and southwestern Ethiopia.

■ *U. i. hawkeri* (Phillips). Neck and head as well as the back of males are the same shade of reddish brown. The blue area around the eyes is more extended than in the nominate subspecies. The females are lighter brown and have tiny white feathers around the eyes. Distribution: Somalia,

except the northwest; further southeastern Ethiopia and northeastern Kenya.

Habitat: They live in arid open grassland and thornbush country, where they search primarily in pairs or small flocks for termites and grass and weed seeds. They are almost completely insectivorous during the breeding season. This species is parasitized by the Fischer's whydah *Vidua (Tetraenura) fischeri*.

Aviculture: First bred by Mr. E. J. Boosey in England in 1957; breeding successes, however, remain rare. Their free spherical grass nest is often fragile, with a side entrance. These rather intelligent birds prefer half-open or enclosed nest boxes; both sexes build. Soft materials like grass, wool, and feathers are very important. The female lays 3–5 eggs. The incubation period is 13–14 days. Both sexes incubate, the female primarily during the night. The young leave the nest when 20–22 days old; after another two weeks they are independent. For more details, see Violet-eared waxbill. Experience has taught us that a pair can be quite aggressive in a mixed collection. A large aviary, with thick planting, is therefore advisable. Breeding pairs, however, can best be housed in a separate facility where they settle quickly and become surprisingly trustful toward the keeper; they don't even mind an occasional peek in their nest. Their song sounds like that of the violet-eared waxbill but is chirpier and more canary-like. They need a daily water bath and love to play in wet grass.

Food: Normal seed mixture for small finches. During the breeding season various insects such as ant pupae, white worms, maggots, and small, cut-up mealworms, which they favor, are absolutely essential, as are brown bread soaked in water, finch rearing and egg food, sprouted seeds, and millet spray.

Other names: Purple-bellied waxbill, Purple waxbill.

VIOLET-EARED WAXBILL *Uraeginthus (Granatina) granatina* Linnaeus, 1766

DK: Granatastrild, Violoret Granatastrild NL: Granaatastrild FR: Grenadim, Astrild grenadin
DE: Granatastrild IT: Astrilde granata, Granatino

▸ *photos page 102*

Description: Male primarily chestnut, with deep violet ear patches and forehead; eye-ring red. Rump and upper tail and under tail coverts dark blue; wings brownish gray. Chin, throat, vent, and tail black. Eyes reddish brown, beak red, legs brown. The female is duller, with grayish upperparts and yellowish brown underparts. The throat is whitish, the ear patches light violet. There is no blue on the under tail coverts. Young birds resemble the female, but they still have black beaks; the rump, however, is already blue. Males and females have an exceptionally pleasant and clear song. Their communication calls resemble those of the red-cheeked cordon bleu. Length: 5–5½ in (14 cm).

Geographic variations:
■ *U. g. granatina*, as above. Distribution: from central Angola eastward to Zambia and eastern Zimbabwe, and southward to Namibia, Botswana and central South Africa.
■ *U. g. retura* Clancey. Somewhat lighter upperparts; the belly is gray, the throat-patch smaller. The female is lighter than the nominate subspecies; the crown yellowish. Distribution: found in a rather small area covering southern Mozambique.

Habitat: found in thornscrub country and arid areas; in pairs or small flocks, quite often together with *U. angolensis*. These birds build their round nests close to the ground, usually within 3 ft. (1 m), in thorny bushes. The species is parasitized by the Queen whydah *Vidua regia*.

Aviculture: This bird is well-known in aviculture; young birds, however, are difficult to distinguish from *U. angolensis*. The species is very sensitive to disturbances, especially during the breeding season. The best breeding results may be obtained in well-planted, large garden aviaries (don't forget to plant philodendron!). The parents must have access to various insects and finch rearing food. After arrival from Europe the birds must be housed for at least four weeks in a roomy indoor aviary; keep the temperature between 73 and 77°F (23–25°C). After the acclimatization period, the birds may be placed in garden aviaries, provided the outside temperature is no less than 68°F (20°C). In order to maintain a high humidity level, which is recommended in the breeding season, spray your plants daily. Breeding in humidity-controlled birdrooms is strongly recommended.

Although generally friendly toward members of the same genus, they are often hostile and aggressive. A well-planted aviary is the answer if various finch species are kept in the same facility.

We recommend, as indicated already, breeding in indoor aviaries, as during the first days the young don't have much down; temperatures below 77°F (25°C) are often fatal; therefore supply enough nesting material, including wool, grass, coconut fibers, etc., as well as some small feathers, as the male likes to play with them while sitting on the nest. The female lays 4–7 eggs; incubation lasts 13–14 days. After approximately 17–19 days the young leave the nest, but will receive the attention of both parents for another two to three weeks. After 6–8 weeks the young males are fully colored.

Food: Grass and weed seeds, Senegal millet, and spray millet. During the breeding season, small insects, brown bread soaked in water, finch rearing food and egg food are essential. Provide cuttlefish bone throughout the year. See also Red-cheeked cordon bleu (page 92).

Other names:
Violet-eared cordon bleu, Common grenadier, Grenadier waxbill.

U. g. granatina

Genus *Lagonosticta* (firefinches) Cabanis, 1851

AFRICAN FIREFINCH *Lagonosticta rubricata* Lichtenstein, 1823

DK: Mørkerød Amarant NL: Donkerrode vuurvink FR: Amarantha foncee, Sénégali á bec bleu
DE: Dünkelroter Amarant IT: Amaranto del Mozambico, Amaranto becco blu

▶ *photos page 103*

Description: Male. Dark red. Crown, back, and wings brownish red to grayish brown. Along the bend of the wing some little white spots. Yellowish periophthalmic ring. Eyes dark brown; beak black with a reddish sheen, especially the lower mandible; legs black-brown. The female is duller and more light red to yellow in coloration, especially on throat, breast and belly. Young birds are grayish with red upper tail coverts. Both sexes have a nice, clear song. During courtship, the cock spreads his tail like a Chinese fan, while singing almost constantly. Length: 4–4¼ in. (10–11 cm).

Geographic variations:

■ *L. r. rubricata*, as above. Distribution: South Africa (Kaap Province) to southern Mozambique.
■ *L. r. haematocephala* Neumann. Dark red, especially the forehead, crown, neck, and face. Underparts are lighter with many little white dots on breast and flanks. Distribution: Mozambique, except the southern parts, eastern Zimbabwe to central Tanzania and southeastern Zaire, and the border of Angola; from there to northern and eastern Zambia and Malawi.
■ *L. r. ugandae* Salvadori. Dark red, but not as intensive as the previous subspecies; the back is dark olive green. Distribution: northeastern Zaire and the southeastern parts of the Central African Republic, through southern Kenya and Tanzania, with the exception of the south.
■ *L. r. congica* Sharpe. Dark red but with more gray in the back; otherwise almost identical to *ugandae*. The female doesn't have white-colored breast and flank spots. Distribution: western Tanzania, from Burundi and southern Ruanda to central and southwestern Zaire, and further to the northeastern and northern parts of Angola and the western areas of Congo and southern Gabon.
■ *L. r. sannagae* Reichenow. This bird has a very clean, light reddish head, neck and face; the back is warm brown. Distribution: northwestern Zaire, the western half of the Central African Republic, and the southern half of Cameroon.
■ *L. r. polionata* Shelley. Olive brown back with a grayish hue. Red crown with gray; head, face, breast, and flanks carmine. On the breast little white dots, although not always present. In females, all or almost all the red coloration is absent; the lores, however, are usually red. Overall impression is a dull, rather gray bird similar to the female *congica*. Distribution: western Cameroon through Nigeria to the coast of Sierra Leone; also found in Ghana and Togo.
■ *L. r. neglecta* Reichenow. Dark olive brown back and wing coverts, with a gray-reddish head and neck, and light reddish underside. Very little difference from *L. r. polionata*, and we consider these two forms synonymous. Distribution: Guinea and Guinea-Bissau (West Africa).
■ *L. r. virata* Bates. Somewhat lighter than *polionata*. The inside of the second primary flight feather is similar in width to the other primaries, which is not the case in all the other *rubricata* subspecies. In addition, the song of *virata*, as well as certain behavioral characteristics, differ from the other firefinch species. For these reasons, many authorities recognize this form as a full species, the Kulikoro firefinch *Lagonosticta virata*. Distribution: southwestern Mali.

Habitat: Their habitat is savanna, grassland, along forest edges, in neglected agricultural areas, and similar places. The species lives close to the

Lavender waxbill
Estrilda caerulescens
Photo: Pieter van den Hooven   p. 73

Black-tailed lavender waxbill or gray waxbill
Estrilda perreini
Photo: Pieter van den Hooven   p. 74

Black-cheeked waxbill
Estrilda erythronotos
Photo: Pieter van den Hooven   p. 77

Black-cheeked waxbill
Estrilda erythronotos delamerei
Photo: Pieter van den Hooven   p. 77

Red-rumped waxbill
Estrilda charmosyna
Photo: Pieter van den Hooven   p. 79

Orange-cheeked waxbill
Estrilda melpoda
Photo: Pieter van den Hooven   p. 81

Common waxbill
Estrilda astrild
Photo: Pieter van den Hooven   p. 82

Common waxbill mutation. Note the pale beak and reduction of red carotenoids
Estrilda astrild
Photo: Pieter van den Hooven   p. 82

Male red-eared waxbill and female yellow mutation red-eared waxbill
Estrilda troglodytes
Photo: Pieter van den Hooven   p. 85

Red-eared waxbill
Estrilda troglodytes
Photo: Pieter van den Hooven   p. 85

Dufresne's waxbill
Estrilda melanotis melanotis
Photo: Pieter van den Hooven   p. 76

Yellow-bellied waxbill
Estrilda melanotis quartinia
Photo: Pieter van den Hooven   p. 76

Crimson-rumped waxbill
Estrilda rhodopyga
Photo: Pieter van den Hooven   p. 83

Black-headed waxbill
Estrilda atricapilla
Photo: Pieter van den Hooven   p. 84

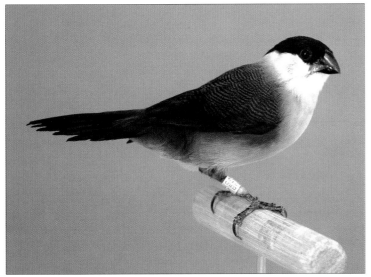

Black-crowned waxbill
Estrilda nonnula
Photo: Pieter van den Hooven   p. 86

Male and female South African gold-breasted waxbills
Amandava subflava clarkei
Photo: Pieter van den Hooven   p. 87

Male Gold-breasted waxbill
Amandava subflava subflava
Photo: Pieter van den Hooven   p. 87

Female gold-breasted waxbill
Amandava subflava subflava
Photo: Pieter van den Hooven   p. 87

Male green avadavat
Amandava (Stictospiza) formosa
Photo: Pieter van den Hooven   *p. 88*

Female green avadavat
Amandava (Stictospiza) formosa
Photo: Pieter van den Hooven   *p. 88*

Male red avadavat (Strawberry finch)
Amandava amandava
Photo: Pieter van den Hooven   *p. 89*

Female red avadavat
Amandava amandava
Photo: Pieter van den Hooven   *p. 89*

Angolan cordon-bleu
Uraeginthus angolensis
Photo: Pieter van den Hooven   *p. 91*

Male red-cheeked cordon bleu with orange cheek patches.
Uraeginthus bengalus
Photo: Pieter van den Hooven   *p. 92*

100

Male red-cheeked cordon bleu
Uraeginthus bengalus
Photo: Pieter van den Hooven   p. 92

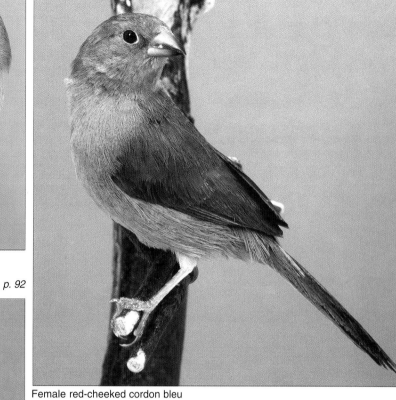

Female red-cheeked cordon bleu
Uraeginthus bengalus brunneigularis
Photo: Pieter van den Hooven   p. 92

Female red-cheeked cordon bleu
Uraeginthus bengalus
Photo: Pieter van den Hooven   p. 92

Male blue-capped cordon bleu
Uraeginthus cyanocephalus
Photo: J.G. Blasman   p. 92

Blue-capped cordon bleu (Blue-headed waxbill), male and female
Uraeginthus cyanocephalus
Photo: Pieter van den Hooven   p. 92

101

Male purple grenadier
Uraeginthus ianthinogaster
Photo: Pieter van den Hooven   p. 94

Female purple grenadier
Uraeginthus ianthinogaster
Photo: Pieter van den Hooven   p. 94

Female violet-eared waxbill
Uraeginthus granatina
Photo: Pieter van den Hooven   p. 95

Male violet-eared waxbill
Uraeginthus granatina
Photo: J.G. Blasman   p. 95

Male violet-eared waxbill
Uraeginthus granatina
Photo: Pieter van den Hooven   p. 95

Male African firefinch
Lagonosticta rubricata
Photo: Pieter van den Hooven   *p. 96*

Female African firefinch
Lagonosticta rubricata
Photo: Pieter van den Hooven   *p. 96*

Kulikoro firefinch
Lagonosticta rubricata virata
Photo: Pieter van den Hooven   *p. 96*

Speckled-breasted firefinch
Lagonosticta rufopicta
Photo: Pieter van den Hooven   *p. 148*

Female red-billed firefinch
Lagonosticta senegala
Photo: Pieter van den Hooven   *p. 149*

Male red-billed firefinch
Lagonosticta senegala
Photo: Pieter van den Hooven   *p. 149*

103

Male vinaceous firefinch
Lagonosticta vinacea vinacea
Photo: Pieter van den Hooven   p. 147

Female vinaceous firefinch
Lagonosticta vinacea vinacea
Photo: Pieter van den Hooven   p. 147

Nestling vinaceous firefinches
Lagonosticta vinacea nigricollis
Photo: Pieter van den Hooven   p. 147

Fledgling vinaceous firefinches
Lagonosticta vinacea nigricollis
Photo: Pieter van den Hooven   p. 147

Abyssinian firefinch
Lagonosticta rhodopareia
Photo: Pieter van den Hooven   p. 148

Male vinaceous firefinch
Lagonosticta vinacea nigricollis
Photo: Pieter van den Hooven   p. 147

Female and male (front) black-bellied firefinches
Lagonosticta rara
Photo: Pieter van den Hooven   p. 151

Male red-faced crimson-wing
Cryptospiza reichenovii
Photo: Pieter van den Hooven   p. 152

Female red-faced crimson-wing
Cryptospiza reichenovii
Photo: Pieter van den Hooven   p. 152

Female and male Ethiopian crimsonwings
Cryptospiza salvadorii
Photo: Pieter van den Hooven   p. 153

Juvenile red-faced crimson-wing
Cryptospiza reichenovii
Photo: Pieter van den Hooven   p. 152

Gray-headed olivebacks
Nesocharis capistrata
Photo: Pieter van den Hooven   p. 155

Gray-headed oliveback
Nesocharis capistrata
Photo: Pieter van den Hooven   p. 155

Chestnut-breasted negro-finch
Nigrita bicolor
Photo: Pieter van den Hooven   p. 159

Pair of crimson-breasted bluebills
Spermophaga haematina
Photo: Pieter van den Hooven   p. 157

Male crimson-breasted bluebill
Spermophaga haematina
Photo: Pieter van den Hooven   p. 157

106

Female crimson-breasted bluebill
Spermophaga haematina
Photo: Pieter van den Hooven   *p. 157*

Juvenile crimson seedcracker
Pyrenestes sanguineus
Photo: Pieter van den Hooven   *p. 162*

Male crimson seedcracker
Pyrenestes sanguineus
Photo: Pieter van den Hooven   *p. 162*

Female crimson seedcracker
Pyrenestes sanguineus
Photo: Pieter van den Hooven   *p. 162*

Female West African quailfinch
Ortygospiza atricollis atricollis
Photo: Pieter van den Hooven   *p. 164*

Male West African quailfinch
Ortygospiza atricollis atricollis
Photo: Pieter van den Hooven   *p. 164*

Female quailfinch subspecies
Ortygospiza atricollis muelleri
Photo: Pieter van den Hooven
p. 164

Male quailfinch subspecies
Ortygospiza atricollis muelleri
Photo: Pieter van den Hooven
p. 164

Juvenile Ethiopian quailfinches
Ortygospiza atricollis fuscocrissa
Photo: Pieter van den Hooven
p. 164

Yearling pair of quailfinches
Ortygospiza atricollis muelleri
Photo: Pieter van den Hooven
p. 164

Male Ethiopian quailfinch
Ortygospiza atricollis fuscocrissa
Photo: Pieter van den Hooven
p. 164

Peters's twinspot mutation
not yet described
Photo: Pieter van den Hooven
p. 169

108

Male brown twinspot
Clytospiza monteiri
Photo: Pieter van den Hooven
p. 166

Female brown twinspot
Clytospiza monteiri
Photo: Pieter van den Hooven
p. 166

Male pink-throated twinspot
Hypargos margaritatus
Photo: Pieter van den Hooven
p. 168

Female and male pink-throated twinspots
Hypargos margaritatus
Photo: Pieter van den Hooven
p. 168

Female Peters's twinspot
Hypargos niveoguttatus
Photo: Pieter van den Hooven
p. 169

Male Peters's twinspot
Hypargos niveoguttatus
Photo: Pieter van den Hooven
p. 169

Male green-backed twinspot
Mandingoa nitidula nitidula
Photo: Pieter van den Hooven
p. 170

Female green-backed twinspot
Mandingoa nitidula nitidula
Photo: Pieter van den Hooven
p. 170

Male Schlegel's twinspot
Mandingoa nitidula schlegeli
Photo: Pieter van den Hooven
p. 171

Female Schlegel's twinspot
Mandingoa nitidula schlegeli
Photo: Pieter van den Hooven
p. 171

Female Chubb's twinspot
Mandingoa nitidula chubbi
Photo: Pieter van den Hooven
p. 170

Male Chubb's twinspot
Mandingoa nitidula chubbi
Photo: Pieter van den Hooven
p. 170

Dybowski's twinspot
Euschistospiza dybowskii
Photo: Pieter van den Hooven p. 167

Aurora finch (Red-winged pytilia)
Pytilia phoenicoptera
Photo: Pieter van den Hooven p. 171

Female melba finch
Pytilia melba melba
Photo: Pieter van den Hooven p. 172

Male melba finch
Pytilia melba melba
Photo: Pieter van den Hooven p. 172

Male melba finch
Pytilia melba belli
Photo: Pieter van den Hooven p. 173

Orange-headed mutation orange-winged pytilia
Pytilia afra
Photo: Pieter van den Hooven p. 175

Female orange-winged pytilias, normal and mutation
Pytilia afra
Photo: Pieter van den Hooven
p. 175

Male orange-winged pytilia
Pytilia afra
Photo: Pieter van den Hooven
p. 175

Female yellow-winged pytilia
Pytilia hypogrammica
Photo: Pieter van den Hooven
p. 174

Male yellow-winged pytilia
Pytilia hypogrammica
Photo: Pieter van den Hooven
p. 174

Male yellow-winged pytilia
Possibly a hybrid
Photo: Pieter van den Hooven
p. 174

Normal and isabel (autosomal recessive) cut-throat finches
Amadina fasciata
Photo: Pieter van den Hooven
p. 178

Male cut-throat finch
Amadina fasciata fasciata
Photo: Pieter van den Hooven   p. 178

Female cut-throat finch
Amadina fasciata fasciata
Photo: Pieter van den Hooven   p. 178

Male Ino cut-throat finch (heredity still not clear)
Amadina fasciata
Photo: Pieter van den Hooven   p. 178

Orange-banded cut-throat finch (autosomal recessive)
Amadina fasciata
Photo: Pieter van den Hooven   p. 178

Female cut-throat finch
Amadina fasciata alexanderi
Photo: Pieter van den Hooven   p. 178

Male cut-throat finch
Amadina fasciata alexanderi
Photo: Pieter van den Hooven   p. 178

113

Male red-headed finch
Amadina erythrocephala
Photo: Pieter van den Hooven   p. 180

Female red-headed finch
Amadina erythrocephala
Photo: Pieter van den Hooven   p. 180

Black munia
Munia (Lonchura) stygia
Photo: Pieter van den Hooven   p. 182

Juvenile black munias
Munia (Lonchura) stygia
Photo: Pieter van den Hooven   p. 182

Variation of the pallid munia
Lonchura pallida pallida
Photo: Pieter van den Hooven   p. 182

Pallid munia
Lonchura pallida pallida
Photo: Pieter van den Hooven   p. 182

Variation of black munia
Lonchura stygia
Photo: Pieter van den Hooven   p. 182

114

White-crowned mannikin
Light form (mostly males)
Photo: Pieter van den Hooven   p. 183

White-crowned mannikin
Dark form (mostly females)
Photo: Pieter van den Hooven   p. 183

Male white-crowned mannikin
Munia (Lonchura) nevermanni
Photo: Pieter van den Hooven   p. 183

Juvenile white-crowned mannikin
Munia (Lonchura) nevermanni
Photo: Pieter van den Hooven   p. 183

Female white-crowned mannikin at nest
Munia (Lonchura) nevermanni
Photo: Pieter van den Hooven   p. 183

Five-colored mannikin
Munia (Lonchura) quinticolor
Photo: Pieter van den Hooven   p. 184

Juvenile Grand Valley munias
Munia (Lonchura) teerinki teerinki
Photo: Pieter van den Hooven   p. 185

115

Female Grand Valley munia
Munia (Lonchura) teerinki teerinki
Photo: Pieter van den Hooven   *p. 185*

Female Grand Valley munia
Munia (Lonchura) teerinki teerinki
Photo: Pieter van den Hooven   *p. 185*

Juvenile Grand Valley mannikin
Munia (Lonchura) teerinki teerinki
Photo: Pieter van den Hooven   *p. 185*

Chestnut-breasted mannikin
Munia (Lonchura) castaneothorax castaneothorax
Photo: Pieter van den Hooven   *p. 185*

Chestnut-breasted munia
Munia (Lonchura) castaneothorax assimilis
Photo: Pieter van den Hooven   *p. 185*

Little chestnut-breasted munia
Munia (Lonchura) castaneothorax sharpii
Photo: Pieter van den Hooven   *p. 185*

Chestnut-breasted munia mutation,
Red-brown, perhaps fawn, autosomal recessive mutation
Photo: Pieter van den Hooven   *p. 185*

Nestling chestnut-breasted munias
Munia (Lonchura) castaneothorax
Photo: Pieter van den Hooven   p. 185

Juvenile hooded munia (above) and juvenile chestnut-breasted munia (below)
Photo: Pieter van den Hooven   p. 191, 185

Yellow-rumped munia
Lonchura flaviprymna
Photo: J.G. Blasman   p. 187

Cinnamon yellow-rumped munia
A sex-linked recessive mutation
Photo: Pieter van den Hooven   p. 187

White-headed munia, dark and light forms
Munia (Lonchura) maja
Photo: Pieter van den Hooven   p. 187

White-headed munia, dark form
Munia (Lonchura) maja
Photo: Pieter van den Hooven   p. 187

White-headed munia, light form
Munia (Lonchura) maja
Photo: Pieter van den Hooven   p. 187

Black-throated munia
Munia (Lonchura) ferruginosa
Photo: Pieter van den Hooven   *p. 188*

Pair of black-throated munias
Munia (Lonchura) ferruginosa
Photo: Pieter van den Hooven   *p. 188*

Black-headed mannikin
Munia (Lonchura) malacca atricapilla
Photo: Pieter van den Hooven   *p. 189*

Tricolored mannikin
Munia (Lonchura) malacca malacca
Photo: Pieter van den Hooven   *p. 189*

Variations of the tricolored mannikin
Munia (Lonchura) malacca malacca
Photo: Pieter van den Hooven   *p. 189*

Chestnut munia
Munia (Lonchura) malacca sinensis
Photo: Pieter van den Hooven   *p. 190*

Brown-headed munia
Munia (Lonchura) malacca brunneiceps
Photo: Pieter van den Hooven   *p. 190*

Great-billed mannikin
Munia (Lonchura) grandis heurni
Photo: Pieter van den Hooven   p. 190

Juvenile great-billed mannikin
Munia (Lonchura) grandis heurni
Photo: Pieter van den Hooven   p. 190

Juvenile chestnut munia
Munia (Lonchura) malacca brunneiceps
Photo: Pieter van den Hooven   p. 190

White-spotted mannikin
Lonchura leucosticta
Photo: Pieter van den Hooven   p. 192

Juvenile white-spotted mannikin
Lonchura leucosticta
Photo: Pieter van den Hooven   p. 192

New Britain (Hooded) munia
Lonchura spectabilis mayri
Photo: Pieter van den Hooven   p. 191

New Britain (Hooded) munia
Lonchura spectabilis gajduseki
Photo: Pieter van den Hooven   p. 191

White-bellied mannikin
Lonchura leucogastra leucogastra
Photo: Pieter van den Hooven   p. 194

Streak-headed mannikin
Lonchura tristissima tristissima
Photo: Pieter van den Hooven   p. 192

Red-brown Moluccan mannikin
Autosomal recessive mutation
Photo: Pieter van den Hooven   p. 196

Moluccan mannikin
Lonchura molucca molucca
Photo: Pieter van den Hooven   p. 196

Javan mannikin
Lonchura leucogastroides
Photo: Pieter van den Hooven   p. 196

Left to right: Javan, white-rumped, and dusky munias
Lonchura leucogastroides, L. striata, L. fuscans
Photo: Pieter van den Hooven   p. 196, 197, 200

120

Spice finch
Lonchura punctulata punctulata
Photo: Pieter van den Hooven `p. 193

Chinese spice finch
Lonchura punctulata topela
Photo: Pieter van den Hooven p. 193

Spice finch
Lonchura punctulata yunnanensis
Photo: Pieter van den Hooven p. 193

Spice finch
Lonchura punctulata nisoria
Photo: Pieter van den Hooven p. 194

Spice finch
Lonchura punctulata baweana
Photo: Pieter van den Hooven p. 194

White-rumped mannikin
Lonchura striata striata
Photo: Pieter van den Hooven p. 197

121

Sharp-tailed mannikin
Lonchura striata acuticauda
Photo: Pieter van den Hooven   p. 197

White-rumped mannikin subspecies
Lonchura striata swinhoei
Photo: Pieter van den Hooven   p. 197

Gray society finch
Autosomal recessive mutation
Photo: Pieter van den Hooven   p. 198

Creme-Ino society finch
Sex-linked and recessive mutation
Photo: Pieter van den Hooven   p. 198

Original black-brown ("wild") form society finch
Lonchura striata var. *domestica*
Photo: Pieter van den Hooven   p. 198

Masked black-brown society finch
Selected brown, autosomal dominant mutation
Photo: Pieter van den Hooven   p. 198

Red-brown society finch
Autosomal recessive mutation
Photo: Pieter van den Hooven   p. 198

Diluted-wing red-brown society finch
Autosomal recessive mutation
Photo: Pieter van den Hooven   p. 198

Young society finches ready to leave the nest

Photo: Pieter van den Hooven   p. 198

Dusky mannikin
Lonchura fuscans
Photo: Pieter van den Hooven   p. 200

Dusky mannikin chicks in nest
Lonchura fuscans
Photo: Pieter van den Hooven   p. 200

Juvenile dusky mannikin
Lonchura fuscans
Photo: Pieter van den Hooven   p. 200

Black-throated mannikin
Lonchura kelaarti kelaarti
Photo: Pieter van den Hooven   p. 201

Timor sparrow
Padda fuscata
Photo: J.G. Blasman   p. 202

123

White Java sparrow
Autosomal recessive mutation
Photo: Pieter van den Hooven   p. 201

Java sparrow
Padda oryzivora
Photo: Pieter van den Hooven   p. 201

Opal Java sparrow
Autosomal recessive mutation
Photo: Pieter van den Hooven   p. 201

Pastel Java sparrow
Sex-linked recessive mutation
Photo: Pieter van den Hooven   p. 201

Unnamed mutation Java sparrow
All blue has disappeared
Photo: Pieter van den Hooven   p. 201

Isabel Java sparrow
Autosomal recessive mutation
Photo: Pieter van den Hooven   p. 201

124

Female pictorella finch
Heteromunia (Lonchura) pectoralis
Photo: Pieter van den Hooven   *p. 203*

Male pictorella finch
Heteromunia (Lonchura) pectoralis
Photo: Pieter van den Hooven   *p. 203*

Madagascar mannikin
Lepidopygia (Lemuresthes) nana
Photo: Pieter van den Hooven   *p. 204*

Bronze-shouldered mannikin
Spermestes (Lonchura) cucullata
Photo: Pieter van den Hooven   *p. 205*

Juvenile bronze-shouldered mannikin
Spermestes (Lonchura) cucullata
Photo: Pieter van den Hooven   *p. 205*

Bronze-shouldered mannikin
Normal and unnamed sex-linked mutation
Photo: Pieter van den Hooven   *p. 205*

Black-and-white mannikin
Spermestes (Lonchura) bicolor bicolor
Photo: Pieter van den Hooven   *p. 206*

Fernando Po mannikin
Spermestes (Lonchura) bicolor poensis
Photo: Pieter van den Hooven   *p. 206*

Red-backed mannikin
Spermestes (Lonchura) bicolor nigriceps
Photo: Pieter van den Hooven   *p. 206*

Magpie mannikin
Spermestes (Lonchura) fringilloides
Photo: J.G. Blasman   p. 207

African silverbill
Euodice (Lonchura) cantans cantans
Photo: Pieter van den Hooven   p. 209

Gray-headed silverbill
Odontospiza caniceps (Lonchura griseicapilla)
Photo: Pieter van den Hooven   p. 208

East African silverbill
Euodice (Lonchura) cantans orientalis
Photo: Pieter van den Hooven   p. 209

Gray gray-headed silverbill
Autosomal recessive mutation
Photo: Pieter van den Hooven   p. 208

Red-brown gray-headed silverbill
Autosomal recessive mutation
Photo: Pieter van den Hooven   p. 208

126

Dark-bellied African silverbill
Autosomal recessive mutation
Photo: Pieter van den Hooven *p. 209*

Cinnamon (brown) African silverbill
Sex-linked recessive mutation
Photo: Pieter van den Hooven *p. 209*

Ino African silverbill
Sex-linked recessive mutation
Photo: Pieter van den Hooven *p. 209*

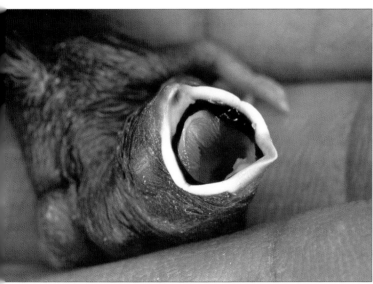

Mouth marking of nestling African silverbill
Euodice (Lonchura) cantans
Photo: Pieter van den Hooven *p. 209*

Indian silverbill
Euodice (Lonchura) malabarica
Photo: Pieter van den Hooven *p. 210*

Opal Indian silverbill
Autosomal recessive mutation
Photo: Pieter van den Hooven *p. 210*

Cinnamon (brown) Indian silverbill
Sex-linked recessive mutation
Photo: Pieter van Hooven *p. 210*

Autosomal recessive pastel silverbills;
color varies due to width of the design
Photo: Pieter van den Hooven *p. 210*

127

Diamond sparrow
Zonaeginthus (Stagonopleura) guttata
Photo: Pieter van den Hooven   p. 211

Orange-billed diamond sparrow
Autosomal recessive mutation
Photo: Pieter van den Hooven   p. 211

Isabel diamond sparrow
Sex-linked mutation
Photo: Pieter van den Hooven   p. 211

Pastel diamond sparrow
Autosomal recessive mutation
Photo: Pieter van den Hooven   p. 211

Female painted firetail finch
Emblema picta
Photo: Pieter van den Hooven   p. 252

Male painted firetail finch
Emblema picta
Photo: Pieter van den Hooven   p. 252

Male crimson finch
Neochmia phaeton phaeton
Photo: Pieter van den Hooven   *p. 220*

Male white-bellied crimson finch
Neochmia phaeton evangelinae
Photo: Pieter van den Hooven   *p. 220*

Female white-bellied crimson finch
Neochmia phaeton evangelinae
Photo: Pieter van den Hooven   *p. 220*

Orange white-bellied crimson finch
Autosomal recessive mutation
Photo: Pieter van den Hooven   *p. 220*

Red-browed firetail finch
Aegintha (Neochmia) temporalis
Photo: J.G. Blasman   *p. 237*

Bicheno's finch (Owl finch),
Stizoptera (Poephila or Taeniopygia) bichenovii
Photo: J.G. Blasman   *p. 232*

Parson finch (Black-throated finch)
Poephila cincta cincta
Photo: Pieter van den Hooven   p. 221

Diggle's finch
Poephila cincta atropygialis
Photo: Pieter van den Hooven   p. 221

Nestling parson finches
Poephila cincta cincta
Photo: J.G. Blasman   p. 221

Brown (cinnamon) parson finch
Sex-linked mutation
Photo: Pieter van den Hooven   p. 221

Creme-Ino parson finch
Sex-linked mutation
Photo: Pieter van den Hooven   p. 221

White-eared grassfinch
Poephila personata leucotis
Photo: Pieter van den Hooven   p. 223

Masked grassfinch
Poephila personata personata
Photo: Pieter van den Hooven   p. 223

Long-tailed grassfinch
Poephila acuticauda acuticauda
Photo: Pieter van den Hooven   p. 222

Heck's (red-billed long-tailed) grassfinch
Poephila acuticauda hecki
Photo: Pieter van den Hooven   p. 222

Isabel long-tailed grassfinch
Autosomal recessive mutation
Photo: Pieter van den Hooven   p. 222

Long-tailed and Heck's grassfinches
P. a. acuticauda; P. a. hecki
Photo: Pieter van den Hooven   p. 222

Gray long-tailed grassfinch
Autosomal recessive mutation
Photo: Pieter van den Hooven   p. 222

Pale-billed long-tailed grassfinch
Autosomal dominant mutation
Photo: Pieter van den Hooven   p. 222

Male zebra finch subspecies
Poephila guttata guttata (front) and P. g. castanotis
Photo: Pieter van den Hooven   p. 224

Selected pied or marked gray male zebra finches
Autosomal recessive mutation
Photo: Pieter van den Hooven   p. 224

Male zebra finch, normal or wild color
Poephila (Taeniopygia) guttata castanotis
Photo: Pieter van den Hooven   p. 224

Female zebra finch, normal or wild color
Poephila (Taeniopygia) guttata castanotis
Photo: Pieter van den Hooven   p. 224

Male and female brown zebra finches
Sex-linked recessive mutation
Photo: Pieter van den Hooven   p. 224

Zebra finches nesting on aviary floor. The birds constructed their own nest.
Poephila (Taeniopygia) guttata castanotis
Photo: Pieter van den Hooven   p. 224

132

Male orange-breasted brown zebra finch
Autosomal recessive mutation
Photo: Pieter van den Hooven   *p. 224*

Male black-cheeked gray zebra finch
Autosomal recessive mutation
Photo: Pieter van den Hooven   *p. 224*

Male pastel gray zebra finch
Autosomal dominant mutation
Photo: Pieter van den Hooven   *p. 224*

Male black-breasted gray zebra finch
Autosomal recessive mutation
Photo: Pieter van den Hooven   *p. 224*

Male pearl gray zebra finch
Sex-linked recessive mutation
Photo: Pieter van den Hooven   *p. 224*

Male black-cheeked black-faced gray and male orange-breasted black-faced gray zebra finches; Autosomal recessive mutations
Photo: Pieter van den Hooven   *p. 224*

Female isabel cherry finch
Autosomal recessive mutation
Photo: Pieter van den Hooven   *p. 238*

Female cherry finch
Aidemosyne (Neochmia) modesta
Photo: Pieter van den Hooven   *p. 238*

Male cherry (plum-headed) finch
Aidemosyne (Neochmia) modesta
Photo: Pieter van den Hooven   *p. 238*

Nestling cherry finches
Aidemosyne (Neochmia) modesta
Photo: J.G. Blasman   *p. 238*

Male and female cherry (plum-headed) finch
Aidemosyne (Neochmia) modesta
Photo: J.G. Blasman   *p. 238*

Male isabel cherry finch
Autosomal recessive mutation
Photo: Pieter van den Hooven   *p. 238*

134

Female star finch
Bathilda (Neochmia) ruficauda
Photo: Pieter van den Hooven   p. 240

Male star finch
Bathilda (Neochmia) ruficauda
Photo: Pieter van den Hooven   p. 240

Female orange-headed star finch
Bathilda (Neochmia) ruficauda
Photo: Pieter van den Hooven   p. 240

Male orange-headed star finch
Bathilda (Neochmia) ruficauda
Photo: Pieter van den Hooven   p. 240

Isabel star finch
Sex-linked mutation
Photo: Pieter van den Hooven   p. 240

Pale-billed star finch
Recent mutation with total reduction of carotenoids
Photo: Pieter van den Hooven   p. 240

Male black-headed Gouldian
Chloebia gouldiae
Photo: Pieter van den Hooven
p. 233

Male red-headed Gouldian finch
Chloebia gouldiae
Photo: Pieter van den Hooven
p. 233

Female red-headed and black-headed Gouldian
Chloebia gouldiae
Photo: Pieter van den Hooven
p. 233

Yellow (orange) headed green Gouldian finch
Autosomal recessive mutation
Photo: Pieter van den Hooven
p. 233

Male white-breasted red-headed Gouldian finch
mutation
Photo: J.G. Blasman
p. 233

Male black-headed pastel Gouldian finch
Sex-linked dominant, single factor
Photo: Pieter van den Hooven
p. 233

Red-headed yellow Gouldian finch
Sex-linked dominant, double factor
Photo: Pieter van den Hooven
p. 233

Male and female blue red-headed Gouldian finches
Autosomal recessive mutation
Photo: Pieter van den Hooven   *p. 233*

Wild-colored and cinnamon Gouldian females
Normal and sex-linked recessive mutation
Photo: Pieter van den Hooven   *p. 233*

Lutino black-headed Gouldians
Sex-linked recessive mutation
Photo: Pieter van den Hooven   *p. 233*

Black-headed white-breasted Gouldian finch
Autosomal recessive mutation
Photo: Pieter van den Hooven   *p. 233*

Combination possibilities: Lilac-breasted + pastel + sea green Gouldian finch
Chloebia gouldiae
Photo: Pieter van den Hooven   *p. 233*

137

Nestling Gouldian finches
Chloebia gouldiae
Photo: Pieter van den Hooven   p. 233

Gouldian chicks showing mouth markings
Chloebia gouldiae
Photo: Pieter van den Hooven   p. 233

Mouth markings of Gouldian chick
Chloebia gouldiae
Photo: Pieter van den Hooven   p. 233

Mouth markings of Papuan parrotfinch chick
Amblynura (Erythrura) papuana
Photo: Pieter van den Hooven   p. 248

Mouth markings of nestling long-tailed grassfinch
Poephila acuticauda
Photo: Pieter van den Hooven   p. 222

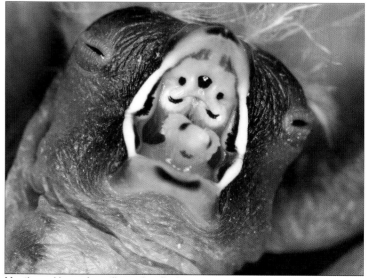

Mouth markings of nestling zebra finch
Poephila (Taeniopygia) guttata castanotis
Photo: Pieter van den Hooven   p. 224

Nest of the red-eared waxbill
Note cock's nest on top of main nest
Photo: Pieter van den Hooven
p. 85

Nest of the gray-crowned munia
Lonchura nevermanni
Photo: Pieter van den Hooven
p. 183

Nest and nestlings of the zebra finch
Poephila Taeniopygia guttata castanotis
Photo: Pieter van den Hooven
p. 224

Left to right:
White-capped, gray-crowned, black-headed munias
Lonchura ferruginosa, L. nevermanni, L. malacca atricapilla
Photo: Pieter van den Hooven
p. 188, 183, 189

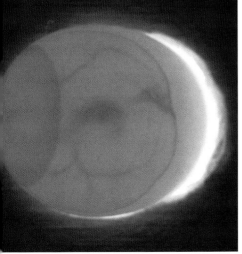

Fertilized zebra finch egg showing early
embryonic development
Photo: Pieter van den Hooven
p. 224

Male green-tailed (Bamboo) parrotfinch
Reichenowia (Erythrura) hyperythra hyperythra
Photo: Pieter van den Hooven   p. 241

Female green-tailed parrotfinch
Reichenowia (Erythrura) hyperythra hyperythra
Photo: Pieter van den Hooven   p. 241

Female green-tailed parrotfinch
Reichenowia (Erythrura) hyperythra microrhyncha
Photo: Pieter van den Hooven   p. 241

Male green-tailed parrotfinch
Reichenowia (Erythrura) hyperythra microrhyncha
Photo: Pieter van den Hooven   p. 241

Male green-tailed parrotfinch
Reichenowia (Erythrura) hyperythra brunneiventris
Photo: Pieter van den Hooven   p. 241

Female green-tailed parrotfinch
Reichenowia (Erythrura) hyperythra brunneiventris
Photo: Pieter van den Hooven   p. 241

Male pin-tailed parrotfinch
Erythrura prasina prasina
Photo: Pieter van den Hooven   p. 243

Female pin-tailed parrotfinch
Erythrura prasina prasina
Photo: Pieter van den Hooven   p. 243

Male yellow-tailed pin-tailed parrotfinch
Autosomal recessive mutation
Photo: Pieter van den Hooven   p. 243

Female yellow-tailed pin-tailed parrotfinch
Erythrura prasina prasina
Photo: Pieter van den Hooven   p. 243

Par-Blue pin-tailed parrotfinches
Probably a modification
Photo: Pieter van den Hooven   p. 243

Many-colored parrotfinch
Amblynura (Erythrura) coloria
Photo: Pieter van den Hooven   p. 245

141

Male tricolored parrotfinch
Amblynura (Erythrura) tricolor
Photo: Pieter van den Hooven
p. 245

Female tricolored parrotfinch
Amblynura (Erythrura) tricolor
Photo: Pieter van den Hooven
p. 245

Par-Blue tricolored parrotfinch
Recent mutation; heredity unclear
Photo: Pieter van den Hooven
p. 245

Female blue-faced parrotfinch
Amblynura (Erythrura) trichroa
Photo: Pieter van den Hooven
p. 246

Male blue-faced parrotfinch
Amblynura (Erythrura) trichroa
Photo: Pieter van den Hooven
p. 246

Lutino blue-faced parrotfinch
Sex-linked mutation
Photo: Pieter van den Hooven
p. 246

142

Pied red-throated parrotfinch
Autosomal recessive mutation
Photo: Pieter van den Hooven   p. 248

Juvenile red-throated parrotfinch
Autosomal recessive mutation
Photo: Pieter van den Hooven   p. 248

Normal and par-blue red-throated parrotfinches
Autosomal recessive mutation
Photo: Pieter van den Hooven   p. 248

Male red-throated parrotfinch
Amblynura (Erythrura) psittacea
Photo: J.G. Blasman   p. 248

Male Papuan parrotfinch
Amblynura (Erythrura) papuana
Photo: Pieter van den Hooven   p. 248

Female Papuan parrotfinch
Amblynura (Erythrura) papuana
Photo: Pieter van den Hooven   p. 248

Juvenile Papuan parrotfinch
Amblynura (Erythrura) papuana
Photo: Pieter van den Hooven   p. 248

Papuan and blue-faced parrotfinches
Amblynura papuana; A. trichroa
Photo: Pieter van den Hooven   p. 248, 246

143

Peale's (Fiji) parrotfinch
Amblynura (Erythrura) pealii　　　　　　　　　　　p. 249
RIGHT: Normal and Par-Blue Peale's parrotfinches
Autosomal recessive mutation
Photo: Pieter van den Hooven　　　　　　　　　　　p. 249

Samoa parrotfinch
Amblynura (Erythrura) cyaneovirens
Photo: J.G. Blasman　　　　　　　　　　　　　　　　　　　　　　p. 250

ground, in dense, thorny bushes, where it searches for small insects and various small seeds. The nest is usually built in thorny bushes, or in thick grass clumps, and consists of a rather flimsy dome-shaped structure with an outer layer of coarse grass and an inner shell of fine, dried grass. The outer layer is constructed by the male, the inner by the female. Parasitized by the variable indigobird *Vidua funerea*.

Aviculture: Especially well-suited for indoor aviaries. Imported birds must be acclimatized at a temperature of approximately 68°F (20°C). Breeding successes are very possible (see Red-billed firefinch, page 149). The female lays 3–6 eggs; both parents incubate for 11–12 days. After 16–19 days the young leave the nest but will be fed by both parents for another 14–17 days. A pair usually uses a nesting box, although they sometimes build a dome-shaped nest in a dense bush close to the ground. In order to promote successful breeding, both parents and later their young will need an ample supply of insects. The species is rather peaceful toward other birds.

Food: See Red-billed firefinch.

Other names: Dark firefinch, Blue-billed firefinch, Ruddy waxbill, Lilac firefinch, South African ruddy waxbill.

BROWN FIREFINCH *Lagonosticta nitidula* Hartlaub, 1886

DK: Stor Punktamarant NL: Grote puntastrild FR: Grand Sénégali à poitrine barrée
DE: Grosser Pünktchenamarant, Braunbürzelamarant IT: Amaranto punteggiato maggiore

Description: Male, gray-brown. Face and breast red; the latter with little white dots. Eyes brown, beak red, legs gray-brown. The female has less red. Young birds lack the white spots and still have a black beak; their general plumage is brownish. Length: 4 in. (10 cm).

Geographic variations:

■ *L. n. nitidula*, as above. Distribution: northern Angola, southeastern Zaire, and northern and western Zambia.
■ *L. n. plumbaria* Clancy. More grayish than the nominate subspecies; under tail coverts and near the rump white. The red colors are lighter. Some little spots on the flanks. The red color in the female is duller, the many spots are smaller than in the nominate form. Distribution: southern part of Angola, northeastern Namibia, northern Botswana and southwestern Zambia.

Habitat: Grass and reeds. They build their grassy domed nests in dense bushes, close to the ground; but also utilize old finch nests as well as nests from weavers and sunbirds. Parasitized by the violet widowbird or Zaire indigobird *Vidua (Hypochera) incognita*.

Aviculture: In recent years, irregularly available in the trade. They are excellent birds for well-planted indoor aviaries. They breed in half-open nest boxes as well as free-standing nests in thick bushes. It sometimes happens that a pair of brown firefinches takes over the nest of other birds, but in general they are very peaceful and won't present any problems if we supply them with various old finch nests and enough half-open nest boxes. Clutch, 3–6 white eggs; incubation period, 12–14 days by both parents. Both also take care of the young, which leave the nest after 18–20 days. The parents feed their offspring for another 7–10 days after fledging.

Food: See Red-billed firefinch, page 149. Experience has taught us that this species seldom accepts cut-up mealworms, but rather feeds on ant pupae and white worms, rearing food, sprouted grass and weed seeds, and brown bread soaked in water.

LANDANA FIREFINCH   *Lagonosticta landanae* Sharpe, 1890

DK: Landana Amarant NL: Donkerrode vuurvink FR: Sénégali de Landane DE: Landana Amarant
IT: Amaranto del Landane

Description: Looks similar to the dark firefinch, *Lagonosticta rubricata*; only the upper mandible is gray, the lower mandible red with a black tip. The hen has the same colored beak. Young seem to look like the youngsters of the dark firefinch. Length: 4.3 in. (11 cm).

Distribution and habitat: Cabinda, and western and central Angola; in pairs and family groups. Seen in grassland, along the borders of forests, near farms and settlements. The landana firefinch is the host of the atlas widow finch, *Hypochera funerea* and the subspecies *H. f. nigerrima*. The female widow finch may enter the nest and lay her egg with very little opposition, while the firefinch is inside. More than one widow finch may parasitize the same nest. Not much is known about this firefinch.

Aviculture: Unkown.

MASKED FIREFINCH   *Lagonosticta larvata* (Ruppell, 1840)

DK: Larveamarant NL: Zwartmasker astrild FR: Amaranthe masquée d'Abyssinie
DE: Larvenamarant IT: Amaranto mascheranto di Abissinia

Description: Male. Black face and throat; forehead, crown, and neck dark gray-brown; upper tail coverts and central tail feathers deep red; under tail coverts dark gray. The rest of the body is brownish wine-red, with little white spots on the breast and flanks. Eyes dark brown with a blue periophthalmic ring; beak steel blue, legs dark gray-brown. The female is duller and has a grayish yellow throat and cheek; back and crown are brown-gray. Young resemble the female. Length: 4 in. (10 cm).

Distribution and habitat: Savanna belt from Gambia to Ethiopia and the northern parts of Uganda, in grassland and bamboo. They like to use plant fibers, moss, and small feathers for their cone-shaped, free-standing nest. It is primarily the female which does the nest building. Although the male brings practically all the materials, he seldom assists in the actual construction. It takes the birds three to five days to complete their nest.

Aviculture: This beautiful species is extremely suitable for indoor facilities. It becomes friendly toward its keeper and toward other small finches in no time at all. A pair likes to use canary nest boxes and baskets, and other small half-open nest boxes. Low, free-standing nests in dense bushes are made out of grass, wool, moss, plant fibers, hay, small feathers, etc. The 3–4 eggs hatch in approximately 11 days; both parents take turns in brooding, but spend their nights cozily together on the nest. When the young are approximately 19 days old they leave the nest, but will be nourished for yet another week. After still another week we must separate them from their parents. Don't check nests, eggs or young while the parents are on or very close to the nest as they are susceptible to disturbances and might abandon their eggs or offspring.

Food: See Red-billed firefinch, page 149. Insects as well as various commercial fine-grade softbill mixtures, soaked and germinated seeds, and seeding grasses are absolutely essential both in and out of the breeding season.

Other names: Black-faced firefinch, Black-throated firefinch.

VINACEOUS FIREFINCH *Lagonosticta vinacea* Hartlaub, 1857

DK: Vinrød Amarant NL: Wijnrode astrild FR: Astrild vineux, Bengali vineux
DE: Weinroter Amarant IT: Amaranto vinoso

▸ *photos page 104*

Description: Male. Black face mask; forehead, crown and neck gray-blue; wings brownish black with wine-red borders; upper tail coverts and center tail feathers deep red; under tail coverts black. The rest of the body is dark wine-red with little white spots on the flanks. Eyes dark brown with a blue-white periophthalmic ring; beak steel blue; legs gray brown. The female is much duller, and has a grayish yellow throat and cheek; back and crown are dull wine-red. Young resemble the hen. Length: 4 in. (10 cm).

Geographic variations:

■ *L. v. vinacea*, as above. Distribution: from the south of Senegal and southwestern Mali, through Gambia to the northern parts of Guinea.

■ *L. v. togoensis* Neumann. Male has more gray on head, back, and wings than the nominate form. The wing feathers have gray-brown borders; breast and belly are reddish blue-gray with little white spots around and on the wings. The female has a grayish underside, and closely resembles the hen of the nominate form. Distribution: Ghana, through Togo to Nigeria (but not on the coast), and the northeastern parts of Cameroon.

■ *L. v. nigricollis* Heuglin. Male has a darker back than *togoensis*; the wings are also darker but with more brown. Underside rather light, especially in the hens. Distribution: Central African Republic, southwestern Sudan, and northern Uganda.

Habitat: All the above birds live in bamboo bushes, savannas, and around farms, in pairs or small family groups. They prefer to look for food on the ground (millets, grass seeds, small insects, etc.). The nest is constructed from grass and fibers, and lined with small feathers and dry grass. The great atlas widow finch *Hypochera camerunensis* lays her eggs in the nest of the vinaceous finch and its subspecies.

Aviculture: Well-known aviary birds, however they are only suited for indoor, well-planted aviaries. These birds like to use canary nest boxes, baskets and other similar small, half-open nest boxes, or old finch nests, which are placed in dense, low bushes. The male usually carries a grass blade in his beak to impress his female, but the latter seldom if ever pays any attention to his behavior. The male doesn't sing during courtship. The tree nest is rather small and round, with an entrance on the side. Here again, the male is the active builder while the hen acts rather calmly and composed, as she plays the real architect. Coconut fibers, dry grass, small pieces of bark, sisal and hemp fibers, and small roots are gladly taken. The female lays 4 eggs which will be incubated for 11–13 days. After 18–19 days the young usually leave the nest, but sometimes not until 21 days, like most other *Lagonosticta* species. Most pairs don't tolerate nest inspection; they become very nervous and will often refuse to feed their young.

The youngsters don't yet have the dark mask, and are rather gray-brown when they leave the nest. There is only some red in the borders of the wing feathers and tail feathers; belly and under tail coverts are brownish black. There are no white little dots either. The young hens have yellowish gray underside.

Adult birds call each other with a rather soft "tschee-tschee" (ee as in sea) or a short "zit-zit" (i as in it). Their warning call sounds like "tschit-tschit-tschit" (i as in it), or "twik-twik-twik-ik-ik-ik." The song interpretation is like "tippi-tippi-tippi" or "schippi-schippi-schippie", interjected with "beri-beri-beri" (e as in bear, i as in sea) or "you-you-you."

Food: Spray millet and small insects throughout the year are essential, as are sprouted and germinated seeds and a variety of green. Regarding the insects, we think of white worms, ant pupae, small cut-up mealworms, and a trusted commercial food for soft-billed birds. Place most of the food on the bottom of the indoor aviary, or on a few bricks. Supply fresh drinking water several times per day.

SPECKLED-BREASTED FIREFINCH *Lagonosticta rufopicta* (Fraser, 1843)

DK: Punktamarant NL: Puntastrild FR: Sénégali à poitrine, barrée Amaranthe pointillée   ▸ *photo page 103*
DE: Punktchenamarant IT: Amaranto punteggiato

Description: Male very similar to the red-billed firefinch (see page 149), only the red is less intense. Primaries are much lighter; crown, neck, shoulders, and back brown with a yellowish sheen. On the breast small white, sickle-shaped dots. Eyes brown to red-brown, periophthalmic ring blue-yellow to blue-white, legs reddish brown. The female has red underparts and cheeks; the rest of the body is brownish gray. Length: 4 in. (10 cm).

Geographic variations:

■ *L. r. rufopicta*, as above. Distribution: from northwestern Zaire through the Central African Republic to southern Chad and central Cameroon, and from Nigeria to Senegal and Sierra Leone.
■ *L. r. lateritia* Heuglin. Male has more gray, especially on the belly, and on the under tail coverts and back. The little white dots which are present in the previous subspecies appear in this race as little horizontal stripes. The female is duller, and has a longer point-design, like little tears, on the breast. Distribution: eastern part of the Central African Republic, southern Sudan, southeastern Ethiopia, western Kenya, northwestern Uganda, and northeastern Zaire.

Habitat: This firefinch lives in savannas, bushes close to villages, and in large gardens and parks, in pairs or small flocks.

Aviculture: As for the previous species. The female lays 3–5 white eggs, and in the wild sometimes up to seven, which are incubated by both parents. The young hatch after 10–11 days, and leave the nest when approximately 17 days old. They should be kept inside during fall and winter.

Food: As for the black-faced firefinch (see page 146); small insects are essential throughout the year, but especially during the breeding season. Germinated seeds, finch rearing food, and extra vitamins and minerals are recommended.

Other name: Bar-breasted firefinch.

ABYSSINIAN FIREFINCH *Lagonosticta rhodopareia* Heuglin, 1868

DK: Rosenamarant NL: Rose vuurvink FR: Amaranthe de rose   ▸ *photo page 104*
DE: Rosenamarant IT: Amaranto roseo ali nere

Description: Some remarks beforehand: This species is closely related to *L. rubricata* but there are some minor differences, especially regarding the inside of the second primary feather, which is not narrowed; further, the under tail coverts are black; the belly feathers start out in olive gray-brown but turn to black on the under tail coverts. Belly and tail coverts in *rubricata* are both black.

The male Abyssinian firefinch has carmine red lores, throat, breast, and first part of belly. Flanks and upper tail coverts are also carmine red. Forehead, neck, and the sides of the neck are grayish brown or black with some reddish hue. Back and under wing coverts brown; primaries and secondaries dark olive brown. The inside of the primaries is beige brown. Latter part of the belly is olive gray-brown; under tail coverts and tail are black with some red hue on the outer tail coverts. Breast with little white spots, which are often absent. Eyes dark brown, with a reddish eye ring; beak steel blue, upper mandible darker with black tip; feet gray-brown. The female has a gray-brownish head, neck and neck sides. Red in lores and upper tail coverts. Belly olive gray, under tail coverts dark gray. Length: 4–4¼ in. (10–11 cm).

Geographic variations:

■ *L. r. rhodopareia*, as above. Distribution: northern and southwestern Ethiopia; also in southeastern Sudan, eastern Uganda and northern Kenya.

■ *L. r. jamesoni* Shelley. Known as Jameson's firefinch, a name sometimes used for the entire species. The brownish forehead, crown, neck, sides of neck, back, and wings have a reddish hue; lores, area around the eyes, and underside soft deep red. Breast and flanks often with white little spots. The female has yellowish red lores, a reddish hue on the upperparts, and pale yellowish red in the underside. Distribution: southeastern Kenya through Tanzania to Swaziland (South Africa), and to eastern Botswana, eastern Zambia, and southeastern Zaire.

■ *L. r. ansorgei* Neumann. Rather a dark-colored bird. Light red around the eyes; same color for the lores. Dark brown on forehead, back and primaries, but with some reddish hue. Female has dark red lores; head, neck, and sides of the neck are brown. Distribution: Western half of Angola, Lower Congo River and in Cabinda.

■ *L. r. bruneli* (Erard & Roche). Very similar to nominate form, but forehead, crown, neck, and side of neck are gray; back and secondary flight feathers chestnut red. The female has a well-bordered grayish head and neck; the upperparts are reddish brown. Distribution: discovered by Dr. J. Brunel in 1973 in the region of Baibokoum in southern Chad, near the Cameroon border and the Central African Republic. This subspecies is regarded by some authorities as a full species, and given the name Reichenow's firefinch *Lagonosticta umbrinodorsalis*.

Habitat: These are typical savanna birds, searching for small seeds and insects on the ground, in low, dense bushes, or in grass clumps. The spherical-shaped grass nest with a side entrance near the top is built in thorny bushes.

Aviculture: This firefinch is only occasionally available. It is an excellent indoor aviary bird, as it likes roomy well-planted facilities; cages are unsuitable. This rather delicate bird is very susceptible to temperature changes. The birds like to search for tidbits near the bottom of the aviary or in low bushes. They are kind toward other small finches. The pairing dance of the male is interesting to watch; he dances on the ground around the hen with a long blade in his beak, while his tail feathers are spread out like a Chinese fan. Clutch consists of 3–4, occasionally 5, white eggs; incubation period is 12 days. Both partners incubate, but we have discovered that the female broods exclusively during the night, while the male roosts outside on a branch very near to the nest. The young leave the nest after 17–20 days. For more details, see Red-billed firefinch (page 149).

Food: Without animal protein, breeding results will be rare. This species needs small insects such as white worms, cut-up mealworms, ant pupae, small maggots, etc. throughout the year, but especially during the breeding and rearing period.

Other names: Jameson's firefinch, Pink-backed firefinch.

RED-BILLED FIREFINCH *Lagonosticta senegala* (Linnaeus, 1766)

DK: Senegalamarant, Amarant NL: Vuurvink FR: Amaranthe, Sénégali rouge
DE: Senegalamarant, Amarant, Roter Amarant IT: Amaranto del Senegal, Amaranto rosso

▸ *photos page 103*

Description: Male, crimson; darker, sometimes reddish brown on back and wings. All primaries have light edges. Rump, flanks, cheeks, and throat light red. Belly whitish with a red hue. Tail brownish red to dark red. Near the bend of the wing and on the breast tiny white spots. Eyes reddish brown with a small yellow periophthalmic ring, beak light red, legs light brown. The female is brownish gray with some white spots on the sides of the breast; her mask is crimson. There is a reddish sheen on the breast. Tail dark brown. Young birds are fully colored after approximately five months; initially they are very similar to the female, although young males show the small white spots at an early age. Length: 3½–4 in. (9–10 cm).

Geographic variations:

■ *L. s. senegala*, as above. Distribution: Senegal

L. s. senegala

and Gambia to Sierra Leone, Liberia, Mali, the northern portion of Ghana and Nigeria to central Cameroon.

■ *L. s. guineensis* Hald-Mortensen. Deeper olive-brown with dark red on face, neck, neck sides, throat, breast, and upperparts. Distribution: West Africa, from Togo, Guinea, and Sierra Leone to southern Senegal.

■ *L. s. rhodopis* (Heuglin). The underside of the tail feathers and most of the backside brownish yellow, without much red hue. Distribution: central and southeastern Niger, northeastern Cameroon, the Central African Republic, most parts of the Sudan to northern Ethiopia, the northern part of Chad and southern Algeria.

■ *L. s. brunneiceps* Sharpe. Head and upperparts brown (therefore, often called the brown-headed Senegal firefinch), sometimes with some reddish hue; under tail coverts and backside grayish brown. Distribution: Ethiopia and Sudan, east of the Nile.

■ *L. s. somaliensis* Salvadori. Duller red with mainly brown-grayish upperparts. Distribution: southern Somalia and northern and northeastern Kenya.

■ *L. s. zedlitzi* (Grote). Upperparts yellowish brown; under tail coverts and backside quite yellow. Distribution: southeastern Kenya to eastern Tanzania and northern Mozambique.

■ *L. s. rendalli* Hartert. A richness of little white spots in males and females. Generally duller red than the nominate form. Distribution: southern Tanzania to eastern Zimbabwe and northern Mozambique.

■ *L. s. pallidicrissa* Zedlitz. Duller red, but nevertheless almost impossible to differentiate from the previous subspecies. Distribution: southern Angola and northern Namibia. We consider this subspecies synonymous to *rendalli*.

■ *L. s. ruberrima* Reichenow. Male, light wine red; much darker brown-red than the previous subspecies in forehead, crown, neck, back, and primaries. Last part of the belly and under tail coverts earth-brown, the latter with white end borders. None or sometimes a few white little spots on breast and flanks. The hen looks much like the previous subspecies but has a darker backside and under tail coverts; clear red lores, and some red in cheeks and ear patches. Distribution: southern Sudan, western Kenya, Tanzania, northern Malawi, and Zimbabwe through Zambia and northeastern Angola, southeastern and southern Zaire to Uganda. This subspecies is often called the beautiful firefinch.

Habitat: These firefinches inhabit grasslands, open savannas, and large gardens and parks; always near human habitation in country towns and villages. The species is parasitized by the Senegal combassou or village indigobird *Vidua chalybeata*, which may even enter the nest while the female firefinch is inside to lay her own egg. The firefinch hen offers little opposition toward the intruder. More than one combassou may parasitize the same firefinch nest!

Aviculture: This rather shy bird builds its nest of hair, grass, wool, moss, leaves, sisal fibers, stems, rootlets, and other fibers; the lining is made from small feathers. Both sexes share nest-building duties. The nest is quite roughly constructed and bullet-shaped. They will also use nesting boxes, old weaver and finch nests, etc., and will even build a nest under the eaves of the night shelter. In an indoor aviary they will also breed during the winter months, but if they do, we should not allow them to continue breeding in the summer. The hatching period is about 12 days; the 3–6 young leave the nest after approximately 18 days, but they will still be fed by their parents for another 18–20 days. The hens are generally weaker than the cocks, so that the aviculturist should keep an eye out for egg binding. It is certainly best to wait a year after buying a pair before allowing them to breed so that all this unpleasantness is avoided. In the wild as well as in captivity, the birds prefer to stay on the ground, where they search for small insects, spiders, and grass and weed seeds.

Birds that are not yet acclimatized find it difficult to tolerate drafts and cold. They fare best at an even temperature of 68°F (20°C). During the fall and winter, we prefer to house our birds inside in roomy cages or indoor aviaries at room temperature. During the breeding season, the male's display is very interesting to watch as he dances in front of his bride with a blade of grass or sometimes a small feather in his beak. Copulation usu-

ally takes place on the ground. Prior to this act, the male pecks his partner gently in the neck feathers; she answers by moving her tail from right to left. A nest box placed in a little thicket will be accepted sooner than one that is hung against one of the walls of the aviary. Never allow more than three broods per season, which runs from April to the middle of September; later broods must be discouraged.

Food: All small millet varieties, spray millet, a good commercial seed mix, grass and weed seeds, fresh, sprouted and germinated, greens such as lettuce, chickweed, spinach, dandelion, etc., small insects, including white worms, daphnia, cut-up mealworms, small maggots, spiders, and ant pupae, egg and rearing foods for finches and soft-billed birds, cuttlebone, vitamins and minerals.

Other names: Common firefinch, Senegal firefinch.

BLACK-BILLED WAXBILL *Lagonosticta rara* (Antinori, 1864)

DK: Sortbuget Amarant NL: Zwartbuikvuurvink FR: Sénégali à ventre noir
DE: Schwarzbauchamarant, Seltener Amarant IT: Amaranto raro ventre nero

▸ *photo page 105*

Description: Male, dark red; underparts, under tail coverts, and tail black. Wings brownish. Eyes brown; beak black, lower mandible with red on the sides; legs brown. The female is brownish, as are the young. The male has a melodious song, which he seldom performs, however. Length: 4½ in. (11.5 cm).

Geographic variations:
■ *L. r. rara*, as above. Distribution: from western Kenya, northern Uganda, and southern Sudan to northern Zaire and the Central African Republic.
■ *L. r. forbesi* Neumann. Somewhat smaller than the nominate subspecies. Length 4 in. (10 cm). Lighter blood red, with much red on the primaries and rest of wing feathers. Deep black underparts. Eye ring yellowish white, feet and legs black. The female is darker red than the nominate form, especially the upperparts, breast, and flanks. Throat

and chin are dark grayish red. Distribution: central Nigeria, eastern Sierra Leone, northern Liberia and southern Guinea. Some small populations are irregularly seen in southern Senegal, Ghana and other western states.

Habitat: Lives primarily on the ground in pairs or small families. Builds its loosely woven spherical grass nest in thorny bushes or low trees, as well as under cane roofs.

Aviculture: Infrequently available. This bird, especially in the beginning, is extremely shy and even with excellent care and management never becomes totally familiar with its keeper or other birds. Therefore only suitable for large, well-planted indoor aviaries. May also be housed outdoors in our warmer areas. It will come to breeding if enough half-open nesting boxes are made available. It often happens, however, that the parents neglect their young, even if enough animal protein is provided. The birds often construct their own nest in a low bush or use an old finch nest which they patch up with grass and coconut fibers; the inside will be lined with small feathers. The typical clutch is 2–4 eggs; both parents incubate during the day but the female only during the late evening hours and night. In the meantime, the male will roost near the nest on a branch, a familiar behavioral pattern with firefinches. Incubation time is 11 days. After 20 days the young leave the nest but the parents will still feed them for another 20 days.

Food: See Red-billed firefinch (page 149).

Other name: Black-billed firefinch, Black-bellied firefinch.

Genus *Cryptospiza* (crimson-wings) Salvadori, 1884

RED-FACED CRIMSON-WING *Cryptospiza reichenovii* (Hartlaub, 1874)

DK: Reichenows Biergastrild NL: Reichenow's bergvink FR: Bengali vert à face rouge
DE: Reichenows Bergastrild, Bergastrild IT: Astro montano di Reichenow

▸ *photos page 105*

Description: Male, lores red, as are the areas around the eyes, the back, the wing coverts, the rump, the upper tail coverts, and the flanks. Throat greenish; the rest of the body is grayish green. Eyes dark brown with a red periophthalmic ring; beak black; legs brownish black. The female has a yellowish eye ring, and the colors of the entire coat of feathers are less intense. Young birds are brownish green and the red on the back is still lacking. Length: 4½ in. (11.5 cm).

Geographic variations:

■ *C. r. reichenovii* (Hartlaub), as above. Distribution: southwestern Cameroons to west central Angola.
■ *C. r. australis* Shelley. Light olive-green. Duller red areas; the red around the eyes is often absent. Distribution: southern Uganda through eastern Zaire and Tanzania to northeastern Zambia, southern Malawi, northwestern Mozambique and northeastern Zimbabwe.
■ *C. r. homogenes* Clancey. This subspecies is somewhat larger in size. Upperparts dark olive-green; head, neck, and face duller. All the red areas are rather bright. Distribution: eastern Zimbabwe and bordering Mozambique.

Habitat: The species can be found higher than 6000 ft. (2400 m), in woodland, particularly in the underbrush; also in tea plantations and in the foothills. There they hunt for small insects and various small seeds. They can frequently be found in thorn bushes, where they will also build their keg-shaped nests; occasionally found nesting alongside red-ant *Pheidole* species.

Aviculture: All the crimson-wings are mountain dwellers and therefore good candidates for outside aviaries because they can withstand the cold relatively well. However, when temperatures drop below 65°F (18°C), they should be brought indoors. All crimson-wings become trusting toward their keeper in a very short time, and they are also friendly toward other small birds. The red-faced crimson-wing will breed in a well-planted aviary. The nest is placed rather low, up to 9 ft. (3 m) from the ground, and is built from grass, moss, and fibers. By preference, it is located in a dense shrub or occasionally in a half-open nest box. Clutch, 3–4 white eggs. Incubation period, 12–13 days. Both parents incubate and feed the young, which leave the nest when approximately 22 days old; after that the father will mostly take care of the fledglings for another two weeks.

Food: Provide a good mix of tropical seeds with a heavy proportion of small millet species. Panicum millet, millet spray, etc. must be supplied daily, as well as grass and weed seeds, which should also be given in sprouted form. Protein from animal sources is essential, especially in the breeding season.

Other names: Nyasa crimson-wing, Reichenow's crimson-wing.

JACKSON'S CRIMSON-WING *Cryptospiza jacksoni* Sharpe, 1902

DK: Jacksons Bjergastrild NL: Jackson's bergvink FR: Bengali de Jackson
DE: Jacksons Bergastrild, Jacksonastrild IT: Astro montano di Jackson

Description: Dark gray to black, especially on wings and tail; forehead and cheeks are red, as are the back, rump, and upper tail coverts. Flanks somewhat orange-red. Eyes dark brown, beak black, legs brown. The female can be distinguished from the male by a somewhat lesser intensity in the red of the head. Young birds lack this red and they possess an overall browner coat of feathers. Length: 5 in. (12 cm).

Distribution and habitat: central Africa, in northeastern Zaire, western Uganda, and western Ruanda and Burundi. The species lives in the mountains up to a height of 9000 feet (2700 m) or more, principally in meadows and on the edges of forests.

Aviculture: This species occasionally has been offered for sale, but we know of no cases where it has successfully been bred in captivity. Males have been observed doing a mating dance with a blade of grass in the beak, but mating and nest building did not ensue.

Food: Provide small millet only in sprouted form. Then, offer weed and grass seed in the ears and a good supply of live food in the form of ant pupae, white worms, fly larvae, and small, cut-up mealworms, plus a good brand of egg food or rearing food for small tropical finches, which should be enriched with insects, preferably ant pupae and little maggots.

Other name: Dusky crimson-wing.

ETHIOPIAN CRIMSON-WING *Crytospiza salvadorii* Reichenow, 1892

DK: Salvadoris Bjergastrild NL: Bergvink FR: Bengali vert
DE: Salvadoris Bergastrild, Salvadoriastrild IT: Astro montano di Salvadori

▶ *photo page 105*

Description: Similar to the red-faced crimson-wing, except there is no red on the head. In general, the feathers are a little browner. Length: 5 in. (13 cm).

Geographic variations:

■ *C. s. salvadorii*, as above. Distribution: East Africa, from central and southern Ethiopia to northern Kenya.
■ *C. s. ruwenzori* W. Sclater. More gray, also in the underparts. Back and wing coverts reddish. Chin and throat are somewhat lighter than in the nominate form. Distribution: Ruwenzori Mountains of Zaire and bordering Uganda, as well as in western Ruanda and Burundi.

■ *C. s. kilimensis* W. Sclater. Upperparts darker gray; underside light gray with an olive-green hue. Distribution: southeastern part of the Sudan, northeastern Uganda, northwestern and western Kenya and northern Tanzania.
■ *C. s. crystallochresta* Desfayes. Upperparts light reddish. Throat bright olive-green. Distribution: southwestern Ethiopia.

Habitat: The birds are typical mountain dwellers, found up to a height of 9000 feet (2700 m).

Aviculture: This species is best kept in an inside aviary with a variety of plants in pots. They are quite trusting and friendly toward birds of their own and other species. They will regularly breed in the aviary. The male does a mating dance, circling with a long blade of grass in the bill. For nesting material, furnish grass, moss, coconut fibers, and leaf veins. The keg-shaped nest generally is built in bushes, preferably thorny ones, but the birds will also move into half-open nest boxes. For more details, see previous species.

Food: See Red-faced crimson-wing (page 152).

Other names: Abyssinian crimson-wing, Salvadori's crimson-wing, Crimson-backed forest finch.

SHELLEY'S CRIMSON-WING *Cryptospiza shelleyi* Sharpe, 1902

DK: Shelleys Bjergastrild NL: Shelley's bergvink FR: Bengali vert de Shelley
DE: Shelleys Bergastrild, Rotmantelastrild IT: Astro montano, di Shelley

Description: Upperparts red, with brownish black on wings and upper tail coverts. Tail black; underside yellowish green. Eyes dark brown, as are the legs; the beak is red, a deviation from the other crimson-wings. The female lacks the red in the head, which is yellowish green instead. Length: 5 in. (13 cm).

Distribution and habitat: Eastern Zaire, in the Ruwenzori Mountains, southwestern Uganda, and in Ruanda and northern Burundi.

Thick wooded areas up to 6000–9000 ft. (1800–2700 m).

Aviculture: This bird became available to the European trade in the 1970s, and has since remained available at high prices. For more details see the above crimson-wing species.

Food: See Red-faced crimson-wing (page 152).

Other name: Red-billed crimson-wing.

Genus *Nesocharis* (olive-backs or chickadee finches) Alexander, 1903

WHITE-COLLARED OLIVE-BACK *Nesocharis ansorgei* (Hartert, 1899)

DK: Lysbuget Mejseastrild NL: Ansorge's meesastrild FR: Bengali vert de Ansorge
DE: Halsbandastrild, Ansorges Olivastrild IT: Astrilde dal collare bianco

Description: Head black; white, rather small neck band and gray-blue neck feathers. Breast grayish green-yellow. Back, rump, upper tail coverts and wings olive-green. Tail black, belly grayish blue, as are the under tail coverts. The female has a grayish underside with no yellow in the breast; the neck band is absent or very small. Eyes and legs dark brown, beak steel black. Length: 4 in. (10 cm). Closely resembles the Fernando Po olive-back *N. shelleyi*, which is smaller, and widely separated geographically.

Distribution and habitat: northeastern Zaire to Uganda and northern Burundi, in grass-

land and along forests, close to water. Up to 7000 ft. (2100 m) high in the mountains.

Aviculture: Excellent for well-planted indoor aviaries with a high humidity (75%). Seldom in the trade. Offer old weaver and finch nests, as well as nesting boxes (see Bengalese). They rarely come to breeding, however. For more details see Melba finch (page 172).

Food: See Melba finch (page 172).

Other name: Olive weaver-finch.

FERNANDO PO OLIVE-BACK *Nesocharis shelleyi* Alexander, 1903

DK: Mørkbuget Mejseastrild NL: Meesastrild FR: Bengali vert à tête noire, Dos-olive de Shelley
DE: Meisenastrild, Shelley's Olivastrild IT: Astrilde Shelleyi

Description: Very similar to the preceding species. Male, entire head black, as are the chin, throat, and sides of the neck. Nape and neck gray, with a small white streak on the sides of the throat. Upperparts olive-green, with a golden hue on the upper tail coverts and rump. Tail black; breast greenish yellow; belly, flanks, and under tail coverts gray. Female duller, without the golden sheen in the upperparts; underparts gray-blue. Bill gray with dark tip; eyes brown; legs and feet brownish. Young similar to female but browner overall. Length: 3¼ in. (8.5 cm).

Geographic variation:
- *N. s. shelleyi*, as above. Distribution: Fernando Po and west Cameroon.

- *N. s. bansoensis* (Bannermann). Slightly larger and darker than the nominate form. Distribution: Cameroon highlands and possibly southeastern Nigeria.

Habitat: Brushy areas, forest edges, and clearings. Forages in trees, only occasionally descending to the ground. Feeds on various seeds, insects, and fruit.

Aviculture: As for other olive-backs.

Other names: Little olive weaver, Shelley's olive-back.

GRAY-HEADED OLIVE-BACK *Nesocharis capistrata* (Hartlaub, 1861)

DK: Hvidkindet Meiseastril NL: Witwangastrild FR: Bengali vert à joues blanches
DE: Weisswangenestrild, Weisswangen-Olivastrild IT: Astrilde guance bianche

▶ *photo page 38, 106*

Description: Cheeks and forehead light gray to white; rest of head gray. Black chin and throat, which forms a triangle and borders the cheeks. Neck, breast, and belly anthracite gray. Flanks, wings, and back fox brown with golden-yellow; the borders of the primaries and secondaries are dark with a greenish hue; inside blackish brown. Eyes red brown, beak black, feet dark pinkish. Both male and female are alike in coloration. Length: 4½ in. (11.5 cm).

Distribution and habitat: From Gambia through Nigeria, Cameroon to southern Sudan, Uganda and northern Zaire, in pairs or small family groups; in woods, swamps, savannas, and in thick bushes and groups of high trees in parks and large gardens. The birds hang on branches in the same manner as chickadees and also feed the same way, holding fruits down on the ground with one foot. Nest up to 9 ft. (3 m) from the ground. The ususal clutch consists of 4 dull-white eggs. Breeding season lasts from July till October.

Aviculture: Was first imported to the Netherlands in 1977. Very friendly bird toward keeper and other small finches. First breeding results in 1982 recorded by Mr. Neutkens, a relative of the authors, although the young were reared by society finches. Later results were accomplished with the natural parents. Clutch, 3–4 eggs; incubation time, 15–16 days; both partners incubate the eggs, although the female more than the male. Young hatch after 15–16 days and leave the nest when approximately 23 days old. The fledglings will start eating millet spray and sprouted small seeds, including millet, canary grass seed, etc., when they are about 24–30 days old. The young are independent after about 3 months.

Food: Millet spray, millet varieties, niger, and canary grass seed can all be provided in both dry and germinated form. Also offer apple and similar fruits, cut-up small mealworms, white worms, maggots, ant pupae, and a good commercial brand egg food and/or rearing food. Provide bird vita-mins, minerals, cuttlefish bone, and oystershell grit throughout the year.

Other names: White-cheeked olive-back, White-cheeked olive weaver, White-cheeked wax-bill.

Genus *Oreostruthus* (mountain finches) De Vis, 1898

CRIMSON-SIDED MOUNTAIN FINCH *Oreostruthus fuliginosus* De Vis, 1897

DK: Bjerg Amandine NL: Bergamandine FR:Djamant des montagnes
DE: Bergamadine IT: Diamante delle montagne

Description: Male. Head, neck, back, wings, and upperparts dark olive-green; face lighter with more gray. Tail brownish black; underside of wings gray-brown with a red hue. Breast, flanks and belly red with dark olive-green wide horizontal bars; the same red on rump and upper tail coverts. Eyes and beak red; feet brown. Female is lighter with only vague barring on the flanks and breast; she is mainly light olive-green with a red rump and upper tail feathers. Length: 5 in. (13 cm).

Geographic variations:

■ *O. f. fuliginosus*, see above. Distribution: southeastern New Guinea, in the Wharton and Owen Stanley Mountains.
■ *O. f. hagenensis* Mayr & Gilliard. Lighter brown with a red hue on the upperparts; belly beige brown; under tail coverts cinnamon brown with reddish wingtips. Distribution: Mt. Hagen, and possibly other areas in the central highlands of New Guinea. This subspecies is somewhat smaller.
■ *O. f. pallidus* Rand. More brown than nominate form, and with less red on the belly than the previous subspecies; however, all red coloring is much brighter. Distribution: western New Guinea, north of the Oranje Mountains, and the Snow and Hindenburg mountains, Irian Jaya. Length: 5 in. (13 cm).

Habitat: This bird is a mountain dweller, occurring up to 10,000 ft. (3000 m). The species is extremely shy, and therefore difficult to observe. They live in pairs in thick bushes, on the ground, in light wooded areas, and along roads, looking for seeds and small insects. Bamboo seeds are their main food.

Aviculture: The birds were first imported in 1967 to the Netherlands, and have been irregularly available in Europe since then; unfortunately not longer readily obtainable in the US. They can best be housed in indoor aviaries at room temperature or somewhat higher, although we have had three pairs in an outdoor aviary with a connected night shelter which was heated to 73°F (23°C). This species is rather popular in Japan and Malaysia; most fanciers cover the bottom of the aviary with grass tussocks, reeds, and thick bushes.

Food: See Red-headed parrotfinch (page 248).

Other names: Red-sided mountain finch, Mountain firetail.

Genus *Spermophaga* (bluebills) Swainson, 1837

GRANT'S BLUEBILL *Spermophaga poliogenys* Ogilvie-Grant, 1906

DK: Grants Frøknaekker NL: Grant's blauwsnavelastrild FR: Loxie de Grant
DE: Grantsamenknacker IT: Becco azzurro di Grant

Description: The male has a red face, breast, back, and upper tail coverts as well as tail; the rest of the feathers are black. The strong blue-gray beak has a red tip; feet light brown-gray. The female is black with white spots on the underparts; the chin and breast are red. Length: 5–5½ in. (13–14 cm).

Distribution and habitat: central and northeastern Zaire, in forest undergrowth and woodland.

Aviculture: Care similar to *Lagonosticta* species. Dr. Burkard imported a pair in 1962. Unlike other bluebills, this species is very devoted to each other, and pairs stay together through thick and thin. They like to sit close together on a perch, although they very seldom preen each other. This species is rather rare in aviculture.

Other name: Grant's forest weaver.

CRIMSON-BREASTED BLUEBILL *Spermophaga haematina* (Vieillot, 1805)

DK: Rødbrystet Frøknaekker NL: Roodborst blauwsnavelastrild FR: Astrild à gros bec bleu, Rouge-noir,   ▸ *photos page 106, 107*
Gros-bec sanguis DE: Rotbrust-Samenknacker, Rotbrüstiger Samenknacker IT: Becco azurro petto rosso

Description: The male is black with a red breast in the shape of a square, and red flanks, chin, and throat. Bill blue with red tip and cutting edges during breeding season. Legs and feet, brown to blackish or olive; eyes brown or chestnut with pale bluish eyelids. The black parts in the female are more grayish, tinged with a reddish or orange hue; underparts with white spots. Young males show more red than young females. Length: 5–5½ in. (13–14 cm).

Geographic variation:
■ *S. h. haematina*, described above. Distribution: western Gambia and southwestern Senegal to southern Mali, Sierra Leone, Liberia, and Ghana.
■ *S. h. pustulata* (Voigt). Male differs from nominate race in having the red of the chin and throat extend to the ear coverts and lores. Uppertail coverts crimson. Females have less red on the forehead than the nominate form, with more red or orange-red on the face and uppertail coverts. Distribution: southeastern Nigeria, Cameroon, Central African Republic to Zaire and Congo, and northwestern Angola.

■ *S. h. togoensis* (Neumann). Males are intermediate between *haematina* and *pustulata*, retaining the black face of the former and the red upper tail coverts of the latter. Females resemble those of *pustulata*, with some variation toward the nominate form. Distribution: from Togo to southwestern Nigeria.

Habitat: These rather shy birds inhabit forest edges, dense thickets, and other damp, overgrown areas. They feed on or near the ground in low bushes and vines, eating insects, spiders, and seeds, including rice.

Aviculture: This beautiful bird has been known to aviculture since 1878. Imported birds are rather nervous and while in quarantine should be housed in a roomy box cage with only an open front. The cage should be "decorated" with a few fir branches. After a rather short period, the birds become extremely tame. Members of this species keep in constant contact with a sharp "zeeee, zeeee, zeeee, zip, zip, zip, shap, zeeee" call. When danger threatens, they warn each other with a sharp "tzec, tzec" ("e" as in "bed").

We consider these birds fine aviary residents; they do very well when the aviary is planted with thick bushes and such. Since they like to search for food on the ground, various feeding stations on the bottom of the aviary are necessary. They are very friendly toward other finches, although other species with much red in their plumage may feel differently about this friendliness, especially during the breeding season; firefinches and various twinspots often have a hard time!

The first young were hatched in captivity in 1879, but unfortunately died within a week due to insufficient food and low temperatures; the parents tend to leave the young unprotected for protracted periods, so they cool off quickly. Allow these birds to breed only in mid-spring. The nest is constructed mainly by the female, using materials brought by the male, such as dry grass, coconut fibers, and hemp fibers. Half-open nest boxes are often preferred. Both parents assist in incubating the clutch of 4 white eggs for 14–16 days, sometimes longer (up to 19 days). These birds should be left in peace while rearing young, particularly during the first three weeks after hatching. However, both parents should be watched carefully when the nestlings are 4–5 days old, as this is the time

they may leave the nest for rather long periods, allowing the chicks to chill. The reason for this behavior is still unknown. It is because of this that we recommend delaying breeding until later in the year, when the weather is warmer. Indoor breeding is advisable, with a room temperature of approximately 81°F (27°C). The young leave the nest when they are 20–23 days old. Young females will start molting at about two months of age, and the young males at three months. In both sexes, the molt takes about 6 weeks. Young males are particularly susceptible to cold during the molt, which manifests itself in diarrhea.

Live food such as ant larvae and white worms is especially necessary during the breeding season, as is a good egg food or rearing food. Small seeds, including grass and weed seeds, thistle seed, millet spray, etc., and commercial softbilled bird food are essential throughout the year.

These bluebills love to bathe. They prefer lukewarm water given in a large ceramic bowl. The water level should be approximately 2 in. (5 cm).

Other names: Western bluebill, Red-breasted bluebill, Blue-billed weaver.

RED-HEADED BLUEBILL *Spermophaga ruficapilla* (Shelley, 1888)

DK:Rødhovedet Froknaekker NL: Roodkop blauwsnavelastrild, roodkopkernbijter FR: Loxie à tête rouge
DE: Rotkopf -Samenknacker IT: Becco azurro petto rosso (same as for the Crimson-breasted Bluebill)

Description: Male, entire head and breast crimson red, extending to flanks; uppertail coverts darker red; remainder of plumage black. The female is similar, but reds are less intense and black replaced by slate gray, with numerous white spots on the underparts. Bill blue-gray with red tip and cutting edges. Length: 6 in. (15 cm).

Geographic variation:

■ *S. r. ruficapilla*, described above. Distribution: northern Angola and Zaire, western Kenya and Tanzania, Uganda and southern Sudan.
■ *S. r. cana* (Friedmann). Males have the black areas of the nominate race replaced by gray, even paler than the nominate female. The gray may

extend to the nape in some specimens. Primaries, secondaries, and flanks have brownish hue, and red areas are less intense. Bill purple with red tip and cutting edges. Females are paler than nominate race, with more barring than spotting on the underparts. Distribution: Usambara Mountains of northwestern Tanzania. This race is totally isolated from the nominate form.

Habitat: Forest edges, clearings, thickets, and overgrown cultivated areas. Prefer dense cover low to the ground in damp, but not wet, areas, up to 8000 ft. (2400 m). Feeds on or near the ground, on grass seeds and insects, especially termites.

Aviculture: This species is friendly toward other finches, and can be kept in an indoor or garden aviary. They are often rather quarrelsome toward their own kind. Imported birds are nervous, and have a tendency to fly against the glass, walls, and mesh. Therefore, keep their surroundings peaceful.

Pairs of this species do not keep in as close contact with each other as those of other bluebill species. During the breeding season the male tries to impress the female by carrying a blade of grass in his beak while making bowing movements in front of her. The female lays 4 white eggs; incubation lasts 16–18 days. The young leave the nest 20 days after hatching. Small insects should be provided throughout the breeding season, as well as commercial egg food and softbill rearing food. Small seeds and such, as for the previous species, are necessary.

Other name: Red-headed forest weaver.

Genus *Nigrita* (negro finches) Strickland, 1843

CHESTNUT-BREASTED NEGRO-FINCH *Nigrita bicolor* (Hartlaub, 1844)

DK: Brunbrysted Skovfinke NL: Bruinborst astrild FR: Nègrette à dessous châtain, Bengali brun ventre roux
DE: Zweifarbenschwarzling, Braunburstschwarzling IT: Negrillo del Bengali petto bruno

▸ *photo page 106*

Description: The male is dark wine-red with dark blue-gray upperparts, wings and tail. The female is duller and somewhat lighter in color. Beak black, feet dark gray-brown. Length: 4½–5 in. (11–12 cm).

Geographical variation:
■ *N. b. bicolor*, described above. Distribution: southwestern Senegal, Guinea, Sierra Leone, Liberia, Ghana, and southern Mali.
■ *N. b. brunnescens* Reichenow. Duller in overall color than nominate race, with upperparts tinged brown or gray-brown. Slightly larger than nominate. Distribution: southern Nigeria, Principé Island, Cameroon, western Kenya and Uganda, northern Zaire and northwestern Angola.

Habitat: Tropical forest canopies. They apparently are associated with certain palm tree varieties, especially the species *Elaeis guineensis*, and feed on their fruits, as well as on other small fruits, seeds and a large variety of insects.

Aviculture: Care similar to *Lonchura* species; mealworms and various pupae are essential. This species is rather rare in aviculture. During quarantine, and later during the breeding season, live food and small seeds are, as already stated, of great importance. The female prefers a nest box with a small, round entrance. In the wild, this species constructs round nests. Even two males or two hens will construct a nest, especially when the aviary includes live plants such as *Ficus benjamina* or *F. pumilla*. The normal clutch is 4 eggs. It is not known whether both partners share incubation duties, but most likely the female does the bulk of the brooding, as is the case with other *Nigrita* species. The youngsters leave the nest after 21–22 days. Small mealworms, whiteworms, and fly larvae are favorites! Greens and fruits, particularly berries, are also appreciated by these birds.

PALE-FRONTED NEGRO-FINCH *Nigrita luteifrons* Verreaux & Verreaux, 1851

DK: Hvidpandet Skovfinke NL: Bleekvoorhoofd astrild FR: Mgrette à dessous gris, Bengali negre à front jaune
DE: Blassstirnschwarzling IT: Negrillo del Bengali fronte gialle

Description: The male is light gray on the upperparts, darker to black around the eyes and cheeks, as well as in primaries and tail. The forehead is yellowish or pale buff. Underparts entirely black. Bill black; eyes red; feet and legs flesh colored to gray-brown. The female is much lighter gray, with gray, rather than black, underparts. Retains the yellowish forehead of the male, but dark coloration in the face restricted to the area around the eyes. Darker on the wings and tail. Length: 4 in. (10 cm).

Geographical variations:
- *N. l. luteifrons*, as above. Distribution: southwestern Nigeria, Cameroon, and Central African Republic to eastern Zaire and western Uganda.
- *N. l. alexanderi* Ogilvie-Grant. In this race, the pale buff or yellowish forehead extends further back to the crown and nape. The eye is black, instead of red. Slightly larger than nominate subspecies. Distribution: Fernando Po.

Aviculture: See Chestnut-breasted negro-finch.

GRAY-HEADED NEGRO-FINCH *Nigrita canicapilla* (Strickland, 1841)

DK: Gråhovedet Skovfinke NL: Grijskop astrild FR: Nègrette à front noir, Bengali nègre
DE: Graunackenschwarzling IT: Negrillo nuca nera del Bengali

Description: Male and female are both black with a silvery gray crown and upperparts, lighter, almost white, on the rump. Upper tail covers dark gray with lighter tips, tail black. The gray of the crown and sides of neck bordered by white. White spots in flight feathers. Beak black, eyes red, feet brown. The female has a more slender bill. Length: 5½–6 in. (14–15 cm).

Geographic variations:
- *N. c. canicapilla*, described above. Distribution: southern Benin, southern Nigeria, Fernando Po, Central African Republic, western Zaire and Uganda.
- *N. c. emiliae* Sharpe. Lacks the white border separating the black underparts from the gray crown and nape. Rump almost same color as back. White spots greatly reduced in number and size. Smaller than birds of nominate race. Distribution: West Africa, in Guinea , Sierra Leone, Togo and Ghana.
- *N. c. angolensis* Bannermann. Differs from nominate race having darker gray upperparts. White spots at tips of greater coverts well-marked. Distribution: northwestern Angola and southwestern Zaire.
- *N. c. schistacea* Sharpe. Similar in appearance to preceding subspecies, but the white spots on the greater wing coverts lacking or greatly reduced.

Distribution: northern Zaire, northern Tanzania, Uganda, western Kenya and southeastern Sudan.
- *N. c. diabolica* (Reichenow & Neumann). Upperparts more sooty; underparts dark grayish black. White spots at tips of greater wing coverts as in *angolensis*. Distribution: highlands of central and southeastern Kenya and northern Tanzania.
- *N. c. candida* Moreau. Resembles *schistacea*, but the upperparts are much lighter silvery gray. Distribution: mountains of western Tanzania.

Habitat: Primary and secondary forests, and forest margins and clearings. Prefers tall forests near water. Found up to 5000 ft. (1500 m) through most of its range. Subspecies in Kenya and Tanzania found at higher altitudes, from 5400 ft. (1700 m) up to 10,000 ft. (3350 m). Eats mostly fruit and oil palm husks, also, some insects, caterpillars, and seeds.

Aviculture: As for other negro-finches, but live food and softbill rearing food essential. These birds should be kept in roomy indoor or garden aviaries, as they are known to become sluggish in cages. The 3–4 white eggs are incubated by the hen for 12–13 days. Bengalese will serve as excellent foster parents for this species.

WHITE-BREASTED NEGRO-FINCH *Nigrita (Percnopis) fusconata*
(Fraser, 1843)

DK: Hvidbrystet Skovfinke NL: Witborstastrild FR: Nègrette à dessous blanc, Bengali brun à ventre blanc
DE: Mantelschwärzling, Weissbrustschwarzling IT: Negrillo del Bengali a petto bianco

Description: The male has a blue-black forehead, crown, and nape; the mantle, back, and wings are earth brown. The rump and tail are glossy blue-black. Underside entirely white. The female looks like her partner but has lighter upperparts. Eyes dark brown or dark red. Beak black, legs and feet gray. 4–4½ in. (10–11.5 cm).

Geographic variations:

■ *N. f. fusconata*, as above. Distribution: Fernando Po, Gabon, Cameroon, southeastern Nigeria, Angola , northern Zaire, and the Central African Republic to Uganda and western Kenya.
■ *N. f. uropygialis* (Sharpe). Differs from nominate subspecies in having the lower back and rump pale buff rather than blue-black, the brown shades much tawnier, and the feet and legs dark brown rather than gray. Distribution: Liberia, southeastern Guinea, southern Ghana, and southwestern Nigeria.

Habitat: Gallery forests, forest margins, and understories of forests up to an altitude of 4600 ft. (1400 m). Inhabits the forest canopy in pairs, family parties, or as singles. Highly insectivorous, but also eats some fruit and seeds.

Aviculture: This species was first imported by C. Webb for the London Zoo in the 1930s. Care is as for other members of the genus. Insects are essential.

Genus *Parmoptila* (antpeckers) Cassin, 1859

WOODHOUSE'S ANTPECKER *Parmoptila woodhousei*, Cassin, 1859

DK: Myrefinke NL: Mierenpikker FR: Astrild formilier DE: Ameisenpicker,,
IT: Astrilde di Woodhousei, Formichierer di Woodhousei

Description: The male has a rust-brown face; underside whitish with small brown triangular-shaped dots. Upperparts dark brown, feathers with lighter tips and shaft streaks. The female is duller overall, the reddish face replaced by warm brown. Young birds similar to female, but underparts reddish brown; thighs and under tail coverts buffy. Beak black, feet light brown to grayish. Length: 4¼ in. (11 cm).

Geographic variations:

■ *P. w. woodhousei*, as above. Distribution: western and central Zaire northward through the Central African Republic, Cameroon, and southeastern Nigeria.
■ *P. w. ansorgei* Hartert. More olive brown upperparts, usually paler than nominate form, with less red on the forehead. Larger than nominate species. Distribution: southwestern Zaire and northern Angola.

Habitat: Woodlands and forest undergrowth, edges of damp lowland forests. Very quiet bird, usually found in small parties or mixed species feeding flocks, foraging on or near the ground for ants and other small insects. Slender bill and brush tongue adapted for gathering ants. May also take small fruits and some seeds.

Aviculture: Virtually unknown in captivity. Should this species become available, consideration would have to be taken to its specialized feeding habits and diet.

Other names: Antpecker, Flowerpecker weaverfinch.

RED-FRONTED ANTPECKER *Parmoptila rubrifrons* (Sharpe & Ussher, 1872)

Only known under its scientific name

Description: Male, upperparts olive-brown with pale tips to feathers, flight and tail feathers somewhat darker. Underparts rich cinnamon. Small white spots on face. Forehead and forecrown bright red. Bill black; eyes red to red-brown; legs and feet grayish or brown. Female, lacks red on crown and forehead, which are spotted with white like the face. Remaining upperparts similar to male. Underparts entirely white with dark spots. Young birds resemble adult male, but with no red on forehead and no white facial spots. Length: 4–4¼ in. (10–11 cm).

Geographic variations:

■ *P. r. rubrifrons*, described above. Distribution: Liberia, southern Mali, and central Ghana.
■ *P. r. jamesoni* (Shelley). Males have entire face same color as underparts. Distribution: northern Zaire, western Uganda, eastern Congo.

Habitat: Forest margins, dense scrub and brushy areas. Forages in pairs, small parties, or mixed species flocks. Feeds basically on ants and other small insects, and a few seeds.

Aviculture: See Woodhouse's antpecker. This species is very seldom available. The female lays 3–4 white eggs. The incubation period lasts approximately 21 days. Small live insects and small seeds are essential throughout the year, but especially during the breeding period.

Other name: Red-fronted flowerpecker weaver-finch.

Genus *Pyrenestes* (seedcrackers) Swainson, 1837

CRIMSON SEEDCRACKER *Pyrenestes sanguineus* Swainson, 1837

DK: Karmesin Astrild NL: Robijn astrild FR: Gros-bec ponceau (à ventre brun)
DE: Karmesinastrild, Karmesinroter or Liberia-Purpurweber IT: Pirenete sanguigno

▸ *photos page 38, 107*

Description: Male, head, neck, breast, flanks, upper tail coverts crimson; nape, mantle, back, and wings earth brown. Tail brown with central feathers crimson and outer feathers edged reddish. Belly, vent, and under tail coverts dark brown. Bill large and steel blue to black. Feet and legs light brown. Eyes dark brown with prominent white eye ring. In the female, the crimson is less extensive. The brown of the mantle extends to the nape and hindcrown; lower breast, belly, flanks, and under tail coverts olive-brown. Eye ring yellow. Length: 5½ in. (14 cm).

Geographic variations:

■ *P. s. sanguineus*, as above. Distribution: Gambia through Guinea-Bissau, southern Senegal, southern Mali, Sierra Leone and the Ivory Coast.
■ *P. s. coccineus* Cassin. Slightly smaller with smaller bill. Female has less crimson, but shows a reddish wash in the flanks and nape. Length: 5 in. (13 cm). Distribution: Liberia, Sierra Leone, and the Ivory Coast.

Habitat: Marshy areas and thick growth along streams. Occurs in pairs or small parties, sometimes feeding in the open, often in company of bluebills *Spermophaga* spp.

Aviculture: Eats seeds, including relatively large, hard seeds. Female lays 3–4 eggs in a free grass nest or half-open nest box. Incubation: 16 days. Young leave the nest in 21–24 days. Half-ripe and sprouted grass seeds, especially seeds from spray millet, white worms, cut-up mealworms, and pupae of ants, flies, etc., as well as a good brand finch rearing and egg food are required for successful rearing.

BLACK-BELLIED SEEDCRACKER *Pyrenestes ostrinus* (Vieillot, 1805)

DK: Purpur Astrild NL: Purperastrild, purpervever FR: Pyrèneste ponceau à ventre noir, Gros-bec ponceau
DE: Purpurastrild, Purpurweber, Schwarzbauch-Purpurweber IT: Pirenete ostrino

Description: Male. Head, neck, breast, and flanks scarlet; lower rump and uppertail coverts crimson. Central tail feathers crimson, outer tail feathers edged crimson. Remaining upperparts and underparts black. Bill large and blue-black. Eyes red or reddish brown, with bluish eye ring. Legs and feet brown. Female has less extensive red areas, and all black areas of plumage replaced by brown. Length: up to 6 in. (15 cm).

Geographic variations:

- *P. o. ostrinus*, as described above. Distribution: Ghana, Ivory Coast, southern Nigeria, Cameroon eastward to Uganda and southern Sudan, southward to northwestern Zambia, Zaire, Congo, Gabon, and northern Angola.
- *P. o. frommi* Kothe. Plumage identical to nominate form. This and other subspecies have been separated on the basis of size, and on the size of the beak, which varies considerably even within the same geographic region. This subspecies includes birds that are larger in size with a more massive beak. Distribution: found in central Nigeria, Togo, Cameroon, Zaire, and northern Zambia and southwestern Tanzania.
- *P. o. rothschildi* Neumann. Rothschild's seedcracker. These birds are smaller than the nominate form, with smaller bills, but may be found in some of the same areas as the larger-billed forms. The exact status of the various subspecies is still uncertain. Distribution: southern Nigeria, Ghana, Cameroon, Zaire, Uganda, northern Angola, Zambia, and southern Sudan.

Habitat: Dense forests, forest margins, and clearings, sometimes in marshy areas. Feeds on the ground on seeds of various sizes, depending upon bill size, including the seed of sedges, as well as rice and other cultivated grains. Some insects and fruit are also eaten.

Aviculture: See Crimson seedcracker.

LESSER SEEDCRACKER *Pyrenestes minor* Shelley, 1894

DK: Lille Purpur Astrild NL: Kleine robijnastrild FR: Petit Pyreneste, Petit-bec ponceau
DE: Kleiner Purpurastrild IT: Pirenete minore

Description: Male. Forehead, crown, facial, and throat areas red. Rump, upper tail coverts, and central tail feathers red. Remainder of plumage brown. Beak black; eyes brown with white eye ring; legs and feet brown. Closely resembles female black-bellied seedcracker, but smaller, and with smaller beak. Female, similar to male, but red on face confined to forehead, front part of face, chin, and upper throat. Length: 5–5½ in. (13–14 cm.)

Distribution and habitat: portions of Tanzania, Malawi, Zimbabwe, and Mozambique. Occurs in both damp and dry forests and forest margins, *Brachystegia* woodland, dense thickets, and rank grass between 2300–6000 ft. (725–1800 m). Known to feed on rice and grass seed.

Aviculture: See Crimson seedcracker.

Genus *Ortygospiza* (quailfinches and locust finch) Sundervall, 1850

COMMON QUAILFINCH *Ortygospiza atricollis* (Vieillot, 1817)

DK: Agerhønerastrild NL: PatrijsastriLd FR: Astrild Caille DE: Rebhuhnastrild IT: Astro quaglia   ▶ *photos page 107, 108*

Description: Upperparts mottled gray-brown. Forehead and cheeks black. White chin and areas around the eyes. Throat black. Underparts grayish with black and white bars. Abdomen yellowish brown. Eyes brown with usually a white periophthalmic ring and lores, beak red, legs brownish. The female is duller and has small brown bars on the head. Length: 3½ in. (9 cm).

Geographic variation:

■ *O. a. atricollis*, as above. West African quailfinch. Distribution: Senegal, Gambia, Mali, northern Guinea and northern Ghana, portions of Nigeria, and northern Cameroon.

■ *O. a. ansorgei* Ogilvie-Grant. Darker than nominate form; throat color runs into color of the breast; center of the latter has a chestnut-brown spot. Clear white and black wave-design. Slightly larger than nominate. Length: 4 in. (10 cm). Distribution: Guinea-Bissau through Sierra Leone to Liberia.

■ *O. a. ugandae* van Someren. More gray on upperparts and darker than the nominate form. Throat and small eye ring whitish. Eye ring may be absent in some specimens. Distribution: northeastern Zaire and southeastern Sudan through northern and eastern Uganda to western Kenya.

The three races described above are sometimes referred to as partridge quailfinches; the following four races are merely called quailfinches.

■ *O. a. fuscocrissa* Heuglin. Similar to next subspecies, but with darker, warmer upperparts; delicate white wavy design with brown center on the breast. Slightly larger than previous races. Length:

4–4½ in. (10–11 cm). Distribution: Ethiopia southward to northern Kenya.

■ *O. a. muelleri* Zedlitz. Similar to *atricollis*, but a broader eye ring, large thin spots; the spots on the upper parts, flanks and the beginning of the breast are more pronounced; center of breast chestnut brown; underparts bright yellowish brown. Length: 4 in. (10 cm). Distribution: This subspecies occupies by far the largest area in Africa of all the quailfinches, from southern Kenya through northeastern and southwestern Tanzania, through northern Malawi and Zambia, and from there to northern Botswana, southern Angola and northern Namibia, through Zimbabwe, eastern Botswana, the southern corner of Mozambique and through the eastern part of South Africa.

■ *O. a. smithersi* Benson. Has the longest spots on the upperside of all subspecies, and is the darkest as well. The white wave design is duller than in the nominate form. Distribution: northern Zambia to eastern and central Angola.

■ *O. a. pallida* Roberts. Much lighter than *muelleri*, with more gray on the upperparts. Underparts lighter to white. Distribution: northern Botswana, and western Zimbabwe.

The following three races are often separated and given full specific status under the name black-chinned quailfinch, or red-billed quailfinch *Ortygospiza gabonensis*. We prefer at this time to retain them as subspecies of *O. atricollis*.

■ *O. a. gabonensis* Lynes. Black-chinned quailfinch. Rather similar to *atricollis*, but without the white chin, hence the common name. Brown cheeks, duller underparts, and lighter brown upperparts. Clear wave-design from the crown to the small secondaries. Length: 4 in. (10 cm). Distribution: southwestern Cameroon through Gabon and the Congo.

■ *O. a. fuscata* W. Sclater. A very dark colored bird; the wave design on the back, neck, and wings is barely visible. Larger stripes at the beginning of the breast, on the flanks, and on the cinnamon-colored under tail coverts. The last part of the breast is chestnut brown. Distribution: from Angola through southern Zaire, northern border of Zambia, and western Tanzania to Burundi. Length: 4 in. (10 cm).

■ *O. a. dorsostriata* van Someren. Colorwise, between the two previous subspecies, darker than *gabonensis* but lighter than *fuscata*. The female has no black on the throat and head. Stripe-design on breast and flanks rather vague and dull. Length: 4 in. (10 cm). Distribution: Ruanda, northwestern Tanzania to southwestern Uganda and eastern border of Zaire.

Habitat: They live in swamps, bogs, marshland, and other wet areas, but also in open grassland, including more arid tussock grassland, and cultivated farm fields, in pairs or small family flocks. During the breeding season in pairs. Feed almost exclusively on small grass seeds, supplemented by a few small insects or spiders.

Aviculture: Small, terrestrial birds, with short tails and strong, long legs. They have a whirring flight. The aviary floor can best be covered with various tussocks of grasses, patches of granulated peat moss, and such. The birds are rather delicate, and must have a variety of small seeds that should be offered in dishes placed on the floor. During the breeding season, live food in the form of ant pupae; cut-up mealworms, green flies, etc. must be available on a daily basis. The female lays 4–6 eggs in a little pear-shaped nest with a side entrance, situated near or on the ground under a grass tussock. Incubation: about 14 days. The young leave the nest after approximately 17–22 days, but will still be fed by both parents for quite some time. These shy birds often fly perpendicularly, so it is necessary to attach some soft fabrics against the inside of the cage roof.

Food: See above, as well as Bengalese, page 198.

Other names: African quailfinch, West-African quailfinch.

LOCUST FINCH *Ortygospiza locustella* Neave, 1909

DK: Rødvinget Vagtelastrild NL: Sprinkhaanastrild FR: Astrild locustelle
DE: Heuschreckenastrild, Rotfügel-Wachtelastrild IT: Astro quaglia ad ali rosse

Description: Male. Face, throat, and breast orange-red; orange patch on wings and red on sides of rump. Upperparts black or brownish black from crown through tail, with small white spots. Underparts blackish gray, with white spots usually on flanks. Bill reddish orange with black culmen; entirely red during breeding season. Eyes yellow; legs and feet light brown. Female more grayish brown on upperparts, with smaller white spots than male. Underparts buff or whitish, with sides of breast and flanks barred with black. Face brownish gray; no red on face, throat, or breast. Brownish orange in wings; sides of rump red as in male. Young similar to female but browner on upperparts, duller buff underparts, black bill, and dark brown eyes. Length: 3½–4 in. (9–10 cm).

Geographic variations:

■ *O. l. locustella*, as above. Distribution: Angola, southern Zaire, Zambia, central and eastern Zimbabwe, Malawi, southern Tanzania, and northern Mozambique.

■ *O. l. uelensis* (Chapin). Differs from nominate race in having no white spots on upperparts or flanks. Distribution: northern Zaire and southwestern Sudan, along the Congo River.

Habitat: Found in grassland and open woodland with grass tussocks, and abandoned agricultural land. Avoids dry areas. Lives entirely on ground. Forms large flocks in non-breeding season, but only found in pairs or family parties when breeding. Eats grass seeds almost exclusively.

Aviculture: Unknown in captivity, but should be treated the same as the common quailfinch.

Other names: Red quailfinch, Marsh finch.

Genus *Clytospiza* (brown twinspots) Shelley, 1896

BROWN TWINSPOT *Clytospiza monteiri* (Hartland, 1860)

DK: Brun Dräbe-astrild NL: Bruine druppelastrild FR: Bengali tacheté à ventre roux
DE: Brauner Tropfenastrild, Monteiroastrild IT: Gemello macchiato

▶ *photos page 109*

Description: Gray-brown; head somewhat lighter and grayer. Upper tail coverts red; tail black. Underside reddish brown, covered generously with white dots. Throat with a red spot in male, replaced by white in the female; the beak in both sexes is black, the eyes are reddish brown with a small blue ring; legs brownish flesh-colored. Young just out of the nest lack the throat spot, and are more subdued in coloring, although the breast is more intense in young females; the tear design not readily visible. Length: 5 in. (13 cm).

Distribution and habitat: The species has two disjunct geographical ranges, although no subspecies have been described. The northern population is found from southeastern Cameroon through the Central African Republic and northern Zaire to northern Uganda, western Kenya, and southern Sudan. The southern population is found in southern Congo through western and southern Zaire and the northern half of Angola. The birds tend to dwell in low bushes and on the ground, in grassland, savannas, parks, and gardens, often close to human habitation, in pairs or small family flocks. In the wild, the birds prefer using the nests of other birds, with repairs and alterations.

Aviculture: This species is suitable only for the more experienced fancier. Breeding this bird in captivity is very well possible and worthy of special attention. The best chance for breeding success is to furnish a roomy and especially quiet indoor aviary with live potted plants, including green tussocks, reeds, bamboo, boxwood, etc., and a low level humidity. Hanging a number of used finch nests in the aviary might stimulate breeding, as these birds, as noted earlier, often take over abandoned nests in the wild. On a number of occasions, a pair of birds had begun to build a nest and started to breed normally. Then, suddenly, without apparent cause, they abandoned the whole thing, frequently beginning a new nest elsewhere. We would furnish several half-open nest boxes hung at different heights on various walls of the aviary. For building material, provide soft grass and hay, small leaves, leaf veins, and especially, coconut fibers. For the rest, care and feeding of these birds should be the same as for the genus *Hypargos* (page 00). The female lays 2–5 eggs; incubation is approximately 13 days. Both partners incubate, the male during the day for short periods of time. He often brings a grass halm or a small feather to the nest.

Brown twinspots must be acclimatized with special care after arrival in a temperate climate. Done properly, there should be little difficulty. Be sure to keep them in a roomy facility at first, that is comfortably warm, without drafts and noise. Inside aviaries are, obviously, the best for this purpose. In winter, keep these birds indoors at a constant minimum temperature of 60°F (15°C). It is important at all times to keep the floor as clean as possible, as the birds like to peck in the sand for hours. Do tie some dry bushes and the like in the corners and at different heights along the wire mesh and wall; they love to hide there if they feel in danger or are too closely observed. When cared for properly, however, the birds become quite trusting and can be safely studied up close, except during the breeding season. They are fun to watch! They tend, as stated before, to stay on the ground a lot, where they move in little hops.

Food: See below.

Genus *Euschistospiza* (dusky twinspots) Wolters, 1943

DYBOWSKI'S TWINSPOT *Euschistospiza dybowskii* (Oustalet, 1892)

DK: Dybowski Dråbeastrild NL: Dybowski's druppelastrild FR: Bengali tâchete à ventre noir   ▸ *photo page 111*
DE: Dybowski's Tropenastrild IT: Astrilde ardesia dorso rosso

Description: Male. Head, neck, and breast slate gray; back and inside wings red. Wings dark slate gray; flanks black with white drop-design; underparts dark brown, upper tail coverts red, tail black. Eyes dark brown, periophthalmic ring red, beak black, legs gray-brown. Females are duller in coloration and have a gray-brownish hue on the underparts; the drop-design is more grayish. Young birds are generally grayer, and the red on back and rump is indistinct; the drop design is also absent. Both sexes have a pleasant song, consisting of tinkling, whistling and chirping tones; the female sings more softly than the male and her concerts won't last as long. Length: 4½ in. (11.5 cm).

Distribution and habitat: West Africa, from Senegal to Guinea and eastern Sierra Leone to the Ivory Coast. Also in Nigeria through Central Africa, northern Zaire to Uganda. The bird is an inhabitant of rain forests, where it lives close to water. It looks for food in low bushes and on the ground. We have seen this bird in pastures, and along not-too-busy roads near small villages as well.

Aviculture: This species is very well suited for large, well-planted indoor vitrines and aviaries. It must be acclimatized with care. The bird may be housed outdoors during warm summer weather, but belongs indoors in the fall and winter months, at a minimum temperature of 50°F (10°C). The bottom of the vitrine or aviary must be covered with grass sods. Due to its nervous nature, this bird is not suitable for cages. It usually comes to breed if there is enough choice in nest boxes and bunches of heather. The mating dance is almost identical to that of the African silverbill *Euodice cantans*; the male often waves to his future bride with a small feather or a blade of grass. The female lays 3–5 eggs; both sexes incubate the eggs, which hatch after 13–14 days. The young leave the nest when approximately 18 days old. After the young have

Euschistospiza dybowskii

left the nest, they will be nourished for another two weeks, primarily by the male. After about four months the young are fully colored.

Food: See Melba finch (page 172). It is important to remember that birds of this genus only take food from the bottom of their vitrine or aviary, and not from feeders hung against the wall. They prefer canary grass seed, as well as various small grass and weed seeds, both fresh and sprouted, a fine-grade insectivorous mixture, of which there are various reliable commercial brands on the market, white worms, cut-up mealworms, fruit flies, green flies, and small maggots. During the breeding season, animal protein remains essential.

Other name: Dybowski's dusky twinspot.

DUSKY TWINSPOT *Euschistopiza (Hypargos) cinereovinacea* (Sousa, 1889)

DK: Skiffergra Astrild NL: Leigrijze astrild FR: Astrild gris ardoise
DE: Schiefergrauer Astrild, Schieferastrild IT: Astrilde ardesia

Description: Head, breast, upperparts, and wings dark slate gray; flanks and upper tail coverts dark wine red; the flanks have a vague drop-design. Lower breast dark slate gray turning to black on the belly, flanks, and under tail coverts, with many white spots (drops). Rest of body black. Eyes red-brown with a reddish or bluish periophthalmic ring, beak black, legs gray-brown. The female is somewhat duller and the drops on the plumage are indistinct. Young birds are gray-brown. The song is similar to that of Dybowski's twinspot. Length: 5 in. (13 cm).

Geographic variations:

■ *E. c. cinereovinacea*, as above. Distribution: central and western Angola.
■ *E. c. graueri* (Rothschild). Darker gray and deeper red coloring; throat, breast, and underparts black. Purple or pink eye ring. The female is also darker than the hen of the nominate form. Distribution: eastern Zaire, Burundi, Ruanda, northwestern Tanzania, and southwestern Uganda.

Habitat: Often high in the mountains, up to 6000 ft. (1800 m) and more, in pairs or sometimes in small flocks; also along the edges of forests, in savannas and grassland, close to water. They look for nourishment in bushes and on the ground.

Aviculture: This is a bird for the expert aviculturist. The species must be housed in a well-planted indoor aviary with a constant temperature of 73°F (23°C). They are only allowed in outdoor facilities during really warm spring and summer weather. The birds were first imported to Europe in 1963, and two years later breeding successes were achieved. The birds are extremely nervous, and won'tt tolerate disturbances during the breeding season. Pairs like half-open nest boxes and bunches of heather, but will also breed in dense bushes, where they construct round nests from plant fibers, grass, wool, moss, small feathers, and little roots. The female lays 3–4 white eggs which primarily she incubates for 13 days. The young fledge after 19–20 days.

Food: See Dybowski's twinspot (page 167).

Genus *Hypargos* (twinspots) Reichenbach, 1862

PINK-THROATED TWINSPOT *Hypargos margaritatus* (Strickland, 1844)

DK: Perleastrild NL: Parelastrild FR: Astrild de Verreaux, Astrild rase
DE: Perlastrild IT: Amaranto rosa

▶ *photos page 109*

Description: Male. Entire face, sides of neck, throat, and breast pink. Upperparts brown, darkening toward rump. Upper tail coverts and lower edges of tail feathers pink; tail dark brown. Belly and flanks black with white spots. Bill black or gray; eyes dark brown with pale blue or pink eye ring; legs and feet dark gray to black. Female similar, but paler, with red of face and throat replaced by grayish buff, which extends through the underparts to the under tail coverts. Eyes dark, eye ring usually pink. Young resemble female but are duller, with reddish wash to rump area. Length: 4¾–5 in. (12–13 cm).

Distribution and habitat: southeastern Africa, from southern Mozambique to northeastern South Africa, in eastern Transvaal, Swaziland, and northern Natal. Inhabits woodland, along the edges of forests, and quiet roads, in pastures and close to small villages. They feed primarily on the ground, eating seeds and small insects.

Aviculture: This excellent vitrine and indoor aviary bird must be acclimatized with the utmost care. Only well-planted housing facilities, with a temperature of at least 50°F (10°C), are appropriate. In captivity, the nest is much larger than in the wild; it is domed and completely made from grasses, and lined with grass and small feathers; sometimes a little circular tunnel toward the top may be included in the construction. For further details see previous species.

Food: See Dybowski's twinspot.

Other names: Rosy twinspot, Verreaux's twinspot.

PETER'S TWINSPOT *Hypargos niveoguttatus* (Peters, 1868)

DK: Rod-Dråbeastrild NL: Druppelastrild FR: Amaranthe emflammée
DE: Roter Tropfenastrild, Peters Tropfenastrild IT: Amaranto fiammante

▶ *photos page 108, 109*

Description: Similar in general appearance and pattern to the pink throated twinspot. Male, forehead and crown gray-brown; face, sides of neck , throat, and upper breast crimson; rump and upper tail coverts dark wine red. Back and wings olive-brown. Tail red with black on the tip. Belly and under tail coverts black. Flanks black with large white spots. Eyes brown with a light gray-blue periophthalmic ring, beak steel blue-gray, legs dark gray. The female has a brownish head, and a red throat and breast; the underside is light brown-gray with little white spots. The young are much grayer than the female and lack the white spots. Both sexes have a pleasant song, but the female's is much softer and sometimes somewhat screeching. Length: 4½–5¼ in. (11.5–13 cm).

Geographic variations:

■ *H. n. niveoguttatus*, as above. Distribution: Mozambique, Zimbabwe, and Malawi.
■ *H. n. interior* Clancey. Lighter brown upperparts; lighter red in face and upper breast. Larger spots. Distribution: northern Zimbabwe, western Mozambique, southwestern Malawi through part of Zambia to eastern Angola and southwestern Zaire.
■ *H. n. macrospilotus* Mearns. Somewhat smaller. Warmer and darker crown and upperparts than in

Hypargos niveoguttatus

nominate form. Smaller and more sparing white spots. Distribution: eastern Mozambique from approximately the city of Beira north to southeastern Malawi and Ottansania to eastern and central Kenya.
■ *H. n. idius* Clancey. There is no visable difference with *macrospilotus*. The bird is somewhat larger than the previous subspecies, and the female has more red on face and in the form of stripes above the eyes. Distribution: northwestern Mozambique along the border of Malawi, northern half of Malawi, northeastern Zambia, western Tanzania, Burundi, Ruanda and southern Uganda.
■ *H. n. centralis* Clancey. Very similar to *macrospilotus*, but with more red coloring on neck and has

stripes above the eyes. Red coloring is mixed with the black on tail, breast, underparts, and under tail coverts. Distribution: northern Zambia through eastern Zaire to the border of Burundi. Length: 5¼ in. (13 cm).

Habitat: These birds can be found in dense bushes, in forests and woods, close to water. They operate in pairs and even occur close to human settlements. Their nests are built in bushes or on the ground.

Aviculture: This friendly bird, both to keeper and other small birds, must be carefully acclimatized at a temperature of approximately 77°F (25°C). After about six weeks, the temperature may be dropped to about 68°F (20°C). The birds don't withstand cold nights, and sleeping boxes must therefore be provided year round. During fall and winter they are best housed indoors at room temperature. When their facilities are well-

planted, breeding successes are very possible; they don't tolerate disturbances, however. Their free-standing globular nests, with a short tunnel, are constructed in a bush or in a half-open nest box of grass, vegetable fibers, and moss, then lined with fine grass and some small feathers. Clutch: 3–6 white eggs; incubation period 12–14 days; both partners incubate; nesting period 19–21 days. During the breeding season, a pair might sometimes be aggressive toward other finches.

Food: See Pink-throated twinspot and Melba finch (pages 168 and 172). A variety of small insects, such as white worms, cut-up mealworms, small maggots, fruit flies, and ant pupae, and a fine-grade commercial insectivorous mixture are essential throughout the year, but especially during the breeding season.

Other name: Red-throated twinspot.

Genus *Mandingoa* (green-backed twinspots) Hartert, 1919

GREEN-BACKED TWINSPOT *Mandingoa nitidula* (Hartlaub, 1865)

DK: Gron Dräbeastrild NL: Groene druppelastrild FR: Bengali vert tâcheté, Bengali vert pointillé
DE: Gruner Tropfenastrild IT: Bengalino verde punteggiato

▶ *photos page 110*

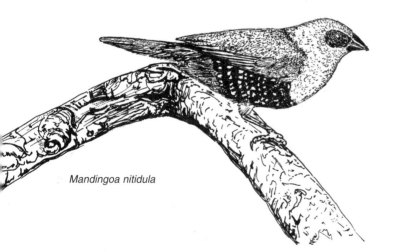

Mandingoa nitidula

Description: Red-orange face and chin; deep olive-green upperparts, wings, breast, and upper tail coverts; some olive-yellow on throat, upper breast, and neck. Olive-green under tail coverts. Blackish underparts with white spots. Eyes brown,

beak black with a red tip, legs brownish. The female is duller and has paler orange on the face. Length: 4–4 ¼ in. (10–11 cm).

Geographic variations:

■ *M. n. nitidula*, as above. Distribution: southeastern South Africa to southern Mozambique.
■ *M. n. chubbi* (Ogilvie-Grant). Chubb's twinspot. Somewhat smaller than nominate form, and more brightly colored. The yellow colors and hues of the nominate are orange in this subspecies; the red-colored face has a golden-yellow chin. A somewhat more slender beak than the nominate, with a red tip and red bill edges. The female has a similar colored beak. Distribution: eastern Africa, from southeastern Sudan and southern Ethiopia through Kenya and Tanzania to northern Mozambique, eastern Zimbabwe and Zaire.

■ *M. n. schlegeli* (Sharpe). Schlegel's twinspot. Somewhat larger than nominate form. Bright red face, throat and upper breast. Pronounced red tip on beak. The flight primaries have an orange-red trace. Some males have more yellow hues instead; in this case, this color variant has also a yellow beak tip. Distribution: western Africa, from Sierra Leone to northern Angola, western Uganda, and eastern and southern Zaire.

■ *M. n. virginiae* (Amadon). The red upperparts are more pronounced. Red beak. Females have red lores and red around the eyes; there is an orange hue in the upperparts. Distribution: Fernando Po.

Habitat: These birds live in small groups along the edges of forests and in thickets. Sometimes found up to 8000 ft. (2400 m) altitude. They feed on small seeds and insects, mainly on the ground.

Aviculture: Lively, hardy birds which feed mainly on the ground. A thickly planted aviary is necessary. They are friendly toward other birds, hence excellent for a community aviary. During the breeding season sometimes quarrelsome toward small finches. They use half-open breeding boxes in which the female lays 4–5 eggs. The young hatch after 13–14 days, and leave the nest 21–23 days later. The first few days, up to a week, they often spend the night in the parental nest. Sometimes young males can be observed carrying nesting materials at 2½–3 months of age. Recently imported birds, coming from Europe, for example, must be housed inside with a temperature of approximately 77°F (25°C). During warm, sunny summers they may be housed in garden aviaries.

Food: Grass and weed seeds, ant pupae and other insects should be available throughout the year. For more details, see Melba finch and Dybowski twinspot (pages 172 and 167).

Other name: Green twinspot.

Genus *Pytilia* (pytilias) Swainson, 1837

AURORA FINCH *Pytilia phoenicoptera* Swainson, 1837

DK: Aurora Astrild NL: Aurora astrild FR: Pytilie à ailes rouges, Diamand aurore
Gem: Aurora-Astrild IT: Melba aurore, Melba ali rosse

▶ *photo page 111*

Description: Ashy-gray upperparts. The somewhat lighter gray head has dark gray streaks and crown. Rump, wings, and upper tail coverts are crimson; central tail feathers crimson also, with brown borders; rest of the tail blackish. Underside dark gray with little white horizontal bars. The female is browner, often lacks all the red but has usually many more white markings on throat, belly, and breast than the male. Eyes brown, beak black or steel gray, legs light red-brown, much lighter in the female. Length: 4¾ in. (12 cm).

Geographic variations:

■ *P. p. phoenicoptera*, as above. Distribution: parts of Senegal, Gambia, Guinea-Bissau, Guinea, Ivory Coast, Ghana, Nigeria, Cameroon, Central African Republic, northern Zaire to northern Uganda, and southern Sudan.

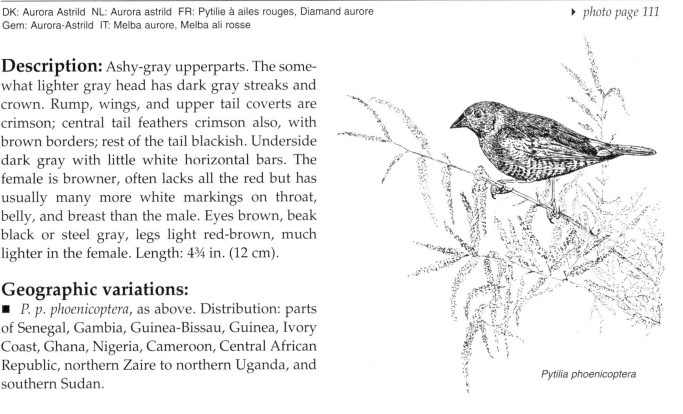

Pytilia phoenicoptera

■ *P. p. lineata* Heuglin. Red-billed aurora finch or Abyssinian aurora finch. This subspecies is somewhat larger in size, and has a red beak; in general, lighter gray in color with more pronounced barring on the underparts than the nominate form. This race is sometimes considered a separate species. Distribution: central and western Ethiopia and bordering Sudan and Kenya.

Habitat: Found in dry savannas, in bushes and tall grass, close to small villages in parks and gardens. They live on insects and seeds. This species is the brood host to the Togo paradise whydah *Vidua (Steganura) togoensis* and the Congo, or long-tailed, paradise whydah *V. (S.) interjecta*. They build untidy, large grass nests which they line with dry grass and some flowering heads. Mostly found in pairs high up in trees as well as on the ground.

Aviculture: These beautiful birds are suitable for cages and aviaries, although the temperature must not fall below 68°F (20°C). Therefore, a pair can best be kept in an indoor, well-planted aviary with other finches. During the breeding season,

they protect their nest very aggressively. The nest is built free in a thick bush, in a dried grass tussock, but some pairs will also use a canary nest pan or nest box. The nest is constructed from grass, hay, coconut fibers, small feathers, etc. Feathers are usually used for lining the inside of the nest, both in captivity and in the wild. A pair breeds well, although they do not like to be disturbed. They are rather peaceful and differ much in behavior in comparison to the melba finch *Pytilia melba* and the orange-winged pytilia *P. afra*.

The male sings a soft, pleasant song practically all day long. In the breeding season, the cock dances around the female with a beautiful raised tail and bowing head.

The hen lays 3–4 eggs; the incubation time is 12 days. About 20 days after hatching, the dark-skinned young leave the nest. After approximately eight weeks, they will have their first molt.

Food: See Melba finch, below.

Other names: Crimson-winged waxbill or pytilia, Aurora waxbill, Red-winged finch (*lineata*).

MELBA FINCH *Pytilia melba* (Linnaeus, 1758)

DK: Broget Astrild NL: Bonte astrild FR: Beau-marquet, Elégante
DE: Buntastrild IT: Melbo

▸ *photos page 111*

Pytilia melba

Description: Upper breast, throat, chin, and forehead scarlet; rest of head gray. Wings and back olive green; rump red; tail red-edged and blackish; upper tail coverts red. Chest olive to golden yellow. Underside gray with many white, wavy, horizontal lines. Eyes brown, beak scarlet, legs grayish brown. The female is duller, lacks all crimson, and has no red in the mask. Length: 4¾–5¼ in. (12–13 cm).

Geographic variations: Two groups of subspecies are recognized, those with gray lores and those with red lores; all in all, some 13 subspecies.

Gray-lored pytilias:
■ *P. m. melba* (Linnaeus), as above. Distribution: from Cabinda through the Congo and Zaire as far

P. m. grotei

as Malawi, southwestern Tanzania, Namibia, and Transvaal, South Africa.

■ *P. m. damarensis* Neunzig. Somewhat larger. Male has a beautiful yellow upper-breast, a very pronounced cross-beam design but little or no white in the center of the belly, lighter on the under tail coverts. The female is light gray with a pronounced cross-beam design on the throat. Distribution: Zimbabwe, western Mozambique to southern Transvaal and the northern part of the Orange Free State (South Africa) through Botswana and northern Namibia to southwestern Angola.

■ *P. m. thamnophila* Clancey. Duller red an forehead and throat than nominate race; upper part of the breast dull yellow-ocher; belly dark with vague beam-design which is totally absent in the under tail coverts. Distribution: southern Mozambique, northeastern South Africa through Swaziland to Natal.

■ *P. m. grotei* Reichenow. Similar to previous subspecies; upper part of breast greenish yellow; under tail coverts white without beam-design. Females have barred design in the throat area as well. Distribution: northeastern Mozambique and eastern Tanzania.

■ *P. m. percivali* Van Someren. Very similar to the subspecies *jubaensis*, except for the red lores of the latter; most belly area and under tail coverts white. The barred design is rather broad on breast and flanks; throat yellow. Distribution: Tanzania and Kenya.

■ *P. m. jessei* Shelley. Very dull coloration; olive-green upperparts. Barred design is thin and close together; gray-brown. Somewhat larger design on the under tail coverts; the flanks have a more spotty design; the female lacks the barred design altogether. Distribution: northern Ethiopia (Eritrea).

■ *P. m. belli* Ogilvie-Grant. Yellowish red throat; not much white in the belly area; intense barred design, even on the under tail coverts. The latter makes it possible to distinguish this subspecies from *P. m. grotei*. However, the female doesn't have the barred design on the throat. Distribution: northwestern Tanzania, Uganda, southwestern Sudan, and northeastern Zaire, as well as Ruanda and Burundi.

Red-lored pytilias:

■ *P. m. citerior* Strickland. Head red; throat with yellow, becoming rather bright on the upper-breast. Upperparts dull yellowish green; dull barred design; white under tail coverts. Gray barred design on female's throat; upper breast white. Distribution: From Senegal and Gambia through Niger, Upper Volta, Chad, and northern Nigeria to northern Sudan and northwestern Ethiopia.

■ *P. m. clanceyi* Wolters. Similar to *citerior*; but warmer yellow; upperparts are brighter than previous subspecies. Barred design more pronounced and gray-brown colored. Distribution: central Sudan, and to the east around the border of Ethiopia.

■ *P. m. soudanensis* (Sharpe). Face red; very similar to *citerior* and *clanceyi*. Throat yellowish green with some reddish hue. Primary feathers with red borders. Distribution: southwestern Chad and southern Sudan to eastern Uganda and northwestern Kenya.

■ *P. m. affinis* Elliot. Similar to *soudanensis*; red in face more pronounced; the red borders of the primaries are absent. Under tail coverts with clear barred design. Distribution: southern and southeastern Ethiopia.

■ *P. m. jubaensis* Van Someren. Similar to *affinis*; red borders on the primaries and secondaries are absent. Much white on underparts; no barred design in the beige-colored under tail coverts. The throat of the female is more pronounced than in *soudanensis*. Distribution: northern Kenya and southern Somalia.

■ *P. m. kirki* Shelley. Primary borders red, upper-parts like *soudanensis*; a reddish hue on the upper breast; breast deep gold-yellow, often with a greenish touch. Dark under tail coverts with barred design. Distribution: from Mozambique, southern Kenya, and the southeastern tip of Somalia toward the Tana River.

Habitat: This species inhabits thorny thickets and long grass, mostly near water. The birds live on small seeds, and termites and other insects, especially during the breeding season. This species serves as brood host to the Eastern paradise why-dah *Vidua (Steganura) paradisea* and three subspecies of the Northern paradise whydah *V. (S.) orientalis*.

Aviculture: After acclimatization at a temperature of about 77°F (25°C), and no green foods for at least two weeks, the birds can be housed in an indoor, well-planted, and sunny aviary. An outside aviary is suitable only during the hot summer months. This species is usually quite aggressive toward other birds, even outside the breeding season, so it is advisable to keep only one pair in a community aviary. The male has a soft, sweet song. These finches spend a lot of time on the ground, looking for small insects and spiders, seeds, and such.

They build a little domed grass nest low in a thicket or bush; seldom do they use a commercial wooden nest box. The inside of the nest is lined with small feathers. The female lays 3–6 eggs; both parents incubate the clutch for approximately 12 days and rear the black-skinned young, which are covered with dark gray down for another three weeks. It sometimes happens that couples, even

when they are well-adjusted to aviary life, throw 3–4 day old youngsters out of the nest, even when the food is right. The only way to prevent this is to offer a rich variety of insects and small seeds, and hope for the best. These birds are also very particular about rearing and egg food; therefore offer different commercial brands and see which ones are being preferred.

It is advisable to house only species without red masks together with the melba finch in a community aviary, as experience has taught us that red-faced birds will be attacked; star finches, for example, are one of the species they like to chase after; even injured birds are not safe. Neither will they tolerate their orange-winged cousins; they coexist, however, peacefully with smaller tropical finches like firefinches of the genus *Lagonosticta*, or waxbills of the genus *Estrilda*.

Food: A good commercial seed mix, with a rich variety of millets; also canary grass seed, spray millet and, especially, grass and weed seeds. Greens, including chickweed, dandelion, and spinach, are essential, although not all birds like it. Throughout the year a variety of insects, such as cut-up mealworms, white worms, small maggots, fruit flies, ant pupae, tubifex, spiders, and waxmoth larvae are necessary. Commercial rearing and egg foods are not always accepted by pytilias. During the breeding season, brown bread soaked in water, cuttlebone, crushed egg shell, and mineral block are important, and help to prevent egg binding. Vitamins and minerals should also be provided.

Other names: Green-winged pytilia, Crimson-faced waxbill.

YELLOW-WINGED PYTILIA *Pytilia hypogrammica* (Sharpe, 1870)

DK: Rødmasked Astrild NL: Roodmaskerastrild FR: Pytilie à ailes jaunes

DE: Rotmaskerastrild IT: Melba ali giallo

▸ *photos page 112*

Description: Very similar to the orange-winged pytilia. Rusty red face, chin, and throat; olive-yellow primary wing feathers; rest of wing somewhat darker. Rump and upper tail coverts red. Tail blackish, often with some red in the outer

feathers. Belly, flanks, and under tail coverts with thin white horizontal stripes. Beak black, gray on the base of the lower mandible; eyes brown, feet pinkish brown. There is also a red-winged variation, scientifically often named as *lopezi*. Females are duller and darker, and lack the red face-mask. The little white stripes start already under the chin. Length: 4¾ in. (12 cm).

Distribution and habitat: Confined to a

small evenly formed strip from Sierra Leone in the west through central southern Nigeria and central Cameroon to western Central African Republic, in pairs and small flocks; often together with other finch species, although very seldom found with closely related species. They live in tree and bush savannas, parks, large gardens, abandoned farmland and neglected cultivated areas near water. We have seen them feeding at the side of a road, especially in the early morning and late afternoon. They are rather silent but males can be extremely aggressive toward other males of the same family. When the birds are disturbed, they quickly retreat to cover in thorny thickets, long grass, or trees. They are almost entirely ground-feeders, except for hawking insects from a perch.

This species builds a three-layered nest in thickets or in dense foliage of low trees. The outer layer consists of blades of grass, the inside layer of stalks and stems, and the innermost layer of grass and small feathers. This species serves as brood host to the Togo whydah *Vidua (Steganura) togoensis*.

Aviculture: This beautiful finch is irregularly available but easy to breed in a garden aviary well-planted to bamboo, reeds, boxwood, etc. They thrive best at a temperature of about 68°F (20°C) and up. They are extremely peaceful. Both parents incubate the eggs, although the female incubates exclusively during the night, and both feed the young. Clutch consists of 3–4 white eggs which hatch after 12–13 days. They often use a half-open nest box or build a small round nest in a thick bush or grass thicket; offer coconut fibers, grass stalks, and the like, as well as chicken down feathers, which they will use to line the inside of the nest. Success can only be achieved when the parents have access to a variety of insects and other animal protein; if the parents don't have this food, they will refuse to feed their young and soon, after three to four days, throw them out of the nest. Sprouted seeds are also very important during the breeding season for both parents and young. Most pairs also appreciate green food.

Other names: Golden-winged pytilia, Red-faced pytilia.

ORANGE-WINGED PYTILIA *Pytilia afra* (Gmelin, 1789)

DK: Wieners Astrild NL: Wienersastrild FR: Pytilie à dos jaune
DE: Wienerastrild, Wieners Astrild, Sansibarfink   IT: Melba dorso giallo

▶ *photos page 111*

Description: Head with a striking red throat and mask which runs till behind the eyes; rest of head is gray. Wings and upperparts olive-yellow; primaries and secondaries sand brown with copper-red or orange-red borders. Underside has horizontally scalloped design with gray; rump, upper tail feathers, and first part of the tail red; under tail coverts with yellowish white crossbeams. The female lacks the red coloring, and the barred design starts on the throat. Beak and eyes red, feet pinkish brown.

Distribution and habitat: southern and central Ethiopia to Mozambique, and through Zimbabwe to Angola, Zaire, and Congo, in pairs

and family groups, but also solitary. Found in moist grassland, along forests, in large parks with high trees and undergrowth, always close to water. The birds build their grass nests in the second half of the rain season. The male has an interesting display during the breeding season. In order to impress his partner, he jumps over the female in a kind of leap-frog game (which can also be seen with Gouldian finches *Chloebia gouldiae*). The species serves as a brood host for the broad-tailed paradise whydah *Vidua (Steganura) orientalis*.

Aviculture: This rather peaceful species, which forages for grass seeds and insects on the ground, should be housed in a densely planted garden aviary with a temperature-controlled shelter kept in the 68–72°F (20–22°C) range, as these birds are very susceptible to temperature changes. The species builds their nest in a dense bush or half-open nest box. The normal clutch is 3–4 white eggs. Incubation time 12–13 days. The parents are very reliable brooders but do need animal protein to raise their young. According to Koepff, the fledglings are fed with more and more seeds as they get ready to leave the nest.

Food: See Melba finch (page 172).

Other names: Yellow-backed pytilia, Golden-backed pytilia, Red-faced finch.

Subfamily Amadinae

Introduction

The Amadinae is a large subfamily of the Estrildidae. Members of this group are usually dully colored, as most of them are inhabitants of dry steppe country. The African silverbill *Euodice cantans* and the Indian silverbill *E. malabarica* are good samples. Birds in this group are sometimes referred to as weaverfinches, as many ornithologists believe that they share a common origin with the true weavers. The cut-throat finch *Amadina fasciata* and the red-headed finch *A. erythrocephala* are apparently close in appearance to the ancestral weavers. Both species, however, have a poorly developed nest-building drive compared to the real weavers; these species prefer to use old weaver nests, which they sometimes reline, and often alter by making the entrance smaller. In the large communal nests of the sociable weaver *Philetairus socius* from southern and southwestern Africa, various finch species will raise their young in the nest chambers. Outside the breeding season, both the finch species and the weaver species can be found wandering around in large flocks in search of waterholes. The song is a ventriloquial purring which can only be heard at a short distance (H. Wendt).

Most of the weaverfinches belong to the genera *Lonchura* and *Munia*, the latter genus often merged into the former. These birds are found in southeastern Asia and New Guinea, and are characterized by a strong, dark colored keg-shaped beak. Their main feathers are sharply bordered black; dark brown and/or white areas with yellow or brownish-red edges on the tail. The tail itself has two or more central feathers which are usually pointed; therefore we refer to them as lancet-tailed finches, an obvious translation of the scientific name *Lonchura*.

The *Lonchura* members are all very acrobatic and chickadee-like, and will skillfully move up and down on vertical reed stalks and such. They usually live in huge flocks of thousands of birds that roost like starlings in trees, or preferably, in dense bushes, in contrast to most other members of the subfamily Amadinae, which prefer to spend the night in sleeping nests.

In *Grzimek's Animal Life Encyclopedia*, Volume 9, Wendt comments on the remarkable songs of the various *Lonchura* species, noting that in some species the song is not audible to the human ear. The movements of the beak are the only indication that the bird is singing, except near the end of the song, when a few soft, high-pitched tones can sometimes be discerned. It has not been determined whether other birds of the species can actually hear the songs, and if so, at what distances. It is speculated that some segments of the song may indeed be soundless, while the beak movements may serve as visual stimuli. Wendt further points out that all other calls of these species fall within the normal sound frequency range and can often be heard for considerable distances.

All members of this subfamily are known for their fast nail growth. Cage and aviary must have reeds and flagstones, so the birds can keep their nails worn short. "Sickle" nails develop if the birds' nails do not get sufficient wear. If perches and other types of roosts are too smooth and too thin, the ever growing nails will not be touching the surfaces and, if left untreated, can even grow into a long spiral. The answer is, as stated, to provide reeds and flagstones as well as perches of varying thicknesses, so that all parts of the toes and nails continually are coming into contact with a surface as the bird moves from one location to the next. Overgrown nails can be dangerous as they can catch in mesh and wire, and possibly cause the struggling bird to break a limb.

After fitting the aviary with a suitable variety of perches, the overgrown nails must be trimmed back to a manageable length using a sharp pair of nail scissors or clippers. To accomplish this, hold the bird in the palm of the left hand (if you are right-handed), restraining it with three fingers, while the thumb and forefinger are used to manipulate one toe at a time. Hold the toe so that the light shines through the nail and clip just below

the quick (blood vessel). If you clip into the quick accidentally, you must stop the bleeding at once with a styptic preparation, though if you are careful this will not be necessary. The clipped edge can be filed gently to a new point with a nail file.

Genus *Amadina* (cut-throat finches) Swainson, 1827

CUT-THROAT FINCH *Amadina fasciata* (Gmelin, 1789)

DK: Båndfinke NL: Bandvink FR: Cou coupé DE: Bandfink, Bandamadine IT: Gola tagliata   ▸ *photos page 112, 113*

Description: More robust in appearance than other estrildines. Male: light fawn; each feather marked with a small black edge. Underside chocolate; tail gray, throat whitish, with a pronounced red horizontal stripe; a dull cinnamon patch on the belly. The hen lacks the red throat band and the chocolate abdomen. Eyes brown, beak and legs light flesh color. Length: 4–5 in. (11.5–13.0 cm).

Geographic variations:

■ *A. f. fasciata*, as above. Distribution: south of the Sahara in both West and East Africa, from Senegal and Gambia through southern Mali, Niger, and northern Nigeria to Cameroon and Chad.

■ *A. f. furensis* Lynes. Somewhat paler in color and markings than the nominate. Distribution: central Chad through Sudan and northward to Ethiopia, then southward to northwestern Uganda and northeastern Zaire.

■ *A. f. alexanderi* Neumann. Back and wing coverts are grayer that in the nominate race; the underside and tail markings are much broader. Belly patch smaller. Distribution: Ethiopia (except the north and northwest), northern and western Somalia, southeastern Sudan, northern Uganda and northern Kenya.

■ *A. f. candida* Friedmann. Similar to previous subspecies but with a light sand-brown primary color. Distribution: northeastern and southwestern Tanzania.

■ *A. f. meridionalis* Neunzig. Light head; feather tips black. Upper- and undersides gray red-brownish without the brownish sand color. Striking black upper- and underside markings. The red throat band is bordered with white. Distribution: various areas along the east coast of Tanzania and Mozambique; also in southern Malawi, eastern and southern Zambia, northern and western Zimbabwe, and northern Botswana.

■ *A. f. contigua* Clancey. Almost identical to previous subspecies, but with less reddish brown, more sand color. The red throat band is bordered at the bottom by white. Dark wave-design. Distribution: eastern Botswana, southwestern Zimbabwe, southwestern and northeastern South Africa.

Habitat: The species lives in pairs or large flocks freely associating with weavers and waxbills (Brickell). They build their nests, which are spherical, of grass, moss, and various fibers in low bushes or thick trees; they also will use abandoned and even current weaver nests.

Aviculture: This charming bird is commonly kept by novice as well as experienced fanciers. The finch is easy to acquire, relatively inexpensive, and uncomplicated to keep in a roomy cage as well as in an aviary. In either facility, it can be brought to breed easily. Do be sure to provide this species with a steady supply of minerals and cuttlebone, since the hen is rather susceptible to egg binding. In general however, the cut-throat finch has a strong constitution. It has a soft, trilling song, performed with puffed-up neck and throat feathers, and often utters its summoning call, "chirp, chirp."

During the breeding season, these finches, unfortunately, tend to pester other breeding pairs. They visit other nests, causing a certain disquiet that may lead the owners to abandon their nests. Cut-throat finches have been known to steal building materials from other birds, which causes a great deal of consternation among those that are already incubating eggs or raising young. This behavior, by the way, is not restricted to birds in captivity; it is also common in wild birds. We have seen birds robbing the lining out of the nest of a red-billed buffalo-weaver *Bubalornis niger* and bringing it to another nest; rather often we saw cut-throats trying to enter occupied weaver nests, usually with success, and leaving with some lining or such. The species also likes to use old nests as roosting places. Usually the work of nest building is divided between the sexes, the male carrying material to the nest while the female arranges it. During the whole breeding process, the male will often carry a small feather to the nest. Their nests are always nicely lined with soft materials, like thin grass and feathers. In order to find this nesting material, they visit the nests of bird species which use soft lining as well, such as the lesser masked weaver *Ploceus intermedius*, the spotted-backed weaver *P. cucullatus*, the already mentioned red-billed buffalo-weaver, the sociable weaver *Philetairus socius*, and the red-billed quelea *Quelea quelea*. It is obvious that the cut-throat finch should have a constant supply of nesting material throughout the breeding season.

The female lays 4–7 eggs, which she incubates with the aid of the male for about 12–14 days. There are occasions where the female produces extra large clutches. We have seen nests with eight and nine eggs. If you encounter such large clutches, and you have obviously more than one female cut-throat, it is best to take a few eggs away.

During incubation, and this is essential, the birds need absolute quiet. We say this with emphasis, because if disturbed, they will abandon eggs or young sooner or later. After about a month, the young leave the nest and are then fed mainly by the male for another 20 or so days. The youngsters look a lot like the female at the start, although sometimes a little red or brown can be distinguished in immature males. After some 70–75 days however, they attain their adult plumage.

The late Carl Aschenborn, a well-known German aviculturist and author, cites an observation by Karl Neunzig, one of Germany's best known aviculturists/bird painters, which you can easily verify for yourself: in captivity, young males leave the protection of the nest only when they can be readily distinguished from the females by their first brown chest spots and red throat stripe. These features are, of course, not as clearly visible as in mature adult males. You will be able to get three to four sets of young from a breeding pair, so that 20 or more young in one breeding season are not unusual. The late Dr. Karl Russ cites a champion breeding pair that raised 176 young in three years without any break. We definitely don't recommend, however, that you try to achieve a record of this type. We mention this piece of information mainly to inform you, without any intention to motivate you to duplicate it. We would strongly recommend up to three clutches per breeding season, just to prevent egg binding.

Cut-throat finches are relatively cold-tolerant, once they have been acclimatized. However, they should always be kept in a separate cage or aviary. Females should be at least nine months to a year old before they are started into breeding. For nesting material furnish dry grass, plant fibers (agave), strips of bark (willow), small feathers and coconut fibers. This species is extremely partial to dust bathing in the aviary. This is not so strange as they behave similarly in the wild, where they take daily sand baths in their rather arid habitats.

Food: All varieties of small millet, canary grass seed, and similar seeds; also sprouted seeds, spray millet, green food, sprouted seeds, half-ripe grass and weed seed. Provide small cut-up mealworms, white worms, maggots, a well-established commercial rearing and egg food and other protein sources all year round, but especially during the breeding season. Some birds like fruit such as apple, pear, and berries, but a wide variety of greens is of the first importance! To prevent egg binding, supply the females with cod-liver oil and various vitamins and minerals. As stated before, cuttlefish bone is essential throughout the year.

Other name: Ribbon finch.

RED-HEADED FINCH *Amadina erythrocephala* (Linnaeus, 1758)

DK: Rødhovedet Amadine NL: Roodkopamandine FR: Amadine à tête rouge, Moineau de Paradis
DE: Rotkopfamadine IT: Amadina testa rossa

▶ *photos page 114*

Description: Somewhat resembles the cut-throat finch, but the male's entire head is crimson; the red collar is missing. Lores grayish. Back, wings, and upper tail coverts brownish gray; primaries and wing coverts with clearly visible beige colored spots; similar sized spots on secondaries and upper tail coverts, but blackish brown in color and with a white diagonal line. Throat, breast, flanks, and belly are light brown; the feather tips are white with blackish brown borders. Toward the belly and tail the brownish color changes gradually to beige; the under tail coverts have diagonal stripes. Tail feathers black-brown with white tips and borders. The female has a gray-brown head, and the underside is less intense, and presents a more sand-yellow impression. There is often some brown-red on the crown and nape. The white spots are generally smaller. Young males can be differentiated from the females by the red head feathers. Nestlings have a dark skin with some gray down on the head and back. The mouth markings in the corner of the beak are whitish; along the inside these mouth papillae are bordered by black; the inside of the upper mandible, the palate, has five rather large black papillae (grouped at 12, 2, 5, 7, and 10 o'clock) against a grayish black background. Eyes brown, beak and legs flesh-colored. Length: 5 in. (13 cm).

Geographic variations:

■ *A. e. erythrocephala*, as above. Distribution: northwestern Angola through Namibia, Botswana, southwestern Zimbabwe to Cape Province, Transvaal, and Natal, S.A.

■ *A. e. dissita* (Clancey). The red head color is darker and more pronounced; the upperside is grayer. The female is gray instead of sand colored as in the nominate species. Distribution: southeastern and eastern South Africa, central Botswana and northeastern Namibia.

Habitat: Found in dry open savannas in pairs or small flocks up to approximately 30 birds. Outside the breeding season they gather in very large numbers of more than 1000 birds. They build their own nests only by exception, preferring to move into an abandoned weaver nest, or to evict brooding weavers from their abode. They also build their nests in buildings, like the house sparrow *Passer domesticus*. These finches are colony breeders.

Aviculture: This species has become commonplace in aviaries in Europe, not alone because it breeds well. Like the cut-throat finch, this species is not a good candidate for the group aviary because it has the undesirable habit of visiting and destroying the nests of other birds, including those of its own kind! It is best to house a single pair in a separate, roomy aviary, breeding cage, or vitrine, with plants to provide privacy, so the birds can incubate successfully and in peace! The female is quite sensitive to disturbances. You can't afford to check on eggs or young, even with the utmost care.

Breeding pairs in captivity prefer a half-open nest box, as does the closely-related cut-throat finch, but we have noticed that they will take over and remodel nests of other exotic finches. A breeding pair may build a free-standing nest, which is roomy, almost without shape and often with a small entry way. It's worth noting that young males do not leave the nest until they have achieved some of their distinctive red head color, similar to the situation with cut-throat finches. Red-headed finches will breed only if they have been acclimatized at a favorable temperature, 68°F (20°C). In our experience, the best breeding results are achieved in a roomy box or breeding cage.

The usual clutch consists of 4 white eggs, though clutches of 3–6 are not uncommon. The incubation period is 13–14 days. Both sexes incubate. During the day the male sets longer than the female; during the night both parents are on the nest, although the male sometimes sleeps in another nest, or close by on a branch. After 23–25 days the young will leave the nest. They are able to reproduce after six months, but breeding should be delayed until the birds are at least one year old.

This species has hybridized with the cut-throat finch, and the hybrids are fertile. According to Brickell, the well-known South African aviculturist, this species has been taught to talk, although not as well as a parrot.

The species' voice is rather simple, however. Both lure and contact calls are a repeated "chirup, chirup, chirup", and "chilup" respectively, and are remarkably similar to the song of the house sparrow. When the sexes warn each other, they voice a loud "tech" (e as in bed); when upset or disturbed they often hiss. The song, which is performed with a slightly opened beak, sounds like a soft purring and chirping.

Food: Furnish a good commercial seed mixture with various small grains and millets, and for variety, ripe and half-ripe grass and weed seeds. Supplement this, especially in the breeding season, with insects, rearing food and egg food, small cut-up mealworms, white worms, maggots, ant pupae, lots of greens, sprouted seeds, cuttlebone, vitamins and minerals.

Other names: Paradise sparrow, Red-headed amadina, Red-headed weaver-finch, Aberdeen finch.

Genus *Munia* (munias and mannikins) Hodgson, 1836

Many of the species described below have seldom, if ever, been kept in captivity, and detailed avicultural data are therefore lacking. Should any of these species become available, they should probably be treated and fed in a manner similar to other *Munia* and *Lonchura* species described later in the chapter.

ALPINE MANNIKIN *Munia (Lonchura) monticola* De Vis, 1897

DK: Bjerg Sivfinke   NL: Berg rietvink   FR: Donacola des montagnes
DE: Bergsichilffink, Bergschilfamadine   IT: Donacola della montagnes

Description: Chocolate brown with black face, yellow upper tail coverts and black under tail coverts. Underparts whitish with a small black horizontal stripe over the breast, and black wave-design on flanks. Length: 5 in. (12 cm).

Distribution: southeastern Papua New Guinea (Wharton and Owen Stanley-kette Ranges).

Other names: Alpine munia, Eastern alpine mannikin.

SNOW MOUNTAIN MUNIA *Munia (Lonchura) montana* **Junge, 1939**

DK: Højlands Sivfinke NL: Blauwsnavel non FR: Donacole des hauteurs
DE: Höhenschilffink, Höhenschilfamadine IT: Donacola delle alture

Description: Similar to previous species but with a chestnut breast; the flanks have a more delicate design. Length: 4 in. (11 cm). Distribution: western New Guinea (part of Pegununga Maoke).

Other name: Western alpine mannikin.

BLACK MUNIA *Munia (Lonchura) stygia* **Stresemann, 1934**

DK: Hades Nonne NL: Geelstuit non FR: Nonnette noire
DE: Hadesnonne IT: Donacola nera

▸ *photos page 114*

Description: Black; upperside of tail with yellow feather borders; rump and upper tail coverts are also yellow. Length: 4 in. (11 cm). Distribution: southern New Guinea along the Fly River and around the city of Merauke.

Aviculture: First imported to Germany by Krause in 1981. Rather popular in Europe since 1985.

Other names: Black mannikin, Mountain munia.

PALLID MUNIA *Munia (Lonchura) pallida* **Wallace, 1863**

DK: Bleghovedet Nonne NL: Witkop rietvink FR: Nonnette à tête claire
DE: Blasskopfnonne, Gelbbauchnonne IT: Cappuccina dalla testa pallida

▸ *photos page 114*

Description: Very similar to the yellow-rumped mannikin (see page 187), but with a much lighter head and a mahogany-brown rump, upper and under tail coverts, and tail. Length 4 in. (11 cm). Distribution: Lesser Sunda Islands and southwestern part of Sulawesi. A local subspecies *L. p. subcastanea* (Hartert) has been described from the lower Palu valley in north-central Sulawesi.

Aviculture: Imported into Germany by Platen as early as 1879. Has been bred regularly in Europe since 1977.

Other names: Pallid finch, Pale-headed munia, Celebes munia.

ARFAK MUNIA *Munia (Lonchura) vana* **Hartert, 1930**

DK: Arfak Nonne NL: Arfak non FR: Nonnette de Arfak
DE: Arfaknonne IT: Donacola di Arfak

Description: Light chocolate brown; face whitish, breast, crown and neck gray-yellow; reddish brown underparts. Rump and upper tail coverts yellow. Tail feathers with yellow borders. Length: 4 in. (11 cm). Distribution: northwestern New Guinea in the Arfak Mountains (Vogelkop).

Other names: Arfak mannikin, Gray-banded mannikin.

GRAY-HEADED MANNIKIN *Munia (Lonchura) caniceps* Salvadori, 1876.

DK: Grahovedet NL: Grijskopnon FR: Nonnette à tête grise
DE: Graukopfnonne IT: Cappuccino testa grigia

Description: Gray head, neck and underparts. Upperparts dark brown with lighter primary and secondary borders. Rump, upper tail coverts, and tail yellowish brown. Length: 4 in. (10 cm). Distribution: southern Papua New Guinea (Bowutu, and in the Mount Victoria region). In addition to the nominate race described above, two other subspecies are recognized: *M. c. scratchleyana* (Sharpe), warmer brown on upper parts, crown usually streaky, underparts with buff tinge; *M. c. kumusii* (Hartert), paler above, darker below than nominate form.

Other name: Gray-headed munia.

WHITE-CROWNED MANNIKIN *Munia (Lonchura) nevermanni* Stresemann, 1934

DK: Nevermanns Nonne NL: Witschedel non FR: Nonnette à calotte blance
DE: Weissscheitelnonne, Nevermanns Nonne IT: Donacola a colotta bianca

▸ *photos page 115*

Description: Chestnut brown with lighter head and a reddish hue in the underparts. Length: 5 in. (11.5 cm). Distribution: southern New Guinea (Frederik Hendrik Eiland) and eastward over the border into Papua New Guinea to the Fly River.

Aviculture: First imported into Germany in 1973, and bred the following year.

Other names: Gray-crowned munia, Gray-crowned mannikin.

HUNSTEIN'S MANNIKIN *Munia (Lonchura) hunsteini* (Finch, 1886)

DK: Hunsteins Nonne NL: Hunstein's non FR: Nonne de Hunstein
DE: Hunsteinnonne IT: Donacola di Hunsteini

Description: Very dark brown with light gray scalloping on forehead, crown and neck. Red rump, upper tail coverts, and tail. Primaries and secondaries with reddish borders. Length: 4–4¼ in. (10–11 cm). Distribution: Bismarck archipelago. The nominate race is found on New Ireland; a second subspecies, *M. h. minor* (Yamashina), is found on the Truk Inseln and Ponape. Length: 4 in. (10 cm). Some authorities also consider the following species (New Hanover mannikin) to be a subspecies of Hunstein's mannikin.

Other name: Hunstein's munia.

NEW HANOVER MANNIKIN *Munia (Lonchura) nigerrima* Rothschild & Hartert, 1899

DK: Sort Nonne NL: Moeras non FR: Nonne des James DE: Mohrennonne, Schwarze Nonne IT: Donacola di James

Description: Grayish black with a red rump and upper tail coverts. Some red hue on the breast; wing feathers with reddish borders. Length: 5 in. (12.5 cm). Distribution: New Hanover in the Bismarck archipelago.

NEW IRELAND MANNIKIN *Munia (Lonchura) forbesi* **Sclater, 1879**

DK: Forbes Nonne NL: Forbes' non FR: Nonne de Forbes
DE: Forbesnonne IT: Donacola di Forbes

Description: Chocolate brown with black head and lighter brown somewhat scalloped underparts; under tail coverts black. Rump, upper tail coverts and tail yellowish brown. Length: 5 in. (11 cm). Distribution: the island of New Ireland in the eastern Bismarck archipelago.

Other name: New Ireland finch.

FIVE-COLORED MANNIKIN *Munia (Lonchura) quinticolor* **Vieillot, 1807**

DK: Femfarvet Nonne NL: Vijfkleurennon FR: Nonne quinticolore, Nonne à cinq couleurs
DE: Funffarbennonne IT: Donacola a cinque colori

▶ *photo page 115*

Description: Chestnut head with yellowish brown line-design on cheeks; lores, chin, and throat brownish black. The dark brown neck has vague whitish scalloping. Back and wing feathers dark reddish brown; upper tail coverts yellow. Flanks and thighs black; breast and further underparts white with some cream-yellow hue in the center. Length: 5 in. (11 cm). Distribution: Timor and other islands in the Lesser Sundas.

Other names: Chestnut-and-white mannikin, chestnut-and-white munia, Five-colored munia.

NEW BRITAIN MUNIA *Munia (Lonchura) melaena* **Sclater, 1880**

DK: Tykhovedet Sivfinke NL: Dikkop non FR: Donacole à grosse tete
DE: Dickkopf-Schilffink, Dickkopf-Schilfamadine IT: Donacola dalla testa grossa

Description: Male and female are similar in color. Head, back, upperparts, breast, lower belly, and under tail coverts black. Rump, upper tail coverts, and the edges of the central tail feathers copper-red. Upper tail dark red. Breast and belly light chestnut with a distinct black wave-design on the flanks. Beak dark gray, eyes dark brown, feet slate-gray. The beak of the female is somewhat smaller and duller in coloration. Length: 4¼ in. (11 cm).

Distribution and habitat: New Britain (island northeast of Papua New Guinea, in the Bismarck Archipelago) and Buka Island in the Solomon Islands; the latter population, discovered in 1981, may prove to be an undescribed subspecies, being somewhat darker than the New Britain birds. Found in grassland with bush growth, and even on the beach, where they search for little mussels. They operate in loose colonies, looking for grass and weed seeds. They also construct their round nests in grass tussocks and in low, thick bushes, from leaves, grass and such. There is no specific breeding season. As long as there is enough food, and the circumstances are right, the birds are willing to start a family.

Aviculture: Seldom available. A gentle but attractive bird which needs a quiet indoor aviary with lots of thick bushes and grass tussocks. At a constant room temperature, a pair will start caring for a family any time throughout the year, but allow only three clutches per season to avoid egg binding. The birds will take half-open nest boxes. The female lays 3–6 white eggs; both partners incubate for approximately 14 days. The young leave the nest after 17 days. For more details, as well as for food details, see Bengalese, page 198.

Other names: Thick-billed munia, New Britain

finch, Buff-bellied mannikin, Buff-bellied black mannikin. This species should not be confused with another species that also goes by the common name New Britain mannikin or munia, *Munia (Lonchura) spectabilis*.

GRAND VALLEY MUNIA *Munia (Lonchura) teerinki* (Rand, 1940)

DK: Sortbrystet Sivfinke NL: Zwartborstrletvink FR: Donacole à poitrine noire
DE: Schwarzburst-Schilffink, Schwarzbrust-Schilfamadine IT: Cappuccino petto nero

▶ *photos page 115, 116*

Description: Black head and breast. Neck and upperparts brown; upper tail coverts yellowish brown. Underside white; flanks with some black scalloping. Beak grayish white, eyes brown, feet dark gray-brown. Length: 5 in. (11 cm).

Geographic variations:

■ *M. t. teerinki*, as above. Distribution: central Snow and Oranje Mountains, and southern side of Maoke Mountains, of western New Guinea.
■ *M. t. mariae* Ripley. Darker than the nominate, especially regarding the upperparts and wings. Distribution: western New Guinea, on the northern side of Maoke Mountains; bordering the area where *teerinki* is found.

Habitat: Found in grassland, thick bush country, forest edges, parks and gardens, and up to 8400 ft. (2500 m) in the mountains. Little is known about the wild life and behavior of this species.

Aviculture: The nominate subspecies became rather popular in the late 1980s, especially in Germany. In 1989 H. Mayer, a well-known finch aviculturist and researcher, achieved the first breeding successes. The species is rather timid, but friendly toward other munias and small African finches. The bird likes to use a half-open nest box, but will also construct its own oval-shaped free nest from coconut fibers, grass, small feathers for the inside lining, moss, little leaves, and other plant material. The courtship display starts on a horizontal branch with the male holding a grass stem or other fiber in his beak. The clutch consists of 3–5 white eggs which will be incubated by both partners. Breeding commences after the third egg, and lasts for 14–15 days. The youngsters open their eyes when about 9 days old, and leave the nest when 21–24 days old. After fledging, however, they return to their familiar nest to sleep for the night, but will roost outside on a branch near the nest after approximately a week. At three months of age they start with the molt which will end in 4–5 months. According to Mayer, the young start to sing when 46 days old. It appears that males really like to sing a lot in front of their hens, who seem to listen with much attention. This species enjoys taking water baths during the day, especially during mid-morning.

Food: See Bengalese (page 198).

Other names: Grand Valley mannikin, Black-breasted munia.

CHESTNUT-BREASTED MUNIA *Munia (Lonchura) castaneothorax* (Gould, 1837)

DK: Brunbrystet Sivfinke NL: Bruinbrost rietvink FR: Tisserin à poitrine châtaingne, Donacola commun
DE: Braunbrust-Schilffink, Braunbrust-Schilfamadine IT: Cappuccino petto bruno, Donacola comune

▶ *photos page 116, 117*

Description: Head grayish brown with many light-colored markings; darker brown mantle and wings. Yellowish rump and upper tail coverts. Yellowish tail. Throat, chin, and face blackish brown. Breast white with a vague chestnut hue. Underparts white with black under tail coverts.

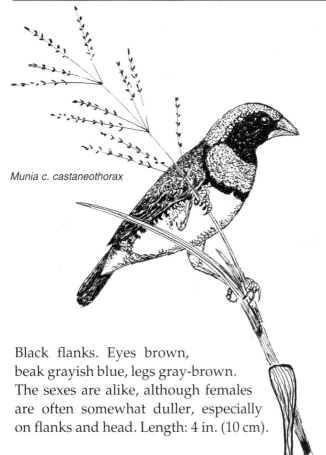

Munia c. castaneothorax

Black flanks. Eyes brown, beak grayish blue, legs gray-brown. The sexes are alike, although females are often somewhat duller, especially on flanks and head. Length: 4 in. (10 cm).

Geographic variations:

■ *M. c. castaneothorax*, as above. Distribution: Australia, from eastern Queensland through eastern New South Wales.

■ *M. c. assimilis* (Mathews). Not as many little stripes on cheeks. Breast chestnut brown; rump and upper tail coverts golden yellow. Distribution: Australia, in northern parts of Northern Territory and West Australia; also Melville Island and Groote Eylandt.

■ *M. c. ramsayi* Delacour (former scientific name: *M. c. nigriceps* Ramsay). Black head with white spots (tips of the feathers); black stripes on the flanks. Length: 4 in. (10 cm). Distribution: southeastern New Guinea.

■ *M. c. sharpii* Madarasz. Little chestnut-breasted munia (or finch). Forehead and crown whitish gray. Only some stripe-design on cheeks. Dark red-brown rump and upper tail coverts. Length: 3½ in. (9 cm). Distribution: northern New Guinea, from Astrolabe Bay to Humboldt Bay, and Manam Island.

■ *M. c. uropygialis* Stresemann & Paludan. Similar to previous subspecies but with lighter rump and

upper tail coverts. Somewhat lighter face. Length: 3¾ in. (9.5 cm). Distribution: limited to a very small area in northwestern New Guinea (Irian Jaya).

■ *M. c. boschmai* Junge. Dark head, dark brown breast, and light yellow upper tail coverts. Distribution: central Irian Jaya, up to 8400 ft. (2500 m) in the mountains.

Habitat: Their habitat is grassland, cane fields, reed beds, and along the coastal districts of northern Australia, where they live in sometimes large flocks. They often destroy whole cereal crops.

Aviculture: Rarely available in the trade, although various European aviculturists are occasionally breeding this amicable bird in well-planted (reeds!), large, outdoor aviaries with a variety of nesting boxes. Before the breeding starts, the male dances in front of his mate, drawing himself up to his full height, while hopping up and down on his branch or perch. This species is excellent for the beginner. There have in the past also been some successes in cross-breeding them with several other mannikins and grassfinches, including the striated munia *Lonchura striata*, the Indian silverbill *Euodice malabarica*, the masked grassfinch *Poephila personata*, and the zebra finch *P. guttata castanotis*. Again, we highly discourage the practice of hybridization.

Chestnut-breasted munias are pleasant, tolerant birds that never get into arguments and bear up quite well in most circumstances. They also need fresh bath water daily, and nail care, like all the other *Munia* and *Lonchura* species! The female lays 4–6, but often up to 8 eggs; the incubation time is approximately two weeks. The young leave the nest after about 22–28 days. The first few evenings, the male delegates his youngsters back to the parental nest, where the whole family spends the night. After about 3 weeks the young are independent.

Food: Small and medium size millets, spray millet, oats, grass and weed seeds, thistle seed, and buckwheat (fresh, sprouted, and germinated). Greens such as chickweed, dandelion, spinach, etc., and apples, pears and oranges. Throughout the year, but especially during the breeding and rearing period, ant pupae, cut-up mealworms, white worms, small maggots, egg and rearing food for finches, and brown bread soaked in water. Additionally, they should have cuttlebone, minerals, and vitamins. Daily fresh drinking and bathing water is essential.

Other name: Chestnut-breasted mannikin, Chestnut-breasted finch.

YELLOW-RUMPED MUNIA *Munia (Lonchura) flaviprymna* (Gould, 1845)

DK: Gul Sivfinke NL: Gele rietvink FR: Donacola à tête grise, Donacola à poitrine
DE: Gelber Schilffink, Gelbbrust-Schilffink IT: Donacola a testa grigia

▸ *photos page 117*

Description: Rump, upper tail coverts, and middle tail feathers rusty yellow; breast reddish brown, underparts brownish yellow. Back and wings chestnut brown. Throat white, crown grayish blue. Eyes dark brown, beak gray-blue, legs dark grayish blue. Length: 4 in. (10 cm).

Distribution and habitat: northern West Australia to the Northern Territory; in grassland, swamps and reedy margins, often in the company of the chestnut-breasted munia; cross-breedings in the wild between those two species are possible.

Aviculture: These very pleasant birds are somewhat easier to breed when three or more pairs are placed in a large, well-planted garden aviary. The female lays 5–6 eggs; the incubation time is 13–14 days. The young leave the nest after approximately 3 weeks. For more information regarding the breeding season and the food requirements, see Chestnut-breasted munia, page 185.

Other names: Yellow-rumped mannikin, Yellow-rumped finch.

WHITE-HEADED MUNIA *Munia (Lonchura) maja* Linnaeus, 1766

DK: Hvidhovedet Nonne NL: Witkopnon FR: Nomette à tête blanche
DE: Weisskopfnonne IT: Cappuccino dalla testa bianca

▸ *photos page 117*

Description: White head; upper breast, back, and wings chestnut; underparts black. Sexes are alike, but sometimes the male's head is brighter. Eyes brown, beak dark blue-gray, legs grayish black. Length: 4½ in. (11.5 cm).

Distribution and habitat: southern Thailand, the Malay Peninsula, and the Indonesian islands of Sumatra, Simeulue, Nias, Java, and Bali. Inhabits grassland, sometimes in enormous flocks. This species constructs nests in grass clumps; their nests are small and made from grass and vegetable fibers.

Aviculture: These birds are very much in demand around the world. Although the breeding results from these birds are only average, it is even-

tually possible that a pair will breed if the cage is in a very quiet and restful spot. There is a better chance of breeding if a pair is housed in a garden aviary; matings with society finches do occur often. Once a pair of white-headed munias starts breeding, you can expect the four to five young in about 13 days; after 25–30 days, the chicks leave the nest, but still take food from the parents for awhile. Their nail growth is rather fast and the nails should be carefully trimmed twice a year; a job that is far from easy (see page 177), but necessary. These birds must have fresh drinking and bathing water daily. This species can grow rather old; we have seen birds of 18 and 20 years of age!

Other names: White-headed mannikin, White-headed nun, Pale-headed mannikin.

BLACK-THROATED MUNIA *Munia (Lonchura) ferruginosa* (Sparrman, 1789)

DK: Sortstrubet Nonne NL: Zwartkeel non FR: Nonnette à poitrine noire
DE: Schildnonne, Schwarzkehlnonne IT: Cappuccino a petto nero

▶ *photos page 118*

Description: Similar to the black-headed munia (see page 189), and regarded by some authorities as a subspecies of that bird. However, only the throat and upper breast are black, unlike any other form of that species. The head and neck are white, more sharply delineated from the brown body than in the white-headed munia. Length: 4 in. (10 cm).

Distribution and habitat: Java and Bali; in reeds and tall grass. They build their nests in grass clumps. This species often becomes a pest in rice paddies, to the great annoyance of the farmers. Sometimes occur in surprisingly large flocks consisting of hundreds of birds.

Aviculture: An excellent bird for the beginner. The species, however, must be housed in a roomy aviary, as they quickly fall ill in small quarters. They are friendly toward their own kind as well as to other small finches. A pair regularly comes to breed, especially if it has company. Excellent results are achieved when three or more pairs are housed in the same aviary. Thick plantings of reeds, tall grass, thick bushes, etc. are necessary. The female lays 3–5 eggs which hatch after 14–15 days. The young leave the nest after about 24 days, but will return to their "cradle" for the night for at least another ten days. After six weeks the young are independent, and after six months look like their parents.

Food: See Bengalese, page 198.

Other names: Java munia, Java mannikin (see also page 196).

CHESTNUT MUNIA *Munia (Lonchura) malacca* (Linnaeus, 1766)

DK: Trefarvet Nonne NL: Zwartbuiknon FR: Jacobin
DE: Schwarzbauchnonne IT: Cappuccino tricolore

▶ *photos page 118, 119*

The chestnut munia is divided into a number of distinctive subspecies, several of which are much better known, especially in aviculture, by other names. The nominate subspecies, for instance, is the popular tricolored mannikin, or tricolored nun, of the bird trade, and the other subspecies are collectively known as black-headed mannikins (or nuns). For easier reference, we will name and describe the important subspecies as if they were separate species. As mentioned above, the black-throated munia *L. ferruginosa* is also sometimes considered a subspecies of this species.

TRICOLORED MANNIKIN *Munia (Lonchura) malacca malacca* Linnaeus, 1776

DK: Trefarvet Nonne (as above) NL: Driekleurnon FR: Jacobin (as above)
DE: Dreifarbennonne IT: Cappuccino tricolore

▶ *photos page 118*

Description: Head, neck, nape, throat, and part of the breast black; flanks and lower breast white; remaining underparts and under tail coverts black. Wing, back, and tail brown. Eyes dark brown, beak light blue-gray, legs grayish black. The white in the female is not as clear as in the male. Length: 4½ in. (11.5 cm).

Distribution and habitat: southern and eastern India and Sri Lanka. Found in grassland and cultivated areas, in sometimes large flocks.

Aviculture: This extremely strong and lively bird is excellent for the beginner. It is, however, far from easy to breed, but in quiet, large garden aviaries well-planted to reeds, corn, grass, and dense bushes it sometimes will use the deserted nests of canaries or other finches, and raise a family. We should leave a few flagstones on the aviary floor (see page 00) to act as "pedicurists," and keep their nails in shape and short. The birds will not tolerate inspections during the breeding cycle. Supply them with perches located high in the aviary, and offer them plenty of insects and rearing food for finches. The female lays 3–5 eggs; the incubation period is 13 days. The young leave the nest after approximately 20 days, but are fed by their parents for another two or three weeks. After six months the young are fully colored.

Food: As for the spice finch (page 193). Provide them with a variety of insects, cuttlebone, weed and grass seeds, egg and rearing food for finches, greens, and stale bread soaked in water.

Other names: Chestnut munia, Tricolored nun, Tricolored munia.

BLACK-HEADED MUNIA *Munia (Lonchura) malacca atricapilla* Vieillot, 1807

DK: Sorthovedet Nonne NL: Zwartkopnon FR: Capuchins à tête noir, Mungal
DE: Schwarzkopfnonne, Schwarzbauch-Nonne IT: Cappuccino a testa nera

▶ *photos page 118, 139*

Description: Head, upper breast, center of belly, and under tail coverts black. Rest of upperparts chestnut brown; reddish on tail coverts and tail. The lower breast and flanks, which are white on the nominate race, are warm brown in this subspecies. The sexes are alike. Eyes brown, beak blue-gray, legs dark blue-gray. Length: 5 in. (13 cm).

Geographic variations:

■ *Munia m. atricapilla*, as above. Distribution: northeastern India and southeastern Nepal,

Munia (Lonchura) malacca atricapilla

Assam, Bangladesh, Manipur, Burma, and north-western Yunnan province, China.

■ *M. m. rubroniger* (Hodgson). Feathers of back, upper tail coverts, and tail have mahogany brown borders, fading to yellowish gold with wear. Distribution: northern India and Nepal up to 6700 ft. (2000 m) in the mountains.

■ *M. m. deignani* Parkes. Upper tail coverts and tail feathers with light mahogany brown borders. Under tail coverts and belly brownish black. Somewhat smaller than *atricapilla*. Distribution: southwestern Yunnan, Thailand, Cambodia, Laos, Vietnam, and southeastern China.

■ *M. m. sinensis* (Blyth). Duller brown, especially the upperparts. Black under tail coverts; underparts brown with black belly. Distribution: southern Thailand through Malaysia and the Sumatran lowlands.

■ *M. m. batakana* (Chasen & Kloss). Like previous subspecies, but with even duller brown. The center of the belly is black. Distribution: the more mountainous areas of Sumatra.

■ *M. m. formosana* (Swinhoe). Formosa munia. Forehead, crown and neck brownish gray; face, breast and under tail coverts black. Some chestnut brown between breast and belly in the form of a small band. Distribution: Taiwan, and the northern Philippines.

■ *M. m. jagori* (Martens). Similar to previous subspecies. Brownish colored head feathers. Intensive chestnut brown belly and flanks. Distribution: the Philippine island of Luzon, except the most northern tip.

■ *M. m. gregalis* Salomonsen. Black forehead, crown and neck. Distribution: the Philippines, except Luzon; also Borneo, northern and northeastern Sulawesi, and Halmahera.

■ *M. m. brunneiceps* (Walden). Brown-headed munia. Chocolate brown with black forehead, crown and neck, chin, throat, and upper breast. Also rump and upper tail coverts are black; the tail with a red hue. Dark underparts and under tail coverts. Length: 5 in. (11 cm). Distribution: southwestern part of Sulawesi.

Habitat: All subspecies are found in grassland and cultivated areas, often in large flocks.

Aviculture: This is an extremely strong, lively, and excellent bird for the beginner. During the winter months, house all munias in quarters with room temperature. Care and management are the same as for the previous subspecies (page 189).

Food: See Bengalese (page 198).

Other names:
Chestnut mannikin,
Black-headed mannikin.

M. m. sinensis

GREAT-BILLED MANNIKIN *Munia (Lonchura) grandis* Sharpe, 1882

DK: Tyknaebsnonne NL: Diksnavelnon FR: Nonnetta à gros bec
DE: Dickschnabelnonne IT: Donacola a becco grosso

▶ *photos page 119*

Description: Black; wings, flanks, and back chestnut brown. Rump, upper tail coverts, and outer edges of the tail feathers ardent yellow-brown. The female is similar to the male, however, the base of the hen's beak is somewhat smaller. Eyes brown-red (some ornithologists state that the eyes of the female are much darker brown), beak silvery gray, legs gray. Length: 5 in. (13 cm).

Geographic variations:

■ *M. g. grandis*, as above. Distribution: southeastern and northeastern Papua New Guinea.

■ *M. g. ernesti* (Stresemann). Rump, upper tail coverts and the edges of the tail light yellow. Distribution: northeastern Papua New Guinea, from the Sepik River to the Astrolabe Bay.

■ *M. g. destructa* (Hartert). Reddish brown edging of the back feathers. Rump and tail feathers with straw yellow borders. Distribution: northern New Guinea and Papua New Guinea (Humboldt Bay).

■ *M. g. heurni* (Hartert). Deep chestnut brown, with light reddish brown edging on rump, upper tail coverts, and tail feathers. Distribution: northwestern New Guinea, between the Mamberamo and Taritatu rivers.

Habitat: Primarily a swamp bird, although sometimes found in grassland. They construct their nest from grass and other plant fibers, usually in grass clumps, but also in thick trees and bushes. Families stay together for a long time and can very often be found some 2000 ft. (600 m) high in the mountains near streams or small rivers. We have sometimes found four to eight nests in one tree. The nest is oval and often has still flowering grass and weed stems in its structure.

Aviculture: This very sociable bird is rather rare in aviculture; we saw the first captive birds in Switzerland in 1970 (Dr. R. Burkard). The birds are shy and like to hide in bushes and such. They like to use nest boxes but will construct their own nests as well. The clutch consists of 3–4 white eggs; the incubation time is 13–14 days. After 21–22 days the young leave the nest, but will sleep during the night in the nest for another 4–5 days. After two weeks they are independent, and four months after they have left the nest, they finish their molt. Care and management are similar to the other mannikin species.

Other name: Grand munia.

NEW BRITAIN MANNIKIN *Munia (Lonchura) spectabilis* Sclater, 1879

DK: Pragtnonne NL: Witbuiknon FR: Nonnette à ventre roux
DE: Prachtnonne, Weissbauchnonne IT: Donacola a ventre rosso

▶ *photos page 119*

This species should not be confused with the New Britain munia *Munia (Lonchura) melaena*, described on p. 184.

Description: Primarily black, except for the reddish, chocolate brown wings and upper tail coverts; the latter, and the tail, are edged yellowish brown; underparts white with some yellowish or brownish sheen. Eyes dark reddish brown, beak gray, legs dark gray. The sexes are alike, although the females are more delicate and their tails are somewhat duller in coloration. The male sings an almost inaudible song, similar to that of the spice finch. When the birds detect danger, they sound a high pitched "geeeec, geeeec" call. Length: 4 in. (10 cm).

Geographic variations:
■ *Munia s. spectabilis*, as above. Distribution: New Britain, Long, and Umboi islands.
■ *M. s. wahgiensis* Mayr & Gilliard. Upperparts chestnut brown; yellowish brown underparts. Upper tail coverts yellow. Distribution: northeastern Papua New Guinea (Wahgi river area).
■ *M. s. mayri* (Hartert). Similar to previous subspecies; upperside, however, rather light brown. Distribution: northern New Guinea (border of New Guinea and Papua New Guinea).
■ *M. s. gajduseki* Diamond. Intense chestnut brown upperparts; yellow under tail coverts and yellowish brown underparts. Distribution: Karimui area of central New Guinea.

Habitat: The birds operate in small groups, even during the breeding season. They feed on grass and weed seeds, and insects. The nests are constructed in dense bushes, in high grass clumps or in reeds.

Aviculture: Since 1970, irregularly available in the trade and through breeders. Excellent species for vitrines and large cages, but, obviously, best for aviaries. They are very friendly toward their own kind and other small species of waxbills and finches. In the wild, small family groups breed in the same tree or bush. Pairs often build sleeping nests, even outside the breeding season. For more details regarding breeding, food, care and management, see Chestnut-breasted munia (page 185).

Other names: Sclater's mannikin (or munia), Chestnut-breasted finch, New Britain munia, Hooded mannikin (or munia).

Genus *Lonchura* (mannikins) Sykes, 1832

WHITE-SPOTTED MANNIKIN *Lonchura leucosticta* D'Alberts & Salvadori, 1879

DK: Perlebroncefinke NL: Gepareld bronzemannetje FR: Capucin a poitrine ecaillee
DE: Perlenbronzemännchen, Schubbenbrust-Bronzemännchen IT: Cappuccino dal petto squamato

photos page 119

Description: Chestnut brown with whitish spots, especially on throat, upper breast, and wings; small stripes on head. Under tail coverts blackish; upper tail coverts and rump yellowish. Eyes dark brown, beak and feet dark silvery gray. Length: 4 in. (10 cm).

Distribution and habitat: In the southern parts of New Guinea and Papua New Guinea, between the Fly and Noord rivers; in grass, bamboo, reeds along the rivers, along the edges of woods, in gardens and clearings. Usually in groups of 100 or more birds. During the breeding season they split into smaller colonies and construct their nests in dense bushes and grass tussocks, from grass, little leaves, and other vegetable matter. The clutch consists of 4–5 white, somewhat oblong eggs (10.8 x 15.7 mm).

Aviculture: Excellent, peaceful aviary bird,

although somewhat shy in the beginning. When placed in an aviary for the first time, hang fir branches against the mesh and from the roof; this will offer them some privacy. Once adjusted to their abode, they will quickly come to breed in a nest box or free nest. The eggs will be incubated for approximately 14 days. For more information, see Chestnut-breasted munia (page 185).

Food: Small millet varieties, spray millet and a good commercial finch seed mixture. Especially during the breeding season, germinated and sprouted grass and weed seeds are essential, as well as animal protein, including various insects, egg food, etc.; green food should also be available throughout the year.

Other name: White-spotted munia.

STREAK-HEADED MANNIKIN *Lonchura tristissima* (Wallace, 1865)

DK: Sørge Broncefinke NL: Weduwe Bronzemannetje FR: Capucin triste
DE: Trauerbronzemännchen IT: Cappuccino triste

▸ *photo page 120*

Description: Both sexes are alike in coloration, as in most *Lonchura* species. Blackish brown with vague little whitish stripes on head and mantle. Yellowish rump and upper tail coverts. Light brown wingtips. Cinnamon colored crossbeam design in wings, back, and flanks. Length: 4 in. (10 cm).

Geographic variations:

■ *L. t. tristissima*, as above. Distribution: north-

western New Guinea, in the Vogelkop Mountains.
■ *L. t. hypomelaena* Stresemann & Paludan. Underparts much darker than nominate form; rump and upper tail coverts much brighter yellow. Distribution: central New Guinea, in the Weyland Mountains.
■ *L. t. calaminoros* (Reichenow). Colorwise, between both previous subspecies. Distribution: This race has by far the largest distribution, ranging from the whole southern part of Papua New

Guinea over the middle to northeastern of New Guinea, where it borders the range of *hypomelaena*.

Habitat: Found in grass, bamboo, reeds, gardens and parks, along wood edges, and up to 6000 ft. (1700 m) in the mountains. They usually operate in relatively small family congregations; outside the breeding season, however, they may form large groups.

Aviculture: Rather rare in aviculture. Kept successfully by the German finch expert R. Heff in 1981/82. Clutch 3–4 eggs. For care, management, and food see Chestnut-breasted munia, page 185.

Other name: Streak-headed munia.

SPICE FINCH *Lonchura punctulata* Linnaeus, 1758

DK: Muskatfinke NL: Muskaatvink, Muskaatvogeltje FR: Capucin damir Muscade
DE: Muskatfink, Muskatamadine IT: Domino

▶ *photos page 121*

Description: Head, throat, and neck reddish chocolate brown; back and wings dark brown; rump light brown; breast, flanks, and under tail coverts white, the feathers with brown edges (scaly); underparts light brown, and white on the abdomen. Tail brown, upper tail coverts dark brown. The sexes are alike but the male's beak is somewhat thicker and heavier; the head is larger and broader. The male also stands out because of the very soft song (see page 177), performed with the head held high and throat feathers puffed out. It is a pity that you can hardly hear anything of his song! Young birds don't have the scaly appearance. Eyes dark red-brown, beak steel grayish black, legs blue-gray. Length: 4½–5 in. (11.5–13 cm).

Geographic variations:

■ *L. p. punctulata*, see above. Distribution: India south of the Punjab and Assam; southern Nepal, Sikkim, Sri Lanka.

■ *L. p. subundulata* (Godwin-Austen). Browner on the upperparts in comparison with the previous subspecies. The scales in the design are larger in the underparts, and grayish brown. The rump doesn't show much scaly-design. Upper tail coverts olive-yellow, as well as the feather edges of the tail. Lower mandible silvery white. Distribution: Bhutan and northeastern India (Assam) to Burma and western and southern Thailand.

■ *L. p. topela* (Swinhoe). Chinese spice finch. Face-mask smaller and duller. Most feathers have a bright, small scaly design. Rump gray-brown; upper tail coverts and tail with yellow edging. Eyes are dark brown, not red-brown. Distribution: eastern Thailand, Cambodia, and Vietnam to southeastern China. Also found in Taiwan, and introduced in parts of eastern Australia in 1942.

■ *L. p. yunnanensis* Parkes. Similar to previous subspecies but with more pronounced and darker scaling. Upper tail coverts brighter yellow than in *topela*. Distribution: the southwestern part of Yunnan province (China), and northeastern Burma.

■ *L. p. fretensis* (Kloss). Pronounced reddish brown head. Close-set, stripe-like scaling on underparts and under tail coverts. Distribution: Malaysia, Sumatra, and surrounding islands.

■ *L. p. cabanisi* (Sharpe) (or *L. p. jagori* Cabanis). Brightly colored bird with intense red-brown stripe-like design on the underparts as well as on the rump; the latter is rather vague. Distribution: the Philippine Islands, and introduced on Palau Islands.

■ *L. p. particeps* (Riley). Duller and lighter brown; underparts reddish brown. Upper tail feathers and tail greenish gray. Distribution: Sulawesi, Indonesia.
■ *L. p. nisoria* (Temminck). Rather similar to the two previous subspecies. Rump brown with dark scaly-design. Upper tail feathers and tail gray. Distribution: Java and Bali (Indonesia).
■ *L. p. baweana* (Hoogerwerf). Like previous subspecies but duller. Scaly-design only on breast and flanks. Belly white; upper tail coverts gray-green. Distribution: Bawean Island (north from Java).
■ *L. p. fortior* (Rensch). Similar to *baweana*, but bigger. Length: 5 in. (12 cm). Upper tail coverts and tail have greenish yellow edging. Distribution: Lombok and Sumbawa in the Lesser Sunda Islands.
■ *L. p. sumbae* Mayr. More pronounced than *fortior*. Overall color and scaly design reddish brown. Under tail coverts with white wave-design. Upper tail coverts and tail bright yellowish green. Distribution: Sumba Island in the Lesser Sundas.
■ *L. p. blasii* (Stresemann). Larger bird with intensive reddish brown neck, head, and face. Very dark scaly-design on underparts, much darker than in *sumbae*; flanks black(!). Upper tail coverts and tail yellowish green to yellow. Length: 4¾ in. (12 cm). Distribution: Flores and Timor (Lesser Sunda Islands) and Tanimbar.

Habitat: Occurs in grassland, parks and gardens, rice paddies, reeds, and bamboo areas along rivers and streams, and along the edges of forests. Usually near human habitation. Feeds on rice, grass and weed seeds, and during the

Aviculture: This bird is practically always available in the trade. It was first imported into Europe in 1758. The species is modest in its demands and is suitable for garden aviaries and large cages and indoor aviaries. In the winter it must be housed indoors in a frost-free area, but this doesn't imply that this species cannot tolerate temperature zones. Experience has shown that, if the birds are given an outside aviary with a sturdily build night enclosure containing felt-lined nest boxes, which also serve as sleeping places, they can spend the winter outdoors. A pair builds a rather large, round nest in a thick bush; they seldom use nest boxes. The female usually lays 4–5 eggs, but sometimes as many as 7–10. Incubation period is 14 days. The hatchlings have a pinkish skin with light gray down on the upperparts, and some of the same on the head. After 3–4 days their begging cries are clearly audible. The first feathers appear after 8–10 days, and after another 1–2 days they will leave the nest, but will return for the night for the next 2–3 days.

For more details, see the various Silverbills. Cross-breeding (which we don't encourage!) is possible with, for example, Bengalese, silverbills, Java sparrows, and various munias. Hens have a tendency to suffer from egg binding, so careful monitoring is essential.

Food: We can keep the birds in excellent health by giving them a variety of insects throughout the year, as well as weed seeds and a tropical seed mix, some cod liver oil, and stale bread soaked in water. For more nutritional information, see Bengalese (page 198).

Other names: Nutmeg mannikin (or munia), Spotted mannikin (or munia), Scaly-breasted munia, Spice bird.

WHITE-BELLIED MANNIKIN *Lonchura leucogastra* (Blyth, 1846)

DK: Hvidbuget Broncefinke NL: Witborst bronzemannetje FR: Capucin à ventre blanc
DE: Weissbauch-Bronzemännchen IT: Cappuccine a ventre bianco

▶ *photo page 120*

Description: Forehead, cheeks, chin, throat, breast, flanks, upper and under tail coverts blackish brown; crown, neck, back, wings and wing coverts dark chestnut brown. The feathers of the neck and wing coverts have long, thin, white shafts. The dark brown tail feathers have rather wide yellow edging. Belly cream white with brownish spots on the sides. Upper mandible dark gray, lower mandible light ivory colored, eyes dark brown, feet slate gray (Bielfeld). Length: 4 in. (10 cm).

Geographic variations:

■ *L. l. leucogastra*, as above. Distribution: Sumatra, Malaysia, southern Thailand and southern Burma (Tanasserim).

■ *L. l. smythiesi* Parkes. Dark grayish brown upperparts with vague stripe-design. Upper tail coverts somewhat brighter. The race is larger than the nominate form. Length: 4.3 in. (11 cm). Distribution: northwestern Borneo.

■ *L. l. castanonota* Mayr. Upperparts chocolate brown with clearly visible stripe-design. Rump and upper tail coverts, face, forehead, throat, breast, flanks and under tail coverts dark brown; belly white. Yellow edged tail feathers. Length: 4 in. (10 cm). Distribution: southwestern Borneo.

■ *L. l. palawana* Ripley & Rabor. Dark brown, even the upper tail coverts. Bib brownish black. Length: 4 in. (10 cm). It is interesting to note that this subspecies has a more slender and shorter beak in comparison with the other subspecies. Distribution: northeastern Borneo, Palawan Island and other small islands in the Philippines.

■ *L. l. manueli* Parkes. Fairly dark brown coloration. Throat and upper tail coverts brownish black. Distribution: the southern islands of the Philippines.

■ *L. l. everetti* (Tweeddale). Chocolate brown with pronounced stripe-design. The tail edging is dull. Kind of fluffy transition between the brownish breast/flank area and the white belly area. Length: 4.3 inches (11 cm). Distribution: the northern islands of the Philippines.

Habitat: Edges of woods, thickets, gardens and parks, and even in the jungle, often far removed from civilization, in pairs or small family groups. This species breeds close to the ground in thick bushes and trees. Little groups stay together, sometimes using the same tree or bush for their round nests, which are constructed from grass, small bamboo leaves, and other vegetable matter. Clutch 4–7 eggs.

Aviculture: These very sociable, friendly birds

L. l. leucogastra

were at one time rather popular, but are not always recognized as a separate species due to their similarities with the black-throated mannikin *Lonchura kelaarti*, the Java mannikin *L. leucogastroides*, the Moluccan mannikin *L. molucca*, and the sharp-tailed mannikin *L. striata*. They are excellent cage and aviary birds. They like to construct free nests in low bushes, but usually settle for nest boxes of 6 x 6 x 6 in. (15 x 15 x 15 cm), which should be placed as close to the roof of the covered part of the aviary as possible. Provide them with grass, hay, vegetable matter, coconut fibers (their favorite building material), and such; the inside will be lined with small down feathers and coconut fibers. Clutch: 4–5 eggs; incubation 14–18 days. After 21–28 days the young will leave the nest; they will be independent in approximately 14 days. They finish their first molt when about three months old.

Breeding successes depend for a great deal on the availability of animal protein: cut-up mealworms, white worms, maggots, and commercial egg and rearing food for finches; also, germinated seeds are essential. For further information regarding care and management, as well as food requirements, see Bengalese, page 198.

Other name: White-breasted mannikin, White-bellied munia.

MOLUCCAN MANNIKIN *Lonchura molucca* **Linnaeus, 1766**

DK: Moluk-Broncefinke NL: Gestreept bronzemannetje FR: Capucin des Moluques
DE: Wellebauch-Bronzemännchen IT: Cappuccino delle Molucche

▶ *photos page 120*

Description: Head, upper breast, and tail black. Neck, shoulders, and back chocolate brown. Rather dark brown wings with lighter feather edging. Breast, belly, and upper tail coverts cream white with dense blackish wave-design. Upper mandible black, lower bluish gray; feet gray. Length 4.3 inches (11 cm). Females often have a lighter rump and back, a smaller, rounder head, and a more slender beak.

Geographic variations:

■ *L. m. molucca*, as above. Distribution: eastern Sulawesi, and surrounding small islands; also found on the islands of Buru, Ceram, and Halmahera, and the islands to the north of the latter.

■ *L. m. vagans* (Meise). This subspecies usually has a small white band between the throat and upper breast. The density of the wave-design is somewhat less, hence the bird gives a much lighter-colored overall impression. Distribution: southern Sulawesi (formerly Celebes), Alor, Wetar, the Kai Islands, and the Ceram-Laut Islands.

■ *L. m. propinqua* (Sharpe). An even wider white band between throat and breast, and less wavy design. Distribution: Flores, Sumba, Sumbawa, and surrounding islands.

Habitat: Inhabits grassland, rice paddies, gardens and parks, and along the edges of forests, up to 4000 ft. (1200 m) in the mountains. The birds operate in small family groups. Our experience with this species is that they were not afraid of humans at all, and came very close while we were feeding them seeds; they like to live in gardens and will stay if the owners will take care of them! They build their round nests in dense bushes or trees with thick leaf-canopies. But we also discovered nests in wall crevices, under roofs, and in climbing wallplants. This species breeds after the rainy season (March-May).

Aviculture: The species became rather popular in the early '80s, but was already known in Europe in 1879, according to aviculturist and author Karl Neunzig. The birds are very trusting, friendly toward other finches and mannikins, and come to breed easily, as long as they have access to nest boxes or dense bushes. Provide coconut fibers, grass, small leaves, and other vegetable material as building matter. The clutch consists of 3–7 white eggs (15.7 x 10.8 mm). Incubation time is 15–16 days. The youngsters leave the nest after 18–19 days, and will be independent in another 10–11 days. Fledglings are rather loud in their cries for food, especially after they have left the nest. Youngsters will end their first molt when approximately 4 months old.

Food: See Bengalese (page 198).

Other names: Moluccan munia, Black-faced munia.

JAVA MANNIKIN *Lonchura leucogastroides* **(Horsfield & Moore, 1856)**

DK: Java Broncefinke NL: Zwartstuit bronzemannetje FR: Capucine de Java
DE: Java-Bronzemännchen, Schwarzburzel-Bronzemännchen IT: Cappuccino di Giavo

▶ *photos page 120*

Description: Crown, breast, and throat black; belly white, blackish toward the tail. Cheeks, wings and back brown. There is a vague stripe-design on the wings. Under tail coverts usually light brown. Eyes brownish red. Upper mandible black, lower mandible gray. Legs gray-brown. The sexes are alike, but the male has a pleasant chirping, somewhat "purring" song. Length: 4 in. (10 cm).

Distribution and habitat: southern Sumatra, Java, Bali, Lombok, and introduced to the Singapore area; in high grass, reeds, and thick bushes, but also along the edges of forests, in agricultural developments, orchards, gardens and parks, and along roads, up to 5000 ft. (1500 m) in the mountains. Their main diet consists of rice, but during the breeding season various small insects and spiders are caught and fed to the young.

Aviculture: A friendly, quiet bird, suitable for large cages, vitrines, and aviaries. A pair usually builds a nest in a thick bush near the ground, although now and again half-open nesting boxes are used as well. The normal clutch is 4–5 white eggs, which are incubated by both partners for approximately 12 days. The youngsters leave the nest in 20–28 days, depending on the foraging of the parents. Animal protein is essential. After fledging, the young are still fed by the parents for another 12–14 days. When about 6 weeks old, the young start the molt, which lasts approximately 12 weeks.

Food: See Bengalese (page 198).

Other names: Javanese mannikin, Javanese white-bellied munia.

WHITE-RUMPED MANNIKIN *Lonchura striata* (Linnaeus, 1766)

DK: Spidshalet NL: Spitsstaart bronzemannetje FR: Domino à longue queue, Capucin domino
DE: Spitzschwanz- Bronzemännchen, Lanzettschwänzchen IT: Domino a coda lunga

▶ *photos page 120, 121, 122*

Description: Head, throat, back, and wings chocolate brown; cheeks, neck, flanks, and breast lighter. The face, throat, upper breast area, and neck have a vague bar (stripe) design. Rump grayish white with little brown bars; underparts white. Eyes reddish brown; upper mandible black, lower mandible light blue-gray; feet gray. The sexes are alike, but the male has a soft song, similar to that of the Bengalese. Length: 4½ in. (11.5 cm).

Geographic variations:
The seven recognized subspecies of *Lonchura striata* are separated into two groups. The first three subspecies constitute the white-rumped mannikins; the last four are the sharp-tailed mannikins.
■ *L. s. striata*, described above: Distribution: southern India and Sri Lanka.
■ *L. s. fumigata* (Walden). Very similar to previous subspecies, but lighter on face and breast. Upperparts duller than in *striata*. Neck feathers often with lighter edging. Distribution: the Andaman Islands.
■ *L. s. semistriata* (Hume). Clear edging, white belly and wave-design on the throat, neck, and upper breast. The back has some cinnamon brown feathers. Distribution: the Nicobar Islands.

■ *L. s. acuticauda* (Hodgson). This is the "real" sharp-tailed mannikin, considered to be the probable wild ancestor of the society finch or Bengalese (see page 00), together with the nominate *striata*. This subspecies has a strong brown wave-design on the throat, upper breast area, and neck, and cinnamon-colored feather edging. The same edging appears on the back feathers. Underparts cream gray; rump cream brown. Distribution: northern India and the southern Himalaya through northern Burma and Bangladesh to northern Thailand.
■ *L. s. subsquamicollis* (Baker). Upperparts darker brown in comparison with previous subspecies, and with almost no wave-design. The belly is deeper cream and blackish brown. Distribution: Burma (Tenasserim), southern Thailand, Sumatra, Laos, Vietnam, the Yunnan province in southern China, and the island of Hainan.
■ *L. s. swinhoei* (= *squamicollis*) (Cabanis). Lighter brown back. Reddish hue on the upper parts of the breast area and neck. Underparts with dark brown feather edging. Distribution: southeastern China.
■ *L. s. phaethontoptila* (Oberholser). A rather light colored subspecies with vague wave-design; often the underparts are all pure white. Distribution: Taiwan (Formosa).

Habitat: All subspecies have their habitat in grass and reeds, gardens, parks, orchards, along roads, and sometimes even close to human settlement. They are also found high in the mountains, up to 6700 ft. (2000 m), along the edges of forests and in agricultural areas; sometimes in large flocks in the rice paddies, where they are often considered a pest!

Aviculture: All the named mannikins in this section are friendly, suitable for cages, vitrines, and aviaries. When there are thick plantings or various nesting boxes, pairs often breed. The male dances around his future bride with ruffled feathers. The female lays 4–6 eggs; both partners incubate the eggs, which hatch after approximately 14 days. After about 21 days the young leave their "cradle," but return for the night to the parental nest. The young are independent after about two weeks, but they can't be put to breeding until they are at least 11–12 months old.

Food: All varieties of millets, fresh as well as germinated or soaked, especially in the breeding season. A rich variety of greens is absolutely necessary, as well as grass and weed seeds; for more details, see Bengalese (page 198).

Other names: Striated munia, White-backed munia, White-rumped munia, Sharp-tailed munia, Hodgson's munia.

BENGALESE or SOCIETY FINCH *Lonchura striata* var. *domestica*

DK: Magefinke NL: Japans meeuwtje FR: Moineau du Japan
DE: Japanische Movchen IT: Cappuccino del Japan

▸ *photos page 122, 123*

Description: This domesticated form, which is not found in the wild, occurs in various shades of brown and white, and there are even some varieties that have a little crest.

Aviculture: A gentle, friendly disposition and an aptitude for breeding and raising families, even in small spaces, has given this domesticated bird its alternate name, society finch. These characteristics have also lent the Bengalese its reputation as an excellent foster parent for more temperamental species.

Eggs from other birds, especially Australian grassfinches, can be given for adoption to society finches to reduce the risk of mishap. It doesn't matter if the eggs have been incubated by the original parents for awhile; in fact, Bengalese will not be upset if the eggs they are brooding hatch after they have been in their care for only, say, 5 or 6 days.

Even young hatchlings abandoned by their true parents can be entrusted to Bengalese for further care, if the adoptive parents have been raising young at more or less the same age and stage of development.

Foster nestlings should be returned to their natural parents once they reach adulthood; otherwise, these young birds will want to stay near society finches and won't associate with their own kind. Such imprinting should be prevented if one intends to breed these birds later.

The use of society finches as foster parents has engendered a good deal of controversy, however, especially with regard to Australian grassfinches, such as Gouldians. J. Trollope (see page 68) states that the Gouldian finch is the main species to be reared by fostering with society finches. He notes that some aviculturists claim this as the reason that infertility sometimes occurs in certain strains of Gouldians, and that others point out the evils of imprinting, suggesting that Gouldians reared by Bengalese react like Bengalese as adults, failing to respond to the reproductive behavior of other Gouldians. Others argue that no evidence has been offered to prove this hypothesis.

Nevertheless, based on their world fame as foster parents, any serious bird fancier interested in rearing finches should have at least two or three pairs of society finches.

When purchasing a pair of Bengalese, however, one must be sure the sales contract permits an exchange if they turn out to be an ineffective couple. Spelling out the exact guarantee is good business for both buyer and seller. These measures are necessary because it's hard to sex Bengalese. Only the song of the male, a rather attractive, soft rasp, can help sex the birds successfully, but there is no similar test for females, besides DNA testing.

To further confound the breeder, two females, when placed together, act like a breeding pair. They build a nest, lay infertile eggs, and take turns incubating. Even two males together can act like a true pair. They don't sing, but build empty nests with brooding chambers, sitting for days on the empty nest as if they were incubating. Although demand is high for these birds, if you pick a reliable breeder and have a little luck, you can acquire trustworthy breeding pairs.

The Bengalese has, as stated, no real counterpart in the wild, but was itself bred from the sharp-tailed munia *Lonchura striata acuticauda* and the striated, or white-rumped, munia *L. s. striata*. The late American aviculturist Allan Silver believed that the African silverbill *Euodice cantans* also was involved in the development of the society finch. Different varieties were bred during its period of domestication, which can be traced back to about 1700, until the Bengalese finally became a very popular ornamental bird. It came to Europe quite late, getting to England in 1860, to Germany in 1872, to the Netherlands in 1874; and to the United States between 1890 and 1895, although it didn't become popular until around 1950.

Society finches are good breeders and are suitable both as aviary and cage birds. They will allow nesting material to be stolen from their nest box, even if they are involved in building or brooding. In fact, Bengalese let themselves be pushed around to the point of giving up their whole nest to other birds. Some society finches will stand up for their rights, but they are the exceptions. In short, Bengalese need support from the fancier to breed successfully, not because the birds are unwilling, but because they don't get the chance. Therefore, these birds should be provided a breeding cage of adequate size, or a spacious aviary with enough protection, in the form of fir branches attached to roof, walls, and mesh, for example, and always

enough nest boxes if the birds share their housing with other birds.

Many aviculturists consistently rear 15–20 young per year from a pair of society finches. Personally, we think this is overdoing things; one should not take advantage of the birds. Unless you intervene, they will continue to breed winter and summer. This is not advisable because the female would be fatally weakened by egg binding and general exhaustion. It is best not to allow more than three broods per season.

Select a breeding time for them, either in spring or summer, that fits your schedule. The winter months also can be used if you supply a spacious, well-lit indoor aviary room or large breeding cage. If they are kept mainly to be used as foster parents for more delicate species, their breeding should be timed to coincide as closely as possible with the breeding season of the birds for whom they are to serve as hosts.

The normal incubation period for Bengalese is 14–16, sometimes as much as 20, days. After another 21 days, the young are ready to leave the nest, but the parents continue to feed them for some time. After about 40 days, when the young are no longer being fed by their parents, they can be removed and placed in a large box cage. Young birds should not be used for breeding until they are at least one year of age.

Society finches occur, as stated already, in various brownish and white colors; some have a little crest. If a breeder prefers a particular color, he will need to continue breeding just that particular color for three to five generations. Or, to keep the lineage as pure (homozygous) as possible, and in lieu of keeping well-organized records, the young could be banded 8–10 days after they have emerged from the eggs. However, these birds are excellent for all kinds of cross-breedings; the resultant hybrids often win high awards at European bird shows.

Again, the breeding itself does not usually pose many problems. In a well-planted aviary, or in a box cage, one can achieve very satisfactory results. Do not disturb the breeding birds, however, even if they are known as birds that allow regular nest inspection. Even society finches find peace a necessary condition. Supply the birds with large nest boxes, 10 x 10 x 10 in. (25 x 25 x 25 cm), of the half-open type, and ample nesting material such as coconut fibers and grass; remember, some society finches will allow other, more aggressive bird species to take an unfair share of these materials.

Bengalese tend to have fast-growing nails, like the other mannikin species, so some flagstones, reeds etc. should be put in the aviary or cage to serve as "nail files." Special attention should be given to perches, since they are so important to foot health. They should be made of good hardwood such as oak, beech, or manzanita; branch-type perches should not be too thin. A diameter of 1–1½ in. (2.5–3.8 cm) is suitable, allowing the bird to clasp its foot around the perch comfortably. Sandpaper perch covers, sleeves that fit over the perches, are widely known, and provided they are used properly could aid in keeping claws trimmed. Don't cover all the perches, however, as constant resting on perches covered with sandpaper sleeves will aggravate the feet. More than half of the available perches should be bare in order to prevent sore feet. All sleeves should be placed in such a way that the slit is on top. Society finches also require fresh bathing water daily, as well as a varied tropical seed mixture and a quickly replenished supply of insects (see below).

Food: Millet varieties, millet spray, canary grass seed, rape seed, flax, poppy seed, hulled oats or oat groats, raw apple, stale wheat bread soaked in water, cracker meal, cracked peanuts, spinach, cracked sunflower seed, weed and grass seeds, and wheat germ. During the breeding season commercial egg food (present various brands and let the birds decide which they like best), fine-grade softbill meal, insectivorous food, finch pellets, gentles (cleaned larva of the blowfly or bluebottle fly), small flies (2–4 per bird per day; 4–6 during the breeding season), small cut-up mealworms, spiders, ant pupae, white worms, and germinated and sprouted seeds. On a daily basis, in order of importance: water, vitamins and minerals, cuttlebone, crushed oyster shell, baked chicken egg shells, mineral grit, and spray millet.

DUSKY MANNIKIN *Lonchura fuscans* (Cassin, 1852)

DK: Borneo Broncefinke NL: Borneo bronzemannetje FR: Munic de Borneo
DE: Borneo- Bronzemännchen IT: Cappuccino del Borneo

▶ *photos page 120, 123*

Description: Similar to the Java mannikin (see page 196), but no white on belly; completely brownish black with darker tips creating a scalloped effect; the lower mandible and legs are blue-gray. Length: 4 in. (10 cm).

Distribution and habitat: Borneo, Natuna Island (northwest of Borneo), and the Sulu Islands (northeast of Borneo); in grassland and savannas, rice fields, gardens and parks, forest edges, along roads, near water and villages. Nests high in thick trees and under tiles of local huts and houses.

Aviculture: This species is occasionally available. It remains shy for a long time, and breeds only rarely. Needs a quiet, well-planted, roomy aviary. Cross-breedings with Bengalese are possible, and their young are fertile. It is a gentle and friendly bird that really deserves much more attention from the more serious aviculturist. They use a half-open nest box or canary nest basket. Supply grass, little leaves, coconut fibers, moss, little roots, etc. as nesting material. The female lays 4–6 eggs which will be incubated by both partners. During the night both sexes stay in the nest. Incubation time is 14 days; the young open their eyes when approximately 10 days old. About 20–23 days after hatching they leave the nest, but will be fed by both parents for at least another two weeks. They go through molt after 8 weeks, which takes approximately 2 months to finish.

Food: See Bengalese (page 198).

Other name: Dusky munia.

BLACK-THROATED MANNIKIN *Lonchura kelaarti* (Jerdon, 1863)

DK: Jerdon Broncefinke NL: Jerdon bronzemannetje FR: Capucin des montagnes
DE: Bergbronzemannchen IT: Cappuccino di montagna

▸ *photo page 123*

L. k. kelaarti

Description: Male and female are similar in color, although the hen has a more graceful body and a more slender beak. Forehead, crown, face, chin, upper part of the breast area, rump, and wing feathers very dark brown. Rump with tiny yellow spots; upper tail coverts golden yellow. Neck and breast orange-brown with a cinnamon wave-design; the same design also on the upperparts. Darker design in V-form on the belly and under tail coverts; in the latter this design gradually changes into little waves. Upper mandible black, lower mandible blue-gray with a whitish base; eyes dark brown; feet light reddish brown. Length: 4¾ in. (12 cm).

Geographic variations:

■ *L. k. kelaarti*, as above. Distribution: central and southwestern Sri Lanka.

■ *L. k. jerdoni* (Hume). Jerdon's black-throated mannikin. Deeper orange on neck and breast, with white stripe-design. The V-form design is more intense, especially on the belly and the beginning of the under tail coverts. Rump dark blue with cinnamon brown stripes. Upper tail coverts reddish brown. Distribution: southwestern India.

■ *L. k. vernayi* (Whistler & Kinnear). This is a questionable subspecies, and is regarded by most ornithologists as synonymous to *jerdoni*. The bird is somewhat lighter, including the underparts. Distribution: a rather small area in eastern India.

Habitat: In mountainous areas, in grassland, along the forest edges, scrubby country, rice pad-dies, tea plantations, and along roads, near farmland, and in orchards. We have seen their round nests under the eaves of homes and buildings; these are constructed from grass, moss and other vegetable matter. The clutch consists of 4–5 white eggs. They operate in pairs or during the breeding season in small family groups.

Aviculture: A friendly, active bird for large cages and aviaries. The birds, once settled, come to breed easily. The clutch consists in captivity also of 4–5, but sometimes 3–7 eggs, which will be incubated by both partners for 13–15 days. After 23–25 days the youngsters leave the nest and are independent in another three weeks, sometimes as much as a week earlier, depending on food and temperature. They can withstand temperatures as low as 64°F (18°C), but not much lower. The birds like to take a water bath several times a day!

Food: See Bengalese (see page 198).

Other names: Hill mannikin (or munia), Sri Lanka hill munia, Rufous-bellied munia, Rufous-breasted munia.

Genus *Padda* (Java sparrows) Reichenbach, 1850

JAVA SPARROW *Padda oryzivora* (Linnaeus, 1758)

DK: Grå Risfugl NL: Blauwe rijstvogel, rijstvogel FR: Padda, Calfat
DE: Reisfink, Blauer Reisfink, Relsamadine IT: Padda

▸ *photos page 124*

Description: Pale blue-gray; head black with white cheek patches. Belly reddish brown; white under tail coverts. Black tail. Eyes brown with a reddish brown periophthalmic ring; beak red with a whitish tip; legs flesh-colored. The female is somewhat smaller; narrower crown and a more

regularly tapered bill. The base of the male's bill is, in the breeding season, more swollen and brighter red. Length: 6 in. (14 cm).

Distribution and habitat: Originally from Java and Bali (Indonesia); now also found in various neighboring islands: Sumatra, Malaysia, southern Indo-China, Borneo, southern Sulawesi, the Moluccas, the Philippines, and Taiwan. Introduced into Sri Lanka, southern Burma, Zanzibar, St. Helena, among other places. Occurs in light wooded and grassy habitats, reeds, and cultivated land, in small groups. We have seen them breeding under the eaves of buildings, and in holes and crevices of buildings, houses, and trees. Free-standing nests in bushes and trees are domed-shaped.

Aviculture: Very popular aviary bird in Europe, South Africa, the US, and Canada. Several

mutations have already been developed. The white, pied, and brown mutations have gained quite a following, and in 1973 we came across a black-headed Java sparrow in Herentals, Belgium.

Java sparrows are ideal large cage and aviary inhabitants. They prefer using half-open nest boxes measuring 12 x 10 x 10 in. (30 x 25 x 25 cm), or beechwood blocks used often for parakeets. The entrance hole should have a diameter of at least 2 in. (5 cm). If nothing is done to prevent it, the birds will breed throughout the year, which, of course, could lead to egg-binding problems. Limit the breeding period to May through July, and no more than four clutches per season. The clutch consists of 4–7 white eggs. The incubation time is 13–14 days. When approximately 10 days old, the youngsters will open their eyes. If the aviary is fairly peaceful, with only a few fellow inhabitants, success is guaranteed. To discourage fighting, do not hang the breeding boxes close together. Never house two pairs in one cage or aviary; always keep just one pair, or three or more pairs. The white mutation is by far the easiest to breed. The male has a nice bell-like song.

Food: Although the Java sparrow sometimes raises its young with little animal protein, nevertheless it is advisable to present the full menu offered to Bengalese (see page 198).

Other name: Jave rice bird.

TIMOR FINCH *Padda fuscata* (Vieillot, 1807)

DK: Brun Risfugl NL: Bruine rijstvogel FR: Padda brun
DE: Timor Reisfink, Timor Reisamadine, Brauner Reisfink IT: Padda di timor

▶ *photo page 123*

Description: Mainly chocolate brown, with a whitish cream belly and under tail coverts; head and throat black, cheeks white. Length: 5 in. (13 cm).

Distribution and habitat: Timor and other islands in the Lesser Sundas. Inhabits grassland, along the edges of forests, and cultivated (rice!) land, in pairs or small flocks.

Aviculture: This species has rarely been imported in the USA; it seems also rather rare in the wild. In captivity they like to use nest boxes, but will occasionally construct a free nest in a thick bush. The clutch may be 3–8, but usually 4–6, white eggs; incubation 13–16 days. Like the Java sparrow, they need animal protein during the breeding season. Although fast-growing, the young leave the nest rather late, between 21–34 days. After 3–4 months the youngsters have their adult plumage. This species needs a large aviary; more pairs together is recommended.

Food: As for Java sparrow, above.

Other names: Timor sparrow, Timor dusky sparrow.

Genus *Heteromunia* (white-breasted pictorellas) Mathews, 1913

PICTORELLA FINCH *Heteromunia (Lonchura) pectoralis* (Gould, 1840)

DK: Hvidbrystet Sivfjnke NL: Witborstrietvink FR: Donacole à poitrine blanche
DE: Weissbrust-Schilffink IT: Cappuccino petto bianco

▶ *photos page 125*

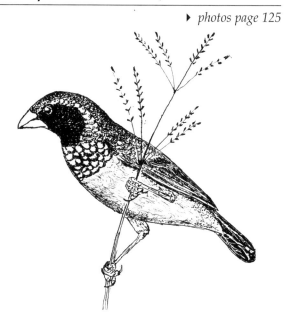

Description: Crown, neck, back, and wings grayish green; rump somewhat lighter; breast, belly, and under tail coverts light reddish brown. Rump somewhat lighter gray-green; cheeks and throat black. An orange-brown stripe from above the eye to the cheeks and neck. White scallop-design on the breast; along the flanks some black-brownish scalloping with white edges; the same along the black tail feathers. The top side of the tail is grayish. Primaries black with gray-brown edges; the greater wing coverts with little white spots and black edges. The cheeks and throat of the female are brownish black; the breast is decorated with smaller scalloping. Eyes brown, beak blue- gray, feet pinkish red. Length: 5 in. (13 cm).

Distribution and habitat: northwestern Australia and Northern Territory; in grassland and savannas, usually in extremely dry areas. The nest is built low between grass clumps. The species forages primarily on the ground, in small groups.

Aviculture: Rather rare in aviculture. The bird is very friendly toward its keeper as well as toward other small birds. The mating dance of the male is performed on the ground; he dances around his future bride while bobbing his head and sometimes touching the female's bill, or picking in the sand. The wings are carried low and the tail goes from right to left. These birds use half-open nesting boxes, which must be partially filled with nesting materials. Hang these boxes low, between 30–40 in. (70–100 cm) above ground level, in dense bushes. It is advisable to have corn plants,

reeds, tall grasses, and bushes as the main plantings in the aviary. The female lays 4–5 eggs, which will be hatched in about 13 days; both partners incubate, and relieve each other every two hours during the day; at night only the hen sits on the eggs. Don't disturb the breeding birds as they are bound to leave the nest and start, after a while, somewhere else. The young leave the nest after approximately 22 days but will be fed by both parents for another week to 10 days. After about 40 days the young are fully capable of looking after themselves.

Newly arrived birds must be acclimatized with care at a temperature of about 77°F (25°C). Birds born in captivity are hardy but must be placed indoors when the temperature drops below 65°F (18°C).

Food: Similar to all the other *Lonchura* species from Australia: grass and weed seeds, millets, canary grass seed, poppy seed, hemp seeds if available, egg and rearing food for finches, greens (see Bengalese, page 00), wheat bread soaked in water, cuttlebone, grit, charcoal, cut-up mealworms, ant pupae, small spiders, green flies, small maggots, and similar invertebrates.

Other names: Pictoral mannikin, White-breasted finch.

Genus *Lepidopygia* (dwarf mannikins) Reichenbach, 1862

MADAGASCAR MANNIKIN *Lepidopygia (Lonchura* or *Lemuresthes) nana*
Pucheran, 1845

DK: Dvaergskadefinke NL: Dwergekstertje FR: Spermète naine
DE: Zwergelsterchen IT: Piccola nonna, Nonnette nana

▶ *photo page 125*

Description: Olive-brown; black lores, throat, and chin; gray face, crown, and neck; underparts with red-brown; coverts with vague wave-design. Rump and upper tail coverts olive-greenish yellow. Wings black-brown. Sexes are alike. Eyes brown; upper mandible black, lower mandible gray-blue; legs horn-colored. Length: 3½ in. (9 cm).

Aviculture: These birds are well-known in Europe, but rather rare in the United States. They are easy to breed in a well-planted outdoor aviary. The male dances before its hen and sings a soft, pretty song consisting of four phrases repeated three or four times. They also like to chase each other as well as other birds, especially when the latter come too close to their nest. For this reason, we prefer to keep them in a small separate aviary, instead of in a community one, although they are far from aggressive birds. Their nests are usually built in thick bushes. They also accept nest boxes. The female lays 3–5, sometimes up to 7, white eggs. Incubation period is 11–13 days; both partners incubate the eggs. During the night both partners sit in the nest. After 21–25 days (sometimes longer; it seems that feeding animal protein increases their growth positively) the youngsters leave the nest, but will be cared for by both parents for another 12–14 days before they become independent. They do not attain full adult plumage for two years. During the breeding season, live insects and germinated seeds are essential.

Food: See Bengalese (page 198).

Other names: Nana, Madagascar munia, Dwarf mannikin, Bib finch, African parson finch.

Genus *Spermestes* (magpie mannikins) Swainson, 1837

BRONZE-SHOULDERED MANNIKIN *Spermestes (Lonchura) cucullata*
Swainson, 1837

DK: Lille Skadefinke NL: Ekstertje FR: Spermète à capucho
DE: Kleinelsterchen IT: Nonnetta

▸ *photos page 125*

Description: Head, neck, and throat glossy black; upperparts dark brown. Upper tail coverts and sides with dark brown stripes; underside buff; scapulars metallic green. Eyes brown; upper mandible black, lower light blue-gray; legs dark gray. The bill of the female is often more regularly tapered than that of the male. Length: 4 in. (10 cm).

Geographic variations:

■ *S. c. cucullata*, as above. Distribution: Senegal through West Africa, and southward to northern Angola, eastward to southern Sudan, Uganda (except the northeastern part), southwestern Kenya, northwestern Tanzania, and northern and eastern Zaire. The species has been introduced to the Comoro Islands, and various islands in the Gulf of Guinea; also Puerto Rico.

■ *S. c. scutata* Heuglin. Less glossy. More brown on throat and upper regions of the breast. Distribution: eastern Sudan, Ethiopia, northeastern Uganda, Kenya and Tanzania, Malawi, eastern Zambia and Mozambique through Zambesi.

■ *S. c. tessellata* Clancey. Delicate wave-design on rump, upper tail coverts, throat, and upper breast area. Not as glossy as the nominate form. Distribution: Angola (except the extreme northern and southern parts), southern Zaire, Zambia, Zimbabwe, western and southern Mozambique and eastern South Africa.

Habitat: Found in open country, farmland, plantations, and near villages; in small to medium groups. The birds feed on the ground, on termites and weed and grass seeds. They build a rather untidy, globular nest with a rough roof over the entrance. The nest is often located near wasp or hornet nests, most likely for protection against predators. They also utilize old weaver and finch nests. The pintailed whydah *Vidua macroura* has been recorded as parasitizing this species.

Aviculture: These are very friendly, lively little birds, although they can be, and usually are, aggressive during the breeding season, even attacking larger birds. Even a singleton male, kept in a community aviary, can be a real tyrant toward all of his colleagues! The male dances and sings a barely audible purring call during the spring and summer. The bird doesn't breed easily, however. To increase chances of breeding success, a well-planted, quietly situated outdoor aviary, housing this species only, should be provided. Commercial nest boxes, and a wide variety of building materials such as dry grass, hay, wool, hemp, moss, etc. are necessary. The 4–6 eggs, occasionally up to 8, will hatch in 14–16 days; both sexes share the task of rearing the young. After 18–22 days the young leave the nest, but both parents continue to feed them for another 14 days. After this time, however, they must be separated from their parents to prevent fighting.

Food: See Bengalese (see page 198).

Other names: Bronze-winged mannikin, Bronze mannikin, Hooded finch.

BLACK-AND-WHITE MANNIKIN *Spermestes (Lonchura) bicolor*
(Fraser, 1843)

DK: Glansskadefinke NL: Glansekstertje FR: Spermète bicolor
DE: Glanzelsterchen, Zweifarbenelsterchen IT: Nonnetta bicolore, Nonnette dorso nero

▶ *photos page 125*

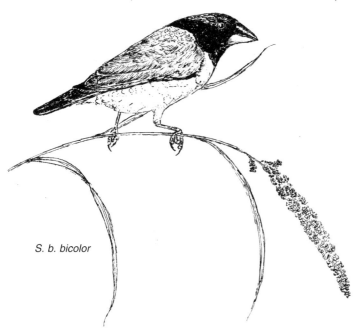

S. b. bicolor

Description: Head and upperparts black tinged glossy bronze green; throat and upper breast black, lower breast and the remaining underparts white; flanks black with white scalloping. Tail black with greenish blue hue. Under tail coverts white. The sexes are alike. Eyes brown, beak light blue-gray, legs black. Length: 4 inches (10 cm).

Geographic variations:

■ *S. b. bicolor*, as above. Distribution: from Gambia to northern Senegal through western Africa to southern Nigeria and western Cameroon.

■ *S. b. poensis* (Fraser). Fernando Po mannikin. Similar to the nominate form, but with a white bar-design in the wings. Distribution: Fernando Po and from southwestern Cameroon along the coast and inland to Zaire, southwestern Uganda, Ruanda, Burundi, northwestern Tanzania, and back to southern Cameroon and northwestern Angola.

■ *S. b. stigmatophorus* Reichenow. Dark-backed mannikin. Similar to *poensis*, but with brownish black upperparts instead of black. Distribution: southwestern Ethiopia southwestward to northern Uganda and the northern banks of Lake Victoria, and eastward from there to western Kenya.

■ *S. b. woltersi* (Schouteden). Wolters' brown-

backed, or red-backed, mannikin. This subspecies is characterized by a red rump and dark brown upperparts with a white tear-design on the flanks. Distribution: parts of Zaire, Angola and Zambia.

■ *S. b. minor* Erlanger. Lesser brown-backed mannikin. The smallest of the subspecies, but otherwise identical to the previous subspecies. Length: 3½ in. (9 cm). Distribution: southern Somalia.

■ *S. b. rufodorsalis* Peters. Somewhat smaller than the nominate form. Back red-brown (see scientific name!), and pure white underparts. Distribution: central and southern Mozambique, southern Malawi, southeastern Zambia, eastern Zimbabwe, and eastern South Africa.

■ *S. b. nigriceps* Cassin. Brown-backed, or rufous-backed, mannikin. Similar to previous subspecies but with a chestnut brown back, wing coverts and inside secondaries; belly and under tail coverts are white. Distribution: central and southeastern Kenya to eastern and central Tanzania, and in westerly direction to northern Malawi and Zambia, as well as in southeastern Zaire.

The various brown-backed subspecies are collectively recognized by some authorities as a separate species, the rufous-backed or brown-backed mannikin, with *nigriceps* as the nominate form, the others becoming subspecies of *nigriceps* rather than *bicolor*.

S. b. nigriceps

Habitat: Frequents savannas, steppes, forest edges and secondary growth, often near water; also high in the mountains, up to 8400 ft. (2500 m).

Aviculture: The cock has a soft song. They are reputed to be fairly good breeders and not quarrelsome, except toward their own kind, when housed in a well-planted aviary together with other small finches. The usual commercial nesting boxes will be accepted, although they often construct a free nest in a thick bush. The building

materials that can be offered are grass, hay, wool, and coconut fibers. The female lays 3–5 eggs, which are incubated by both partners for 13–15 days. The young leave the nest when they are about 18–22 days old, but will be fed for another two weeks by both parents. Animal protein is essential (see previous species).

Food: See Bengalese (page 198).

Other name: Black-breasted mannikin.

MAGPIE MANNIKIN *Spermestes (Lonchura) fringilloides* (Lafresnaye, 1835)

DK: Stor Skadefinke NL: Reuzenekstertje FR: Spermète pie, Grande Nonne
DE: Riesenelsterchen IT: Nonnetta maggiore

▶ *photo page 126*

Description: Head, flanks, rump, upper tail coverts, and tail glossy black. Wings and back dusky; underparts off-white. The feathers of the mantle are brown. Typical lancet-shaped tail. Eyes brown, upper mandible dark gray-black, lower mandible light blue-gray, legs dark gray. The sexes are alike. Length: 4.75–5.1 in. (12–13 cm).

Distribution and habitat: Africa, from Zambia to southern Sudan, and eastward to Kenya. In the west, to southwestern Angola, back to the east to southern Kenya and Tanzania and eastern South Africa. Also in southwestern Ethiopia. Inhabits jungle, grassland, and cultivated areas. Also in the mountains, up to approximately 6700 ft. (2000 m); they like to visit plantations and orchards. They operate in small to medium sized flocks, often together with *Spermestes cucullata* and *S. bicolor*. Culture followers. This finch has one of the largest distributional areas of all known Estrildidae.

Aviculture: These birds can be quite aggressive during the breeding season, especially toward small waxbills. The 4–6 white eggs are incubated for 14–16 days by both sexes. After 21–26 days the youngsters leave the nest; they attain adult plumage in 50–55 days. Care and breeding cycles

parallel that of the Bengalese (see page 198). Aviculturist and ornithologist N. Brickell states that this species, while entering or leaving the nest, will pull feathers over the entrance hole. The species should be brought indoors during the winter months into a lightly heated, roomy area. During the year, but especially during the breeding season, the species should have access to insects and other animal protein.

Food: See Bengalese (page 198).

Other names: Giant mannikin, Pied mannikin.

Genus *Odontospiza* (gray-headed silverbills) Oberholser, 1905

GRAY-HEADED SILVERBILL *Odontospiza caniceps (Lonchura griseicapilla)* (Reichenow, 1879)

DK: Perlehalsamadine NL: Parelhalsamadine, Grijskop zilverbekje FR: Spermète à tête grise
DE: Perlhalsamadine IT: Nonnetta a testa grigia

▶ *photos page 126*

Some authorities merge this genus with *Lonchura*. As the specific name *caniceps* is already taken by another *Lonchura* species, the gray-headed mannikin or gray-headed munia from New Guinea, the present species, when included in *Lonchura*, is designated by the specific name *griseicapilla*.

Description: Head gray; cheeks and throat are covered with small white spots. Mantle and underparts cinnamon brown; under tail coverts cream-white; rump and upper tail coverts white; wing coverts gray; tail and wings black. Sexes are alike, although the male is slightly richer in coloring, especially on the underparts and neck; he also has larger spots on the cheeks and chin. Eyes brown; upper mandible steel gray, lower mandible blue-gray, very light at the base; legs brown-gray. Length: 4¾ in. (12 cm).

Distribution and habitat: southern Sudan and southwestern Ethiopia through northeastern Uganda and Kenya in the southwestern highlands to eastern and central Tanzania; found in savanna, farmland, and near villages, with untidy, large nests often found under roofs and in the walls of huts or in thorny shrubs and hedges; also in trees up to approximately 9 ft. (3 m). Outside the breeding season they usually spend the night in an abandoned weaver nest, but also construct their own sleeping nests. The clutch consists of 4–5, often 6 eggs. The breeding season starts after the rainy season (May and June); they have often 5–6 broods per year.

Aviculture: These birds are indeed easy breeders, also in captivity! They can be placed in community aviaries as well as in large cages. The best breeding results, however, are obtained in aviaries where they can be by themselves. The aviary or cage should be very quiet as they are susceptible to disturbance. Nest inspection is therefore taboo. Both sexes incubate the eggs for 14–15 days. The youngsters leave the nest 24–26 days later. In one season it is not only possible but relatively common to produce 15–20 young from one pair. Limiting them to three broods per year, however, results in the best young, and also lowers the risk of egg binding. Silverbills (below) are extremely suitable foster parents for finches that don't require many insects or a variety of rearing and egg foods. As extras the species prefers chickweed as green food, various small millets and millet spray, and germinated grass and weed seeds; these should be available throughout the year.

The gray-headed silverbill can be crossed with the Indian silverbill *Euodice malabarica* (see page 210), the spice finch *Lonchura punctulata* (page 193), and the society finch *L. striata* var. *domestica* (page 198), although we don't like to encourage this practice, for obvious reasons.

During the breeding season, offer nesting boxes of at least 6 x 6 x 8 in. (15 x 15 x 20 cm). These birds use a variety of building materials, including plant fibers, wool, grass, hay, small feathers, etc. House these birds inside at room temperature during the fall and winter months.

Other names: Pearl-headed silverbill, Pearl-headed amadine.

Genus *Euodice* (silverbills) Reichenbach, 1862

AFRICAN SILVERBILL *Euodice (Lonchura) cantans* (Gmelin, 1789)

DK: Sølvnaeb NL: Zilverbekje FR: Bec d'argent DE: Silberschnäbelchen, Silverfasänchen
IT: Becco d'argento

▸ *photos page 126*

Description: Light rust brown with indistinct mottled appearance. Wings and back dark brown; rump, upper tail coverts, and graduated tail black. Throat and breast buff; further underparts cream to pure white. The sexes are alike, although the female doesn't sing! Young are duller and browner, with a brownish beak. Eyes dark brown; upper mandible silvery gray-blue, not as dark as in *E. malabarica*, lower mandible light gray-blue; legs blue-gray or pinkish. Length: 4–4.5 in. (10–11.5 cm).

Geographic variations:

■ *E. c. cantans*, as above. Distribution: west and central Africa, from Mauretania and Senegal through central Mali, Niger, Chad, and Sudan to Ethiopia.

■ *E. c. orientalis* (Lorenz and Hellmayr). More intensely colored, especially the upperparts. Back and wing coverts clearly mottled. Distribution: eastern Africa, from Sudan through Ethiopia, and eastward into western and southern Arabia, and through eastern Uganda, Kenya, and southwestern Somalia to northern and central Tanzania.

Habitat: They occur in savannas, farmland, and near human settlements in gardens, parks, plantations, rice paddies, and orchards. The nests are built under roofs and/or in the walls of the huts occupied by the natives; also in low, thick shrubs or in old weaver nests.

E. c. cantans

Aviculture: This species, formerly considered conspecific with the Indian silverbill *E. malabarica*, is an excellent bird for large cages and community aviaries. They are easy to keep and become steady breeders. The best breeding successes are obtained in well-planted outdoor aviaries, although these facilities must be located in a quiet place, as breeding pairs are very susceptible to disturbances. Avoid, therefore, nest inspection. The female lays only 3–6 eggs; both sexes incubate them for 12–14 days. After 20–22 days the young leave the nest. For further details see the species below. Crossings are possible with Bengalese, Indian silverbills, common waxbills *Estrilda astrild*, and rufous-backed mannikins *Spermestes bicolor* ssp., but, as stated before, we are not in favor of this practice. When care and management are up to par, this species becomes very friendly toward its keeper; during the winter months they must be housed inside at room temperature, a minimum of 65°F (18°C). This is one of the best species for a beginner!

Food: During the year but especially during the breeding season various grass and weed seeds, both fresh and sprouted, millet spray and other small millets, and a commercial seed mixture for small finches are essential. Furthermore, greens, egg and rearing foods, animal protein, brown (wheat) bread soaked in water, cuttlebone, crusted egg shells, vitamins and minerals. Germinated grass and weed seeds are considered a treat and should be available throughout the year.

Other name: Black-rumped silverbill.

E. c. orientalis

INDIAN SILVERBILL *Euodice (Lonchura) malabarica* Linnaeus, 1758

DK: Malabar Amadine NL: Loodbekje FR: Bec de plomb DE: Malabarfasänchen IT: Becco di piombo   ▸ *photos page 127*

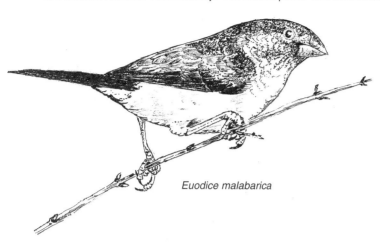

Euodice malabarica

Description: Light brown; rump white; breast and throat yellowish brown; underparts white. Wings chocolate brown with darker primaries. Under tail coverts white with black edges. Eyes dark brown; beak silvery gray-blue, darker than that of *E. cantans*; the upper mandible somewhat darker; legs gray-blue, often with a pinkish sheen. The sexes are alike. Length: 4–4.5 in. (10–11.5 cm).

Distribution and habitat: India, Nepal, Pakistan, Sri Lanka, and southern Afghanistan; also in Oman. Mainly in open country, gardens, parks, orchards, and savannas, but usually close to water. The birds breed in low, dense bushes; often two clutches in one nest! One pair usually has a large clutch of 6–8 eggs, sometimes more (up to 10).

Aviculture: An excellent cage and aviary bird for both beginner and experienced aviculturist; it doesn't demand much and is a prolific breeder. The bird looks very similar to the African silverbill. Sexes can only be distinguished by the almost inaudible, somewhat muttering song of the male, and during the mating season, when he dances around his bride with a grass stem in his beak. A true pair will build a free, small nest in a bush or in a nest box, but they also like to use old weaver nests, which they furnish with a long and narrow entrance. They are inoffensive toward their own kind as well as toward other small finches. Therefore they are very suitable for a community aviary. In captivity, the female may lay up to 12 eggs (hence, even more eggs than in the wild); both parents incubate the eggs, which hatch after 12–14 days. After 21 days the young leave the nest, and will be fed by the parents for another 12–14 days. They should be restricted to no more than three broods per year, to avoid egg binding.

Food: See previous species.

Other names: White-rumped silverbill, White-throated munia.

Subfamily Erythrurae

Introduction

The members of this small subfamily are very colorful indeed, and always in demand with serious aviculturists the world over. Species such as the zebra finch *Poephila guttata*, the Gouldian *Chloebia gouldiae*, the diamond sparrow *Zonaeginthus guttatus*, and the star finch *Bathilda ruficauda* are now considered domesticated, and various fascinating color mutations are well established in aviculture. In the wild, Erythrurae members live in open country, with the exception of most parrotfinches, which prefer bamboo groves. The sexes are alike, or very nearly so, in most species.

GRASSFINCHES

Genus *Zonaeginthus* (diamond sparrows and firetails) (Shaw, 1796) or *Staganopleura* Reichenbach, 1850

DIAMOND FINCH *Zonaeginthus guttatus (Staganopleura guttata)* (Shaw, 1796)

DK: Diamantfinke NL: Diamantvink FR: Diamant à goutellettes DE: Djamantfink, Diamantamadine
IT: Diamante guttata, Diamante guttato, Diamante picchiettato

▸ *photos page 39, 128*

Description: The head and neck of the male are grayish blue; back and wings olive-brown; rump and upper tail coverts crimson; throat white; breast with a wide, black band that runs along the flanks and is bordered by the wings; underside whitish; flanks black with white spots (diamonds); the second part of the scientific name, *guttatus*, means "spotted" and *zona*, in *Zonaeginthus*, is the Latin word for "band"; the Greek *cigintha* is a "kind of bird." Beak maroon; the lores are black. The eyes are bordered with a conspicuous red eye-ring, the same color as the iris. Legs and feet are grayish brown. The hen is usually difficult to distinguish from the male; with enough comparative material the hen's head and body seems generally slighter in structure. The lores are brown instead of black; this is a good distinguishing mark in older birds. The eye-ring is generally lighter in color, as is the beak, which is pinkish red. The immature birds are generally less colorful, with greenish brown wings and back; the rump and upper tail coverts are carmine red; the tail feathers are not black, but brownish black; unlike the conspicuous ash blue head of the adults, in juveniles it has a greenish wash, as has the sides of the head. The flanks are greenish brown with large gray-white bars and spots; the underside of hens is light gray, in young cocks, however, much lighter, almost white. The beak of young hens at about three months of age is generally light red, that of young cocks is dark red with a violet tinge. The rump and upper tail coverts of young hens are dull red; those of young cocks are lighter red with a pale sheen. These color differences can sometimes be seen in older birds, especially when not in breeding condition. A cock bird ready for mating however, is easy to distinguish by his frequent singing and his vivid red eye-rings. Should the bird moreover take a grass stem in the beak, stand high on the legs, and press the beak down against the breast, it is definitely a male. During this performance he will also let his song be heard. The cock sometimes sings outside the breeding season, but much less frequently. Also, outside the breeding season, the hen takes no notice of the male's singing; she just keeps to herself.

Apart from the male song, sexes of young birds are difficult to determine outwardly. Even the white spots on the flanks, which are sometimes larger in hens, are no sure indication. The only sure way, as we have said, is the song of the male. Length: 4½ in. (11.5 cm), sometimes a little smaller, sometimes to 4¾ in. (12 cm); tail 1.7 in. (4.3 cm); wings 2½–2¾ in. (6–7 cm).

Distribution and habitat: Australia, central and southern Queensland, and via the Great Dividing Range in New South Wales, through Victoria to western South Australia (Eyre Peninsula); also on Kangaroo Island, a large island south of Adelaide, South Australia. They live in open terrain, including grassland, mallee thickets, gardens, parks, and open woodland, generally in the immediate neighborhood of water. We have seen these birds on Kangaroo Island close to the little towns, especially in gardens and parks. In Queensland we have also frequently seen them close to human habitation. In Adelaide we observed them especially in the sparsely wooded

hills, where they had plenty of space to move about. By leg-banding numbers of birds over a two year period, we ascertained that they were largely sedentary and almost never left the area in which they were hatched and reared. It seems that most pairs build a new nest in the same shrub in which they nested the previous year. We observed some pairs even repairing or rebuilding their old original nests and reusing them. It is therefore understandable that in some areas, where the habitat is in their favor, they remain all year round. Juveniles usually also stay in the area in which they were reared, breeding locally when they mature. In spite of this, continual urbanization is gradually forcing populations of the birds further inland. We observed a typical example of this when, on Kangaroo Island in 1983, diamond finches were forced more than 1100 yards (about 1 km) further inland in a single year.

Diamond finches are very strong on the wing; they fly powerfully with the flowing, light undulation that is characteristic of birds that live in open terrain and must be quick on the wing to escape from predators. This typical kind of flight can be seen in many Australian finches, but especially in all firetail species, like the diamond finch. However, it has to be said that the flight of the diamond finch is the most beautiful of all.

Diamond finches are mainly seed eaters. Like sparrows, the finches hop on the ground in search of seeds, but they also jump up to the heads of seeding grasses with some success. During the breeding season, the birds supplement their menu with insects which they also find on the ground or pluck from the foliage of plants. In captivity, diamond finches will be content with a commercial seed mixture as the main part of the diet, but they show a preference for white and Japanese millets, especially outside the breeding season. During the breeding season, sprouted seeds and seeding grass heads are taken avidly; millet sprays and bunches of seeding weeds can also be given in the aviary (see page 39). It is recommended that such seed heads are offered throughout the year. If they are offered only in the breeding season it is possible that the birds will eat too much of them and become too fat. Providing such seed heads on a regular basis discourages the birds from eating these seeds exclusively, and they will also seek out other food. In this connection, it should be noted that hemp is also one of their favorite seeds. But this should be given only sparingly, even when the birds are in a large aviary with plenty of exercise space.

In the wild, various termites and other insects and their larvae are taken by the breeding adults and fed to their nestlings. In the cage or aviary, small mealworms or maggots can be given; these larvae should first be killed by immersing them in boiling water in a net or a piece of old nylon pantyhose. Fruit flies and white worms *Enchytraeus* spp. can also be given, as can commercial egg food. Grit must be available throughout the year, and a mineral block should also be available. In the wild we have seen the birds eating pieces of charcoal. In captivity we would therefore also recommend that charcoal is made available. Grains of charcoal are present in some commercial grit mixtures, but it is also available separate in little boxes. However, charcoal should be given very sparingly and cautiously. The necessity of a daily supply of charcoal is questionable, as it is suspected of absorbing vitamins A, B_2 and K from the intestinal tract. If this is correct, it means that charcoal can cause vitamin-deficiency disease.

During the breeding season, we also like to give our birds some brown bread soaked in water, although this item must be removed after a few hours, as it will sour rapidly. Put commercial egg food, soaked bread, and other quickly perishable foods in the sheltered part of the aviary so they don't spoil too quickly. Never soak bread in milk, as many birds cannot tolerate it.

As in the wild, captive birds drink regularly, but especially in the early hours of the morning. Unlike most birds, but in common with zebra finches, Gouldian finches, doves, and pigeons, members of this subfamily suck the water up. This method works very well early in the morning or after light rain, when dewdrops hang from the foliage; the birds can suck up the water directly from the leaves, or from a concave stone, etc. Birds that live in areas subject to drought are often able to suck up water in such a way. In an aviary you may often see these birds gently hopping along twigs after a rain shower, sucking up drops of

water that hang from the leaves. We have also seen both aviary inmates and wild finches jumping up to hanging dewdrops, catching them on the tip of the beak, and swallowing as they land. In the aviary, the birds are very partial to running water. A little fountain with fresh running water is indeed a luxury for most fanciers, but will not only be good for the health of their birds, but influences behavior strongly and positively as well. It also cuts out the danger of spoiled, infected water. In spite of this, we give our diamond finches, and other birds, of course, a fresh dish of water in which a dose of vitamin/mineral supplement is dissolved, twice per day.

Before the breeding season actually gets underway, the cock is already charming his spouse with a simple song. The song is somewhat harsh sounding and consists of a series of simple notes which we can best describe as "qweat, qweat, qweat-the-qweat-the-qweat," (ea as in sea); sometimes one can hear small variations. In the wild, as well as in the aviary, one can hear the contact calls, not only when a group, usually consisting of 20–30 birds, including the current year's offspring, is togther, but also when one or more birds have strayed too far away from the group and are being warned to return. Such contact calls have a nasal character; they are fairly consistent but quite urgent, beginning with a high tone and then gradually descending into the second syllable: "whoo-oo-oo-hee-ee-ee" (oo as in wood; ee as in heat). A similar, somewhat softer, call is used for contact between cock and hen. During the breeding season, and particularly near the nest, the call of the cock, especially, is higher and louder. The cock identifies himself with such a call when he approaches the nest, so that the hen is not alarmed. Normal contact calls are used when the birds seek shelter from the midday heat, and also in the evenings when they assemble to roost.

In this connection, it is worth mentioning the "snoring call," first described by the ornithologist J. Welschke. This is a call uttered by one of a pair before flying from the food hopper to the nest in order to relieve his/her mate. This snoring call is actually uttered before the bird takes to the wing, and the bird in the nest answers in a similar fashion. We have observed this behavior, together with the snoring call, several times in large cages, especially in outdoor aviaries, and even once in the wild, in Queensland, when one of the birds, about 5 ft. (1½ m) from the nest and about 12 ft. (3.5 m) from where we were concealed, was acrobatically removing some seeds from grass heads. Once the bird finished eating, it sat dead still on the ground, uttering a low toned, somewhat drawn-out "chrou-chrou-chrou" (ou as in ought), which was answered almost immediately by the bird in the nest. Welschke, as well as Immelmann, is convinced that the answer from the bird in the nest means that all is safe and well, and that the relief can take place without danger. This behavior can also be seen in the red-eared firetail finch *Zonaeginthus oculatus* (see page 00). We agree with both of these ornithologists, having observed the behavior ourselves several times. Immelmann is right in pointing out that this form of communication, which is shared by several other species of Australian finches, including the zebra finch and the red-eared firetail finch, has evolved as a result of the long entrance tunnel to the nest, in which a bird in the nest would have absolutely no visual contact with the outside world.

In the case of a nest not yet fully completed, the bird can look outside and see possible danger in time, whereas a bird in a fully completed nest with a tunnel cannot see such danger itself and requires assistance. The tunnel is thus constructed first, before the nest, and we must note further that the birds continue to add to the nest even when they have eggs or youngsters. The so-named "snoring call" is something like the somewhat harsh song of the cock, only it is not so long, and is interspersed with an "ee" (as in deep) sound: "kwee-ou-kwee-ou, kwee-ou-thee-ou-thee-kwee," and the possible variations on this.

Another call is the lure call, used by the birds when approaching each other. The call of the cock is higher than that of the hen, and is held longer; it sounds like: "woo-ooh-ee-ee, woo-oh-ee-ee" (oo as in too; ee as in sea).

Diamond finches are very temperamental, and this shows during courtship. In Australia they can sometimes breed throughout the year, when suitable conditions prevail. However, breeding captive birds for such an extended period is not advised, as sooner or later you will be confronted with egg binding, weak youngsters, or other problems.

It has been determined that diamond finches pair up early in life and that the pair bond is sustained for life. We consider the courtship display of the diamond finch to be exceedingly pronounced. The cock repeatedly makes a spectacular display. Before beginning his dance, he seeks out a long stalk of grass, which he then holds in his beak. Thus "kitted-out," he flies to a high, thin branch. Once there, he sits bolt-upright and bobs up and down with the stem in his beak! We have observed birds, with stems over 4½ ft. (135 cm) long in the bill, trying to balance, and even falling off the perch! The head is stretched up as far as it will go, but with the beak pointing down toward the breast, and all the time trying not to lose the stem! Additionally, he spreads out his flank and belly feathers imposingly, and appears almost doubled in size. Once in this position, he begins to make bobbing movements as his legs and feet are bent and stretched in turn, like a bouncing ball, as described by Immelmann. His toes always hang tightly onto the twig during this performance; in other words, the whole display takes place in one spot. While performing, he lets out his harsh "kweet, kweet, kweet, kweet" calls. As soon as the hen reacts and comes into his sight, the cock makes the last deep movement and stretches his neck like a youngster begging for food. (Compare this with the well-known begging behavior of young zebra finches!) He also lets out his "kweet, kweet" sound while doing this. This behavior can be best observed with birds in a large outdoor aviary.

The diamond finch often builds its rough nest under the huge nests of eagles and other birds of prey. We have also found their nests among the thickly packed twigs of crows' nests. Twice we have found nests of diamond finches under the eaves of a derelict barn used by cattle at night; five times in a lemon tree in a friend's garden; eight times in a rose bush, three times in an orange tree, once in the nest of a crested hawk *Aviceda subcristata*, and many times in eucalyptus trees infested with mistletoe. You can thus imagine that these birds are not particularly fussy with regard to nesting sites.

Generally, however, the bottle-shaped nests are found in thick shrubs or other undergrowth, sometimes in high spots, even in trees. We have found nests sometimes as high as 83 ft. (25 m) up in trees. The nest itself has a tunnel-like entrance up to 3 in. (8 cm) long, and the main nest is about 6 in. (15 cm) in diameter, with the nest chamber about 3 in. (8 cm) in diameter. The nest is made from grass stalks and strips and similar items. We have found that stalks up to 18 in. (45 cm) long are sometimes used, but also thin twigs and strips of bark are utilized. The inner chamber is lined with soft grass and feathers. Both cock and hen continue to strengthen and repair the nest, even when there are eggs or young in it. From this you can well imagine that diamond finches are very active birds, which in captivity must have an aviary or at least a very roomy cage, otherwise they are likely to pine away.

Outside the breeding season the birds are kept busy building dormitory nests or practice nests. When a number of these have been constructed, they restore, repair, rebuild, strengthen, lengthen tunnels, etc. We saw several sleep/breeding nests that had an extra tunnel, often opposite the main entrance but sometimes in the roof or one of the sides. These were probably used as emergency exits. Since Australia has a large population of snakes and lizards, these emergency exits are no mere luxury in the view of many ornithologists. The extra tunnel is, at first, kept closed; the opening in the wall or roof is first made after the young have hatched. It is interesting to note that, as Immelmann observed, many African waxbills, such as cordon bleus *Uraeginthus* spp., etc., build a similar nest.

The clutch normally consists of 5–8 eggs, but may range from 4–9 eggs, each about 18 x 13 mm. The birds start to incubate after the second egg has been laid. The sexes take turns incubating, but usually both parents incubate at night. The incubation period is approximately two weeks.

In their native Australia, the main natural breeding season stretches from August to well into January, which are of course spring and summer in the Southern Hemisphere. Sometimes these birds nest additionally in autumn, from March to the end of May, and exceptionally, in winter, dur-

Diamond Finch / *Zonaeginthus guttatus*   Photo: Matthew M. Vriends

ing June and July, depending on weather conditions and availability of food.

It is thus possible for a pair to rear three broods in the year. The young leave the nest at about a month of age, but sometimes as young as 21–26 days. However, they are still fed by the parents for a considerable time after fledging. They attain full adult plumage in one to three months, and are then difficult to distinguish from their parents.

As we have already mentioned, the birds live in groups of about 30 outside the breeding season, though odd isolated pairs may still be seen occasionally. They inhabit mallee scrub, eucalyptus woodland, farmland and riverine areas. During the breeding season the groups remain in loose contact, often building their nests in close proximity, sometimes even in the same shrub or tree!

In the aviary, as we will see, the situation is quite different. Pairs are best kept singly, as males are prone to fight, and we cannot afford such risks with breeding birds. It would only take two cocks fighting to destroy the harmony of all birds in the aviary.

In the wild we saw the birds in groups repeatedly drinking together, foraging for food, even helping each other out in nest building and feeding the fledglings.

Aviculture: The diamond finch is not really suitable as a cage bird, being a very active bird, it would soon get too fat in a confined space. Trying to breed with obese birds will not be very successful. Small aviaries with numbers of other finch-like birds are also not very suitable, as diamond finches have the nasty habit of vandalizing nests, disturbing eggs and nestlings, and generally interfering with breeding. However, we must honestly say that we have come across several pairs of diamond finches that were quite friendly and sociable; but strong behavioral differences mean that fanciers must keep a close eye on diamond finches when they are kept in a community aviary, so that any potential problem can be swiftly nipped in the bud.

Many breeders, including ourselves, like to place several diamond finches of both sexes together in a large aviary and allow them to pair up themselves. This is recommended because diamond finches are strongly monogamous; wild birds often pair bond, even before they have their full adult plumage. It is quite easy to follow this method if you have leg banded your birds with bands (rings) of various colors. As soon as a pair has formed, it must be immediately removed to a large cage placed out of hearing of the other diamond finches. The pairs can be returned to aviaries when they are completely rested and at least one year old. If you want to breed selectively (breeding mutations for example), you must place chosen pairs together, this is quite easy as long as

you keep them out of sight and sound of the other bird until the pair is in breeding condition.

Diamond finches are not particularly difficult birds to breed, and, with a little insight and knowledge, even the beginner can be successful. Incidentally, the first captive breeding results in Europe were in France about 1855, and the Netherlands from 1865, with Mr. Cornelly being the first breeder.

As we have said, the most ideal housing for diamond finches is a large, well designed aviary, so that the birds can take cover if necessary. You can keep other finches in such an aviary, but bear in mind that certain individuals can cause trouble. Some breeders, who have an aviary at least 26 ft. (8 m) long, use already formed pairs to form a colony. This will be successful, as long as we remove any trouble-makers. Such an aviary will house seven or eight pairs of diamond finches along with other finch species.

The aviary must always be dry and draft-free, protected from cold winds. In areas with prolonged rainy periods, it is recommended that at least half of the outside flight is roofed over with transparent roofing material, so that the floor stays dry. The length of the aviary must always be enough to allow the birds adequate flying room, without hitting something once in flight. Medium sized shrubs, clumps of grass, and similar low plantings are recommended, so that birds can take shelter if there is any trouble.

Furthermore, it is important, as we have mentioned above, to provide a fountain with running water so that the birds always have fresh water. It would be ideal to install a sprinkler system in the open part of the flight, not only for the benefit of the plants; the birds will also use it. It is a wonderful sight seeing the finches taking a shower! However, the floor of the aviary must not be permanently wet. Many fanciers have the sprinkler system only in the open part of the flight and set it to work in the morning, say from 10:00 A.M. to noon , allowing the midday sun to dry everything up again before evening, so that the birds don't have to go to roost in a wet environment. If for some reason or other you cannot supply running water or a sprinkler system, you must give water in large, shallow, earthenware dishes so that there is no danger of the birds drowning. Such dishes must naturally be cleaned and refilled with fresh water several times per day.

An adequate temperature is important for the well-being of the birds. Temperatures below 60°F (15°C) are not well tolerated. Birds housed in outdoor quarters must therefore be taken indoors as soon as temperatures start to drop in early fall.

Diamond finches need adequate nesting material at breeding time. You must keep a good eye on the birds, who will steal materials from other nests if they don't have enough! Such behavior can be detrimental to other broods as the thieves don't make any distinction between empty nests or those containing eggs or young!

Cocks in breeding condition will perform their courtship dance, and partners will be continually preening each other. Preening is a very important activity in the life of the diamond finch, and is carried out between partners at all times of the day. Newly fledged young start preening themselves and each other almost immediately. Preening is a family affair, pairs or siblings rarely carrying this out with unrelated members of the group.

In Australia, well cared for captive diamond finches will breed throughout the year, but in Europe and the US, we should stick to no more than three broods per annum, beginning in April or May. Many fanciers start breeding only when they are sure they have a constant supply of grass and weed seeds plus insects. The birds will show they are in breeding condition by courtship dances by the cock, and by collecting nesting materials. A large amount of nest material is used by diamond finches, often three to four times more than other Australian finches! So make sure they have enough. Experience has shown that long, pliable grass stems are a favorite for building the nest chamber, interwoven with small down feathers (chicken feathers are prized). Hay, small twigs, and wool may also be offered.

The nest is bulky and usually bottle-shaped, with one entrance. Frequently one or two extra nests are built on top or on the sides for roosting purposes. Both partners build the nest. Make sure you have thick shrubs in the aviary, approximately 6 ft. (2 m) high; these will be used as nesting sites in preference to nest boxes. However, it is advisable to also offer a number of nest boxes at various sites, with minimal measurements 6 x 6 x 6 in. (15 x 15 x 15 cm). You never know!

Four young are usually reared per clutch. Diamond finches are regarded as excellent parents, but are not tolerant of too many nest inspections, especially after the young have hatched. It is therefore recommended that youngsters are first leg banded just before they fledge. Young that leave the nest too early rarely return for the night and there is a great risk that they will succumb to the cold.

It may be prudent to point out that the first eggs of young breeding pairs will do better if fostered out to society finches *Lonchura striata* var. *domestica*. We have noticed that if allowed to rear their own chicks, first-time breeding pairs often abandon them after only a couple of days feeding.

In Australia, we noticed that many breeders divided a brood of diamond finches among two or three pairs of society finches (or placed them in the nest of diamond finches that had only one or two young), as it is impossible for these foster parents to rear a whole brood of diamond finches. Young diamonds eat a lot more than young society finches, so the food supply of the foster parents is inadequate to feed them all properly.

The young are fed by both parents, and are never left alone in the nest! So, when one parent is foraging for food the other stays in the nest, only leaving when the partner has returned. Only after 12–14 days will it happen that both parents leave the young alone for short periods. After foraging, they always stay awhile in the nest, but this period also shortens and when the young are about 20 days old, both parents will be busy going backward and forward keeping them fed! This behavior encourages the young themselves to leave the nest, especially when one of the parents sits outside with food in its beak, luring the youngsters out. The strongest youngster makes the first break into the wide world. As soon as the other youngsters see this, especially when they are also hungry, they will follow suit.

Shortly after the youngsters have fledged, the parents will become extremely agitated, as the fledglings do not stay easily together, but seem to disappear into every corner of the aviary. It is interesting to watch with binoculars how the parents try to get the young together where they will have more control over them. After a few hours they usually give up these attempts and feed their brood in a somewhat calmer manner. They continue to feed the young a variety of foods for about three weeks before they become independent. Evenings and nights the parents and young return to the old nest or to a sleeping nest to roost. After leaving the nest early in the morning, they have a mutual preening session before going to eat and drink.

Diamond finches remain fertile for a relatively long time; five years is about the average. They should not, however, be allowed to breed until they are at least 12 months old. Average life expectancy for a diamond finch is 7–8 years, providing it receives optimum housing, care, and feeding.

Three color mutations are known at the present time. In the recessive yellow, the conspicuous red rump of the normal form is replaced by orange. The second mutation is the sex-linked fawn, and the third, obviously, the yellow split for fawn (yellow/fawn).

Food: Diamond finches may be fed on various kinds of millets and sorghum, but they prefer white and Japanese millet, especially during the breeding season and in the colder months of the year. Canary grass seed, seeding grass heads both ripe and unripe, and weed seeds can all be offered. Ripe seed heads will be taken greedily if you place them in bottles of water set into the ground. Millet and canary grass seed can also be given in soaked or sprouted form. Greenfood such as spinach, chickweed, endive, chicory, and so on should be offered. Although not all birds will take them, insects are an important part of the diet; commercial rearing and egg foods for canaries can also be offered, not only in the breeding season, but throughout the year. Yet, as we have already said, we have known diamond finches that ignored insects as long as they had seeding grass heads available. In spite of this, we recommend that insects such as the following are made available: ant pupae, small cut-up mealworms, enchytrae, maggots, spiders, and similar. Fruit flies *Drosophila* spp. are taken avidly; you can attract these and other insects with a piece of banana or other fruit laid in the sun and covered with mesh to stop the birds coming into contact with it. The birds will catch the insects hovering around the fruit or sitting on the mesh. The fruit should be changed every couple of days. Finally, the birds must have a mineral block, salt wheel (available commercially), cuttlefish bone, oyster shell grit, and some charcoal (but not too much of the latter; see page 59). We offer our birds stale wholegrain bread soaked in water twice a week, but beware of mold, and a good brand of vitamin/mineral supplement in powder form that we sprinkle over the bread or greenfood.

Other names: Diamond sparrow, Diamond firetail finch, Spotsided finch.

BEAUTIFUL FIRETAIL *Zonaeginthus bellus (Stagonopleura bella)* (Latham, 1801)

DK: Ildhalefinke NL: Vuurstaartamadine FR: Diamant à queue de feu
DE: Feuerschwanzamadine IT: Diamante coda di fuoco

Description: Upperparts olive-brown with finely lined brown-black wave-designs, finer and closer on the chin. Wings chocolate brown with the same wave-design. Back, rump, and upper tail coverts crimson. Tail feathers dark brown with brown-blackish wave-design. Forehead and ear black; chin and throat whitish brown. Breast, flanks and underside white with wave-design. Under tail coverts black. Eyes dark brown with an opal-blue periophthalmic ring, beak red, legs pinkish. The female's ear-stripe is less intense; also there is less black in the mid-belly. Length: 5 in. (12 cm).

Distribution and habitat: Australia, from Newcastle to Victoria and the east coast of South

Australia, Kangaroo Island and Tasmania (where the species is its only indigenous finch); in swamps, grassland, bushes, parks and gardens. The bird is fully protected by law in the states where it occurs.

The beautiful firetail is primarily a coastal species, although it has been recorded inland in the valleys of the Great Dividing Range and some 2000–2300 ft. (600-700 m) above sea level in the Blue Mountains.

Aviculture: Rarely available in Europe and the USA; some experienced breeders in Australia are working with this difficult bird. It needs a large, well-planted aviary, without other birds. According to avicultural literature, it is unlikely that this species will ever become established in captivity outside Australia.

RED-EARED FIRETAIL *Zonaeginthus oculatus (Steganopleura oculata)*
Quoy & Gaimard, 1830

DK: Rødøret Amadine NL: Roodooramadine FR: Astrild à oreillons rouges
DE: Rotohramadine IT: Diamante dalle orecchie rosse

Description: Looks very similar to the beautiful firetail, but has a small red ear patch and the underparts are scalloped rather than having the wavy barring of *bellus*. The male has an olive-brown head, back, and breast; finely barred with black. Wings have the same color, but with lighter edging. Underparts from the lower breast down black spotted with white; the same for the under tail coverts. Upper tail coverts and tail scarlet; central tail feathers brownish barred. Lores and forehead black. Crimson patch behind the eye. Periophthalmic ring blue; beak scarlet, legs dark brown. The female is somewhat duller with an orange-scarlet eye patch, which becomes especially evident in the breeding season. Length: 4½–4¾ in. (11–12 cm).

Distribution and habitat: From the extreme southwestern part of Western Australia. For those Australian aviculturists who look for fascinating detailed information, we would like to refer you to *Finch Breeders Handbook: The Australians* (see page 00), one of the very best books ever published

about Australian finches in captivity. The red-eared firetail lives in habitats similar to those of the beautiful firetail.

Aviculture: Like the previous species, this bird is extremely rare in aviculture. It requires the same care, management, and diet as the diamond sparrow (see page 211).

Genus *Neochmia* (crimson finches) Gray, 1849

CRIMSON FINCH *Neochmia phaeton* (Hombron & Jacquinot, 1841)

DK: Solastrild NL: Zonneastrild, Australische vuurvink FR: Phaeton, Rubin d'Australie
DE: Sonnenastrild, Sonnenamadine IT: Diamante fetonte, Diamante rosso

▸ *photos page 129*

Neochmia phaeton

Description: Red, with a grayish sheen on the upperparts; blackish crown. Wings anthracite with gray-brown edging. Often a few little white spots on the flanks and breast. Belly and under tail coverts black. Underside of wings yellow. The female is grayish; cheeks and throat are wine red; rump and upper tail coverts red with black feather edging. Wings grayish red with dark brown edging. Eyes brown-red with a black iris; light pink periophthalmic ring; beak red, lighter on the female, with white on the base; legs grayish yellow. Length: 5–5½ in. (13–14 cm).

Geographic variations:

■ *N. p. phaeton*, as above. Distribution: northeastern West Australia through Northern Territory to northwestern Queensland.

■ *N. p. iredalei* Mathews. Brighter in coloration, without the black crown. Neck and crown have the same color. Distribution: from Cape Melville in northeastern Queensland to Proserpine, and southeastern Cape York Peninsula.

■ *N. p. albiventer* Mathews. A very brightly colored bird, much like the previous subspecies.

Crown, nape, and neck red with a grayish hue. Underside and under tail coverts white; therefore sometimes called the pale-bellied crimson finch (waxbill). The bases of the upper and lower mandibles are white. Length: 4.3–4.7 in. (11–12 cm). Distribution: northern and western Cape York Peninsula, northeastern Australia.

■ *N. p. evangelinae* D'Albertis & Salvadori. Much like the previous subspecies; underparts cream-white, ochre or yellowish; by many ornithologists seen as a golden variety of the nominate form. Crown and neck with gray-green hue. Very brightly colored red bill with shiny white bases. Distribution: southern Papua New Guinea, north of Cape York Peninsula.

Habitat: Grassland, reed and coastal plains. Sometimes in trees and bushes, where they like to build their rather bulky nest, which doesn't have a tunnel. The female lays 5–8 white eggs, averaging 14 x 12 mm, which will be incubated for approximately 14 days by both parents, each for approximately two-hour shifts during the day. During the night, only the hen broods while the male roosts near the nest on a branch.

Aviculture: Rather rare in the USA, more common in Europe. The species is not polygamous, however, they will accept alternative mates for different seasons. As a general rule, these birds should only be kept in single pairs with no other birds, as they have a reputation for being extremely pugnacious. However, some are less pugnacious than others and can be kept either colonially or in a mixed species aviary, provided the other occupants are equally robust. When the temperature drops below 60°F (15°C), they must be housed indoors at room temperature. The species is very nervous while breeding, so very susceptible to disturbances. They like to take canary baskets as their "maternity room", although we have had more success by offering them large nest boxes, 10 x 10 x 10 in. (25 x 25 x 25 cm), with a half-open front; place the nests in thick bushes as high as possible. Their free nests are constructed from coarse grasses, wool, pieces of bark, and moss; the lining is made from soft feathers, preferably white. A free nest is a bold structure measuring about 6 in. (15 cm) long, 4 in. (10 cm) high and 6 in. (15 cm) wide. The female is the main architect. The nest may be used at various times, but be prepared; hygiene is not their biggest virtue! As we stated before, we consider it the most aggressive of all Australian grassfinches. Nevertheless, it is a beautiful and most interesting species, and worth all the effort of getting them to breed. Watch the birds while alarmed; they twitter their alarm call and flick their tail back and forth, a feature that is probably the reason why they are often called pheasant finches!

The species is very susceptible to drafts, cold weather and nasty winds; they like sunshine and should only be housed in a garden aviary when the weather is warm and sunny. The preferred aviary is the one that is well-planted and not too large, and without colleagues. Fresh water at all times is essential; they like to take a bath several times a day. When kept indoors, a mist sprayer should be used; the birds will get familiar with it in a surprisingly short time.

Allow no more than three broods per season. The 5–6 eggs are incubated for approximately 14 days by both partners (see above), and the youngsters leave the nest after about 21 days. The first few nights they will sleep in the nest, although all the young do not always return; after two weeks they are independent, and after three months, or sometimes a couple of weeks longer, they have finished their molt.

Food: See Bengalese (page 198). Live food and germinated seeds are essential.

Genus *Poephila* (grassfinches) Gould, 1842

PARSON FINCH *Poephila cincta* Gould, 1836

DK: Korthalet Baelteflnke DK: Gordelgrasvink FR: Diamant a bavette
DE: Gürtelgrasfink, Gürtelgrasamadine IT: Diamante bavette

▶ *photos page 130*

Description: Silverish gray head; black throat and lores. Fawn back, somewhat brownish on the wings. Black tail and bar over the white rump. White upper tail coverts. Breast and underparts cinnamon; first part of the under tail coverts white. Black patch on the flanks. Eyes dark brown, beak dark gray, legs flesh-colored. Length: 4¼ in. (10 cm).

Geographic variations:
■ *P. c. cincta*, as above. Distribution: eastern Australia; overlaps widely with the following subspecies in the southern part of the Cape York Peninsula in the north, extending southeastward through Queensland into northern New South Wales.
■ *P. c. atropygialis* Diggles. Diggles's parson finch. Differs from nominate race in having a black rump and upper tail coverts. Distribution: Cape York Peninsula, except the extreme northern point.
■ *P. c. nigrotecta* Hartert. Chocolate Diggles parson finch. Black rump and a more intensive overall clear brown coloration. Distribution: extreme northern portion of Cape York Peninsula.

Habitat: These birds live in forest, woodland, and scrubby country, near watercourses, and open plains. They occur near the coast in small flocks.

Aviculture: Sociable, but sometimes aggressive in captivity. They need space; hence a large, well-planted aviary is necessary. Keeping more pairs together (which means at least three pairs, never only two) stimulates social behavior and nest construction. They build a bottle-like nest of grass, feathers, and plant fibers, with an entrance tunnel, but prefer using a nest box or the old nests of other birds. They like to have a choice, so supply plenty of nesting facilities. The female lays 5–9 eggs; both sexes incubate for approximately 13 days. The young leave the nest after three weeks and are fed by both parents.

Food: See Zebra finch (page 224). In addition to small ripe and half-ripe seeds, insects are essential during the breeding season.

Other name: Black-throated finch.

LONG-TAILED FINCH *Poephila acuticauda* (Gould, 1839)

DK: Spidshalet Baeltefinke   FR: Diamant à longue queue   DE: Spitzschwanzamadine, Spitzschwanz-Gürtelgrasfink   ▸ *photos page 131*
IT: Djamante coda lunga

Description: Similar in appearance to the parson finch, but the black tail has two long central feathers like fine needles. Eyes dark brown, beak yellow, legs red. The female has a slightly smaller bib; her call is lower in pitch and much softer. Length: 7 in. (18 cm), including the tail; body length: 5 in. (13 cm).

Geographic variations:

■ *P. a. acuticauda*, as above. Distribution: northern West Australia, and overlapping the border of the Northern Territory.
■ *P. a. hecki* Heinroth. Heck's grassfinch or Red-billed long-tailed finch. Differs by having a red or orange-red beak, rather than yellow as in the nominate form. Distribution: from the border of West Australia and Northern Territory in the north, and from there into northern Queensland.

Habitat: These birds live in high eucalyptus trees and along open forests; rarely in open grassland and scrub country. Always found near water courses. They exhibit a rather strong pair bonding and stay together for life.

Aviculture: Extremely sociable in the wild, but sometimes troublesome in an aviary. Can best be kept with larger birds in a well-planted aviary. They must be housed indoors during the fall and winter. A spacious area encourages the growth of the two long central tail feathers. The female lays 5–6 white eggs; the sexes take alternate shifts incubating for 13–14 days. Give the birds as many different nest boxes as possible; they must be positioned high and far apart, behind natural cover.

The birds will construct roosting nests as well, so be sure to provide enough building materials. Sometimes different pairs will sleep together in these nests.

Although sexing is not easy, males usually have a more heart shaped throat patch, while hens have a pear-shaped bib which is somewhat smaller as well. The best method of sexing the birds is to observe which of them sings the crowing and mating song. Stimulate breeding by supplying grass and weed seeds as well as live food. Restrict a pair from breeding after two or three clutches. The hen should be at least one year old before being placed in the breeding program.

The courtship display of the male begins with frequent bowing and head-bobbing toward the female, often with a stem of grass in his beak, like the African waxbills. During this dance, his body feathers are fluffed, accentuating his features, particularly the black throat patch. The female responds with similar head-bobbing and bowing. The male then sings his little song, which has been described as ascending to a louder and clearer series of soft notes. The female accepts his advances by leaning forward and quivering her tail to solicit copulation. After mating, the pair will usually indulge in further bobbing and mutual preening.

Food: See Zebra finch (page 224).

Other names: Blackheart, Blackheart finch, Shaft-tailed finch (grassfinch).

MASKED FINCH *Poephila personata* Gould, 1842

DK: Maskebaeltefinke NL: Maskeramadine FR: Diamant à masque
DE: Maskenamadine IT: Diamante mascherato, Diamante, nera

▶ *photos page 130*

Description: Male. Chestnut, darker on the wings; rosy brown cheeks, neck and underside; white upper tail and under tail coverts. Black band across the lower back to the sides. Eyes dark brown, beak pale yellow, legs light brownish pink. The black mask of the female is smaller. Length: 5–5½ in. (13–14 cm).

Geographic variations:

■ *P. p. personata*, as above. Distribution: northern Australia, from Derby in the west to the mouth of the Flinders River in the east.
■ *P. p. leucotis* Gould. White-eared grassfinch. Part of the lower cheeks white; chin and throat black, bordered by a white band which flows into the cheeks. Cinnamon upperparts. Black flank patch. Distribution: from the east coast of the Gulf of Cape York Peninsula, in savanna-type country, close to basalt rock ridges. In Australia, this sub-species is rather popular as an aviary bird.

Poephila personata
P. cincta
P. acuticauda

Habitat: The birds live on dry savanna woodland, open forests and grassy plains, always near water courses. Due to its constant search for water, this bird is also found in gardens and parks in sometimes large groups, composed of pairs (their pair bonds last at least throughout the breeding season).

Aviculture: Excellent, sociable, but somewhat noisy bird, which needs a large, well-planted aviary. They live mainly on the ground in search for food, but spend their mating season high between the branches of dead scrub and trees. Their nest is bulky, close to the ground, and constructed from grass, small feathers, plant fibers, and wool. In the nest-sites, pieces of charcoal are incorporated for hygroscopic reasons. The female lays 4–6 eggs; both sexes incubate for 13–14 days. After 21 days the young leave the nest but will be fed for another two weeks by both parents before they are independent. In 3–4 months they finish their youth molt and their beaks will be yellow. Around this time the young males start to sing. For more details see other *Poephila* species.

Food: See Zebra finch (page 224).

ZEBRA FINCH *Poephila guttata castanotis* (Gould, 1842)

DK: Zebrafinke NL: Zebravink FR: Diamant mandarin DE: Zebrafink IT: Diamante mandarino   ▸ *photos page 132, 133, 139*

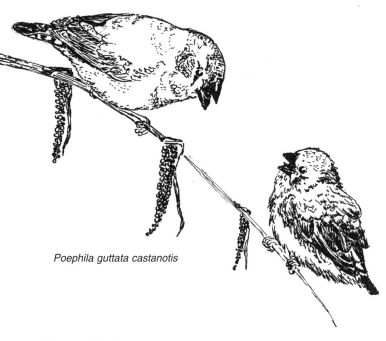

Poephila guttata castanotis

Description: The male is mainly softly grayish above, more gray-blue on the head and neck, gray-brown on the back, with a conspicuous orange or chestnut cheek patch which is bordered from below the eye with a narrow, black vertical line ("tear"). A further narrow black line edges the base of the beak, and the area between the two black lines is white. The wings are dark gray-brown. The throat and upperpart of the breast are marked with horizontal, dark gray to black, narrow wavy lines which are bordered below with a wider dark breast band or bar that runs across the width of the chest. The lower underside is beige-white, the flanks orange-red with round white spots. The tail is black with white diagonal bands. The rump and under tail coverts are white. The beak is coral red, the eyes red, the feet orange-brown. The hen is gray above with a gray, sometimes almost white, ear spot. The area between the black tear-line and the narrow black line around the base of the beak is white, as in the cock. The throat, neck, chest, and sides are gray; the underside white-beige. The tail is similar to that of the male, as are the white rump and under tail coverts. The beak is much lighter red colored than that of the male; the eyes are red, the feet orange-yellow. Length: 4–4½ in. (10–11cm).

The attentive zebra finch fancier will notice that there are some variations of the above descriptions among domestic stock. For example, domesticated birds have dark brown, rather then red eyes. The gray in the cock of domesticated normals (= gray or wild color) is more brownish while the underside of the wild hen is frequently much paler than that of her domesticated counterpart; the same can be said about the cheeks. Domesticated birds are also usually more robust and elongated than wild specimens.

On fledging, the young already bear a resemblance to adult hens; only the black lines round the cheeks and beak are missing and this area is colored gray rather than white. Hatchlings have a pink, flesh-colored skin, with or without sparse white down; the beak is horn-colored. In approximately 3 weeks the skin gradually darkens, and a week later is almost black. In about 12 days the beak is quite black. The primaries appear after 7 days, the tail feathers on the tenth day, and small contour feathers on the eleventh to twelfth days. The vanes on the primaries can be seen at this time.

Geographic variations:

■ *P. g. castanotis*, as above. Although it is somewhat of a departure to describe a subspecies other than the nominate first, this is justified by the fact that the domesticated stock of this common avicultural bird derives from *castanotis* rather than from *guttata*. Distribution: Australia. This subspecies is common and widespread over most of the Australian continent. It is absent only from coastal northern Australia, Cape York Peninsula, the extreme southeastern area, including Tasmania, and the rainforests of extreme southwestern Australia.

■ *P. g. guttata* Vieillot. Timor zebra finch. This bird is brownish yellow, and the top and sides of the head are darker than in the Australian race. The females of the Timor zebra finch also have a darker breast and back. This bird is somewhat smaller than the Australian bird. Distribution:

Lesser Sunda Islands, including Timor and Flores, Alor, Wetar, and Sumba.

Dr. Jean Delacour, the late French ornithologist and aviculturist, regarded all zebra finches, including this Indonesian variety, as being one and the same, but it is now generally accepted that he was mistaken. The English naturalist and artist John Gould was also concerned with the zebra finch, and even before his first trip to Australia in 1838, he had published a detailed description of the species. It is also interesting to note that Vieillot, who quite probably had zebra finches in his own aviaries, described the only subspecies of the finch then recognized, hence the Indonesian race, rather than the Australian form; he made a mistake however, as he states that he was describing the Australian bird! In his earlier two-part work, *Les Oiseaux Chanteurs* (1805-1809), he describes his breeding successes in detail! In his *Nouveau Dictionnaire d'Historie Naturelle* (new edition, 12, page 233) he named the zebra finch *Taeniopygia guttata* (1817): the Greek *tainia* = band, and the Greek *pyge* = rump, tail. The word *guttata* is derived from the Latin *gutta* = spot or drop; *guttata* thus means: spotted, referring to the spotted markings on the flanks. *Castanotis* is derived from the Greek *castanon* = chestnut, and the Greek *otos*, genitive of *ous* = ear, and means as much as: with a chestnut colored ear. It should be noted that many authorities still recognize the genus *Taeniopygia* for this species. L.J.P. Vieillot (1748-1831) was the first biologist who wrote about this interesting and well-known cage and aviary bird, in *Histoire Naturelle des Plus Beaux Oiseaux Chanteurs de Zone Torride*.

In older literature you may come across various scientific names, and at one time up to seven subspecies were recognized. In alphabetical order, these are *alexandrae* (1921), *castanotis* (1837, 1842), *hartogi* (1920), *mouki* (1912), *mungi* (1912), *roebucki* (1913), and *wayensis* (1912). It is now generally recognized, however, that these are in fact all taxonomically identical, though there are some obvious color variants in certain areas. The Australian ornithologist, J. A. Keast proved beyond doubt there is only one subspecies of the zebra finch in Australia, however unlikely this may seem in such a large territory. One possible explanation is that

frequent droughts on the continent, especially in Central Australia, force birds to migrate in search of food and, especially, water, causing a regular intermixing of different bird populations, leading to a standardization of type. However, there are still variations in markings, beak color, and size but these are always seen in individuals and they disappear through pairing in the second generation.

Habitat: In Australia, we were able to ascertain that the denser populations always occurred in the more arid areas; but the species was also present in coastal areas, especially after long periods of inland drought. We have frequently seen flocks of 100 or more birds in the regions of Brisbane and Townsville (Queensland), Campbelltown (New South Wales), Roebuck Bay and Carnarvon (Western Australia).

In the ornithological journal *Emu* (No. 58, pp. 219–246, Melbourne, 1958), Dr. J. A. Keast, in his famous article *Intraspecific variations in the Australian finches*, declared categorically that there are no consistent geographic variations of the zebra finch, as we noted earlier. He came to this conclusion after examining hundreds of skins of the birds from all parts of the continent. Personally, we must agree with his conclusion after examining 48 skins from various geographical locations. This conclusion can be considered to be quite an important ornithological fact, considering, as we said above, the enormous distributional range of the zebra finch.

As long as adequate supplies of water and food are available, this finch is relatively sedentary in its habits. In other words, it stays put as long as conditions are optimum. However, the nature of the Australian continental climate means that drought can occur in almost any region at almost any time. The climate is only theoretically cyclic, and wildlife has to adapt to any sudden emergency. Unseasonal droughts in one area mean that the normally sedentary zebra finches have to move on to more favorable areas. Local migrations mean that separate geographical flocks of birds meet up at regular intervals and are very likely to interbreed, which is why we stated that color variations disappear usually after the first pairing.

This, of course, means that the genes from all populations eventually get together with those of all other populations over periods of years, resulting in a sort of natural standardization of type now generally recognized as the single subspecies *castanotis*. But, as we said, this does not mean that color, pattern, and morphological differences do not occur. These are usually too small to warrant separate subspecific classification. According to Keast, these differences often apply to the size and color of the beak, the size of the body, the amount of striping in the breast pattern, the size of the band separating the breast and belly, and so on.

As we have already discussed, the continental race of zebra finches occurs over much of the Australian mainland. As climate and topography can vary greatly over various parts of the continent, it follows that not all populations of zebra finches have the same lifestyle all of the time. As an example, let us look at the life of zebra finches indigenous to northern Australia. Here it is predominantly grassland, some cultivated, some not, interspersed with small trees and shrubs; the average rainfall is relatively low so that more luxuriant vegetation is out of the question. The zebra finch is also found in relatively open savanna, or sparsely treed grassland. In parts of Central Australia, zebra finches may invade in favorable times, but nearly always head for more suitable areas during the summer drought. In such cases the birds may have to migrate almost to coastal areas in search of adequate water and food. Much of central Australia is rocky, but zebra finches may congregate in stands of scrub, known to Australians as mulga, or in spinifex, a kind of grass with wiry stems, where they can take shelter from the hot sun, build their breeding nests, or roost either among the foliage or in special nests that are specially constructed for this purpose.

During my (MMV) visits to these habitats, I observed quite large numbers of zebra finches, although the conditions could not have been described as ideal, as there was little water, inadequate nesting facilities, etc. We must not forget, however, that zebra finches drink much in the manner of pigeons and doves, by sucking the water rather than scooping like most birds. This gives them the possibility of sucking up dew drops in the early morning. Moreover, zebra finches have a lower metabolic rate than many other birds and thus require less water. They also excrete less water in their droppings and are capable of taking some brackish water without apparent ill effects.

European settlement during the last 200 years has also had a beneficial effect on zebra finches, as well as many other forms of wild life in the central areas of Australia. The installation of dams, bores, troughs, and drains for irrigation and stock (cattle, sheep, horses) watering, has allowed many species of birds to survive in large numbers in areas where this would previously not have been possible. Difficulties are experienced then only by birds living in the real outback, or never-never (described by some Australians as the land that God forgot), which have to migrate to more favorable areas when times become desperate. Large numbers of these finches may also be seen in the more inhabited areas of eastern, southeastern and southwestern Australia, where they occur in parks, gardens and plantations. Such birds have lost much of their natural fear and have become as cheeky as house sparrows *Passer domesticus*, which were introduced into Australia around 1850–1860 and have spread through Victoria to Tasmania, South Australia and Queensland, and now inhabit the whole eastern half of Australia with the exception of western Cape York Peninsula.

Zebra finches forage mostly on the ground, less often in trees and shrubs. They do not walk like a starling, but hop like a sparrow with both feet together. Their flight is rapid, relatively direct, and slightly undulating. They are capable of flying quite considerable distances without stopping to rest.

Like the vast majority of the Australian grass finches, zebra finches are basically seed eaters, but they do not live exclusively on seeds as is frequently believed. In addition to half ripe and ripe grass seeds of both wild and cultivated varieties, they will eat the seeds of many other plants as well as a variety of small insects. Several times we have observed them feeding on termites, small moths, and flies, which they sometimes caught in flight; in addition to seeking insects on the ground, they also sought them among the foliage of trees and shrubs where a quantity of larvae (caterpillars and grubs) are taken. Although they do not take so many insects outside the breeding season, hatchlings are fed almost exclusively on insects for the first few days of their lives.

As we have already discussed, zebra finches are good at conserving water, and drink like doves; by sucking up the water they are able to take in the morning dew from grass and foliage. This, of course, allows them not only to survive, but actually to thrive and reproduce in what to us seems like very inhospitable climatic conditions. This does not mean that our domestic zebra finches can be kept without water or with a very sparse water supply; they have to have a daily supply of fresh water.

The characteristic, somewhat monotonous tin-trumpet call of the zebra finch can hardly be called a song, but is nevertheless not unattractive. The cock birds can sometimes be heard, especially in the evening time, uttering a sort of short solo song.

The most important call, designated by Immelmann as the identity call, is a nasal, trumpet-like "tiah." This is the species' most common vocalization, both in the wild and in the cage or aviary. Individual birds use the call, as well as large groups, usually in flight, and we have seen and heard groups of 40–100 birds using the identity call. Should one of the birds from the group lag behind, then the call becomes conspicuously more urgent in tone. During the breeding season this call can be continuously heard at, or close to the nesting sites, as pairs hold aural contact with each other. In the case of approaching danger, the call becomes more penetrating and urgent.

Immelmann recognizes a communication call similar to the "tiah" but softer, and perhaps resembling a repetitive "tet, tet, tet." In our opinion this call is not so urgent or alarming as the "tiah" call; it is used in smaller groups of say 10–20 birds and especially by pairs in flight. During mating, this call is also used, but is even softer and occasionally sounds as if it is being uttered with difficulty! The call is often used by the cock simultaneously as he spreads his tail to display the "zebra" markings of his rump, and is thus designed to impress the female. Later, the action may be used to reassure the hen during nest building or during incubation.

Another call, a hissing "west" likened by Immelmann to the ripping of a piece of cotton cloth, is used by birds to warn off other birds, both of their own and other species, that approach nesting sites too closely.

Finally, there is the "song," or what bird fanciers describe as the song. This vocalization consists of a series of harsh, low, nasal trills of up to two seconds in duration. Immelmann compares these with "stomach talking," something that we find difficult to agree with. It must be noted here that this song, frequently heard in captive birds, is hardly ever heard in the wild, except with males that do not have partners.

Before actual copulation takes place, the cock courts the hen with a dance. It is a rather simple dance when compared to that of other Australian grassfinches, and consists of the cock springing from twig to twig in the vicinity of the hen. At the same time, the cock points his beak in the direction of the hen, sometimes even rubbing his beak against hers. The cock's tail is also regularly bent in the direction of the hen, sometimes so that it passes over her body. The hen usually perches quietly on a twig and allows the performance to proceed. We rarely saw the hen playing a great part in the ceremony, actually; she usually played a very passive part. Sometimes the hen flits off to another perch and the cock continues the hopping performance as he follows her, his movements rapid and constant, so that a certain rhythm is followed. During the display, the feathers of the crown, the sides of the head, the cheeks, and even the belly, are regularly fluffed out. After some time the hen, if receptive, will respond by rapidly raising and lowering her tail; this is a sign that she is ready to mate.

Copulation usually occurs on the ground, on a large stone, on rocks, or in trees or shrubs with a large amount of dead wood so that the foliage does not get in the way. Copulation may occur several times during the mating period. Whether zebra finches pair for life or regularly change partners is a point that is still not determined by ornithologists, but most do believe, like we do, that pairing is for life. In the aviary, this is of course not the case, especially with regard to the forced matings required for color breeding. It is generally accepted that pairs and groups of zebra finches stay together even outside the breeding season, sharing all of their daily activities, mutually preening, and even sleeping in pairs in their special roosting nests. We have occasionally seen pairs outside the breeding season disappearing into their roosting nests in order to avoid the hot midday sun!

Zebra finches seem to have no special preference for nesting sites; we have seen nests in the most amazing places, but generally they build their nests in the thick foliage of small trees and shrubs. We often found nests in thorn scrubs, and it is interesting to observe that in southwestern Australia, zebra finches almost exclusively use the thorny shrub *Hakea preissii* in which to build. Such a nesting site gives good protection against predatory birds and other animals. In the eastern areas, the birds often use introduced shrubs, including brambles and roses; some even nest in citrus trees, according to Immelmann. Aside from foliage, zebra finches may nest on the ground, among grass tussocks, in hollow limbs, and in termite mounds. In Queensland and Central Australia, we have even found nests in abandoned rabbit burrows! Zebra finches like to recycle nest material and will demolish one nest in order to construct another. In some cases they will use old nests again, and we have often found completely new pairs laying their eggs in long abandoned nests. Young pairs may even use the nests in which they were born, after their parents move out, as has been proved with marked birds. Nests are occasionally found in the eaves of houses and other buildings, in abandoned vehicles, old tin cans, cooking vessels and so on! The height of the nest from the ground does not seem to be a major concern and may range from ground level to higher than 26 ft. (8 m).

The nest is a simple construction; nest material includes grass, moss and feathers. There are no hard and fast rules, and research has shown us that the main nest material used will depend on what is available in the habitat. Green grass may be used as well as dried grass, and in the absence of grass, small twigs may be used. The nest is lined especially with small down feathers and we have often also found rabbit hairs, sheep wool, moss,

and small twigs. Immelmann dissected nests and counted their constituent parts. Nests were constructed from 300–450 individual lengths of grass ranging from 4¾–6 in. (12–15 cm) in the outer layers, and 2–2½ in. (5–6 cm) in the inner layers. The longest grass stem the ornithologist found was almost 12 in. (30 cm)!

Some birds, interestingly, hardly build a nest, selecting instead old zebra finch nests which they refurbish with a new roof, etc., or the nest of other birds, including other grassfinches and swallows. Nests found in tree hollows and similar places have no roof and are built simply as a loosely packed, untidy cup. Zebra finches also build a roosting nest, also simple in construction but frequently with a roof and a tunnel-like entrance. Old, abandoned nests are sometimes used as roosting nests.

Although both sexes will collect nesting materials, it is usually the cock that collects most of these, while the hen concerns herself mainly with the inner nest architecture. The cock often helps with the outer framework of the nest but the majority of the internal work is done by the hen. In the drier areas of Central Australia, we noted that both sexes were concerned with building the whole nest, perhaps a reflection on the urgency of completing a brood during the short wet season when adequate food and water is available. In areas where plenty of water and food are available over longer periods, the nest takes 13–15 days to build, whereas when both birds build in a hurry it can take as little as 3–6 days.

The success of a clutch depends largely on the rainfall; thus the availability of water and food. Therefore breeding begins even in the driest parts of Australia as soon as the rains come, whatever time of the year it happens to be. It is possible in some areas for zebra finches to raise one clutch after another throughout the year, sometimes totaling seven, eight, or even more. This is perhaps the reason why well cared for captive zebra finches are so ready to breed at any time of the year. In the wild it can sometimes also happen, especially in Central Australia, that zebra finches miss out a whole year of breeding altogether during bad times.

The wet season in the north begins in November or December and ends in March or

April, and zebra finches in that area breed continually during this time, stopping only as the rains diminish. In southwestern Australia we find a similar situation, but in addition to the rainfall, the temperature also plays a part here; indeed the latter can have a great influence on breeding. According to Serventy and Marshall (*Emu* 1957), the following situation exists: the particular rainfall in the winter months is inadequate to allow the birds to breed but in spring and autumn the birds breed. During the summer months, breeding is not possible as there is little or no rainfall; while in the winter, the temperature is too low. Occasionally, unseasonal summer rainfall will trigger off a bout of breeding, but results are often poor due to premature ending of suitable conditions. In eastern Australia, similar situations may arise.

It is a well known fact that captive zebra finches lay variable numbers of eggs in a clutch. In the wild, the variation of clutch sizes may not be so great, but it is still difficult to make any hard and fast rules, though the smallest and largest clutches we found consisted of three and ten eggs, respectively. According to our notes, we examined some 160 nests over a period of three years. The average clutch size was 4–5 and the size of the eggs varied from 9.7 x 15. 6 to 11.5 x 16 mm.

Observations have shown that both sexes begin incubating after the fourth egg has been laid. Each bird does an average shift of 2–2½ hours, although actual shifts may sometimes be less than one hour or more than three hours on the nest during the day. At night, both parents stay in the nest together. There seems to be no hard and fast rules regarding the change of shift, but this is probably influenced by things such as hunger, thirst, tiredness, temperature, broodiness, etc. As soon as the incubating bird hears its partner's voice, it leaves the eggs and flies off, leaving the partner to take over. Subsequent changes occur in a similar manner.

We often observed cock birds bringing a piece of nest material, a grass stem, feather, little twig, etc., to the nest at the beginning of his shift so that he could while away his incubation time working it into the nest structure. We never saw the hens performing this behavior.

The incubation time is influenced by tempera-

ture, humidity, broodiness and so on, but the average time is 12–16 days. Newly hatched youngsters are covered sparsely with down and have flesh colored skin. The skin darkens after the third day and by the end of the week is almost black. The horn colored beak changes to black by the 12th day.

The eyes first open after 8–11 days. In 7–8 days, the first primary feathers appear. The young are silent for the first three days but thereafter the begging calls, which one of our researchers likened to the sound of a nail file being dragged over a nail, can be heard, softly at first but increasing in volume as the chicks grow older. As soon as the begging calls start, the parents become more active in feeding the young. Both parents share in this chore; half-ripe grass seeds and plant seeds, plus insects, form the bulk of the food. The young leave the nest in 21–23 days, depending on the amount of available food, and thus the rate of development.

During the first week after fledging, the parents guide the young back to the nest in the evenings so that they may spend the night relatively safely. They are often brought back near to, or into, the nest and fed there during the day, probably to help lighten the evening muster! This habit no longer occurs in captive birds.

Even after becoming independent, the youngsters spend a long time with, or near, their parents, and roost with them at night. The parents often construct a new nest for the next brood so

Poephila guttata

that the first brood can continue to roost in their own nursery.

The first molt starts after the seventh week, and after a further 4–6 weeks they have their adult plumage and the characteristic red beak, which darkens to full adult color by the tenth week. As we have mentioned several times above, zebra finches are extremely social birds. This can be seen by their tendency to live in groups of 40–100 or more individuals. The group usually stays together in the same area as long as conditions are acceptable, but in times of drought, lack of water and food will force the flock to migrate together to more favorable areas. During the afternoon, the birds congregate together at a certain site in order to sing together and mutually preen. At dusk, the same birds huddle together to roost for the night at the roosting sites. In severe droughts, groups can congregate together, forming flocks of 1000 or more individuals; these groups can unfortunately cause enormous damage if they should descend onto cultivated areas, especially seed crops.

During the breeding time, groups split up into smaller parties of 6–22 pairs; however, they always remain in contact with the other groups. It is interesting to note that rarely is more than one breeding nest, plus a roosting nest, to be found in the same tree or shrub; it can thus be surmised that each pair has its own mini-territory and therefore a certain amount of privacy. In the more arid zones, however, where nesting sites may be scarce,

Zebra Finch / *Poephila guttata*   Photo: Matthew M. Vriends

a different situation arises, and sometimes 10–20 nests may be found in the same tree or shrub.

Members of the group always keep in some form of contact with each other. The late Dr. Klaus Immelmann once told me (MMV) that the birds certainly can recognize each other from their calls, and while neighbors may freely visit each other in their nests, strangers are driven energetically away. Most members of the colony congregate together at water sources several times a day in order to drink and bathe and mutually preen. Similarly, they fly in groups to the feeding grounds, which may be up to 330 ft. (100 m) away from the nesting sites.

Aviculture: Let's start with a "potted" history of the zebra finch in aviculture. The French ornithologist Vieillot (see page 225) was, as we stated, perhaps the first person to keep and, especially, to breed zebra finches in captivity. Whatever the case, the German magazine *Die Gefiederte Welt* reported about zebra finch breeding as though it was the most usual thing in the world, in its first year of publication (1872). In his book *Prachtfinken* (Estrildid Finches), published in 1879, the well-known German ornithologist and aviculturist Dr. Karl Russ stated that "the experience derived from breeding zebra finches is fundamental to the breeding of all other cage birds." The English aviculturist C. W. Gedney gave a comprehensive description of the care and breeding of zebra finches in his book *Foreign Cage Birds*, also published in 1879. All in all, we can assume that zebra finches have been known in Europe for about 200 years and they were probably imported even earlier than budgerigars.

Mr. H. Rensenbrink of the famous Artis zoo in Amsterdam, Netherlands, told us that the first zebra finches, still known then under the scientific name of *Taeniopygia castanotis*, arrived there in 1859. They were given the name *mandarin amandina*, which was probably derived from the French *diamant mandarin*. Rensenbrink was unable to tell us the exact date of the first specimens arriving in Europe, but did find a report that Vieillot had bred them in Paris (see above).

A former director of the Burger's Zoo (Arnhem, The Netherlands), Dr. R. A. Th. van Hooff, told me

(MMV) that the first zebra finches were brought to London, "but when this occurred cannot be determined, since it concerned just a little insignificant bird. The 'Zoo' in Antwerp (Belgium) probably got one soon after London, as did 'Artis,' while it is probable that Berlin (Germany) had one of the first. As far as I can trace back, our park received its first zebra finches in 1928; and in 1929 and 1930 we bred them. Where and when the first was bred is extremely difficult to say. Perhaps it was done by a bird enthusiast privately, or it could have occurred in the animal parks of London, Berlin or Antwerp. One of the first–if not the first–importers of these finches to Holland was the firm of Blaser of Rotterdam. I don't know if the firm exists anymore. They were bird dealers, and later sold other large animals worldwide too."

Zebra finches became popular and desirable as breeding birds all over western Europe during the latter half of the 19th century. However, it is still not known where and when the first zebra finch was bred in captivity, even in Australia. We do know, however, that the first mutation, the white zebra finch, was bred in Australia. As reported by C. af Enehjelm of the zoo in Helsinki (Finland) in his article in *Foreign Birds* (September, 1956), the white color first appeared during 1921 in a community aviary owned by A. J. Woods of Sydney. The three white birds were sold by Woods to a fellow citizen named H. Lyons who standardized the mutation and bred several hundred birds. The first white zebra finches arrived in Europe in the mid-1930s. The silver, or dilute normal, mutation also originated in Australia; the first examples reaching the western world before the second world war. Enehjelm did not, unfortunately, report precisely who bred this mutation, nor where or when it was bred.

Enehjelm thought it possible that the first fawn or normal brown mutation was bred in Australia, but the late aviculturist C. Stork (Eindhoven, The Netherlands) puts this down to F. Mills of Johannesburg, South Africa, in 1942. Enehjelm also stated that the first pied or variegated zebra finch was hatched in the aviaries of U. Nilsson (Copenhagen) in the early 1930s. Whitehouse, of Brisbane, Australia, first saw the chestnut-flanked white zebra finch in the wild, and in 1937 was fortunate in producing the mutation in his captive

breeding stock. However, only females were produced at first and it was several more years before he succeeded in producing a male. This was one of the last mutations to become known in Europe. At the present time (2002) there are more than 40 recognized color mutations and at least ten more are theoretically possible.

Zebra finches are particularly well suited for anyone who is just beginning to keep birds. Keeping a single pair in a large cage for their song or color, or keeping several pairs (three or more, never two pairs) together for breeding is not a difficult task, and there isn't any magic connected with it. Zebra finches not only demand little in the way of care, but have a bright and vigorous song and are easy to breed. And, without a doubt, zebra finches also win the hearts of many experienced bird fanciers and breeders because they offer endless opportunities to achieve fascinating color varieties through breeding experimentations. Zebra finches are prolific breeders in outdoor aviaries and breeding cages, but only three or four broods per season are recommended. Remove all nesting materials (grass, plant fibers, small down feathers, moss, wool), as soon as the nest is completed, to prevent further construction. The free nest is bottle-shaped, with an entrance tunnel. They like to use all types of nest boxes and such. The female lays four to five eggs, which are incubated by both sexes for about 13–16 days. The young leave the nest after 20–22 days.

Youngsters should be close banded between the 10th and 12th day after hatching (please ask an experienced fancier to help you the first time). When the young are between 5–6 weeks old and their beaks are turning red, they should be taken away from their parents. They must be carefully watched, however, to ensure that they can feed themselves. Don't breed with zebra finches until they are at least eight months to one year old; when not breeding, males and females should be separated from the age of three months onward.

Food: See Bengalese (page 198), and text above, especially page 226.

Other names: Chestnut-eared finch, Chestnut finch, Spotted-sided finch.

Genus *Stizoptera* (double-bar finches) Oberholser, 1899

BICHENO'S FINCH *Stizoptera (Poephila) bichenovii* (Vigors & Horsfield, 1827)

DK: Ringastrild NL: Ringastrild FR: Diamant de Bicheno DE: Ringelastrild, Ringelamadine IT: Bicheno-astrild   ▸ *photo page 129*

Habitat: This species is found in long grass and scrub (pandanus), near water; also in cane fields, parks and gardens, never moving more than approximately 2 miles (3.2 km) from a permanent watering place.

Aviculture: An extremely friendly and peaceful aviary bird that must be housed indoors during fall and winter. They are often found on the ground, and it is advisable to have a leaf-mold compost heap in one of the corners. This heap should give the birds the opportunity to look for insects, satisfying their urge for scratching.

This species should choose their own partners. They build their own little nests from grass and small feathers in thick shrubbery, or use a nesting box. The female lays 4–5 white eggs which are incubated for 12–14 days by both sexes. During the night, both partners sit on the nest. When hatched, the young have a yellowish flesh-colored skin and some gray down. After approximately 4 days, the pigmentation of the skin is finished and the young look blackish. They leave the nest after some 19–25 days. In addition to insects, standard seed mixtures are needed. They drink by sucking, as do zebra finches. When the young are fed, sitting on a perch, they will lift their wings as though trying to shield the remainder of the clutch from the parent bird (Iles). In the wild, both subspecies will interbreed.

Description: Male. Crown, neck, shoulders, and further upperparts gray-brown, with very fine bars. Black wing coverts with white dots. Tail black; rump white. Forehead black; one black band across the throat and bordering the cheeks; another black bar bordering the breast from shoulder to shoulder. Throat, face, and underparts white; the latter with a buff sheen. Eyes dark brown, beak gray, legs dark gray-brown. The female's breast is slightly paler; blackish gray wing coverts. This species is the smallest of all Australian grassfinches. Length: 3–4 inches (8-10 cm).

Food: See Zebra finch (see page 224). Limit the feeding of mealworms to only 2 per day per bird, and only one for each chick in the nest.

Other names: Banded finch, White/Black-rumped finch, Double-barred finch, Owl-faced finch, and Owl finch. In North America, owl finch is the name most commonly used.

Geographic variations:

■ *S. b. bichenovii*, as above. Distribution: Australia, in southeastern New South Wales, Queensland (except the southwestern part), and northern area of Northern Territory.

■ *S. b. annulosa* (Gould). Black rump. Distribution: Australia, in the most northern part of Northern Territory.

Genus *Chloebia* **(Gouldian finch) Reichenbach, 1862**

GOULDIAN FINCH *Chloebia gouldiae* **(Gould, 1844)**

DK: Gouldsamadine NL: Gouldamadine FR: Diamant de Gould
DE: Gouldamadine IT: Diamante di Gould

▶ *photos page 136, 137, 138*

Description: Three color morphs characterize the wild Gouldian finch in Australia: the red headed, the black-headed, and the yellow-headed. All varieties are 5–5½ in. (12.5–14 cm) in length. Apart from their spectacular colors, males are recognized by their long, pointed middle tail feathers, which are about 1½ in. (4 cm) long. Hens' tail feathers are about ¾–1 in. (2–2.5 cm) long.

Personally, we find the red-headed Gouldian finch to be the most attractive of the trio. In the historical literature, this bird is often referred to as *C. g. mirabilis*, as the color morphs were at first thought to represent subspecific variations. However, as the forms interbreed freely in the wild, always producing the genetically correct color morph with no intermediates, the concept of subspecies cannot be considered valid. We repeat the obsolete names here only to enable readers to understand the early literature should they care to pursue further research.

In the red-headed cockbird, the deep red mask is bordered on the crown by a thin, black band, which broadens on the throat and runs into the black chin. The black band is followed by a light, sky blue band, which is twice as wide on the crown and sides of the head as it is on the chin. The breast is lilac or lilac-blue. The remaining under parts are deep yellow or orange-yellow, running into white around the area of the legs. The under tail coverts are white; the tibia is a brighter white. The nape, back, and wings are grassy green. The rump and upper tail coverts are light blue. The tail and primary wing feathers are black, the latter having green edges; the tail feathers are marked with white dots. The underside of the wings are silvery gray. The middle, black tail feathers are like needle-points. The eyes are dark brown and are surrounded by a thin, lilac periophthalmic ring; the beak is horn-colored with a conspicuous red tip; the legs and feet are pinkish. The hen is altogether duller in appearance, and usually lacks the blue neckband. Her tail is lighter

lilac, the underside paler. Her red mask is not nearly as brightly colored as the male's.

The second variety is the black-headed Gouldian finch, which is the most abundant variety in the wild, and the one from which the species was originally described. It therefore became the nominate subspecies *C. g. gouldiae* when further forms were named, but as mentioned above, subspecific differentiation is no longer considered valid, and all three variations are merely color morphs of one monotypic species. Apart from its black mask, the bird's coloration is similar to that described above. In this case, the hen also has a deep black head.

The third variety is the yellow-headed Gouldian finch, which was given the now-obsolete racial name *C. g. armitiana*. It is very scarce in the wild, representing less than 0.05% of the population. Although it is not rare in captivity, it is less abundant in domestic collections than the other varieties of Gouldians. The yellow-headed variety is similar in color to the other varieties except it has an orange-red to orange-yellow mask, which is frequently intermingled with black feathers.

The colors of juvenile birds are somewhat different than the adults. A young Gouldian that has just hatched from its egg is flesh-colored, having no feathers. In the angles of its jaw are two blue and one yellow, wart-like, light-reflective papillae (see also page 233). It has five black spots on its palate, two on its tongue, two on the inside of the point of the upper mandible and a horsehoe-shaped marking on the inside of the lower mandible. Biologically speaking, these markings are characteristic of the species. Similar, but not identical, markings are found in closely related finch species. In other words, a Gouldian finch does not have the same papillae and mouth markings (quantity, color, form, size, etc.) as a zebra finch, a blue-faced parrotfinch or a diamond firetail finch. In the dim light of the nest or nest box, these papillae and markings reflect the sparse available light and indicate to the parent birds the way to the crop. After the young birds leave the nest, the papillae and markings are lost, respectively, from the beak corners, inside the bill, and on the tongue, and will totally disappear when the birds are 2½–3 months old.

Before the first molt, juvenile Gouldians are easy to distinguish from adults. They are mainly olive green above, with more gray. Their upper tail feathers are gray, washed with blue; the edges of the feathers are lighter gray, and are easily seen when the wings are closed. The tail and wings are dark gray with olive green edges. The long, pointed, middle tail feathers can not yet be distinguished in length from the other tail feathers. The cheeks and forehead are gray to greenish gray, while the chin, throat, most of the belly and underside of the tail are whitish. The center of the tail is light gray-blue or yellow-gray; in some birds, it is rose-brown, but this color is lighter on the edges, usually light yellowish. The dark eyes are ringed with a featherless, thin, light blue border. The legs and feet are rose-colored, the beak is horn-colored, sometimes with a little red or yellow. It is impossible to distinguish the sexes of the juveniles according to their colors. However, as the cocks begin to try out their vocal cords, first hesitantly, then enthusiastically, we can distinguish them from the silent hens. We do not have to wait long for the cocks to start singing; they will start when they are 28–29 days old, as early as 5–7 days after leaving

the nest. Often they will sing all day long, provided they are left undisturbed.

It is interesting to note that cocks begin shaking and bobbing their heads at about 35 days, often accompanied by a beautiful little song. At this point, it makes sense to leave the newly emerged youngsters completely in peace for a few days. If they are disturbed, they may panic and fly around, possibly injuring themselves on the aviary wire or any nearby obstructions. The birds should be left alone to peacefully explore and become accustomed to their surroundings. They will then have every opportunity to remain secure, content, and become well adjusted birds. After a few days, the young birds will begin to feed themselves. After the second week, they will become more or less independent.

Distribution and habitat: Generally the birds occur in the tropical part of northern Australia, from Derby eastward to the Gulf of Carpentaria and to Charters Towers. Especially the Kimberley District is rich in these birds. They move around a great deal, so an exact range is hard to describe. They live on the grassy plains, often near water courses; also in mangrove swamps and thickets. Their numbers are, sadly enough, rapidly declining in the wild.

Aviculture: There is no doubt that Gouldian finches, famous for their remarkable, almost unnaturally colored plumage, can be accepted as the most beautiful of all the finches. They have always generated an interest among the bird loving public. However, the Gouldian finch is not recommended for beginning bird fanciers with little or no avicultural experience. As we discovered during trips to Australia, aviculturists there and around the globe have called the Gouldian a problem bird due to various husbandry and breeding problems. Happily, generations of dedicated bird-keepers have experimented to reduce the severity of these problems. Still, anyone who wants Gouldians should first gain experience with the hardier birds, such as zebra finches or Bengalese (society finches), then thoroughly acquaint themselves with Gouldians through avicultural societies, the literature, and other avenues of available information.

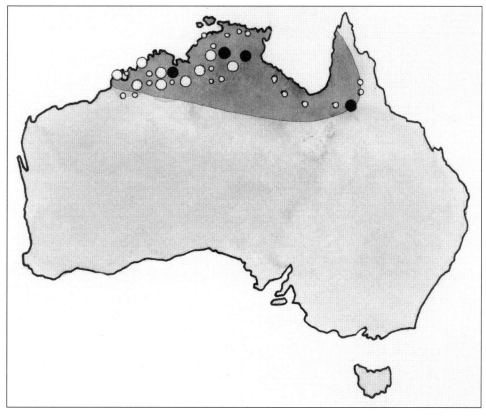

Distribution of the Gouldian Finch

Based on an RAOU (Royal Australian Ornitholocal Unim, 1983).

▓ Normally accepted distribution.

○ Recorded by less than 11% of the surveyors.

◯ Recorded by 11–40% of the surveyors.

● Recorded breeding by more than 40% of the surveyors.

(Redrawn from The Atlas of Australian Birds *by M. Blakers, S. J. J. F. Davies and P. N. Reilly, Melbourne University Press, 1984.)*

Nevertheless, the Gouldian finch is one of the most satisfying cage birds providing, of course, that it receives all it requires in order to remain in top condition. The owner of a pair of acclimated Gouldian finches in top condition will soon discover how trusting they are. After a few weeks in a roomy cage or an aviary, and after they have become accustomed to their new surroundings, the birds will remain unflappable. The key is to treat them with the respect they deserve. If approached calmly and kindly, the birds will respond in a similar manner.

Gouldian finches are in every respect excellent birds to keep in a cage or aviary. Currently, they are extremely popular due in part to the many fascinating color mutations that have been developed over the past 40 years. The beautiful Gouldian finch originated in tropical northern Australia, especially the Kimberley District. It was first described by John Gould, the English naturalist, who saw the birds during a sojourn in Australia. Gould was so excited that he mistakenly drew and colored a pair of hens together with a juvenile specimen, rather than a true pair. The finch had not been previously described, so Gould decided

to honor his wife, the former Miss. J. Coxon, a gifted wildlife artist who illustrated many of Gould's early publications, by calling the bird *Amadina gouldiae*, or Mrs. Gould's amadine. Later, Gould wrote: "It was with feelings of the purest affection that I ventured to dedicate this lovely bird to the memory of my late wife, who for many years, laboriously assisted me with her pencil, accompanied me to Australia, and cheerfully interested herself in all my pursuits."

The Gouldian finch is the keystone of many serious collections. Gouldians are easy to acquire, in part because of heavy importation from Europe. Of course, there are many excellent American and Canadian breeders as well!

A single pair can be induced to breed in a roomy cage, but breeding success can also be achieved in a garden aviary or indoor aviary. In an aviary, several pairs can be housed together; the minimum is three, the maximum is five. Gouldian finches are pleasant toward other small birds, and there is no reason not to house them with other Australian grassfinches, such as zebra finches. Gouldians require a nest box measuring at least 6 x 6 x 10 in. (15 x 15 x 25 cm). The nest box should

Gouldian Finch (male, red mask) / *Chloebia gouldiae*
Photo: Matthew M. Vriends

John Gould

Between 1832 and 1880, John Gould produced a total of 41 large folio books, with no less than 2,999 hand-colored plates. As Gould himself was a mediocre artist, he gladly allowed his wife, as well as Edward Lear, H. C. Richter, and William Hart to do the finer work. Richter and Hart worked for him as illustrators for about 30 years. The first living Gouldian finches arrived in England in 1887, and were first seen on the continent at the great bird exhibition in Berlin in 1896–1897.

Since that time, Gouldian finches have really taken the bird fancy by storm, and avian specialists continue to discover new facts on the care, breeding and color mutations of this incredibly beautiful Australian bird. In the 1930s, after many disappointments and failures, P.W. Teague, an English aviculturist, built up a healthy stud of Gouldian finches. Teague rightly is known as the most successful Gouldian finch breeder of all time, and his articles in *Avicultural Magazine*, published between 1931 and 1946, are still recognized as classic guides to the successful care and breeding of these birds.

have an entry hole 2 in. (5 cm) in diameter, or it should be half-open. They use either dry or fresh grass for nesting material, and seem to especially prefer hay, leaf veins, sisal rope and coconut fibers. In order to prevent the birds from becoming entangled, don't furnish material in lengths greater than 4 in. (10 cm). Supply ample amounts of nesting materials, because some birds like to build large nests.

Clutches produced in captivity usually consist of 5–6 white eggs. However, clutches can be as small as 3 or as large as 8 eggs. Eggs are incubated by both parents for about 14 days. The new generation leaves the nest at 21–24 days of age. The first molt occurs at 8–10 weeks, and at 5 months the young will show their adult colors.

Remember, these birds cannot tolerate low temperatures. The best breeding results occur at temperatures above 77°F (25°C). To achieve a good molt, the temperature should never drop below 72°F (22°C). Sick birds should be isolated and kept at a temperature of at least 77°F (25°C). However, in our own experiences, a constant 86°F (30°C) is the best for these situations. During molt, birds are very sensitive to temperature changes and will even stop the molt if temperatures drop below 70°F (21°C). Humidity also is extremely important. At a temperature of 77°F (25°C), the humidity should be kept at 70% You should have a good thermometer and hygrometer to monitor the environment.

Some pairs are prolific breeders, but for others, society finches must be used as foster parents.

Food: See Zebra finches (page 224).

Genus *Aegintha* (red-browed finches) Cabanis, 1851

RED-BROWED FINCH *Aegintha temporalis* (Latham, 1801)

DK: Tornastrild NL: Doornastrild FR: Astrild à cinq couleurs
DE: Dornastrild, Dornamadine IT: Astro di Sydney

▶ *photo page 129*

Description: The adult male is olive-yellow above with yellowish golden shoulders; underside gray with olive-yellowish reflection; lores and eyebrows are orange or bright red and somewhat broader than in the female. Rump and part of the back and upper tail coverts crimson; nape and crown light beige. Ear-coverts, throat, and underside bluish gray. Upper wing coverts and inner secondaries olive-yellow. Eyes reddish brown; beak red with triangular-shaped black patches on culmen and on the lower mandible; legs and feet high flesh colored. Length: 5 in. (12 cm). The adult female is somewhat duller; the red eyebrows are smaller and shorter. The young are much like the female, with a gray head and wings, the latter with dark olive outer webs. Rump and upper tail coverts dull crimson. No eyebrow coloring; black beak; underside of the body grayish brown.

Geographic variations:

■ *A. t. temporalis*, as above. Distribution: Cape York Peninsula in eastern Australia to the southeastern coast of South Australia.

■ *A. t. minor* (A. J. Campbell). Back and flight feathers are more yellowish green; the sides of the head toward the back lighter green than in the nominate subspecies. Underside, from chin to belly, grayish white. Under tail coverts dark gray to black. Somewhat smaller in total length. Length: 4¼ in. (11 cm). Distribution: Along the coast of eastern Australia between Cape York Peninsula and MacKay, where, interestingly, mixed populations (*temporalis* x *minor*) can be found. An additional, rather small population in western Australia to approximately Inkerman on the Gulf of Carpentaria may have developed from avicultural escapees.

■ *A. t. loftyi* Mathews. Much more brownish on the head than in the nominate subspecies; female with yellow-brown underside. Distribution: Kangaroo Island and Mount Lofty range (hills outside Adelaide, South Australia) in small populations.

Habitat: The edges of forests, in gardens and parks, and along the banks of rivers and lakes. Outside the breeding season in small to large flocks of up to some 100 birds.

Aviculture: This species is a slender and quick little bird; it does best in a good sized outdoor aviary with a rich planting. The bird doesn't do too well in cages and indoor vitrines. Nevertheless, the red-browed finch is extremely sensitive to cold; be sure the temperature is never allowed to drop below 65°F (18°C). It is also sensitive to high humidity, so during the fall it should be housed in a roomy indoor aviary. Males as well as females share in nest building, although the female concentrates more on the nest cup. Generally, they like a half-open or enclosed nest box or a coconut-type nest. It does happen repeatedly that they build a free bottle-shaped nest in one of the bushes, from freshly cut and dry grass, hair, moss, wool, coconut fibers, small feathers, and the like. Shortly after the nest is completed, the female starts laying her eggs. Both male and female are extremely sensitive to disturbances, and if these occur, the birds usually abandon the nest, even if they already have eggs or young. Under favorable conditions, the female lays 3–8 eggs, which are incubated for 13–14 days by both parents. The young leave the nest when approximately 22 days old. For the night, the parents direct them back into the nest, and after approximately 10 days they will look for perching places in the cage or aviary. While being fed by the parents the young will flap their wings and make begging sounds. When hungry they will follow their parents around. During the second breeding round, the young often disappear into the nest, visiting their parents and in doing so, may consequently damage eggs or nestlings. It is thus advisable at this stage to place the youngsters in a separate flight or aviary. After around two months, the first red feathers will appear. After 3½ months, the young will have completed their final molt; at this point they are very difficult to distinguish from their parents.

The male has interesting, clear, and somewhat monotonous but still appealing whistles that he utters before mating. He also makes amusing steps during the mating dance, which he performs with the body erect and the tail atilt. He usually carries a long stalk in his beak. At the end of the dance both parents point their tails toward each other and the female stretches her neck upward, a symbolic nest building-movement. The entire performance is extremely rewarding to watch but doesn't take a long time at all.

Only Japan and Europe continue to be sources of these birds, and many times they are not available. Australia has had an export ban in effect since the early 1960s. As a consequence, we must treat the birds now in this country with the utmost care, especially since it is extremely difficult to keep these birds alive and well without half-ripe seeds and, particularly, live food such as ant-pupae, aphids, small cut-up mealworms, spiders, etc. House the birds in a large, well-planted open garden aviary rather than in a large cage as the birds will remain shy in the latter and will seldom come to breed there. Although the species can easily be kept with other small finches, and usually doesn't interfere with other breeding species, they do have the habit of constructing their nest in the immediate vicinity of other birds' nests, and will vigorously defend it when necessary. The species sometimes suffers from air-sac mite and scours (watery diarrhea), and is known to be susceptible to low temperatures. The red-browed finch can be expected to live for 4–6 years.

Food: See Star finch, page 240. Provide the birds daily with fresh drinking and bath water. Dripping or running water is preferred, as these birds like to bathe at least three times a day. The birds indeed love water and will sit in the rain for long periods of time. Birds kept indoors should be sprayed with a mister; a simple mist spray system in a corner above your plants is obviously the ideal solution.

Casuarina seeds

Australian aviculturists should be warned against the unlimited feeding of *Casuarina* seeds, the seeds of the cassowary tree. Although the seed is an important part of the bird's natural diet, overfeeding may induce aggressive behavior. However, the birds are generally known as active and sociable, and a great deal of time is spent preening one another.

Other names: Red-headed finch, Firetail finch, and Temporal finch. The often seen name Sydney waxbill is confusing as there seems to be no close relationship with the African waxbills.

Genus *Aidemosyne* (cherry finches) Reichenbach, 1862

CHERRY FINCH *Aidemosyne modesta* (Gould, 1837)

DK: Ceresastrild NL: Ceresamadine, Ceresvink FR: Diamant modeste, Modeste
DE: Zeresfink, Zeresastrild, Ceresastrild, Zeresamadine IT: Diamante zebrato, Diamante modesto

▶ *photos page 134*

Description: Male is similar in plumage to female. Crown, chin, and forehead dark red to red-brown; nape and back olive brown; rump feathers and upper tail coverts are lighter, often off-white; poorly formed wave designs. Primaries brown with white tips. Ear coverts white with brown wavy design. Lores and tail black with white spots on the outer feathers. Underparts white with small olive-brown bars. Abdomen and under tail coverts white. Eyes dark brown, beak black, legs and feet brownish pink. The female lacks the claret forehead and chin spots, and has a thin white line above and to the rear of the eye. Length: 4–4¼ in. (10–11 cm).

Distribution and habitat: Eastern Australia, from Townsville in Queensland to the central region of New South Wales and to the border of Victoria; in gardens, shrubs, and grassland, near water. Outside the breeding season in large groups, often together with Bicheno's finches, but always near water.

Aviculture: These rather timid and passive birds have become popular in recent years but are still very expensive; yet it is worth the money from the viewpoint of their color and their fascinating behavior. They can be kept in a mixed collection, and are eminently suitable for colony breeding. Acclimatization of imported birds, such as those coming from Europe or Japan, for example, can cause difficulties; only experienced finch hobbyists should give these birds a try. They build a tidy, closely woven round nest, lined with small feathers, often in bushes, but also in canary nest boxes and the like.

The female lays 4–7 white eggs which are incubated by both partners, although the female does most of the brooding. The young hatch in 11–12 days. Absolute quiet is a prime requirement. To avoid brooding problems, one could use either Bengalese or Indian silverbills *Euodice malabarica* as breeders and foster parents. Personally, we prefer to use the latter because they are close relatives; in fact, the two species have frequently been hybridized, but the cherry finch has also been crossed with zebra finches, long-tailed finches, masked finches, and double-bar finches. As stated elsewhere, we are not in favor of cross-breeding; let us keep all species pure!.

Breeding cherry finches in the colder or even milder states is best done indoors. The birds like heat and don't do well in temperatures below 65°F (18°C). Their aviary should have ample plantings, because they tend to be shy, particularly during the breeding season. Although they are nervous

about outside disturbances, they tolerate other finches quite well. It is important to always keep these finches in pairs, because as singletons they pine away. In order to obtain good breeding pairs, give the species the opportunity to choose their own partners; therefore colony breeding (6–12 pairs) is usually very successful. As soon as the nest is completed, remove most of the excess building material; the same applies when the birds are using a nest box; this is done to avoid the tendency of this species to constantly indulge in nest building, often at the expense of egg laying! The young leave the nest when they are about 21 days old; they will be independent in another two weeks. They are mostly olive brown without any red markings on the head; the underside is grayish white with some vague barring. After three months, however, they are identical to their parents. Young males start singing in approximately 6 weeks.

Food: Ripe and half-ripe seeds, sprouted millets, small berries, greens, a variety of live food and rearing food, cuttlefish bone, vitamins and minerals.

Other names: Modest finch (grassfinch), Plain-colored finch, Plum-headed finch; sometimes Plum-capped finch or Diadem finch.

Females can be distinguished from males only by means of a clear-white lore, about 5 millimeters in width, which runs from the beak above the eyes; males lack the lores (Rubner).

Genus *Bathilda* (star finches) Reichenbach, 1862

STAR FINCH *Bathilda (Neochmia) ruficauda* (Gould, 1837)

DK: Sivastrild NL: Biezenastrild, Binsenastrild FR: Diamant ruflcauda, Djamant à quene rousse

DE: Binsenastrild, Binsenamadine IT: Diamante coda rossa

▸ *photos page 135*

Description: Face red, as are crown and throat; the back of the head, the neck, and shoulders are grass green with a blue hue. Rump rose-red with whitish rose-red scalloped design. Wings grass green with light edges; pin feathers of the wings dark green. Tail black-red; breast and flanks yellow-green. Belly yellow to whitish yellow. Face, breast, and flanks are richly covered with white dots. Eyes red, beak dark red, legs yellowish. Length: 4–4½ in. (10–11.5 cm).

Geographic variations:

■ *B. r. ruficauda*, as above. Distribution: northern Australia, down to the Ashburton River on the west and northern New South Wales in the east (Cayley).

■ *B. r. clarescens* (Hartert, 1899). The colors in this subspecies are more pronounced, but the red mask, especially cheeks and chin, are less intense. The little dots are gray-green. The female is also stronger in color. Distribution: northern and northwestern Queensland to northern Western Australia.

Habitat: Found in large flocks, always near water in tall grass, rice and sugar-cane fields, swamps, bushes and trees; often together with crimson finches (see page 220). During the heat of the day, the whole flock will adjourn to shady bushes.

Aviculture: This species, being bold and venturesome by nature, is quite popular throughout the world. The female is not easy to distinguish from the male, but with experience, sexing can be done quickly because the red on the throat of the female is less intense. Cheeks and forehead are not as intensely red. Star finches are easy to breed, provided they are kept in a well-planted, quiet aviary. For planting, select tall grass, reeds, ivy, and dense bushes; the birds will quickly select a display area where the cocks will perch and sing, thereby presenting their owners with many hours of enjoyment. The birds are exceptionally friendly to fellow inhabitants. In roomy outside aviaries, they usually will build a free nest in a little bush. Don't disturb them there, as they are quite sensitive. With any luck, you will be able to count on three clutches per season. The clutches consist of 3–5 eggs, which are incubated for 12–14 days. The young leave the nest after 18–25 days, are very shy at first, and will attempt to hide at the first sign of disturbance. After 3–4 weeks they are fully independent, and should be removed from the parents so the latter can start on the next clutch. The young start their molt, which can last for some time, at the age of 2½ months, but should be finished in approximately 8 months.

During fall and winter, star finches must be housed indoors at room temperature; minimum temperature 60°F (15°C). This temperature is essential, as this species does not normally roost in a nest or nest box. It is advisable to separate the pairs outside the breeding season to prevent untimely attempts at nesting, resulting in a possible loss of the hen through egg-binding. Keep accurate records, because in the wild, as well as in captivity, pair-bonding is very strong. During courtship, the juvenile female will circle round the cock carrying a blade of grass in her beak, frequently flying so close to her selected partner that the grass will be dragged across his back. This display, according to Iles, appears to be a preliminary to pair-bonding, and mostly occurs among unmolted birds. When the pairs are formed, the cock takes over the grass carrying. Nests are constructed in long grass or reeds, or in a half-open nest box. In the box we like to place a canary nest pan as a base, half-filled with grass and other fibers. The hen does the construction, the male carries nesting material. The nest is usually very neat.

Food: During the breeding season, a rich variety of insects and their larvae, sprouted seeds, greens, commercial egg and rearing food, grit, cuttlefish bone, vitamins and minerals must be available at all times; the birds tend to throw their young from the nest when the food is not to their liking. The birds should have daily access to clean bath and drinking water.

Other names: Ruficauda finch, Red-tailed finch, Red-faced finch, Rufous-tailed finch.

PARROTFINCHES

Genus *Reichenowia* (green-tailed parrotfinches) Poche, 1904

BAMBOO PARROTFINCH *Reichenowia (Erythrura) hyperythra* (Reichenbach, 1862)

DK: Bambus Papagøjeamadine NL: Groenstaart-papegaaiamadine, Berg-nonpareil FR: Diamant à queue verte   ▸ *photos page 140*
DE: Bambus-Papageiamadine, Berg-Papageiamadine IT: Diamante del bambu

Description: Males are intensive moss green in neck and back; this applies also to the wing coverts but these have yellow hues. Forehead and face, past the eyes, turquoise; beak is bordered with a small black band. Beak 11 mm and straight. Rump and upper tail coverts ochre-yellow. Chin, cheeks, breast, belly, and under tail coverts ochre-brown. Wings and tail black with green edging; central tail feathers green on top. Eyes dark brown, beak black-gray, legs pink. The female is visibly paler in coloration and has a brown stripe across the beak; the male has a black one. The young are even paler than the female. Length: 4.3 in. (11 cm).

Geographic variations:
- *R. h. hyperythra*, as above. Distribution: Java.
- *R. h. intermedia* (Hartert). Somewhat smaller in size than nominate form. Blue forehead, less intensive on face and neck. Rump, upper tail coverts and wing coverts with yellow hue. Beak 9 mm and straight. Distribution: island of Lombok in the Lesser Sundas (Indonesia).
- *R. h. obscura* Rensch. Similar to previous subspecies but with more yellow on neck, back, and wing coverts. Pale blue forehead; cheeks brown. Beak 8 mm, thick and compact. Distribution: Flores and Sumbawa in the Lesser Sunda Islands.

- *R. h. ernstmayri* Stresemann. Smaller than nominate form, and very similar to *obscura*. Upperparts light yellow-green, rump and upper tail coverts very light yellowish green. Underparts dull orange-brown with yellow hue; belly and under tail coverts with green. Distribution: southern Sulawesi.
- *R. h. microrhyncha* Stresemann. Little area of forehead greenish blue. Grass green back, rump, and upper tail coverts. Underparts orange-yellow-brown. Beak 8 mm, short, slender. Distribution: northern and central Sulawesi.
- *R. h. brunneiventris* (Grant). Upperparts, including rump and upper tail coverts, deep grass green; flanks and breast also grass green but with a blue hue. Intense blue forehead, which runs past the eyes. Face and underparts ochre-brown. Beak 8 mm. Length: 4.3–4¾ in. (11–12 cm). Distribution: islands of Luzon and Mindoro in the Philippines.
- *R. h. borneensis* (Sharpe). Upperparts light yellow-green. Light blue face (past cheeks), forehead and crown. Ochre underparts with greenish hue. Beak 12–13 mm, long and elevated. Distribution: northern Borneo (Sabah and Sarawak).
- *R. h. malayana* (Robinson). Upperparts light yellow-green. Less blue in face than previous subspecies; cheeks chestnut. More yellow on under-

parts than *borneensis*. Beak 12–13 mm, long and elevated similar to previous subspecies. Distribution: Malaysia.

Habitat: All of the subspecies are typical mountain dwellers, reaching more than 9000 ft. (2700 m) above sea level. These birds live in pairs, even outside of the breeding season, or else they form small groups of two or three pairs. They eat principally all types of bamboo seed, grass and weed seeds, some small insects and greens such as buds, little flowers, sprouts; they also like to visit rice paddies, and pick at small berries.

Aviculture: This beautiful bird was first imported into Germany in 1930 and then, in 1965, to Switzerland (Dr. R. Burkard). It seems that over the years various subspecies were imported into Europe and that *hyperythra*, *obscura* and *microrhyncha* were the most successful breeders, especially when kept in box-type breeding cages and indoor aviaries at room temperature, although Burkard has various species outdoors, but with access to a well-closed-in night shelter.

The birds lay rather large white eggs (13 x 17 mm) which are incubated for approximately 14 days; when the youngsters are about 9 days old they open their eyes, and leave the nest, quite late, when 23–26 days old. Two weeks later they are independent and should be separated from their parents. At 3–4 months old they finish their molt and are then similar to the adults. Birds should be at least one year old before being placed in a breeding program.

Food: Includes all types of small millets, especially panicum. Also canary grass seed, and grass and weed seeds. The birds utilize little of other seeds and they don't seem to want much protein of animal origin, like maggots and small mealworms. Ant pupae, however, especially small ones, are much appreciated, as well as a good commercial brand egg food or rearing food.

Other name: Green-tailed parrotfinch, Tawny-breasted parrotfinch.

Genus *Erythrura* (real parrotfinches) Swainson, 1837

GREEN-FACED PARROTFINCH *Erythrura viridifacies*
(Hachisuka & Delacour, 1937)

DK: Manila Papagøjeamadine NL: Mani-papegaaiamadine FR: Pape à tête verte, Pape de Manile
DE: Manila-Papageiamadine IT: Diamante dalla testa verde

Description: Upperparts grass green; lighter green underparts. Upper tail coverts and elongated central tail feathers red; rest of tail feathers dark gray with green edging, except for the outer ones, which have reddish edges. Underside of wings and under tail coverts ochre-brown. Gray primaries with green-yellowish edging. Beak black, eyes dark brown, legs light pinkish red. The female is duller in coloration, especially regarding the underside; the central tail feathers are shorter. Length: 4¾ in. (12 cm).

Distribution and habitat: Luzon and Negros Islands, Philippines. The status of this species is rather uncertain due to the many eruptions of the volcano Pinatubo, where the birds used to live in rather large flocks. We found the species also around the capital Manila in parks and gardens but also in the mountains and in rice paddies and bamboo fields. Not much is known about the life of this rather timid bird.

Aviculture: This species is obviously rare in aviculture. It was first imported to California in 1935 in rather large numbers, but all birds died within the year. Only Mr. W. S. Sheffler from Los Angeles had some success; he was the first to breed with a healthy pair, but unfortunately the young, as well as the parents, died the next year (1936). In 1979 the German aviculturist Horst Bielfeld (see page 00) received a pair which was housed in a well-planted aviary. The couple did pretty well, and even raised young three times during the first season. Regrettably, the parents refused to forage for animal protein, although a variety of insects was available, and all young died prematurely. The next year only infertile eggs were laid but no breeding attempts were made. As far as we know, there are momentarily no green-faced parrotfinches in aviculture.

Food: See Pin-tailed parrotfinch, below.

Other name: Manila parrotfinch.

PIN-TAILED PARROTFINCH *Erythrura prasina* (Sparrman, 1788)

DK: Løggrøn Papegøjeamadine NL: Indische Nonpareil FR: Quadricolore, Pape des prairies
DE: Lauchgrüne Papageigmadine IT: Diamante quadri colore

▶ *photos page 141*

Description: Forehead, the area around the eye, cheek, and upper part of the throat ink blue. On the lores and around the beak the color darkens to black. Nape, neck, back, and wings dark grass green. Primaries black, edged in yellow. Under tail coverts and tail scarlet. Underside yellow with a red sheen, so that one seems to see a dim orange. Belly almost orange-red. Eyes dark brown, beak black, legs pink. The female has no red on the breast and further is less brightly colored. Length: 5½–6 in. (14–15 cm).

Geographic variations
■ *E. p. prasina*, as above. It is important to point out that this species comes in two color phases, the one with the red underside (above), and one with a yellow belly, previously recognized in the nomenclature as *Spermestes hauthi*. This yellow-bellied mutation is regularly seen in wild flocks and interbreeds with red-bellied specimens. Distribution: Burma, Thailand, Laos, Cambodia, Malaysia, Sumatra, and Java.
■ *E. p. coelica* Baker. Less and lighter blue on the face; the breast is duller red than in the nominate form. Distribution: northern Borneo.

Habitat: The birds live in groups ranging from a few pairs to rather large flocks, in the underbrush, at the forest edges, in bamboo thickets, up to 6600 ft. (2000 m) high in the mountains. There have been many reports of birds in rice fields, where they can be a true pest. They crawl around in rough branches and the like, so that their nails

wear down regularly. It is therefore essential to provide these birds, and all other parrotfinches, with reeds and flagstones, to help keep their nails trimmed.

Aviculture: This beautiful bird is really well suited only to experienced fanciers; it is difficult to keep alive and in good condition. Acclimatization requires much effort and experience. Until recently, birds shipped from their native land were fed principally on paddy rice during the journey, and new arrivals suffered from one-sided feeding. They required much more (and still do!), for example vitamins B and D. Unfortunately, casualties were high! Immediately after arrival, these wonderful birds must be housed in roomy flight (breeding) cages kept at a constant minimum temperature of 77°F (25°C). The cages must be equipped with infrared lamps. Once the birds recover (which will take a few weeks, at least), the temperature can be dropped to 68°F (20°C). You will be able to tell that the birds feel happy when you see them make agile movements and you hear the male singing. If it is possible to acclimatize the birds in inside, well-planted aviaries, we would prefer this above large flight cages. Even if the care is first-rate, don't expect the birds to become trusting, even though they are curious and will allow you to approach them closely. In inside aviaries, avoid glass walls and screens, as the birds are likely to fly against them, often with disastrous consequences.

Breeding is a real task, especially considering that the birds molt twice a year. The molt, however, doesn't last long, but that of both partners

Pin-tailed Parrot Finch (male) / *Erythrura prasina*
Photo: Matthew M. Vriends

should coincide in order to achieve copulation. The mating dance is well worth studying. The male repeatedly makes races toward the female, meanwhile making small bows with his body and beating his tail from left to right. Sometimes he runs sideways like a crab for several paces. He performs his song with enthusiasm and sometimes it looks as if he whispers something into his mates' ear. The couple builds a sizeable nest from fibers, bast, grass leaves, leaf veins, and the like. They rarely use nest boxes but prefer to build a free nest in thick bushes, broom branches, or tufts of tall, thick grass. The female lays 2–5 eggs, which she incubates for about two weeks. Both parents feed the young quite diligently, especially with sprouted seeds and small pieces of fresh greens, as well as some insects. After three weeks, the young leave the nest, but after two to three days of being out-in-the-world, they become easily frightened, start fluttering with their wings, and call out in high twitters. After a week or so this behavior will gradually disappear. We don't know of any other parrotfinch with this kind of behavior. The temperature must be maintained around 77°F (25°C), and infrared lamps should be used during the entire breeding season. We have found that it is best to keep three or five pairs in a single, roomy, well-planted aviary to achieve successful breeding.

Food: Provide paddy rice and an abundance of oats, canary grass seed, millet spray, silver millet and panicum millet, plus groats and wheat, which is very important. All these seeds may also be furnished germinated and sprouted, especially during the breeding period. Put a multi-vitamin preparation in the drinking water or, in powder form, mixed in with rearing food and greens. Also, furnish a daily supply of cuttlebone, grit, and limestone, grass and weed seed, greens (chickweed, lettuce), fruit (apple, cherry, orange), and pieces of cucumber. After some time, you can get away from paddy rice altogether. Especially during the breeding season, don't forget to supply animal protein, such as cut-up mealworms, white worms, ant pupae, and commercial egg food and rearing food.

Other name: Pin-tailed nonpareil.

Genus *Amblynura* (South China Sea parrotfinches) Reichenbach, 1862

TRICOLORED PARROTFINCH *Amblynura (Erythrura) tricolor* (Vieillot, 1817)

DK: Blagrøn Papegøjeamadine NL: Forbes-papegaaiamadine FR: Diamant de Tanimbar
DE: Forbes-Papageiamadine, Blaugrune Papageiamadine IT: Diamante tricolore di tanimbar

▸ *photos page 38, 142*

Description: Cobalt blue head, neck, throat, cheeks and underside. Back, wing coverts, and inside secondaries green. Rump, upper tail coverts, and the tail itself, red. Eyes brownish red, beak black, legs dark pink. The female is somewhat lighter in color. Fledglings lack the blue and have a pale green underside. Length: 4 in. (10 cm).

Distribution and habitat: The islands of Timor, Wetar, Damar, Babar, and Tanimbar in the Lesser Sundas (Indonesia). Lives in the mountain woods, up to about 5000 ft. (1500 m).

Aviculture: This bird is unquestionably beautiful and resembles the blue-faced parrotfinch. The species is seen from time to time in aviculture. It remains a difficult bird to keep well. Fanciers G. and M. van Boeckel, The Netherlands (1991) had three hens and two males. They placed one pair in a large breeding cage; the male followed his partner throughout the cage with a long grass stem in his beak and, once perched, stretched himself at full length. He sang enthusiastically high, vibrating notes. After this courtship, the birds immediately started to construct a nest in a nest box, finishing it in only 3 days! The clutch consisted of 5 eggs (17.7 x 13.1 mm), and the incubation time was 14 days. The young left the nest after 17 days; they were independent in 21 days.

Food: See Pin-tailed parrotfinch (page 243).

Other names: Blue-fronted parrotfinch, Three-colored parrotfinch.

MANY-COLORED PARROTFINCH *Amblynura (Erythrura) coloria*
(Ripley & Rabor, 1961)

DK: Mangefarvet Papegøjesmadine NL: Veelkleuren-papegaaiamadine FR: Diamant des montagnes
DE: Buntkopf-Papageiamadine IT: Diamante a guanee rosse e blue

▸ *photo page 141*

Description: Green; blue forehead, face, and cheeks. There is a unique half-moon shaped red collar running from the ear toward the neck. Rump, upper tail coverts, and the central tail feathers deep red. Tail and wings blackish, the feathers of the latter with green edging. Eyes dark brown, beak black, legs gray flesh-colored. The female is somewhat duller and the young even more so, with a green reflection on the upperside; they also lack the red and blue. After a year the colors of the females brighten and then can no longer be distinguished from the adult male. It pays to color-band young birds so that they can be sexed easily when they get older. Length: 4 in. (10 cm).

Distribution and habitat: Mindanao Island, Philippines. Gonzales first discovered and caught this bird in 1960. It occurs in open places of light forests and along the edges of forests in the mountains. There it feeds on small insects and fine grass and weed seeds.

Aviculture: This bird was first imported into Europe in 1964, and a number of breeders then acquired some pairs which quickly were bred successfully. This species is rather well known in the USA. The birds are not the least bit shy, and probably for this reason can easily be bred, provided breeding birds are properly acclimatized. They can be kept in roomy cages as well as aviaries. Provide half-open nest boxes, in which the birds will usually build a relatively large and rather rough nest from coconut fibers, grass, hay, and small down feathers. The clutch consists usually of 2, but occasionally 3, eggs, which are incubated for two weeks. Fledglings are still fed by their parents for approximately 14 days after they leave the nest. After five months, the young acquire the adult colors. Care requirements are as for the red-

headed parrotfinch. Dr. Burkhard of Switzerland has identified this bird as one of the most reliable breeders among the parrotfinches in captivity. It is highly desirable to breed this bird with the greatest of care, because it is quite unlikely that many new importations will be possible.

Food: Furnish canary grass seed, both dry and in sprouted and germinated form, panicum millet, millet spray, and other small millet varieties. During the breeding season, add grass and weed seeds, even though not all birds will make much use of these. Also provide cut-up small mealworms, small ant pupae, white worms, boiled eggs (well diced), egg food and rearing food, and some greens, which these birds gladly consume, especially during the breeding season.

Other names: Red-eared parrotfinch, Mindanao parrotfinch, Mt. Katanglad parrotfinch.

BLUE-FACED PARROTFINCH *Amblynura (Erythrura) trichroa* Kittlitz, 1835

DK: Trefarvet Papegøjeamadine, Blåhovedet Papegøjeamadine NL: Driekleur-papegaaiamadine
FR: Diamant tricolor de Kittliz DE: Dreifarbige Papageiamadime, Dreifatben-Papageiamadine IT: Diamante di Kittlitz

▶ *photos page 142, 143*

Description: Cheeks and forehead bright cobalt blue. Crown light green; the nape much darker green. The central tail feathers, which are somewhat longer than the others, and upper tail coverts are dark red. The wings are grass green. Primaries dark brown with light green and black edges. Tail feathers black with red borders. Many races (see below) don't have the attractive soft

green, but there are all grades of intermediary colors up to nearly yellow, especially on the neck and on the thigh (tibia) feathers. Eyes dark brown, beak black, legs light gray-brown. The female is duller in coloration, with less blue on the face. Length: 4½–4¾ in. (11.5–12 cm).

Geographic variations:
■ *A. t. trichroa*, as above. Distribution: Kusaie Island in the Carolines.
■ *A. t. cyanofrons* Layard. Cobalt-blue head much more intensive than previous subspecies. Upperparts dark green with some yellow hue. Underparts grass green. Distribution: Loyalty Islands, Banks Island, and New Hebrides.
■ *A. t. sanfordi* Stresemann. Elevated upper mandible. Violet-blue face. Underparts green-yellow; upper tail coverts reddish orange. Distribution: central Sulawesi, up to 8400 ft. (2500 m) high in the mountains.
■ *A. t. modesta* Wallace. Similar to previous sub-

species but with a more slender upper mandible. Length: 5.1 in. (13 cm). Distribution: northern Moluccas, on the islands of Halmahera, Batjan, Ternate, and Tidore.

■ *A. t. pinaiae* Stresemann. Cobalt blue face. Overall color bluish green; ochre-brown in upperparts. Somewhat smaller in size than *modesta*. Length: 4.3 in. (11 cm). Distribution: southern Moluccas, on Ceram and Buru.

■ *A. t. sigillifera* (de Vis). This subspecies now includes the former subspecies *goodfellowi* from New Guinea and the former subspecies *macgillivrayi* from northeastern Australia. Similar to previous subspecies, but with bright dark red upper tail feathers. Length: 5.1–5.5 in. (13–14 cm). Distribution: Cape York Peninsula of northeastern Australia; also New Guinea, up to 13,000 ft. (4000 m) high in the mountains.

■ *A. t. clara* Takatsukasa & Yamashina. Light blue face; color doesn't pass the eyes, however, as is the case with all previous subspecies. The light blue color is the brightest by far of all subspecies, with a yellowish hue on the neck and rump. The underparts are yellowish green. Distribution: Truk and Ponape islands in the Carolines.

■ *A. t. eichhorni* Hartert. Cobalt blue face, reaching barely past the eyes. Mainly grass green with red-orange upper tail coverts. Distribution: St. Matthias Island in the Bismarck Archipelago.

■ *A. t. pelewensis* Kuroda. Long and elevated upper mandible. Cobalt blue face, reaching just behind the eyes. Dull green upperparts, with a blue hue, especially on the chin; upper tail coverts red. Length: 4.75–5.1 in. (12–13 cm). Distribution: Palau Islands.

■ *A. t. woodfordi* Hartert. Small bluish face; neck without yellow hue; underparts light bluish green. Dull yellow-orange upper tail coverts. Length: 4¾ in. (12 cm). Distribution: Guadalcanal.

Habitat: Found in woods in the mountains, up to 6000 ft. (1800 m), some subspecies higher as indicated, and also in gardens and plantations, coastal plains, rain forests, and mangroves. They feed principally on grass and weed seeds. Their nest is preferably built high in the trees; it is rectangular in shape and constructed of grass, moss, leaf veins, and dry leaves.

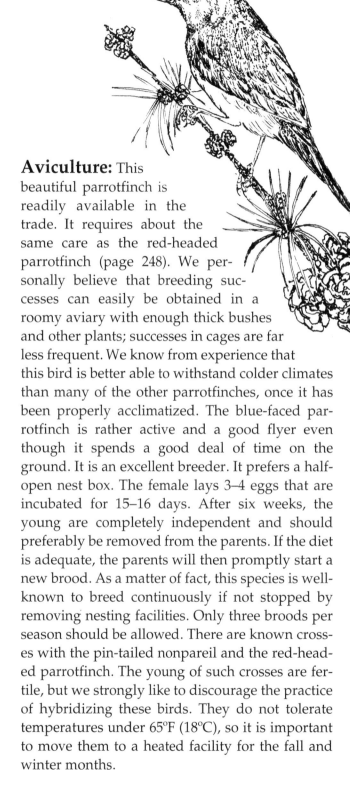

Aviculture: This beautiful parrotfinch is readily available in the trade. It requires about the same care as the red-headed parrotfinch (page 248). We personally believe that breeding successes can easily be obtained in a roomy aviary with enough thick bushes and other plants; successes in cages are far less frequent. We know from experience that this bird is better able to withstand colder climates than many of the other parrotfinches, once it has been properly acclimatized. The blue-faced parrotfinch is rather active and a good flyer even though it spends a good deal of time on the ground. It is an excellent breeder. It prefers a half-open nest box. The female lays 3–4 eggs that are incubated for 15–16 days. After six weeks, the young are completely independent and should preferably be removed from the parents. If the diet is adequate, the parents will then promptly start a new brood. As a matter of fact, this species is well-known to breed continuously if not stopped by removing nesting facilities. Only three broods per season should be allowed. There are known crosses with the pin-tailed nonpareil and the red-headed parrotfinch. The young of such crosses are fertile, but we strongly like to discourage the practice of hybridizing these birds. They do not tolerate temperatures under 65°F (18°C), so it is important to move them to a heated facility for the fall and winter months.

Food: see Red-headed parrotfinch (page 248).

Other name: Three-colored parrotfinch.

PAPUAN PARROTFINCH *Amblynura (Erythrura) papuana* **Hartert, 1900**

▶ *photos page 138, 143*

DK: Papua Papegøjeamadine NL: Papua driekleur-papegaaiamadine FR: Diamant de Papua
DE: Papua-Papageiamadine IT: Diamante di papua

Description: Similar in color to the blue-faced parrotfinch (see page 246), but somewhat larger. The green colors are more intensive; the neck and shoulders have a deep yellow hue. In the upper breast and flanks the green color has been touched by blue. Light blue face, chin, and upper throat; rump, upper tail coverts, and central tail feathers red. Tail feathers with red edging. Heavy, cone-shaped beak. Females have a smaller blue facial area, without blue on the chin and upper throat. They are also duller in overall coloration, and have a more slender bill. Length: 6–6.3 in. (15–16 cm).

Distribution and habitat: New Guinea, up to 8400 ft. (2500 m) high in the mountains; found in wood clearings, grass fields, and rice paddies; in pairs or small family groups.

Aviculture: Was kept and studied by R. Neff (1969), a well-known German finch specialist. His birds were very friendly and not nervous while housed in an aviary. One of his main observations was that the two birds were very close, and used to take naps on a branch in the afternoon and even slept close to each other, with actual bodily contact. Adult parrotfinches usually never sit or sleep next to each other and seldom exhibit, just like Gouldians, bodily contact. Mr. Neff's pair went to Dr. R. Burkhard and then to Prof. Dr. V. Ziswiler of the University of Zurich, who at that time was making detailed studies of all the *Erythrura* species (see: V. Ziswiler, H. R. Guttinger, and H. Bregulla (1972): *Monographie des Gattung* Erythrura *Swainson 1837 (Aves, Passeres, Estrildidae,* Bonner Zoologische Monographien, Bonn).

Food: Millet varieties, millet spray, grass and weed seeds, canary grass seed, various small berries, pieces of apple, banana, and figs (Prof. Ziswiler considers fig seeds one of the main foods of wild Papuan parrotfinches); also some insects. Neff's birds were also eating small mealworms when they were approximately three months in captivity, and some time later they even started to eat ant pupae.

RED-HEADED PARROTFINCH *Amblynura (Erythrura) psittacea* **(Gmelin, 1789)**

▶ *photos page 143*

DK: Rødhovedet Papegøjeamadine NL: Roodkop-papegaaiamadine FR: Diamant à tête rouge
DE: Rotkopf-Papageiamadine, Rotköpfige Papageiamadine IT: Diamante pappagallo

Description: Red forehead, part of the crown, and face; lores black. Upper breast, rump, and tail also red. Rest of the body parrot green. Eyes dark brown; beak black, the lower mandible usually brownish; legs light gray-brown. The female is duller with less red on the face. Length: 4¾ in. (12 cm).

Distribution and habitat: New Caledonia, in grassland and shrubbery.

Aviculture: This is a truly bright-colored bird which is exceptionally suited for a roomy aviary with a lot of plants. It must not be exposed to temperatures below 65°F (18°C), so that in the winter months it must always be moved to a heated facility. The best breeding results are achieved in a large indoor aviary, equipped with nest boxes of at least 7 in. (18 cm) square. The birds build a rather sizeable nest, as all parrotfinches do, from grass, fibers, leaf veins, and the like. They lay clutches of 3–6 eggs, of which there are usually a few infertile ones. Incubation time, 13 days. After 21–22 days, the young fly out, and subsequently they sleep close together in the low vegetation. There is no objection to keeping grown-up young with the parents, as long as the whole family is housed in an aviary. In cages the father tends to chase after the youngsters, especially when the female has a new clutch. This species doesn't take nest inspection very well.

Food: Includes various millets, canary grass seed, niger seed, poppy seed, ripe and unripe grass and weed seeds, and oats. Also furnish a rich variety of greens such as spinach, dandelion, and chickweed, fruits such as figs, dates, and oranges, and, importantly, a lot of animal protein, such as cut-up small mealworms, ant pupae, larvae, white worms, wax moths, tubifex, water fleas, and other water insects, plus a good brand egg or rearing food for finches. Some birds also will reluctantly accept old brown bread soaked in water.

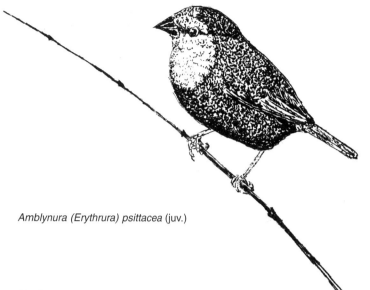

Amblynura (Erythrura) psittacea (juv.)

Other name: Red-throated parrotfinch. While red-headed parrotfinch is the traditional name for this species in both the ornithological and avicultural literature, the name red-throated parrotfinch is the common name applied to this species by much of the current ornithological literature, with the older name red-headed parrotfinch now being used to refer to the Samoa parrotfinch *Amblynura (Erythrura) cyaneovirens*, the species long known aviculturally as the royal parrotfinch. The name royal parrotfinch is now reserved for *A. (E.) regia*, long considered a subspecies of *cyaneovirens*, but now accorded full specific status by most authorities.

PEALE'S PARROTFINCH *Amblynura (Erythrura) pealii*
(formerly known as *Erythrura cyaneovirens pealii*) Peale, 1848

DK: Peales Papegøjeamadine NL: Peale's papegaaiamadine FR: Diamant de Peale
DE: Peales Papageiamadine, Kurzschwanz Papageiamadine IT: Diamante di Peale

▸ *photos page 144*

Description: Green; throat and upper part of breast with a blue hue. Chin black; face, cheeks, forehead, and crown red. Part of the rump, upper tail coverts, and central tail feathers red. Tail reddish black with red edging. Secondaries black-brown with green edges. Eyes dark brown, beak reddish brown, feet light reddish pink. Females are duller with a smaller red facial area. Length: 4½ in. (10 cm).

Distribution and habitat: Fiji Islands; in

the mountains up to 3300 ft. (1000 m) in elevation, in wooded areas, rice paddies, parks and gardens; in bushes and thick trees. They are not shy at all, and we have seen them in Suva near the fish market in the surrounding trees as well as in the center of town. They operate in pairs or small family groups and flocks of up to some 26 birds. They look for seeds, particularly those of figs and casuarina, and don't like to stay on the ground for long periods of time. They nest in bushes or high in trees. The nest is a round structure built from coconut fibers, grass, hay, leaves and other vegetable matter. The female lays 3–4 rather round eggs (15.8 x 11.7 mm). There are usually two broods in January–April.

Aviculture: This species arrived in Germany and Switzerland in the early 1960s (H. Bregally). The birds do like roomy housing; therefore, breeding cages are unsuitable. During the breeding season a pair will usually occupy a half-open nest box or a square parakeet nest box; the birds like to use a lot of nesting materials, including those listed above for wild birds as well as small down feathers, bark, and moss, since their constructions are rather extensive. The eggs are incubated for about 14 days. The youngsters leave the nest when approximately 26 days old. For the first few days after fledging, they like to return to the nest for the night. Three weeks after leaving the nest they are independent, and at about 8 months of age, they are similar to the parents in appearance.

Other name: Fiji parrotfinch.

SAMOA PARROTFINCH *Amblynura (Erythrura) cyaneovirens* (Peale, 1848)

DK: Korthalet Papegøjeamadine NL: Kortstaart-papegaaiamadine, Samoa-papegaaiamadine
FR: Diamant de Samoa DE: Samoa Papageiamadine IT: Diamante petto blu di Samoa

▶ *photo page 144*

Description: Dark red head; black lores. Also red are the last part of the upper tail coverts, the central tail feathers, and the edging of the remaining tail feathers. Chin and underparts turquoise blue; this part of the body is by far the most remarkable feature of this wonderfully beautiful bird. Between the breast and the head runs a somewhat darker turquoise band. Rump, primaries and the inside of the secondaries are green with a turquoise hue. According to the literature, this blue color is at its brightest when the birds are about 20 months old (Bielfeld). Beak black, eyes and legs brown. Length: 4.3 in. (11 cm).

Geographic variations:

■ *Amblynura c. cyaneovirens*, as above. Distribution: Upolu, the principal island of Western Samoa.
■ *A. c. gaughrani* (Crossin). Head lighter red; the green colors are more intense. Distribution: Savaii (largest island of Samoa, part of Western Samoa). We consider this subspecies synonymous to the nominate form.

Habitat: This species is found in lightly wooded areas, grassy fields, and in the mountains up to 3300 ft. (1000 m). Outside the breeding season these birds operate solitarily, although we have seen them in small groups of 8–12 birds at feeding spots. They construct round nests; the clutch consists of 3–4 round, rather large eggs (15.8 x 12.9 mm). Pairs stay together till approximately two weeks after the January–April breeding season ends.

Aviculture: Due to the confusion among scientists in regard to the relationships between Peale's, Samoa, and royal parrotfinches, and the nomenclature of these forms, it was (and is!) not always clear which species the aviculturist was dealing with. We like to follow Dr. Hans E. Wolters' classification, as we have had the opportunity to study all three species in the wild as well as in captivity. We concluded that Dr. Wolters' studies agree with our own findings, and therefore we prefer to recognize these three forms as separate and full species. Readers who wish to consult further literature should keep in mind, however, that many other authorities still regard all three forms as subspecies of one species, or separate only one while leaving the other two together.

The female lays 3–5 eggs which are incubated for 13–14 days; the young leave the nest after 20–22 days, some four days later than their wild counterparts. Two to three weeks after they have left the nest, the youngsters are independent. For more details see previous species.

ROYAL PARROTFINCH *Amblynura (Erythrura) regia* (Sclater, 1881)

DK: Kongepapegøjeamadine NL: Konings-papegaaiamadine FR: Diamant royale
DE: Könings-Papageiamadine IT: Diamante Reale

Description: Not as slender in build as the pintailed parrotfinch; more compact and without elongated central tail feathers. Head and neck bright red; lores black, chin and upper part of the throat deep cobalt blue with black. Rest of the throat, breast, neck, upperparts, and flanks cobalt blue; rump and under tail coverts green. Wing coverts dark cobalt blue with a dark green hue; primaries black with green edging. When the birds are approximately two years old the cobalt blue color changes into deep blue-violet. Last part of the rump, upper tail coverts, and central tail feathers red; the remaining tail feathers dark brown with red edging. Beak black, eyes dark brown, legs reddish pink. Length: 4.3 in. (11 cm).

Geographic variations:

■ *A. r. regia*, as above. Distribution: Banks Island; Vanuatu in the New Hebrides.
■ *A. r. efatensis* Mayr. More green in belly and back; darker red overall; otherwise very similar to nominate form. Distribution: Efate Island in the New Hebrides.
■ *A. r. serena* (Sclater). Like previous subspecies; more green on back and underparts. Both this and the previous subspecies, however, will color more blue in time; most birds we examined, at the age of 10–14 months, had quite some blue in their feathers. Distribution: Aneitum Island in the southern New Hebrides.

Habitat: Found in lightly wooded areas, parks, and gardens. These birds do not like to forage on the ground. We saw birds drinking water from leaves and taking baths in rain showers, perched high-up on a branch. They like the seeds of figs as well as the pulp; also seeds, berries and similar fruits. They only eat insects if they are in the fruit pulp, such as larvae and fruit flies. They construct their nest high in a tree from grass, small leaves, and hair from cattle; the inside is made from coconut fibers and other soft fibers. The clutch consists of 3–4 eggs, which are rather round (16 x 13 mm). Incubation time is 14 days; after 21 days the young leave the nest. After two more weeks they are independent.

Aviculture: This parrotfinch was first imported into Europe in 1934. It can be bred rather easily, provided the right nutrition is offered. Nests are built free in dense bushes. The clutch contains 3–4 eggs. Fledglings are fed by the male for approximately three extra weeks after they leave the nest. Their youth molt starts at about two months of age and lasts two to three months.

Food: This species utilizes a lot of fruit (see above) every day, and also should get canary grass seed, grass and weed seeds, and various small millets and millet spray. It is not easy, however, to convert these birds to a seed diet; fruits, figs, and dates should be on the menu on a daily basis, as well as sprouted seeds.

Other name: Blue-bellied parrotfinch.

PINK-BILLED PARROTFINCH *Amblynura (Erythrura) kleinschmidti*
Finsch, 1878

DK: Kleinschmidts Papegøjeamadine NL: Kleinschmidt's-papegaaiamadine FR: Diamant de Kleinschmidt
DE: Kleinschmidts Papageiamadine IT: Diamante di Kleinschmidt

Description: Male, green; forehead, and around the eyes and chin, black. Crown dark purple. Yellowish behind the black mask. Latter part of the rump as well as the upper tail coverts red; dark brown tail feathers. The black-brown primaries have green edging; inside secondaries green, as is the underside. Eyes dark brown, beak pinkish red, legs dark flesh-colored. The female is somewhat duller in coloration. Length: 4 in. (10 cm).

Distribution and habitat: Viti Levu Island of the Fiji Islands. It is a mountain dweller par excellence, and has been encountered up to 9000 ft. (2700 m) above sea level. It feeds on small seeds, fruits, insects, and flower buds. Their main food is the seed and pulp of the various fig varieties. They operate in pairs or solitarily, sometimes in the company of other softbilled bird species. Nothing is known about their breeding behavior.

Aviculture: This is an extremely brightly colored bird that has been exported only rarely. We know of only some imports to Europe in 1914, and information on their care and feeding is lacking.

Other name: Black-faced parrotfinch.

Genus *Emblema* (firetail finches) Gould, 1842

PAINTED FIRETAIL FINCH *Emblema picta* **Gould, 1842**

DK: Malet Astrild NL: Geschilderde astrild FR: Emblema peint
DE: Gemalter Astrild, Spinifexastrild IT: Diamante variopinto

▸ *photo page 128*

Description: A brown backed, slim finch with a scarlet spotted face, chin, throat, breast, center of belly, upper tail coverts and rump. Rest of the belly is black, as are the flanks, the latter with white spots. Under tail coverts and tail are black. Iris white, becoming darker in captive birds; small, white eye ring. Red lower mandible with blue base; upper mandible black with a red tip; the female has the same colored beak. Legs very light flesh-colored. The female has considerably less red in the face and under-body, except the center of the belly. Chin and throat have very small white spots; breast and flanks large white spots. Length: 4 in. (10 cm).

Distribution and habitat: Central and western Australia through the Northern Territory and into Queensland and northern South Australia. The species can erupt and spread beyond its usual range. The bird occurs particularly in arid areas, grassland, and places with acacia shrub and spinifex, but there will always be water nearby. This finch builds globular nests, utilizing even little stones, pieces of bark and hard earth as building material.

Aviculture: This is an extremely attractive bird, very suited to an aviary. It gets along well with other birds, including those of its own kind, and seldom gets into fights. The aviary should be well planted, a requirement of all Australian grass-finches. Still, there should be open sandy spots as well. The birds tend to sleep on the ground or in low-hanging nest boxes. The species builds nests in the vegetation or in nest boxes, like Hartz canary nests, provided they are placed low to the ground. They tend to use rough nesting materials, as does the crimson finch (see page 220), such as leaves, rough dry grass, and bark, which are incorporated into the foundation. The walls of the nest are made of small twigs, grass, leaf veins, and the like. For padding on the inside, all types of small, soft feathers are used. Nest building can take all of two weeks. There is a small entryway leading to the inside of the nest. The female lays 4–5 eggs; they hatch in 15–18 days, and the young leave the nest at 20–25 days of age. After ten to twelve weeks, the young are adult, but should not be used for breeding until the following spring. Of course, they should be mated to unrelated birds to avoid inbreeding. The male has an interesting mating dance. With an averted head, he circles the female over and over.

These birds tend to be a little shy at first, but if cared for properly, they become quite trusting and are then readily encouraged to breed. For details on care and feeding, see the section on the star finch, page 240.

Other names: Mountain finch, Painted finch.

Classification of the Estrildid Finches—Vriends (after Wolters, et al.)

Family Estrildidae

Subfamily Estrildinae

Estrilda (Glaucestrilda) caerulescens
Estrilda (Glaucestrilda) perreini
Estrilda (Glaucestrilda) thomensis
Estrilda (Neisma) melanotis
Estrilda (Brunhilda) erythronotos
Estrilda (Brunhilda) charmosyna
Estrilda paludicola
Estrilda poliopareia
Estrilda melpoda
Estrilda astrild
Estrilda rhodopyga
Estrilda (Krimhilda) atricapilla
Estrilda troglodytes
Estrilda (Krimhilda) nonnula

Amandava (Sporaeginthus) subflava
Amandava (Stictospiza) formosa
Amandava amandava

Uraeginthus angolensis
Uraeginthus cyanocephalus
Uraeginthus bengalus
Uraeginthus (Granatina) ianthinogaster
Uraeginthus (Granatina) granatina

Lagonosticta rubricata
Lagonosticta nitidula
Lagonosticta landanae
Lagonosticta larvata
Lagonosticta vinacea
Lagonosticta rufopicta
Lagonosticta rhodopareia
Lagonosticta senegala
Lagonosticta rara

Cryptospiza reichenovii
Cryptospiza jacksoni
Cryptospiza salvadorii
Cryptospiza shelleyi

Nesocharis ansorgei
Nesocharis shelleyi
Nesocharis capistrata

Oreostruthus fuliginosus

Spermophaga poliogenys
Spermophaga haematina
Spermophaga ruficapilla

Nigrita bicolor
Nigrita luteifrons
Nigrita canicapilla
Nigrita (Percnopis) fusconata

Parmoptila woodhousei
Parmoptila rubrifrons

Pyrenestes sanguineus
Pyrenestes ostrinus
Pyrenestes minor

Ortygospiza atricollis
Ortygospiza locustella

Clytospiza monteiri

Euschistospiza dybowskii
Euschistospiza (Hypargos) cinereovinacea

Hypargos margaritatus
Hypargos niveoguttatus

Mandingoa nitidula

Pytilia phoenicoptera
Pytilia melba
Pytilia hypogrammica
Pytilia afra

Subfamily Amadinae

Amadina fasciata
Amadina erythrocephala

Munia (Lonchura) monticola
Munia (Lonchura) montana
Munia (Lonchura) stygia
Munia (Lonchura) pallida
Munia (Lonchura) vana
Munia (Lonchura) caniceps
Munia (Lonchura) nevermanni
Munia (Lonchura) hunsteini
Munia (Lonchura) nigerrima
Munia (Lonchura) forbesi
Munia (Lonchura) quinticolor
Munia (Lonchura) melaena
Munia (Lonchura) teerinki
Munia (Lonchura) castaneothorax
Munia (Lonchura) flaviprymna
Munia (Lonchura) maja
Munia (Lonchura) ferruginosa
Munia (Lonchura) malacca
Munia (Lonchura) grandis
Munia (Lonchura) spectabilis

Lonchura leucosticta
Lonchura tristissima
Lonchura punctulata
Lonchura leucogastra
Lonchura molucca
Lonchura leucogastroides
Lonchura striata
Lonchura fuscans
Lonchura kelaarti

Padda oryzivora
Padda fuscata

Heteromunia (Lonchura) pectoralis

Lepidopygia (Lonchura or Lemuresthes) nana

Spermestes (Lonchura) cucullata
Spermestes (Lonchura) bicolor
Spermestes (Lonchura) fringilloides

Odontospiza caniceps (Lonchura griseicapilla)

Euodice (Lonchura) cantans
Euodice malabarica

Subfamily Erythrurae

Zonaeginthus guttatus (Steganopleura guttata)
Zonaeginthus bellus (S. bella)
Zonaeginthus oculatus (S. oculata)

Neochmia phaeton

Poephila cincta
Poephila acuticauda
Poephila personata
Poephila guttata

Stizoptera (Poephila) bichenovii

Chloebia gouldiae

Aegintha temporalis

Aidemosyne modesta

Bathilda (Neochmia) ruficauda

Reichenowia (Erythrura) hyperythra

Erythrura viridifacies
Erythrura prasina

Amblynura (Erythrura) tricolor
Amblynura (Erythrura) coloria
Amblynura (Erythrura) trichroa
Amblynura (Erythrura) papuana
Amblynura (Erythrura) psittacea
Amblynura (Erythrura) pealii
Amblynura (Erythrura) cyaneovirens
Amblynura (Erythrura) regia
Amblynura (Erythrura) kleinschmidti

Emblema picta

Classification of the Estrildid Finches—Sibley, Ahlquist, Monroe*

Family Passeridae

Subfamily Estrildinae

Tribe Estrildini

Parmoptila rubrifrons
Parmoptila woodhousei

Nigrita fusconota
Nigrita bicolor
Nigrita luteifrons
Nigrita canicapilla

Nesocharis shelleyi
Nesocharis ansorgei
Nesocharis capistrata

Pytilia phoenicoptera
Pytilia lineata
Pytilia afra
Pytilia melba
Pytila hypogrammica

Mandingoa nitidula

Cryptospiza reichenovii
Cryptospiza salvadorii
Cryptospiza jacksoni
Cryptospiza shelleyi

Pyrenestes sanguineus
Pyrenestes ostrinus
Pyrenestes minor

Spermophaga poliogenys
Spermophaga haematina
Spermophaga ruficapilla

Clytospiza monteiri

Hypargos niveoguttatus
Hypargos margaritatus

Euschistopiza dybowskii
Euschistopiza cinereovinacea

Lagonosticta rufopicta
Lagonosticta nitidula
Lagonosticta senegala
Lagonosticta rara
Lagonosticta rubricata
Lagonosticta landanae
Lagonosticta virata
Lagonosticta umbrinodorsalis
Lagonosticta rhodopareia
Lagonosticta vinacea
Lagonosticta larvata

Uraeginthus angolensis
Uraeginthus bengalus
Uraeginthus cyanocephala

Uraeginthus ianthinogaster
Uraeginthus granatina

Estrilda caerulescens
Estrilda perreini
Estrilda thomensis
Estrilda quartinia
Estrilda melanotis
Estrilda poliopareia
Estrilda paludicola
Estrilda ochrogaster
Estrilda melpoda
Estrilda rhodopyga
Estrilda rufibarba
Estrilda troglodytes
Estrilda astrildid
Estrilda nigriloris
Estrilda nonnula
Estrilda atricapilla
Estrilda kandti
Estrilda charmosyna
Estrilda erythronotos

Amandava amandava
Amandava formosa
Amandava subflava

Ortygospiza atricollis
Ortygospiza gabonensis
Ortygospiza locustella

Emblema picta

Stagonopleura bella
Stagonopleura oculata
Stagonopleura guttata

Oreostruthus fuliginosus

Neochmia temporalis
Neochmia phaeton
Neochmia ruficauda
Neochmia modesta

Taeniopygia guttata
Taeniopygia bichenovii

Poephila personata
Poephila acuticauda
Poephila cincta

Erythrura hyperythra
Erythrura prasina
Erythrura viridifacies
Erythrura tricolor
Erythrura trichroa
Erythrura coloria
Erythrura papuana
Erythrura psittacea
Erythrura pealii

Erythrura cyaneovirens
Erythrura regia
Erythrura kleinschmidti

Chloebia gouldiae

Lemuresthes nana

Lonchura malabaricca
Lonchura griseicapilla
Lonchura cucullata
Lonchura bicolor
Lonchura nigriceps
Lonchura fringilloides
Lonchura striata
Lonchura leucogastroides
Lonchura fuscans
Lonchura molucca
Lonchura kelaarti
Lonchura punctulata
Lonchura leucogastra
Lonchura tristissima
Lonchura leucosticta
Lonchura malacca
Lonchura ferruginosa
Lonchura quinticolor
Lonchura maja
Lonchura pallida
Lonchura grandis
Lonchura vana
Lonchura caniceps
Lonchura nevermanni
Lonchura spectabilis
Lonchura hunsteini
Lonchura forbesi
Lonchura nigerrima
Lonchura flaviprymna
Lonchura castaneothorax
Lonchura stygia
Lonchura teerinki
Lonchura montana
Lonchura monticola
Lonchura melaena

Heteromunia pectoralis

Padda oryzivora
Padda fuscata

Amadina fasciata
Amadina erythrocephala

Note: The S-A-M classification includes the parasitic widowbirds in the subfamily Estrildinae as a second tribe, the *Viduini*.

Bibliography

Bates, H. & R. Busenbark. 1970. *Finches and Softbilled Birds*. TFH Publications, Inc., Neptune, New Jersey

Bielfeld, H. 1996. *Das Prachtfinken Buch*. Verlag Ulmer, Stuttgart.

Brickell, N. 1986, 1989. *Introduction to Southern African Cage and Aviary Birds*. Vol. I & II, Nadine Publishers, South Hills, 2136, S.A.

Buchan, J. 1976. *The Bengalese Finch*. Isles d'Avon Ltd., Kingswood, Bristol, U.K.

Collier, C. (a.o.). 1987. *Finch Breeders Handbook, Vol. 1, The Australians*. Queensland Finch Society Publications, Woolloongabba, Queensland 4102.

Evans, S. & M. Fidler. 1988. *The Gouldian Finch*. Blandford Press, London.

Grzimek, B. (ed.). 1973. *Grzimek's Animal Life Encyclopedia*, Vol. 9. Van Nostrand Reinhold Company, New York.

Harman, I. & M. M. Vriends. 1978. *All about Finches and related Seed-eating Birds*. TFH Publications, Inc., Neptune, New Jersey.

Iles, G. W. 1975. *Breeding Australian Finches*. Isles d'Avon Ltd., Kingswood, Bristol, U.K.

Immelmann, K. 1965. *Australian Finches in Bush and Aviary*. Angus and Robertson, Melbourne.

Koepff, C. 2001. *The Finch Handbook*. Barron's, Hauppauge, N.Y.

Neunzig, K. 1965. *Fremdländische Stubenvögel*. Asher & Co., Amsterdam.

Restall, R. L. 1975. *Finches and other Seed-eating Birds*. Faber and Faber, London.

Roberts, A. 1961. *Birds of South Africa* (revised ed.). The Trustees of the South African Bird Book Fund, Cape Town.

Rutgers, A. & K. A. Norris (eds.). 1970–1977. *Encyclopedia of Aviculture*, Vol. 1–3. Blandford Press, Poole, Dorset.

Trollope, J. 1992. *Seed-eating Birds: their Care and Breeding*. Blandford, Strand, London.

Vriends, M. M. 1983. *Australische Vinken*. Spectrum, Utrecht.

Vriends, M. M. 1989. *The New Bird Handbook*. Barron's, Hauppauge, N.Y.

Vriends, M. M. 1991. *Gouldian Finches*. Barron's, Hauppauge, N.Y.

Vriends, M. M. 1996. *Hand-feeding and Raising Baby Birds*. Barron's, Hauppauge, N.Y.

Vriends, M. M. 1997. *The Zebra Finch*. Howell Book House, New York.

Vriends, M. M. 1998. *Simon & Schuster's Guide to Pet Birds*, 10th printing. Simon & Schuster, New York.

Vriends, M. M. & Tanya M. Heming-Vriends. 2001. *The Canary Handbook*. Barron's, Hauppauge, N.Y.

Woolham, F. 1987. *The Handbook of Aviculture*. Blandford Press, Poole, Dorset.

Index of Common Names

(Followed by Index of Species and Subspecies by Genera and Multilingual Index of Common Names)

Index of Species and Subspecies by Genera

Multilingual Index of Common Names

(Dansk, Deutsch, Français, Italiano, Nederlands)